STOCK
TRADER'S
ALMANAC
2 0 1 6

Jeffrey A. Hirsch & Yale Hirsch

WILEY

www.stocktradersalmanac.com

Editor in Chief	Jeffrey A. Hirsch
Editor at Large	Yale Hirsch
Director of Research	Christopher Mistal
Production Editor	Steven Kyritz

For general information about our other products and services, please contact our Customer Care Department within the United States at 800-762-2974, outside the United States at 317-572-3993, or fax at 317-572-4002.

Wiley publishes in a variety of print and electronic formats and by print-on-demand. Some material included with standard print versions of this book may not be included in e-books or in print-on-demand. If this book refers to media such as a CD or DVD that is not included in the version you purchased, you may download this material at http://booksupport.wiley.com. For more information about Wiley products, visit our website at www.wiley.com.

ISBN: 978-1-119-11068-2 (paper)
ISBN: 978-1-119-18933-6 (ebk)
ISBN: 978-1-119-18930-5 (ebk)

Printed in the United States of America.

10 9 8 7 6 5 4 3 2 1

This Forty-Ninth Edition is respectfully dedicated to:

Sy L. Harding (1935-2015)
and
Michael L. Burke (1935-2014)

Since the last edition, we have lost these two legends of Wall Street. We were privileged to know both gentlemen and continue to benefit immeasurably from their work. Renowned fundamental and technical analysis, award winning market timing, prolific market research, and distinguished investment newsletters; Sy and Mike will be deeply missed.

Mike was Editor of Chartcraft publications and *Investors Intelligence* from 1982 to 1999 and co-editor with John Gray 2000–2014. He taught fundamental and technical analysis at the New School, New York from 1978–1990 and was a columnist and contributing editor of the *Moneypaper* from 1983–2012. He authored *The Three Box Reversal Method of Point and Figure: Construction and Formations* (Chartcraft) in 1999. Mike developed Point and Figure Relative Strength analysis for stocks. He created the Broad Industry Group Bullish %'s technique for finding depressed stock market sectors about to rally and the industry group Insider Analysis as a leading indicator of what senior corporate executives think about the next moves in their companies' share price. He inaugurated a number of different model portfolios, including the Fidelity Switch Fund concentrating on equities, Fidelity bond and international funds, and three portfolios of individual stocks: Low-Priced, Long-Term, and Income & Appreciation. To this day, we continue to incorporate *Investors Intelligence* research and indicators into our market analysis.

Sy was a true man of all seasons. He was one of the foremost proponents of market seasonality, cycles, and recurring historical patterns, so naturally we were keen on each other's research, analysis, strategies, and systems. Sy enhanced our Best Six Months Switching Strategy (pages 52, 54, 60 and 62) with MACD triggers, dubbing it the "best mechanical system ever." He founded Asset Management Research Corp in 1988 and published the *Street Smart Report*, providing research, analysis, and timing on the stock, gold, and bond markets. With a background in engineering as founder and owner of two high-tech manufacturing firms, it was natural that his research involved technical analysis and charting as well as fundamentals. Sy was frequently ranked in the "Top Ten Market Timers in the U.S." He authored the 1999 book *Riding the Bear: How to Prosper in the Coming Bear Market* (Adams Media), which accurately predicted the 2000–2002 bear market, and *How to Beat the Market the Easy Way!* (Wheatmark) in 2007, just prior to the 2007–2009 bear market, which introduced market-timing strategies for down markets.

INTRODUCTION TO THE FORTY-NINTH EDITION

We are pleased and proud to introduce the Forty-Ninth Edition of the *Stock Trader's Almanac*. The *Almanac* provides you with the necessary tools to invest successfully in the twenty-first century.

J. P. Morgan's classic retort, "Stocks will fluctuate," is often quoted with a wink-of-the-eye implication that the only prediction one can make about the stock market is that it will go up, down, or sideways. Many investors agree that no one ever really knows which way the market will move. Nothing could be further from the truth.

We discovered that while stocks do indeed fluctuate, they do so in well-defined, often predictable patterns. These patterns recur too frequently to be the result of chance or coincidence. How else do we explain that since 1950 all the gains in the market were made during November through April, compared to a loss May through October? (See page 52.)

The *Almanac* is a practical investment tool. It alerts you to those little-known market patterns and tendencies on which shrewd professionals enhance profit potential. You will be able to forecast market trends with accuracy and confidence when you use the *Almanac* to help you understand:

- How our presidential elections affect the economy and the stock market—just as the moon affects the tides. Many investors have made fortunes following the political cycle. You can be sure that money managers who control billions of dollars are also political cycle watchers. Astute people do not ignore a pattern that has been working effectively throughout most of our economic history.

- How the passage of the Twentieth Amendment to the Constitution fathered the January Barometer. This barometer has an outstanding record for predicting the general course of the stock market each year, with only eight major errors since 1950, for an 87.7% accuracy ratio. (See page 16.)

- Why there is a significant market bias at certain times of the day, week, month, and year.

Even if you are an investor who pays scant attention to cycles, indicators, and patterns, your investment survival could hinge on your interpretation of one of the recurring patterns found within these pages. One of the most intriguing and important patterns is the symbiotic relationship between Washington and Wall Street. Aside from the potential profitability in seasonal patterns, there's the pure joy of seeing the market very often do just what you expected.

The *Stock Trader's Almanac* is also an organizer. Its wealth of information is presented on a calendar basis. The *Almanac* puts investing in a business framework and makes investing easier because it:

- Updates investment knowledge and informs you of new techniques and tools.
- Is a monthly reminder and refresher course.
- Alerts you to both seasonal opportunities and dangers.
- Furnishes a historical viewpoint by providing pertinent statistics on past market performance.
- Supplies forms necessary for portfolio planning, record keeping, and tax preparation.

 The WITCH icon signifies THIRD FRIDAY OF THE MONTH on calendar pages and alerts you to extraordinary volatility due to the expiration of equity and index options and index futures contracts. Triple-witching days appear during March, June, September, and December.

 The BULL icon on calendar pages signifies favorable trading days based on the S&P 500 rising 60% or more of the time on a particular trading day during the 21-year period January 1994 to December 2014.

 A BEAR icon on calendar pages signifies unfavorable trading days based on the S&P falling 60% or more of the time for the same 21-year period.

Also, to give you even greater perspective, we have listed next to the date of every day that the market is open the Market Probability numbers for the same 21-year period for the Dow (D), S&P 500 (S), and NASDAQ (N). You will see a "D," "S," and "N" followed by a number signifying the actual Market Probability number for that trading day, based on the recent 21-year period. On pages 121–128, you will find complete Market Probability Calendars, both long-term and 21-year for the Dow, S&P, and NASDAQ, as well as for the Russell 1000 and Russell 2000 indices.

Other seasonalities near the ends, beginnings, and middles of months—options expirations, around holidays, and other significant times—as well as all FOMC Meeting dates are noted for *Almanac* investors' convenience on the weekly planner pages. All other important economic releases are provided in the Strategy Calendar every month in our e-newsletter, *Almanac Investor*, available at our website, *www.stocktradersalmanac.com*.

One-year seasonal pattern charts for Dow, S&P 500, NASDAQ, Russell 1000, and Russell 2000 appear on pages 171 to 173. There are three charts each for Dow and S&P 500 spanning our entire database starting in 1901 and one each for the younger indices. Since 2016 is a presidential election year, each chart contains typical election year performance compared to all years.

The Notable Events on page 6 provides a handy list of major events of the past year that can be helpful when evaluating things that may have moved the market. Over the past few years, our research had been restructured to flow better with the rhythm of the year. This has also allowed us more room for added data. Again, we have included historical data on the Russell 1000 and Russell 2000 indices. The Russell 2K is an excellent proxy for small and mid-caps, which we have used over the years, and the Russell 1K provides a broader view of large caps. Annual highs and lows for all five indices covered in the *Almanac* appear on pages 149–151, and we've tweaked the Best & Worst section.

In order to cram in all this material, some of our Record Keeping section was cut. We have converted many of these paper forms into computer spreadsheets for our own internal use. As a service to our faithful readers, we are making these forms available at our website, *www.stocktradersalmanac.com*.

Election years are the second-best year of the four-year cycle and sixth years of decades have been up double digits four in a row, so 2016 has some solid history behind it. You can find all the market charts of elections since the Depression on page 24. The last nine sixth years of decades appear on page 42. Never-before-shown Eighth Year of Presidential Terms charts appear on page 40. On page 76 is our Best Investment Book of the Year, *Fast Forward: The Technologies and Companies Shaping Our Future* (Fruitful Publications, 2014), which should help increase your trading returns dramatically. Other top books are listed on page 116.

Sector seasonalities include several consistent shorting opportunities and appear on pages 94–98. On pages 34–36, featured for the first time this year, learn how we are now working with professional money managers at Probabilities Fund Management LLC to leverage Almanac probabilities with a strategic and tactical trading system.

We are constantly searching for new insights and nuances about the stock market and welcome any suggestions from our readers.

Have a healthy and prosperous 2016.

NOTABLE EVENTS

2014

Jun 2	Palestine unity government formed
Jun 5	Islamic State begins major offensive through northern Iraq
Jul 9	Israel bombs Gaza, Hamas bombs Israel
Jul 17	Malaysia Air Flight 17 shot down by a missile in Ukraine. All 298 on board killed
Aug 8	U.S. begins military air campaign in northern Iraq
Aug 8	Ebola outbreak in West Africa declared epidemic
Aug 10	Ferguson, MO riots
Aug 26	Israel and Hamas agree to a ceasefire
Sep 22	U.S. and Arab partners begin airstrike campaign in Syria
Oct 3	Cyber-attack on JPMorgan Chase and nine other financial institutions compromises over 83 million accounts
Nov 12	Rosetta spacecraft Philae probe lands on Comet 67P, first landing of its kind
Dec 17	U.S. resumption of normal relations with Cuba
Dec 28	Indonesia AirAsia Flight 8501 crashes into Java Sea killing all 162 people on board

2015

Jan 1	Lithuania adopts the Euro, becomes 19th member of the Eurozone
Jan 1	Eurasian Economic Union established between Russia, Belarus, Armenia, Kazakhstan, and Kyrgyzstan
Jan 7	Terrorist attack on the offices of satirical newspaper *Charlie Hebdo* in Paris
Jan 3-7	Series of massacres in Nigeria by Boko Haram kills more than 2,000
Jan 15	Swiss National Bank abandons the cap on the franc's value relative to the euro

Jan 22	Yemeni president resigns and Houthi forces seize the presidential palace
Feb 12	Russia, Ukraine, Germany, and France ceasefire agreement on Ukraine conflict fails days later
Feb 16	Egypt begins airstrikes on Islamic State in Libya retaliating for beheadings of Egyptian Christians
Feb 27	Russian opposition politician Boris Nemtsov assassinated in Moscow
Mar 6	NASA Dawn probe enters orbit around Ceres, first spacecraft to visit a dwarf planet
Mar 12	Islamic State allies with fellow jihadist group Boko Haram,
Mar 24	Germanwings flight crashes in the French Alps killing all 150 on board
Mar 25	Saudi-led coalition of Arab countries starts military intervention in Yemen
Apr 2	148 killed in mass shooting at Garissa University in Kenya by Al-Shabaab terrorists
Apr 13/19	2 migrant shipwrecks in Mediterranean, over 1,000 drown
Apr 25	Quake in Nepal kills 8,000, leaves over 100,000 homeless, destroys many historic sites
Mar 5-8	Ancient sites of Nimrud, Hatra, and Dur-Sharrukin in Iraq demolished by ISIS
May 11	India's population officially reaches 1 billion
May 11-12	Picasso sells for $179.3 mil; Giacometti sculpture for $141.3 mil, new world records
May 12	Second major earthquake in Nepal, measuring 7.3 on the Richter scale; 200 deaths
May 20	5 major world banks fined US$5.7bn for currency manipulation
May 22	Ireland first country to legalize same-sex marriage by popular vote
May 27	FIFA accused of bribery of hundreds of millions of dollars over 20+ years, 14 indicted

2015 RECAP/2016 OUTLOOK

Five months into 2015, the S&P 500 has come within 5.1 % of the first half high of 2250 we projected last year at this time on an intraday basis. The Dow has come within 3.4% of the 19000 we expected and NASDAQ has exceeded 5000 as we anticipated. The market did rally 3–5% on the S&P 500 and the Dow last summer as we thought it would before the correction. NASDAQ ran higher and the rally kept on running until September when we got about half the 10–15% we were looking for.

We bought rather heavily into the V-bottom, establishing several long ETF sector and individual stock positions. At this writing, with our Seasonal MACD Sell Signal for the Dow and S&P issued on April 30 and NASDAQ's on the verge, most of those longs are closed or on hold with tight stops.

We have also begun to ease into our seasonal defensive positions and shorts in anticipation of the long overdue 10% correction this summer or fall. At the end of May DJIA was up just 1.1% year-to-date and S&P 500 2.2%. At the same point in the year in previous pre-election years, DJIA was up on average slightly more than 8% while S&P 500 was typically up nearly 12%. Tepid economic data leading to so-so earnings forecasts and a Fed that is considering when to raise rates for the first time since 2006 has likely led to this lack of market performance this year versus past pre-election years.

This lagging performance supports our other analysis that the market is getting more prone to a correction some time during the Worst Six Months. Whether we pull back in June or later in the typical August-October dry patch remains to be seen. We may leak higher, but further upside is becoming less likely and harder to come by. The Greek sovereign debt saga and the big headwind from Fed's highly-anticipated rate hike, plus mixed economic data and seasonal forces are likely to catalyze a market pullback. We do not expect anything sinister, but the long-averted 10% correction, give or take a few percentage points is quite likely.

Unfortunately, our outlook for 2016 is less than sanguine. Presidential perspectives on page 20 and throughout this edition paint a low probability for substantial gains in 2016. Election years have been considerably weaker in recent history and eighth years of presidential terms represent the worst of election years since 1920. In eighth years, DJIA and S&P 500 have suffered average declines of –13.9% and –10.9% respectively. Out of these six full years, only 1988 was positive. As a result, eighth years have vastly differed from the typical election-year pattern.

Currently, the best three quarters of the 4-year cycle (midterm Q4 and pre-election Q1–2, page 102) and usual 50% move from the midterm low to the pre-election year high are well below average. After a sideways move through Q3 2015, we should end 2015 near a slightly higher new high. The next bear market may begin near the end of 2015 or in 2016 and take the market 20–30% lower into 2017–2018 in what is likely to be the last cyclical, garden-variety bear market that finally puts an end to this secular bear market that began in early 2000.

We do not expect much upside over the next few years in the market. But after the next bear market, our Super Boom forecast should kick in. We have raised the floor on our initial forecast, but the 500+% move to Dow 38820 by 2025 is still on target.

—Jeffrey A. Hirsch, June 2, 2015

THE 2016 STOCK TRADER'S ALMANAC

CONTENTS

DIRECTORY OF TRADING PATTERNS AND DATABANK

STRATEGY PLANNING AND RECORD SECTION

2016 STRATEGY CALENDAR

(Option expiration dates circled)

	MONDAY	TUESDAY	WEDNESDAY	THURSDAY	FRIDAY	SATURDAY	SUNDAY
JANUARY	28	29	30	31	1 JANUARY New Year's Day	2	3
	4	5	6	7	8	9	10
	11	12	13	14	(15)	16	17
	18 Martin Luther King Day	19	20	21	22	23	24
	25	26	27	28	29	30	31
FEBRUARY	1 FEBRUARY	2	3	4	5	6	7
	8	9	10 Ash Wednesday	11	12	13	14 ♥
	15 President's Day	16	17	18	(19)	20	21
	22	23	24	25	26	27	28
MARCH	29	1 MARCH	2	3	4	5	6
	7	8	9	10	11	12	13 Daylight Saving Time Begins
	14	15	16	17 ♣ St. Patrick's Day	(18)	19	20
	21	22	23	24	25 Good Friday	26	27 Easter
APRIL	28	29	30	31	1 APRIL	2	3
	4	5	6	7	8	9	10
	11	12	13	14	(15) Tax Deadline	16	17
	18	19	20	21	22	23 Passover	24
	25	26	27	28	29	30	1 MAY
MAY	2	3	4	5	6	7	8 Mother's Day
	9	10	11	12	13	14	15
	16	17	18	19	(20)	21	22
	23	24	25	26	27	28	29
JUNE	30 Memorial Day	31	1 JUNE	2	3	4	5
	6	7	8	9	10	11	12
	13	14	15	16	(17)	18	19 Father's Day
	20	21	22	23	24	25	26

Market closed on shaded weekdays; closes early when half-shaded.

2016 STRATEGY CALENDAR

(Option expiration dates circled)

MONDAY	TUESDAY	WEDNESDAY	THURSDAY	FRIDAY	SATURDAY	SUNDAY	
27	28	29	30	1 JULY	2	3	
4 Independence Day	5	6	7	8	9	10	JULY
11	12	13	14	(15)	16	17	
18	19	20	21	22	23	24	
25	26	27	28	29	30	31	
1 AUGUST	2	3	4	5	6	7	
8	9	10	11	12	13	14	AUGUST
15	16	17	18	(19)	20	21	
22	23	24	25	26	27	28	
29	30	31	1 SEPTEMBER	2	3	4	
5 Labor Day	6	7	8	9	10	11	SEPTEMBER
12	13	14	15	(16)	17	18	
19	20	21	22	23	24	25	
26	27	28	29	30	1 OCTOBER	2	
3 Rosh Hashanah	4	5	6	7	8	9	OCTOBER
10 Columbus Day	11	12 Yom Kippur	13	14	15	16	
17	18	19	20	(21)	22	23	
24	25	26	27	28	29	30	
31 🎃	1 NOVEMBER	2	3	4	5	6 Daylight Saving Time Ends	
7	8 Election Day	9	10	11 Veterans' Day	12	13	NOVEMBER
14	15	16	17	(18)	19	20	
21	22	23	24 Thanksgiving Day	25	26	27	
28	29	30	1 DECEMBER	2	3	4	
5	6	7	8	9	10	11	DECEMBER
12	13	14	15	(16)	17	18	
19	20	21	22	23	24	25 Christmas Chanukah	
26	27	28	29	30	31	1 JANUARY New Year's Day	

11

JANUARY ALMANAC

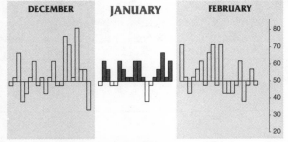

JANUARY								FEBRUARY					
S	M	T	W	T	F	S		S	M	T	W	T	F	S
31					1	2			1	2	3	4	5	6
3	4	5	6	7	8	9		7	8	9	10	11	12	13
10	11	12	13	14	15	16		14	15	16	17	18	19	20
17	18	19	20	21	22	23		21	22	23	24	25	26	27
24	25	26	27	28	29	30		28	29					

Market Probability Chart above is a graphic representation of the S&P 500 Recent Market Probability Calendar on page 124.

◆ January Barometer predicts year's course with .754 batting average (page 16) ◆ 12 of last 16 presidential election years followed January's direction ◆ Every down January on the S&P since 1950, *without exception*, preceded a new or extended bear market, a flat market, or a 10% correction (page 48) ◆ S&P gains January's first five days preceded full-year gains 85.4% of the time, 14 of last 16 presidential election years followed first five days' direction (page 14) ◆ November, December, and January constitute the year's best three-month span, a 4.2% S&P gain (pages 50 & 147) ◆ January NASDAQ powerful 2.7% since 1971 (pages 58 & 148) ◆ "January Effect" now starts in mid-December and favors small-cap stocks (pages 106 & 110) ◆ 2009 has the dubious honor of the worst S&P 500 January on record.

January Vital Statistics

	DJIA		S&P 500		NASDAQ		Russell 1K		Russell 2K	
Rank	6		5		1		5		3	
Up	42		40		29		23		20	
Down	24		26		16		14		17	
Average % Change	1.0 %		1.0 %		2.7%		1.0%		1.7%	
Election Year	0.3 %		0.5 %		2.6%		0.7%		2.3%	
Best & Worst January										
	% Change		% Change		% Change		% Change		% Change	
Best	1976	14.4	1987	13.2	1975	16.6	1987	12.7	1985	13.1
Worst	2009	−8.8	2009	−8.6	2008	−9.9	2009	−8.3	2009	−11.2
Best & Worst January Weeks										
Best	1/9/76	6.1	1/2/09	6.8	1/12/01	9.1	1/2/09	6.8	1/9/87	7.0
Worst	1/24/03	−5.3	1/28/00	−5.6	1/28/00	−8.2	1/28/00	−5.5	1/4/08	−6.5
Best & Worst January Days										
Best	1/17/91	4.6	1/3/01	5.0	1/3/01	14.2	1/3/01	5.3	1/21/09	5.3
Worst	1/8/88	−6.9	1/8/88	−6.8	1/2/01	−7.2	1/8/88	−6.1	1/20/09	−7.0
First Trading Day of Expiration Week: 1980–2015										
Record (#Up – #Down)	24.12		21–15		20–16		20–16		20–16	
Current streak	D2		D3		D3		D3		D3	
Avg % Change	0.10		0.08		0.10		0.05		0.12	
Options Expiration Day: 1980–2015										
Record (#Up – #Down)	19–17		19–17		19–17		19–17		20–16	
Current streak	U5		U1		U1		U1		U1	
Avg % Change	−0.06		−0.06		−0.12		−0.08		−0.07	
Options Expiration Week: 1980–2015										
Record (#Up – #Down)	19–17		15–21		20–16		15–21		19–17	
Current streak	D1		D2		D1		D2		D1	
Avg % Change	−0.18		−0.10		0.21		−0.11		0.22	
Week After Options Expiration: 1980–2015										
Record (#Up – #Down)	19–17		22–14		20–16		22–14		24–12	
Current streak	U1		U1		U1		U1		U1	
Avg % Change	−0.04		0.18		0.12		0.16		0.17	
First Trading Day Performance										
% of Time Up	59.1		48.5		55.6		43.2		45.9	
Avg % Change	0.27		0.17		0.22		0.17		0.09	
Last Trading Day Performance										
% of Time Up	56.1		60.6		62.2		56.8		73.0	
Avg % Change	0.19		0.22		0.25		0.27		0.20	

Dow & S&P 1950–April 2015, NASDAQ 1971–April 2015, Russell 1K & 2K 1979–April 2015.

20th Amendment made "lame ducks" disappear.
Now, "As January goes, so goes the year."

DECEMBER 2015/JANUARY 2016

MONDAY

D 81.0
S 81.0
N 71.4

28

With respect to trading Sugar futures, if they give it away for free at restaurants you probably don't want to be trading it.
— John L. Person (Professional trader, author, speaker, *Commodity Trader's Almanac*, nationalfutures.com, 2/22/2011 TradersExpo, b. 1961)

TUESDAY

D 47.6
S 57.1
N 47.6

29

Wise men are instructed by reason, men of less understanding by experience, the most ignorant by necessity, the beasts by nature.
— Marcus Tullius Cicero (Great Roman Orator, Politician, 106–43 B.C.)

WEDNESDAY

D 42.9
S 57.1
N 42.9

30

War is God's way of teaching Americans geography.
— Ambrose Bierce (Writer, satirist, Civil War hero, *The Devil's Dictionary*, 1842–1914?)

*Last Trading Day of the Year, NASDAQ Down 12 of last 15
NASDAQ Was Up 29 Years in a Row 1971–1999*

THURSDAY

D 42.9
S 33.3
N 42.9

31

We are handicapped by policies based on old myths rather than current realities.
— James William Fulbright (U.S. Senator Arkansas 1944–1974, 1905–1995)

New Years Day *(Market Closed)*

FRIDAY

1

You try to be greedy when others are fearful, and fearful when others are greedy.
— Warren Buffett (CEO Berkshire Hathaway, investor, and philanthropist, b. 1930)

SATURDAY

2

January Almanac Investor Sector Seasonalities: See Pages 94, 96, and 98

SUNDAY

3

JANUARY'S FIRST FIVE DAYS: AN EARLY WARNING SYSTEM

The last 41 up First Five Days were followed by full-year gains 35 times for an 85.4% accuracy ratio and a 14.0% average gain in all 41 years. The five exceptions include flat 1994 and four related to war. Vietnam military spending delayed the start of the 1966 bear market. Ceasefire imminence early in 1973 raised stocks temporarily. Saddam Hussein turned 1990 into a bear. The war on terrorism, instability in the Mideast, and corporate malfeasance shaped 2002 into one of the worst years on record. The 24 down First Five Days were followed by 13 up years and 11 down (45.8% accurate) and an average gain of 0.7%.

In presidential election years this indicator has a solid record. In the last 16 presidential election years, 14 full years followed the direction of the First Five Days.

THE FIRST-FIVE-DAYS-IN-JANUARY INDICATOR

	Chronological Data					Ranked by Performance		
	Previous Year's Close	January 5th Day	5-Day Change	Year Change	Rank	Year	5-Day Change	Year Change
1950	16.76	17.09	2.0%	21.8%	1	1987	6.2%	2.0%
1951	20.41	20.88	2.3	16.5	2	1976	4.9	19.1
1952	23.77	23.91	0.6	11.8	3	1999	3.7	19.5
1953	26.57	26.33	−0.9	−6.6	4	2003	3.4	26.4
1954	24.81	24.93	0.5	45.0	5	2006	3.4	13.6
1955	35.98	35.33	−1.8	26.4	6	1983	3.3	17.3
1956	45.48	44.51	−2.1	2.6	7	1967	3.1	20.1
1957	46.67	46.25	−0.9	−14.3	8	1979	2.8	12.3
1958	39.99	40.99	2.5	38.1	9	2010	2.7	12.8
1959	55.21	55.40	0.3	8.5	10	1963	2.6	18.9
1960	59.89	59.50	−0.7	−3.0	11	1958	2.5	38.1
1961	58.11	58.81	1.2	23.1	12	1984	2.4	1.4
1962	71.55	69.12	−3.4	−11.8	13	1951	2.3	16.5
1963	63.10	64.74	2.6	18.9	14	2013	2.2	29.6
1964	75.02	76.00	1.3	13.0	15	1975	2.2	31.5
1965	84.75	85.37	0.7	9.1	16	1950	2.0	21.8
1966	92.43	93.14	0.8	−13.1	17	2004	1.8	9.0
1967	80.33	82.81	3.1	20.1	18	2012	1.8	13.4
1968	96.47	96.62	0.2	7.7	19	1973	1.5	−17.4
1969	103.86	100.80	−2.9	−11.4	20	1972	1.4	15.6
1970	92.06	92.68	0.7	0.1	21	1964	1.3	13.0
1971	92.15	92.19	0.04	10.8	22	1961	1.2	23.1
1972	102.09	103.47	1.4	15.6	23	1989	1.2	27.3
1973	118.05	119.85	1.5	−17.4	24	2011	1.1	−0.003
1974	97.55	96.12	−1.5	−29.7	25	2002	1.1	−23.4
1975	68.56	70.04	2.2	31.5	26	1997	1.0	31.0
1976	90.19	94.58	4.9	19.1	27	1980	0.9	25.8
1977	107.46	105.01	−2.3	−11.5	28	1966	0.8	−13.1
1978	95.10	90.64	−4.7	1.1	29	1994	0.7	−1.5
1979	96.11	98.80	2.8	12.3	30	1965	0.7	9.1
1980	107.94	108.95	0.9	25.8	31	2009	0.7	23.5
1981	135.76	133.06	−2.0	−9.7	32	1970	0.7	0.1
1982	122.55	119.55	−2.4	14.8	33	1952	0.6	11.8
1983	140.64	145.23	3.3	17.3	34	1954	0.5	45.0
1984	164.93	168.90	2.4	1.4	35	1996	0.4	20.3
1985	167.24	163.99	−1.9	26.3	36	1959	0.3	8.5
1986	211.28	207.97	−1.6	14.6	37	1995	0.3	34.1
1987	242.17	257.28	6.2	2.0	38	1992	0.2	4.5
1988	247.08	243.40	−1.5	12.4	39	1968	0.2	7.7
1989	277.72	280.98	1.2	27.3	40	2015	0.2	??
1990	353.40	353.79	0.1	−6.6	41	1990	0.1	−6.6
1991	330.22	314.90	−4.6	26.3	42	1971	0.04	10.8
1992	417.09	418.10	0.2	4.5	43	2007	−0.4	3.5
1993	435.71	429.05	−1.5	7.1	44	2014	−0.6	11.4
1994	466.45	469.90	0.7	−1.5	45	1960	−0.7	−3.0
1995	459.27	460.83	0.3	34.1	46	1957	−0.9	−14.3
1996	615.93	618.46	0.4	20.3	47	1953	−0.9	−6.6
1997	740.74	748.41	1.0	31.0	48	1974	−1.5	−29.7
1998	970.43	956.04	−1.5	26.7	49	1998	−1.5	26.7
1999	1229.23	1275.09	3.7	19.5	50	1988	−1.5	12.4
2000	1469.25	1441.46	−1.9	−10.1	51	1993	−1.5	7.1
2001	1320.28	1295.86	−1.8	−13.0	52	1986	−1.6	14.6
2002	1148.08	1160.71	1.1	−23.4	53	2001	−1.8	−13.0
2003	879.82	909.93	3.4	26.4	54	1955	−1.8	26.4
2004	1111.92	1131.91	1.8	9.0	55	2000	−1.9	−10.1
2005	1211.92	1186.19	−2.1	3.0	56	1985	−1.9	26.3
2006	1248.29	1290.15	3.4	13.6	57	1981	−2.0	−9.7
2007	1418.30	1412.11	−0.4	3.5	58	1956	−2.1	2.6
2008	1468.36	1390.19	−5.3	−38.5	59	2005	−2.1	3.0
2009	903.25	909.73	0.7	23.5	60	1977	−2.3	−11.5
2010	1115.10	1144.98	2.7	12.8	61	1982	−2.4	14.8
2011	1257.64	1271.50	1.1	−0.003	62	1969	−2.9	−11.4
2012	1257.60	1280.70	1.8	13.4	63	1962	−3.4	−11.8
2013	1426.19	1457.15	2.2	29.6	64	1991	−4.6	26.3
2014	1848.36	1837.49	−0.6	11.4	65	1978	−4.7	1.1
2015	2058.90	2062.14	0.2	??	66	2008	−5.3	−38.5

Based on S&P 500

14

Small Caps Punished First Trading Day of Year
Russell 2000 Down 16 of Last 25, But Up 5 of Last 7

MONDAY

D 66.7
S 47.6
N 66.7

4

Investors operate with limited funds and limited intelligence, they don't need to know everything. As long as they understand something better than others, they have an edge.
— George Soros (Financier, philanthropist, political activist, author, and philosopher, b. 1930)

Second Trading Day of the Year, Dow Up 15 of Last 22
Santa Claus Rally Ends (Page 114)

TUESDAY

D 71.4
S 61.9
N 57.1

5

It was never my thinking that made the big money for me. It was always my sitting. Got that? My sitting tight!
— Jesse Livermore (Early 20th century stock trader and speculator, *How to Trade in Stocks*, 1877–1940)

WEDNESDAY

D 52.4
S 57.1
N 52.4

6

Our philosophy here is identifying change, anticipating change. Change is what drives earnings growth, and if you identify the underlying change, you recognize the growth before the market, and the deceleration of that growth.
— Peter Vermilye (Baring America Asset Management, 1987)

THURSDAY

D 52.4
S 47.6
N 57.1

7

Individualism, private property, the law of accumulation of wealth and the law of competition…are the highest result of human experience, the soil in which society, so far, has produced the best fruit.
— Andrew Carnegie (Scottish-born U.S. industrialist, philanthropist, The Gospel Of Wealth, 1835–1919)

January's First Five Days Act as an "Early Warning" (Page 14)

FRIDAY

D 38.1
S 47.6
N 57.1

8

I will never knowingly buy any company that has a real time quote of their stock price in the building lobby.
— Robert Mahan (Trader commenting on Enron)

SATURDAY

9

SUNDAY

10

THE INCREDIBLE JANUARY BAROMETER (DEVISED 1972): ONLY EIGHT SIGNIFICANT ERRORS IN 65 YEARS

Devised by Yale Hirsch in 1972, our January Barometer states that as the S&P 500 goes in January, so goes the year. The indicator has registered **only eight major errors since 1950 for an 87.7% accuracy ratio**. Vietnam affected 1966 and 1968; 1982 saw the start of a major bull market in August; two January rate cuts and 9/11 affected 2001; the anticipation of military action in Iraq held down the market in January 2003; 2009 was the beginning of a new bull market following the second worst bear market on record; the Fed saved 2010 with QE2; and QE3 likely staved off declines in 2014. (*Almanac Investor* newsletter subscribers receive full analysis of each reading as well as its potential implications for the full year.)

Including the eight flat-year errors (less than +/– 5%) yields a 75.4% accuracy ratio. A full comparison of all monthly barometers for the Dow, S&P, and NASDAQ can be seen in the January 20, 2015 Alert at www.stocktradersalmanac.com. Bear markets began or continued when Januarys suffered a loss (see page 48). Full years followed January's direction in 12 of the last 16 presidential election years. See page 18 for more.

AS JANUARY GOES, SO GOES THE YEAR

Market Performance in January

Year	Previous Year's Close	January Close	January Change	Year Change	
1950	16.76	17.05	1.7%	21.8%	
1951	20.41	21.66	6.1	16.5	
1952	23.77	24.14	1.6	11.8	
1953	26.57	26.38	-0.7	-6.6	
1954	24.81	26.08	5.1	45.0	
1955	35.98	36.63	1.8	26.4	
1956	45.48	43.82	-3.6	2.6	flat
1957	46.67	44.72	-4.2	-14.3	
1958	39.99	41.70	4.3	38.1	
1959	55.21	55.42	0.4	8.5	
1960	59.89	55.61	-7.1	-3.0	flat
1961	58.11	61.78	6.3	23.1	
1962	71.55	68.84	-3.8	-11.8	
1963	63.10	66.20	4.9	18.9	
1964	75.02	77.04	2.7	13.0	
1965	84.75	87.56	3.3	9.1	
1966	92.43	92.88	0.5	-13.1	X
1967	80.33	86.61	7.8	20.1	
1968	96.47	92.24	-4.4	7.7	X
1969	103.86	103.01	-0.8	-11.4	
1970	92.06	85.02	-7.6	0.1	flat
1971	92.15	95.88	4.0	10.8	
1972	102.09	103.94	1.8	15.6	
1973	118.05	116.03	-1.7	-17.4	
1974	97.55	96.57	-1.0	-29.7	
1975	68.56	76.98	12.3	31.5	
1976	90.19	100.86	11.8	19.1	
1977	107.46	102.03	-5.1	-11.5	
1978	95.10	89.25	-6.2	1.1	flat
1979	96.11	99.93	4.0	12.3	
1980	107.94	114.16	5.8	25.8	
1981	135.76	129.55	-4.6	-9.7	
1982	122.55	120.40	-1.8	14.8	X
1983	140.64	145.30	3.3	17.3	
1984	164.93	163.41	-0.9	1.4	flat
1985	167.24	179.63	7.4	26.3	
1986	211.28	211.78	0.2	14.6	
1987	242.17	274.08	13.2	2.0	flat
1988	247.08	257.07	4.0	12.4	
1989	277.72	297.47	7.1	27.3	
1990	353.40	329.08	-6.9	-6.6	
1991	330.22	343.93	4.2	26.3	
1992	417.09	408.79	-2.0	4.5	flat
1993	435.71	438.78	0.7	7.1	
1994	466.45	481.61	3.3	-1.5	flat
1995	459.27	470.42	2.4	34.1	
1996	615.93	636.02	3.3	20.3	
1997	740.74	786.16	6.1	31.0	
1998	970.43	980.28	1.0	26.7	
1999	1229.23	1279.64	4.1	19.5	
2000	1469.25	1394.46	-5.1	-10.1	
2001	1320.28	1366.01	3.5	-13.0	X
2002	1148.08	1130.20	-1.6	-23.4	
2003	879.82	855.70	-2.7	26.4	X
2004	1111.92	1131.13	1.7	9.0	
2005	1211.92	1181.27	-2.5	3.0	flat
2006	1248.29	1280.08	2.5	13.6	
2007	1418.30	1438.24	1.4	3.5	flat
2008	1468.36	1378.55	-6.1	-38.5	
2009	903.25	825.88	-8.6	23.5	X
2010	1115.10	1073.87	-3.7	12.8	X
2011	1257.64	1286.12	2.3	-0.003	flat
2012	1257.60	1312.41	4.4	13.4	
2013	1426.19	1498.11	5.0	29.6	
2014	1848.36	1782.59	-3.6	11.4	X
2015	2058.90	1994.99	-3.1	??	

January Performance by Rank

Rank	Year	January Change	Year's Change	
1	1987	13.2%	2.0%	flat
2	1975	12.3	31.5	
3	1976	11.8	19.1	
4	1967	7.8	20.1	
5	1985	7.4	26.3	
6	1989	7.1	27.3	
7	1961	6.3	23.1	
8	1997	6.1	31.0	
9	1951	6.1	16.5	
10	1980	5.8	25.8	
11	1954	5.1	45.0	
12	2013	5.0	29.6	
13	1963	4.9	18.9	
14	2012	4.4	13.4	
15	1958	4.3	38.1	
16	1991	4.2	26.3	
17	1999	4.1	19.5	
18	1971	4.0	10.8	
19	1988	4.0	12.4	
20	1979	4.0	12.3	
21	2001	3.5	-13.0	X
22	1965	3.3	9.1	
23	1983	3.3	17.3	
24	1996	3.3	20.3	
25	1994	3.3	-1.5	flat
26	1964	2.7	13.0	
27	2006	2.5	13.6	
28	1995	2.4	34.1	
29	2011	2.3	-0.003	flat
30	1972	1.8	15.6	
31	1955	1.8	26.4	
32	1950	1.7	21.8	
33	2004	1.7	9.0	
34	1952	1.6	11.8	
35	2007	1.4	3.5	flat
36	1998	1.0	26.7	
37	1993	0.7	7.1	
38	1966	0.5	-13.1	X
39	1959	0.4	8.5	
40	1986	0.2	14.6	
41	1953	-0.7	-6.6	
42	1969	-0.8	-11.4	
43	1984	-0.9	1.4	flat
44	1974	-1.0	-29.7	
45	2002	-1.6	-23.4	
46	1973	-1.7	-17.4	
47	1982	-1.8	14.8	X
48	1992	-2.0	4.5	flat
49	2005	-2.5	3.0	flat
50	2003	-2.7	26.4	X
51	2015	-3.1	??	
52	2014	-3.6	11.4	X
53	1956	-3.6	2.6	flat
54	2010	-3.7	12.8	X
55	1962	-3.8	-11.8	
56	1957	-4.2	-14.3	
57	1968	-4.4	7.7	X
58	1981	-4.6	-9.7	
59	1977	-5.1	-11.5	
60	2000	-5.1	-10.1	
61	2008	-6.1	-38.5	
62	1978	-6.2	1.1	flat
63	1990	-6.9	-6.6	
64	1960	-7.1	-3.0	flat
65	1970	-7.6	0.1	flat
66	2009	-8.6	23.5	X

X = major error Based on S&P 500

JANUARY

First Trading Day of January Expiration Week, Dow Up 16 of Last 23

MONDAY

D 52.4
S 61.9
N 66.7

11

History is replete with episodes in which the real patriots were the ones who defied their governments.
— Jim Rogers (Financier, *Adventure Capitalist*, b. 1942)

TUESDAY

D 47.6
S 57.1
N 61.9

12

If you are not willing to study, if you are not sufficiently interested to investigate and analyze the stock market yourself, then I beg of you to become an outright long-pull investor, to buy good stocks, and hold on to them; for otherwise your chances of success as a trader will be nil.
— Humphrey B. Neill (Investor, analyst, author, *Tape Reading and Market Tactics*, 1931, 1895–1977)

January Expiration Week Horrible Since 1999, Dow Down 10 of Last 17 Average Dow loss: –1.3%

WEDNESDAY

D 57.1
S 52.4
N 57.1

13

There are many people who think they want to be matadors [or money managers or traders] only to find themselves in the ring with two thousand pounds of bull bearing down on them, and then discover that what they really wanted was to wear tight pants and hear the crowd roar.
— Terry Pearce (Founder and President of Leadership Communication, b. 1941)

THURSDAY

D 52.4
S 52.4
N 52.4

14

The only title in our democracy superior to that of president is the title of citizen.
— Louis D. Brandeis (U.S. Supreme Court Justice 1916–1939, 1856–1941)

January Expiration Day, Dow Down 10 of Last 17 With Big Losses Off 2.1% in 2010, Off 2.0% in 2006 and 1.3% in 2003

FRIDAY

D 61.9
S 61.9
N 47.6

15

There has never been a commercial technology like this [Internet] in the history of the world, whereby the minute you adopt it, it forces you to think and act globally.
— Robert D. Hormats (Under Secretary of State Economic, Business and Agricultural Affairs, 2009–2013, Goldman Sachs 1982–2009, b. 1943)

SATURDAY

16

SUNDAY

17

JANUARY BAROMETER IN GRAPHIC FORM SINCE 1950

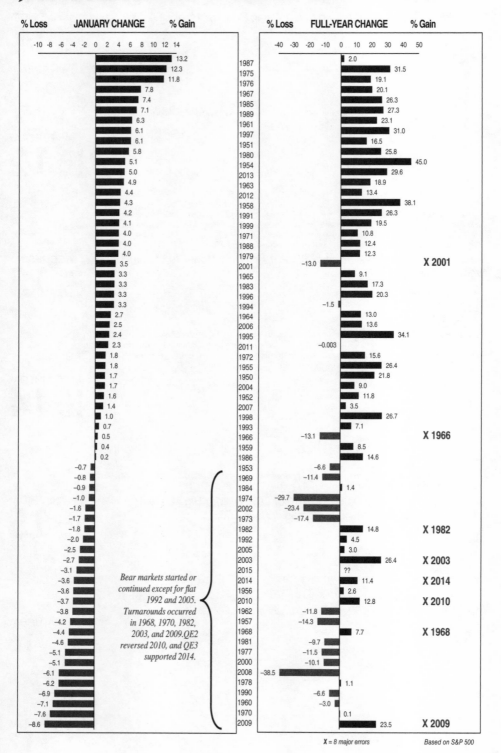

% Loss	JANUARY CHANGE	% Gain

	% Loss	FULL-YEAR CHANGE	% Gain

Year	January	Year	Full-Year
	13.2	1987	2.0
	12.3	1975	31.5
	11.8	1976	19.1
	7.8	1967	20.1
	7.4	1985	26.3
	7.1	1989	27.3
	6.3	1961	23.1
	6.1	1997	31.0
	6.1	1951	16.5
	5.8	1980	25.8
	5.1	1954	45.0
	5.0	2013	29.6
	4.9	1963	18.9
	4.4	2012	13.4
	4.3	1958	38.1
	4.2	1991	26.3
	4.1	1999	19.5
	4.0	1971	10.8
	4.0	1988	12.4
	4.0	1979	12.3
	3.5	2001	−13.0 X 2001
	3.3	1965	9.1
	3.3	1983	17.3
	3.3	1996	20.3
	3.3	1994	−1.5
	2.7	1964	13.0
	2.5	2006	13.6
	2.4	1995	34.1
	2.3	2011	−0.003
	1.8	1972	15.6
	1.8	1955	26.4
	1.7	1950	21.8
	1.7	2004	9.0
	1.6	1952	11.8
	1.4	2007	3.5
	1.0	1998	26.7
	0.7	1993	7.1
	0.5	1966	−13.1 X 1966
	0.4	1959	8.5
	0.2	1986	14.6
	−0.7	1953	−6.6
	−0.8	1969	−11.4
	−0.9	1984	1.4
	−1.0	1974	−29.7
	−1.6	2002	−23.4
	−1.7	1973	−17.4
	−1.8	1982	14.8 X 1982
	−2.0	1992	4.5
	−2.5	2005	3.0
	−2.7	2003	26.4 X 2003
	−3.1	2015	??
	−3.6	2014	11.4 X 2014
	−3.6	1956	2.6
	−3.7	2010	12.8 X 2010
	−3.8	1962	−11.8
	−4.2	1957	−14.3
	−4.4	1968	7.7 X 1968
	−4.6	1981	−9.7
	−5.1	1977	−11.5
	−5.1	2000	−10.1
	−6.1	2008	−38.5
	−6.2	1978	1.1
	−6.9	1990	−6.6
	−7.1	1960	−3.0
	−7.6	1970	0.1
	−8.6	2009	23.5 X 2009

Bear markets started or continued except for flat 1992 and 2005. Turnarounds occurred in 1968, 1970, 1982, 2003, and 2009. QE2 reversed 2010, and QE3 supported 2014.

X = 8 major errors   Based on S&P 500

18

Martin Luther King Jr. Day *(Market Closed)*

MONDAY
18

I learned that courage was not the absence of fear, but the triumph over it. The brave man is not he who does not feel afraid, but he who conquers that fear.
— Nelson Mandela (First President of South Africa, 1918–2013)

TUESDAY
19

D 52.4
S 61.9
N 71.4

You must automate, emigrate, or evaporate.
— James A. Baker (General Electric, b. 1930)

January Ends "Best Three-Month Span" (Pages 50, 58, 147, and 148)

WEDNESDAY
20

D 38.1
S 52.4
N 66.7

Your organization will never get better unless you are willing to admit that there is something wrong with it.
— General Norman Schwarzkopf (Ret. Commander of Allied Forces in 1990–1991 Gulf War, 1934–2012)

THURSDAY
21

D 33.3
S 38.1
N 28.6

It isn't the incompetent who destroy an organization. It is those who have achieved something and want to rest upon their achievements who are forever clogging things up.
— Charles E. Sorenson (Danish-American engineer, officer, director of Ford Motor Co. 1907–1950, helped develop first auto assembly line, 1881–1968)

FRIDAY
22

D 33.3
S 47.6
N 38.1

Drawing on my fine command of language, I said nothing.
— Robert Benchley (American writer, actor, and humorist, 1889–1945)

SATURDAY
23

SUNDAY
24

2016 PRESIDENTIAL ELECTION YEAR PERPECTIVES

ONLY TWO LOSSES IN LAST SEVEN MONTHS OF ELECTION YEARS
Regardless which Party is victorious, the last seven months have seen gains on the S&P in 14 of the 16 presidential election years since 1950. One loss was in 2000 when the election's outcome was delayed for 36 tumultuous days, though the Dow did end higher. Financial crisis and the worst bear market since the Great Depression impacted 2008. *Page 32.*

FIRST FIVE MONTHS BETTER WHEN PARTY RETAINS WHITE HOUSE
Since 1901 there have been 28 presidential elections. When the Party in power retained the White House 17 times, the Dow was up 1.5% on average for the first five months, compared to a 4.6% loss the 11 times the Party was ousted. Since 1950, retaining the White House 8 times brought an average gain of 1.9% compared to –0.1% the other 8 times.

WAR CAN BE A MAJOR FACTOR IN PRESIDENTIAL RACES
Democrats used to lose the White House on foreign shores (1920 WW1, 1952 Korea, 1968 Vietnam, 1980 Iran Crisis). Republicans, on the other hand, lost it here at home (1912 Party split, 1932 Depression, 1960 Economy, 1976 Watergate). Homeland issues dominated elections the last three decades, with the Republican loss in 1992 (Economy), the Democratic loss in 2000 (Scandal), and the Republican loss in 2008 (Economy). As we've learned over the years, it all depends on who the candidates are in 2016.

MARKET BOTTOMS TWO YEARS AFTER A PRESIDENTIAL ELECTION
A takeover of the White House by the opposing party in the past 50 years (1960, 1968, 1976, 1980, 1992, 2000, 2008) has resulted in a bottom within two years, except 1994, a flat year. When incumbent parties retained power (1964, 1972, 1984, 1988, 1996, 2004, 2012), stocks often bottomed within two years as well, except 1984 (three years, 1987), 2004 (one year, flat 2005), and 2012 (no bottom, QE). Whatever the outcome in 2016, we could see a bottom by 2018.

ONLY SIX ELECTION YEAR DECLINES GREATER THAN 5% SINCE 1896
Presidential election years are the second best performing year of the four-year cycle, producing losses of greater than 5% in only six of those 30 years. Incumbent parties lost power in five of those years. Five losses occurred at the end of the second term. FDR defeated Hoover in 1932 and was re-elected to an unprecedented third term as WWII ravaged Europe. Election year 2016 marks the end of the incumbent party's second term, increasing the probabilities of a weak year.

ELECTION YEAR LOSSES OVER 5% SINCE 1896

Year	Party Switch	Average % DJIA Loss *	End of 2nd Term
1920	X	–32.9%	X
1932	X	–23.1%	Market Crash 1st Term
1940	WWII 3rd term	–12.7%	X
1960	X	–9.3%	X
2000	X	–6.2%	X
2008	X	–33.8%	X

MARKET CHARTS OF PRESIDENTIAL ELECTION YEARS
Market behavior last 21 elections including candidates and winners. *Page 24.*

HOW THE GOVERNMENT MANIPULATES THE ECONOMY TO STAY IN POWER
Money faucets get turned on, if possible, in years divisible by "4." *Page 26.*

INCUMBENT VICTORIES VS. INCUMBENT DEFEATS
Markets tend to be stronger when Party in power wins. *Page 28.*

MONDAY

D 57.1
S 52.4
N 42.9

25

The more feted by the media, the worse a pundit's accuracy.
— Sharon Begley (Senior editor *Newsweek*, 2/23/2009, referencing Philip E. Tetlock's 2005 *Expert Political Judgment*)

FOMC Meeting (2 Days)

TUESDAY

D 61.9
S 57.1
N 76.2

26

The mind is not a vessel to be filled but a fire to be kindled.
— Plutarch (Greek biographer and philosopher, *Parallel Lives*, 46–120 A.D.)

WEDNESDAY

D 61.9
S 66.7
N 71.4

27

Cannot people realize how large an income is thrift?
— Marcus Tullius Cicero (Great Roman orator, politician, 106–43 B.C.)

THURSDAY

D 47.6
S 52.4
N 47.6

28

We may face more inflation pressure than currently shows up in formal data.
— William Poole (Economist, president Federal Reserve Bank St. Louis 1998–2008, June 2006 speech, b. 1937)

"January Barometer" 87.7% Accurate (Page 16)
Almanac Investor Subscribers Emailed Official Results (See Insert)

FRIDAY

D 57.1
S 61.9
N 57.1

29

Whom the gods would destroy, they first put on the cover of Business Week.
— Paul Krugman (Economist, *NY Times* 8/17/2001, referring to Enron CEO, cover 2/12, scandal 6/23, quits 8/16, b. 1953)

SATURDAY

30

February Almanac Investor Sector Seasonalities: See Pages 94, 96, and 98

SUNDAY

31

FEBRUARY ALMANAC

FEBRUARY							MARCH						
S	M	T	W	T	F	S	S	M	T	W	T	F	S
	1	2	3	4	5	6			1	2	3	4	5
7	8	9	10	11	12	13	6	7	8	9	10	11	12
14	15	16	17	18	19	20	13	14	15	16	17	18	19
21	22	23	24	25	26	27	20	21	22	23	24	25	26
28	29						27	28	29	30	31		

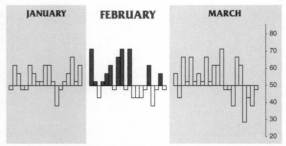

Market Probability Chart above is a graphic representation of the S&P 500 Recent Market Probability Calendar on page 124.

◆ February is the weak link in "Best Six Months" (pages 50, 52, & 147)
◆ RECENT RECORD: S&P up 9, down 6, average change –0.4% last 15 years ◆ Second best NASDAQ month in presidential election years average gain 2.4%, up 7, down 4 (page 157), #9 Dow, up 9, down 7, and #9 S&P, up 9, down 7 (pages 153 & 155) ◆ Day before Presidents' Day weekend S&P down 17 of 24, 11 straight 1992–2002, day after up 5 of last 6 (see pages 88 & 133) ◆ Many technicians modify market predictions based on January's market.

February Vital Statistics

	DJIA		S&P 500		NASDAQ		Russell 1K		Russell 2K	
Rank	8		9		8		9		7	
Up	39		37		25		23		22	
Down	27		29		20		14		15	
Average % Change	0.2%		0.1%		0.7%		0.4%		1.3%	
Election Year	–0.1%		0.1%		2.8%		0.3%		2.5%	
Best & Worst February										
	% Change		% Change		% Change		% Change		% Change	
Best	1986	8.8	1986	7.1	2000	19.2	1986	7.2	2000	16.4
Worst	2009	–11.7	2009	–11.0	2001	–22.4	2009	–10.7	2009	–12.3
Best & Worst February Weeks										
Best	2/1/08	4.4	2/6/09	5.2	2/4/00	9.2	2/6/09	5.3	2/1/91	6.6
Worst	2/20/09	–6.2	2/20/09	–6.9	2/9/01	–7.1	2/20/09	–6.9	2/20/09	–8.3
Best & Worst February Days										
Best	2/24/09	3.3	2/24/09	4.0	2/11/99	4.2	2/24/09	4.1	2/24/09	4.5
Worst	2/10/09	–4.6	2/10/09	–4.9	2/16/01	–5.0	2/10/09	–4.8	2/10/09	–4.7
First Trading Day of Expiration Week: 1980–2015										
Record (#Up – #Down)	21–15		25–11		20–16		25–11		21–15	
Current streak	U1		U1		U2		U2		U2	
Avg % Change	0.26		0.22		0.03		0.20		0.07	
Options Expiration Day: 1980–2015										
Record (#Up – #Down)	18–18		15–21		14–22		16–20		16–20	
Current streak	U1		U1		U1		U1		U2	
Avg % Change	–0.05		–0.13		–0.27		–0.13		–0.09	
Options Expiration Week: 1980–2015										
Record (#Up – #Down)	21–15		19–17		19–17		19–17		23–13	
Current streak	U1		U1		U2		U6		U6	
Avg % Change	–0.05		0.12		0.001		0.13		–0.09	
Week After Options Expiration: 1980–2015										
Record (#Up – #Down)	16–20		16–20		20–16		16–20		19–17	
Current streak	D1		D1		U2		D1		U2	
Avg % Change	–0.31		–0.23		–0.21		–0.20		–0.12	
First Trading Day Performance										
% of Time Up	62.1		62.1		71.1		67.6		67.6	
Avg % Change	0.14		0.16		0.33		0.20		0.34	
Last Trading Day Performance										
% of Time Up	50.0		56.1		51.1		56.8		56.8	
Avg % Change	0.01		–0.01		–0.06		–0.05		0.09	

Dow & S&P 1950–April 2015, NASDAQ 1971–April 2015, Russell 1K & 2K 1979–April 2015.

Either go short, or stay away the day before Presidents' Day.

FEBRUARY

MONDAY

1

D 71.4
S 71.4
N 76.2

A "tired businessman" is one whose business is usually not a successful one.
— Joseph R. Grundy (U.S. Senator Pennsylvania 1929–1930, businessman, 1863–1961)

TUESDAY

2

D 47.6
S 52.4
N 57.1

[A contrarian's opportunity] If everybody is thinking alike, then somebody isn't thinking.
— General George S. Patton, Jr. (U.S. Army field commander WWII, 1885–1945)

WEDNESDAY

3

D 42.9
S 42.9
N 42.9

The average man desires to be told specifically which particular stock to buy or sell. He wants to get something for nothing. He does not wish to work.
— William LeFevre (Senior analyst Ehrenkrantz King Nussbaum, 1928–1997)

THURSDAY

4

D 52.4
S 52.4
N 52.4

Civility is not a sign of weakness, and sincerity is always subject to proof. Let us never negotiate out of fear. But let us never fear to negotiate.
— John F. Kennedy (35th U.S. President, Inaugural Address 1/20/1961, 1917–1963)

FRIDAY

5

D 57.1
S 57.1
N 61.9

No other country can substitute for the U.S. The U.S. is still No. 1 in military, No. 1 in economy, No. 1 in promoting human rights and No. 1 in idealism. Only the U.S. can lead the world. No other country can.
— Senior Korean official (to Thomas L. Friedman *NY Times* Foreign Affairs columnist, 2/25/2009)

SATURDAY

6

SUNDAY

7

MARKET CHARTS OF PRESIDENTIAL ELECTION YEARS

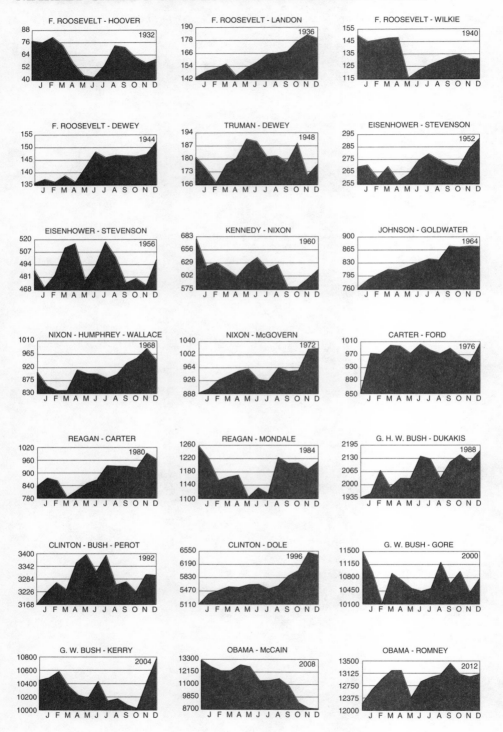

Based on Dow Jones Industrial Average monthly closing prices

MONDAY

D 47.6
S 61.9
N 66.7

8

An inventor fails 999 times, and if he succeeds once, he's in. He treats his failures simply as practice shots.
— Charles Kettering (Inventor of electric ignition, founded Delco in 1909, 1876–1958)

Week Before February Expiration Week, NASDAQ Down 9 of Last 15, 2010 Up 2.0%, 2011 Up 1.5%, 2014 Up 2.9%, 2015 Up 3.2%

TUESDAY

D 57.1
S 47.6
N 47.6

9

Nothing is more uncertain than the favor of the crowd.
— Marcus Tullius Cicero (Great Roman orator, politician, 106–43 B.C.)

Ash Wednesday

WEDNESDAY

D 57.1
S 66.7
N 52.4

10

To achieve satisfactory investment results is easier than most people realize. The typical individual investor has a great advantage over the large institutions.
— Benjamin Graham (Economist, investor, *Securities Analysis* 1934, *The Intelligent Investor* 1949, 1894–1976)

THURSDAY

D 61.9
S 71.4
N 61.9

11

The only function of economic forecasting is to make astrology look respectable.
— John Kenneth Galbraith (Canadian/American economist and diplomat, 1908–2006)

Day Before Presidents' Day Weekend, S&P Down 17 of Last 24

FRIDAY

D 47.6
S 47.6
N 66.7

12

The soul is dyed the color of its thoughts. Think only on those things that are in line with your principles and can bear the light of day. The content of your character is your choice. Day by day, what you do is who you become.
— Heraclitus (Greek philosopher, 535–475 B.C.)

SATURDAY

13

Valentine's Day ♥

SUNDAY

14

HOW THE GOVERNMENT MANIPULATES THE ECONOMY TO STAY IN POWER

Bull markets tend to occur in the third and fourth years of presidential terms while markets tend to decline in the first and second years. The "making of presidents" is accompanied by an unsubtle manipulation of the economy. Incumbent administrations are duty-bound to retain the reins of power. Subsequently, the "piper must be paid," producing what we have coined the "Post-Presidential Year Syndrome." Most big, bad bear markets began in such years—1929, 1937, 1957, 1969, 1973, 1977, and 1981. Our major wars also began in years following elections—Civil War (1861), WWI (1917), WWII (1941), and Vietnam (1965). Post-election 2001 combined with 2002 for the worst back-to-back years since 1973–1974. Plus, we had 9/11, the war on terror, and the build-up to confrontation with Iraq.

Some cold hard facts to prove economic manipulation appeared in a book by Edward R. Tufte, *Political Control of the Economy* (Princeton University Press). Stimulative fiscal measures designed to increase per capita disposable income providing a sense of well-being to the voting public included: increases in federal budget deficits, government spending, and social security benefits; interest rate reductions on government loans; and speed-ups of projected funding.

Federal Spending: During 1962–1973, the average increase was 29% higher in election years than in non-election years.

Social Security: There were nine increases during the 1952–1974 period. Half of the six election-year increases became effective in September eight weeks before Election Day. The average increase was 100% higher in presidential than in midterm election years. Annual adjustments for inflation have been the norm since then

Real Disposable Income: Accelerated in all but one election year between 1947 and 1973 (excluding the Eisenhower years). Only one of the remaining odd-numbered years (1973) showed a marked acceleration.

These moves were obviously not coincidences and explain why we tend to have a political (four-year) stock market cycle. Here are more examples of Election Year "generosity":

- "Nixon plans to pump about $1 billion a month more than originally planned into spending programs designed to put money into the pockets of millions of currently unhappy voters...Such openhanded spending marks Nixon's conversion from unsuccessful policies of conservatism and gradualism to the activist, pump-priming Keynesian economic theory." *Time*, January 31, 1972.
- "[EPA] Administrator Carol M. Browner today announced President Clinton's proposed fiscal year 2001 budget of $7.3 billion for the United States Environmental Protection Agency...the largest increase in the history of the Clinton/Gore Administration in spending for EPA...." EPA press release, February 7, 2000.
- "Like many of its predecessors, the Bush White House has used the machinery of government to promote the re-election of the president by awarding federal grants to strategically important states." *NY Times*, May 18, 2004.
- "Even some conservatives grumble that Bush's tax cuts, expanded drug benefits for seniors and increased military spending have spurred a dramatic increase in the federal budget deficit, projected to be $477 billion in fiscal 2004, according to the Congressional Budget Office." *TheStreet.com*, July 2, 2004.

The United States does not have an exclusive on electoral spending manipulations:

- "An executive increases spending to reward or cultivate loyalty to himself as the party or coalition leader. Evidence from South Korea and Taiwan between the 1970s and 2000 supports the theory. This strategy affects spending outcomes in election years." *Journal of East Asian Studies*, January 2006

As we go to press in mid-2015, the campaign for the White House is well underway. Hillary Clinton currently leads the Democratic hopefuls by a wide margin, but there are about ten Republican candidates who are in a statistical dead heat at the moment. The proverbial pump has been over-primed and flooded since 2008 to keep the U.S. economy solvent and the market humming along. U.S. quantitative easing is over and the Fed is on the threshold of raising interest rates for the first time since 2006. A lame duck Democratic president remains at odds with a Republican Congress. With little left to juice the economy an incumbent-less, wide-open, and contentious race is bound weigh negatively on the market.

Presidents' Day *(Market Closed)*

Change is the law of life. And those who look only to the past or present are certain to miss the future.
— John F. Kennedy (35th U.S. President, 1917–1963)

Day After Presidents Day, NASDAQ Down 14 of Last 21
First Trading Day of February Expiration Week Dow Down 7 of Last 11

Brilliant men are often strikingly ineffectual; they fail to realize that the brilliant insight is not by itself achievement. They never have learned that insights become effectiveness only through hard systematic work.
— Peter Drucker (Austrian-born pioneer management theorist, 1909–2005)

In a study of 3000 companies, researchers at the University of Pennsylvania found that spending 10% of revenue on capital improvements boosts productivity by 3.9%, but a similar investment in developing human capital increases productivity by 8.5%.
— John A. Byrne (Editor-in-Chief, *Fast Company Magazine*)

Let me end my talk by abusing slightly my status as an official representative of the Federal Reserve. I would like to say to Milton [Friedman]: regarding the Great Depression, you're right; we did it. We're very sorry. But thanks to you, we won't do it again.
— Ben Bernanke (Fed Chairman 2006–, 11/8/02 speech as Fed Govenor)

February Expiration Day, NASDAQ Down 12 of Last 16

Doubt is the father of invention.
— Galileo Galilei (Italian physicist and astronomer, 1564–1642)

INCUMBENT PARTY WINS & LOSSES

Since 1944, stocks tend to move up earlier when White House occupants are popular but do even better in November and December when unpopular administrations are ousted.

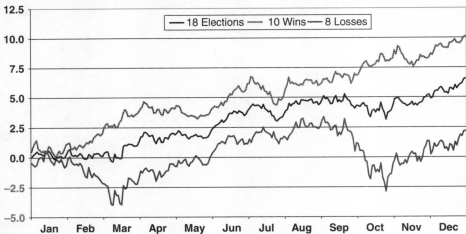

Actual percent changes reveal that March, June, October, and December are best when incumbents stay in power, while July is worst. January, February, September, and October are the worst when they are removed. Ironically, November is best when incumbents are ousted and third worst when they win.

Other interesting tidbits: there were no major losses in October (1984 off fractionally) and only one in June and December when incumbent parties retained the White House. Republican wins in November resulted in total gains of 23.6% (excluding no-decision 2000). Democratic victories produced total losses of 4.6% in November; however, Democrats "gained" 17.1% in December, the Republicans 7.9%.

MONTHLY % CHANGES IN S&P 500 DURING ELECTION YEARS

Incumbents Win

Year	Jan	Feb	Mar	Apr	May	Jun	Jul	Aug	Sep	Oct	Nov	Dec
1944	1.5	−0.3	1.7	−1.2	4.0	5.1	−2.1	0.9	−0.3	N/C	0.4	3.5
1948	−4.0	−4.7	7.7	2.7	7.8	0.3	−5.3	0.8	−3.0	6.8	−10.8	3.1
1956	−3.6	3.5	6.9	−0.2	−6.6	3.9	5.2	−3.8	−4.5	0.5	−1.1	3.5
1964	2.7	1.0	1.5	0.6	1.1	1.6	1.8	−1.6	2.9	0.8	−0.5	0.4
1972	1.8	2.5	0.6	0.4	1.7	−2.2	0.2	3.4	−0.5	0.9	4.6	1.2
1984	−0.9	−3.9	1.3	0.5	−5.9	1.7	−1.6	10.6	−0.3	−0.01	−1.5	2.2
1988	4.0	4.2	−3.3	0.9	0.3	4.3	−0.5	−3.9	4.0	2.6	−1.9	1.5
1996	3.3	0.7	0.8	1.3	2.3	0.2	−4.6	1.9	5.4	2.6	7.3	−2.2
2004	1.7	1.2	−1.6	−1.7	1.2	1.8	−3.4	0.2	0.9	1.4	3.9	3.2
2012	4.4	4.1	3.1	−0.7	−6.3	4.0	1.3	2.0	2.4	−2.0	0.3	0.7
Totals	**10.9**	**8.3**	**18.7**	**2.6**	**−0.4**	**20.7**	**−9.0**	**10.5**	**7.0**	**13.6**	**0.7**	**17.1**
Average	**1.1**	**0.8**	**1.9**	**0.3**	**−0.04**	**2.1**	**−0.9**	**1.1**	**0.7**	**1.4**	**0.07**	**1.7**

Incumbents Lose

Year	Jan	Feb	Mar	Apr	May	Jun	Jul	Aug	Sep	Oct	Nov	Dec
1952	1.6	−3.6	4.8	−4.3	2.3	4.6	1.8	−1.5	−2.0	−0.1	4.6	3.5
1960	−7.1	0.9	−1.4	−1.8	2.7	2.0	−2.5	2.6	−6.0	−0.2	4.0	4.6
1968	−4.4	−3.1	0.9	8.2	1.1	0.9	−1.8	1.1	3.9	0.7	4.8	−4.2
1976	11.8	−1.1	3.1	−1.1	−1.4	4.1	−0.8	−0.5	2.3	−2.2	−0.8	5.2
1980	5.8	−0.4	−10.2	4.1	4.7	2.7	6.5	0.6	2.5	1.6	10.2	−3.4
1992	−2.0	1.0	−2.2	2.8	0.1	−1.7	3.9	−2.4	0.9	0.2	3.0	1.0
2000	−5.1	−2.0	9.7	−3.1	−2.2	2.4	−1.6	6.1	−5.3	−0.5	−8.0*	0.4
2008	−6.1	−3.5	−0.6	4.8	1.1	−8.6	−1.0	1.2	−9.1	−16.9	−7.5	0.8
Totals	**−5.5**	**−11.8**	**4.1**	**9.6**	**8.4**	**6.4**	**4.5**	**7.2**	**−12.8**	**−17.4**	**10.3**	**7.9**
Average	**−0.7**	**−1.5**	**0.5**	**1.2**	**1.1**	**0.8**	**0.6**	**0.9**	**−1.6**	**−2.2**	**1.3**	**1.0**

	Jan	Feb	Mar	Apr	May	Jun	Jul	Aug	Sep	Oct	Nov	Dec
18 Elections	**5.4**	**−3.5**	**22.8**	**12.2**	**8.0**	**27.1**	**−4.5**	**17.7**	**−5.8**	**−3.8**	**11.0**	**25.0**
Average	**0.3**	**−0.2**	**1.3**	**0.7**	**0.4**	**1.5**	**−0.3**	**1.0**	**−0.3**	**−0.2**	**0.6**	**1.4**

Undecided election

FEBRUARY

MONDAY

D 52.4
S 47.6
N 38.1

22

Any fool can buy. It is the wise man who knows how to sell.
— Albert W. Thomas (Trader, investor, *Over My Shoulder*, mutualfundmagic.com, If It Doesn't Go Up, *Don't Buy* It!, b. 1927)

Week After February Expiration Week, Dow Down 11 of Last 17

TUESDAY

D 57.1
S 61.9
N 66.7

23

It wasn't raining when Noah built the ark.
— Warren Buffett (CEO Berkshire Hathaway, investor & philanthropist, b. 1930)

WEDNESDAY

D 33.3
S 38.1
N 52.4

24

Since 1950, the S&P 500 has achieved total returns averaging just 3.50% annually during periods when the S&P 500 price/ peak earnings ratio was above 15 and both 3-month T-bill yields and 10-year Treasury yields were above their levels of 6 months earlier.
— John P. Hussman, Ph.D. (Hussman Funds, 5/22/06)

End of February Miserable in Recent Years, (Page 22 and 133)

THURSDAY

D 42.9
S 47.6
N 52.4

25

Marx's great achievement was to place the system of capitalism on the defensive.
— Charles A. Madison (1977)

FRIDAY

D 47.6
S 57.1
N 52.4

26

Never attribute to malevolence what is merely due to incompetence.
— Arthur C. Clarke (British sci-fi writer, 3001: The Final Odyssey, 1917–2008)

SATURDAY

27

March Almanac Investor Sector Seasonalities: See Pages 94, 96, and 98

SUNDAY

28

MARCH ALMANAC

MARCH						
S	M	T	W	T	F	S
		1	2	3	4	5
6	7	8	9	10	11	12
13	14	15	16	17	18	19
20	21	22	23	24	25	26
27	28	29	30	31		

APRIL						
S	M	T	W	T	F	S
					1	2
3	4	5	6	7	8	9
10	11	12	13	14	15	16
17	18	19	20	21	22	23
24	25	26	27	28	29	30

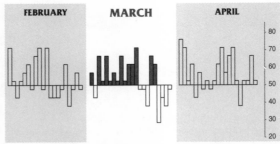

Market Probability Chart above is a graphic representation of the S&P 500 Recent Market Probability Calendar on page 124.

◆ Mid-month strength and late-month weakness are most evident above ◆ RECENT RECORD: S&P 14 up, 7 down, average gain 1.6%, fourth best ◆ Rather turbulent in recent years with wild fluctuations and large gains and losses ◆ March has been taking some mean end-of-quarter hits (page 134), down 1469 Dow points March 9–22, 2001 ◆ Last three or four days Dow a net loser 17 out of last 26 years ◆ NASDAQ hard hit in 2001, down 14.5% after 22.4% drop in February ◆ Second worst NASDAQ month during presidential election years average loss 1.6%, up 6, down 5.

March Vital Statistics

	DJIA		S&P 500		NASDAQ		Russell 1K		Russell 2K	
Rank	5		4		7		4		6	
Up	43		43		28		25		27	
Down	23		23		17		12		10	
Average % Change	1.1%		1.2%		0.8%		1.1%		1.3%	
Election Year	0.6%		0.8%		−1.6%		−0.6%		−2.1%	
Best & Worst March										
	% Change		% Change		% Change		% Change		% Change	
Best	2000	7.8	2000	9.7	2009	10.9	2000	8.9	1979	9.7
Worst	1980	−9.0	1980	−10.2	1980	−17.1	1980	−11.5	1980	−18.5
Best & Worst March Weeks										
Best	3/13/09	9.0	3/13/09	10.7	3/13/09	10.6	3/13/09	10.7	3/13/09	12.0
Worst	3/16/01	−7.7	3/6/09	−7.0	3/16/01	−7.9	3/6/09	−7.1	3/6/09	−9.8
Best & Worst March Days										
Best	3/23/09	6.8	3/23/09	7.1	3/10/09	7.1	3/23/09	7.0	3/23/09	8.4
Worst	3/2/09	−4.2	3/2/09	−4.7	3/12/01	−6.3	3/2/09	−4.8	3/27/80	−6.0
First Trading Day of Expiration Week: 1980–2015										
Record (#Up – #Down)	24–12		24–12		17–19		22–14		19–17	
Current streak	U4		U4		U3		U3		U3	
Avg % Change	0.20		0.08		0.27		0.02		−0.32	
Options Expiration Day: 1980–2015										
Record (#Up – #Down)	19–17		21–15		17–19		19–17		16–19	
Current streak	U1		U1		U1		U1		U1	
Avg % Change	0.07		0.020		−0.04		0.020		−0.04	
Options Expiration Week: 1980–2015										
Record (#Up – #Down)	25–10		24–12		22–14		23–13		20–16	
Current streak	U4		U4		U4		U4		U4	
Avg % Change	0.91		0.77		−0.04		0.71		0.22	
Week After Options Expiration: 1980–2015										
Record (#Up – #Down)	16–20		12–24		18–18		12–24		17–19	
Current streak	D1		D4		D3		D4		D4	
Avg % Change	−0.25		−0.16		−0.001		−0.16		−0.04	
First Trading Day Performance										
% of Time Up	66.7		63.6		62.2		59.5		64.9	
Avg % Change	0.14		0.15		0.21		0.10		0.18	
Last Trading Day Performance										
% of Time Up	42.4		40.9		64.4		48.6		81.1	
Avg % Change	−0.10		−0.001		0.17		0.09		0.39	

Dow & S&P 1950–April 2015, NASDAQ 1971–April 2015, Russell 1K & 2K 1979–April 2015.

March has Ides and St. Patrick's Day;
Begins bullishly, then fades away.

MONDAY

D 42.9
S 47.6
N 33.3

29

What's going on… is the end of Silicon Valley as we know it. The next big thing ain't computers… it's biotechnology.
— Larry Ellison (Oracle CEO, quoted in *The Wall Street Journal* 4/8/03, b. 1944)

First Trading Day in March Mixed, Dow Down 5 of Last 9, −4.2% in 2009, 1996–2006 Up 9 of 11

TUESDAY

D 57.1
S 57.1
N 52.4

1

Mankind is divided into three classes: Those that are immovable, those that are movable, and those that move.
— Arabian proverb (also attributed to Benjamin Franklin)

WEDNESDAY

D 47.6
S 42.9
N 38.1

2

[The Fed] is very smart, but [it] doesn't run the markets. In the end, the markets will run [the Fed]. The markets are bigger than any man or any group of men. The markets can even break a president. …
— Richard Russell (*Dow Theory Letters*, 8/4/04, b. 1924)

March Historically Strong Early in the Month (Pages 30 and 134)

THURSDAY

D 57.1
S 66.7
N 71.4

3

A government which robs Peter to pay Paul can always depend on the support of Paul.
— George Bernard Shaw (Irish dramatist, 1856–1950)

FRIDAY

D 47.6
S 52.4
N 38.1

4

Intellect and Emotion are partners who do not speak the same language. The intellect finds logic to justify what the emotions have decided. WIN THE HEARTS OF PEOPLE, THEIR MINDS WILL FOLLOW.
— Roy H. Williams (*The Wizard of Ads*, b. 1958)

SATURDAY

5

SUNDAY

6

ONLY TWO LOSSES LAST 7 MONTHS OF ELECTION YEARS

Election years are traditionally up years. Incumbent administrations shamelessly attempt to massage the economy so voters will keep them in power. But sometimes overpowering events occur and the market crumbles, usually resulting in a change of political control. The Republicans won in 1920 as the post-war economy contracted and President Wilson ailed. The Democrats came back during the 1932 Depression when the Dow hit its lowest level of the 20th century. A world at war and the fall of France jolted the market in 1940, but Roosevelt won an unprecedented third term. Cold War confrontations and Truman's historic upset of Dewey held markets down through the end of 1948.

Since 1948, investors have barely been bruised during election years, except for a brief span early in the year—until 2000 and then again in 2008. In both years a bubble burst: technology and internet stocks in 2000 and credit in 2008. Barring another massive regulatory failure, financial crisis, political miscalculation, or exogenous event, this is unlikely to occur again in 2016.

The table below presents a very positive picture for the last seven or eight months of election years.

- Since 1952, January through April losses occurred in eight of sixteen election years. Incumbent parties were ousted on six of these eight losses. Ironically, bear markets commenced following four of seven gainers in 1956, 1968, 1973, and 1976.

- Comparing month-end June with month-end April reveals gains in 1952, 1960, 1968, 1988, and 2000 for the sixty-day period, when no sitting President ran for reelection.

- Of the sixteen Julys since 1952, nine were losers (1960, 1968, 1976, 1984, 1988, 1996, 2000, 2004, and 2008). Five were years when, at convention time, no strong incumbent was running for reelection. Note that April through July periods had seven losers, the last five in a row: 1972 by a small margin, 1984 as the market was turning around, 1996 and 2000 as the bubble began to work off its excesses, 2004 and 2008 as the credit bubble burst, and 2012 as the Fed moved from Operation Twist to QE3.

- For a longer perspective, we extended the table to December. Just three losing eight-month periods in an election year are revealed and only two losses in the last seven months of all these years.

S&P 500 DURING ELECTION YEARS

Election Year	% Change First 4 Months	April	May	June	July	Dec	% Change Last 8 Months	Last 7 Months
1952*	−1.9%	**23.32**	23.86	24.96	25.40	26.57	13.9%	11.4%
1956	6.4	**48.38**	**45.20**	46.97	49.39	46.67	−3.5	3.3
1960*	−9.2	**54.37**	55.83	56.92	**55.51**	58.11	6.9	4.1
1964	5.9	79.46	80.37	81.69	83.18	84.75	6.7	5.4
1968*	1.2	97.59	98.68	99.58	**97.74**	103.86	6.4	5.2
1972	5.5	107.67	109.53	**107.14**	107.39	118.05	9.6	7.8
1976*	12.7	**101.64**	**100.18**	104.28	**103.44**	107.46	5.7	7.3
1980*	−1.5	106.29	111.24	114.24	121.67	**135.76**	27.7	22.0
1984	−3.0	160.05	**150.55**	153.18	**150.66**	167.24	4.5	11.1
1988	5.8	261.33	262.16	273.50	**272.02**	277.72	6.3	5.9
1992*	−0.5	414.95	415.35	**408.14**	424.21	435.71	5.0	4.9
1996	6.2	654.17	669.12	670.63	**639.95**	740.74	13.2	10.7
2000**	−1.1	**1452.43**	**1420.60**	1454.60	**1430.83**	1320.28	−9.1	−7.1
2004	−0.4	**1107.30**	1120.68	1140.84	**1101.72**	1211.92	9.4	8.1
2008*	−5.6	1385.59	1400.38	**1280.00**	**1267.38**	903.25	−34.8	−35.5
2012	11.2	1397.91	1310.33	**1362.16**	1379.32	1426.19	2.0	8.8
Totals	**31.7%**						**69.9%**	**73.4%**
Average	**2.0%**						**4.4%**	**4.6%**

*Incumbents ousted, ** Incumbent ousted & undecided Election
Down months are bold

PROBABILITIES FUND MANAGEMENT, LLC

Long/Short Equity
Class A: PROAX
Class I: PROTX
Class C: PROCX
www.probabilitiesfund.com

PROFIT FROM HISTORY

Joseph B. Childrey
Founder, Chief Investment Officer

Investment Overview

The Probabilities Fund Long/Short Equity ("Fund") seeks capital appreciation by systematically investing to gain long, short or leveraged exposure primarily to the S&P 500 through Index ETFs. Since inception in January 2008, the strategy utilized by the Fund has produced attractive absolute, relative and risk-adjusted returns over multiple time periods with average to below average volatility to our benchmark. The strategy places special emphasis on risk management limiting loss by using disciplined, systematic methods. There is no guarantee that any investment will achieve its objectives, generate positive returns, or avoid losses.

Jeffrey A. Hirsch
Investment Committee Consultant

Cumulative Growth Chart

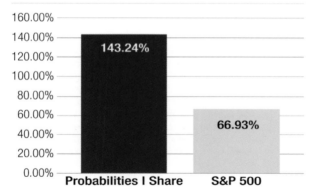

- Probabilities I Share: 143.24%
- S&P 500: 66.93%

Past Performance is no indication of future returns. Since inception, January 1, 2008 to present.

Performance

As of 06/30/2015 (Greater than one year, annualized)

	YTD	1 Year	3 Years	5 Years	Since Inception*
Probabilities Fund (Class I)	-4.24%	1.31%	10.28%	13.74%	12.59%
Probabilities Fund A at NAV	-4.26%	1.12%	N/A	N/A	0.84%
Probabilities Fund A at ML**	-9.76%	-4.71%	N/A	N/A	-3.21%

*A share since inception 1/16/14 to present. I share since inception 12/12/13 to present.
**ML refers to maximum load.

6289-NLD-7/23/2015

Strategic Rules + Tactical Signals

Strategic Rules:
- Historical "best six months".
- Historical "worst six months".
- Quarterly window dressing.
- Pension plan flows.

Tactical Signals:
- Momentum indicators (MACD).
- Pre-fed announcement drift.
- Congressional effect.
- Cross market exchange.

Strategy Highlights

People:
- Thought leadership in the trend following space.
- Over 100 years cumulative experience.

Philosophy:
- Be out of the market during periods when there is a high probability of downside risk.
- Be in the market during periods when there is a high probability of upside reward.

Process:
Directional funds of funds structure utilizing ETFs. Approximately 75% of the time the fund is either 1X or 100% cash.

- Long 1X - approximately 45% of the time.
- Cash - approximately 30% of the time.
- Leveraged - approximately 20% of the time.
- Short - approximately 5% of the time.

Disclosures

Investors should carefully consider the investment objectives, risks, charges and expenses of the Probabilities Fund. This and other important information about the Fund is contained in the Prospectus, which can be obtained by contacting your financial advisor, or by calling 1.888.868.9501. The Prospectus should be read carefully before investing. Probabilities Fund is distributed by Northern Lights Distributors, LLC member FINRA/SIPC. Princeton Fund Advisors, LLC and Northern Lights Distributors are not affiliated.

Performance shown before the inception date of the mutual fund, December 12, 2013, is for the Fund's predecessor limited partnership. The prior performance is net of management fee and other expenses, including the effect of the performance fee. The Fund's investment goals, policies, guidelines and restrictions are similar to the predecessor limited partnership. From its inception date, the predecessor limited partnership was not subject to certain investment restrictions, diversification requirements and other restrictions of the Investment Company Act of 1940 which if they had been applicable, it might have adversely affected its performance. In addition, the predecessor limited partnership was not subject to sales loads that would have adversely affected performance. Performance of the predecessor fund is not an indicator of future results.

Mutual Funds involve risk including the possible loss of principal.

ETFs are subject to investment advisory and other expenses, which will be indirectly paid by the Fund. As a result, your cost of investing in the Fund will be higher than the cost of investing directly in the ETFs and may be higher than other mutual funds that invest directly in stocks and bonds. Each ETF is subject to specific risks, depending on its investments. Leveraged ETFs employ leverage, which magnifies the changes in the value of the Leveraged ETFs, which could result in significant losses to the Fund. The Fund invests in Leveraged ETFs in an effort to deliver daily performance at twice the rate of the underlying index and if held over long periods of time, particularly in volatile markets, the ETFs may not achieve their objective and may, in fact, perform contrary to expectations. Inverse ETFs are designed to rise in price when stock prices are falling. Inverse ETFs tend to limit the Fund's participation in overall market-wide gains. Accordingly, their performance over longer terms can perform very differently than underlying assets and benchmarks, and volatile markets can amplify this effect.

The co-advisor's judgments about the attractiveness, value and potential appreciation of particular security or derivative in which the Fund invests or sells short may prove to be incorrect and may not produce the desired results. Equity prices can fall rapidly in response to developments affecting a specific company or industry, or to changing economic, political or market conditions. A higher portfolio turnover may result in higher transactional and brokerage costs. The indices shown are for informational purposes only and are not reflective of any investment. As it is not possible to invest in the indices, the data shown does not reflect or compare features of an actual investment, such as its objectives, costs and expenses, liquidity, safety, guarantees or insurance, fluctuation of principal or return, or tax features. Past performance does not guaranteed future results.

The S&P 500 Index is an unmanaged composite of 500 large capitalization companies. This index is widely used by professional investors as a performance benchmark for large-cap stocks. Alpha is a measure of the excess return of a fund over an index. Beta is a measure of a fund's volatility relative to market movements. Sharpe Ratio is a measure of risk adjusted performance calculated by subtracting the risk-free rate from the rate of return of the portfolio and dividing the result by the standard deviation of the portfolio returns. A risk free rate of 2.00% was used in this calculation. Standard Deviation is a statistical measurement of volatility risk based on historical returns. Maximum Drawdown represents the largest peak-to-trough decline during a specific period of time. Correlation is a statistical measure of how two investments move in relation to each other. Up and Down Capture ratios reflect how a particular investment performed when a specific index has either risen or fallen. Long positions entail buying a security such as a stock, commodity or currency, with the expectation that the asset will rise in value. Short positions entail a sale that is completed by the delivery of a security borrowed by the seller. Short sellers assume they will be able to buy the stock at a lower amount that the price at which they sold short.

🐂 **MONDAY**

D 66.7
S 66.7
N 47.6

7

The symbol of all relationships among such men, the moral symbol of respect for human beings, is the trader.
— Ayn Rand (Russian-born American novelist and philosopher, from Galt's Speech, *Atlas Shrugged*, 1957, 1905–1982)

TUESDAY

D 47.6
S 52.4
N 47.6

8

Life does not consist mainly of facts and happenings. It consists mainly of the storm of thoughts that are forever blowing through one's mind.
— Mark Twain (pen name of Samuel Longhorne Clemens, American novelist and satirist, 1835–1910)

Dow Down 1469 Points March 9–22 in 2001

WEDNESDAY

D 61.9
S 57.1
N 47.6

9

There is only one side of the market and it is not the bull side or the bear side, but the right side.
— Jesse Livermore (Early 20th century stock trader and speculator, *How to Trade in Stocks*, 1877–1940)

THURSDAY

D 61.9
S 52.4
N 47.6

10

In politics as in chess, or in the military or in business, when you have the advantage you must press it quickly – or lose it. For the first time in history, we are in a position to checkmate tyranny. Momentum is largely on the side of democracy.
— Garry Kasparov (World Chess Champion 1985–2000, b. 1963)

🐂 **FRIDAY**

D 52.4
S 66.7
N 66.7

11

Great spirits have always encountered violent opposition from mediocre minds.
— Albert Einstein (German/American physicist, 1921 Nobel Prize, 1879–1955)

SATURDAY

12

Daylight Saving Time Begins

SUNDAY

13

LEVERAGE THE PROBABILITIES FUND (PROTX) STRATEGIC AND TACTICAL TRADING SYSTEM

One of the first tactical and strategic maneuvers Yale Hirsch made upon completion of the first *Stock Trader's Almanac* in the summer of 1967 was to hire a salesman to go door-to-door on Wall Street to all the brokerage firms and wire houses to introduce them to this tour de force. So while Jimi Hendrix shrouded the airwaves and the Monterey Pop Festival with "Purple Haze" and the Beatles rocked the music landscape with groundbreaking concept albums and took the world on a Magical Mystery Tour of love, peace, and controversy, Yale's *Almanac* salesman pounded the pavement of lower Manhattan during the Summer of Love, turning the investment world on to the efficacy and validity of market patterns, seasonality and cycles, and Yale's brilliant creation, *The Stock Trader's Almanac*. The rest, especially in our case, is history.

Decades later, in 1999, Joe Childrey, at the time a branch manager for A.G. Edwards in La Jolla, California, was heading out on a long-planned African safari vacation. Departing from his office and having left his reading material at home, he grabbed the *Stock Trader's Almanac* that had been sitting on his desk and conference table annually for years—a gift from his boss, the late Ben Edwards, a wise man Joe respected very much. While Joe had perused it and shared it with clients, he had never really delved deep into the *Almanac*.

Traveling for two weeks with nothing to read but the *Almanac*, Joe came back a changed man and a converted market pattern devotee. Upon his return he began to trade his own account using the Best Six Months/Worst Six Months Switching Strategy (pages 52 and 54) with a solid degree of success. In 2007 Joe went out on his own and founded Probabilities Fund, LP. This private investment partnership went live on January 1, 2008, and outperformed the S&P in 2008. While the S&P 500 lost 37.0%, including dividends, during the worst bear market in a generation in 2008, Probabilities Fund gained 5.3% net of management fee and other expenses, including the effect of the hedge fund performance fee.

After five more years of continued success Joe was compelled to make the Probabilities Fund available to more people, especially registered investment advisors and their clients and individual investors. On December 12, 2013, Probabilities Fund became a fully registered mutual fund under the Investment Company Act of 1940, following the same strategy used to manage the hedge fund. **Probabilities Fund** (PROTX) leverages market patterns, seasonality and cycles with a data-driven, rules-based, strategic, and tactical trading system.

As of June 30, 2015 Probabilities Fund was up 143.2% since inception on January 1, 2008 versus 65.4% for the S&P 500 over the same timeframe. Annualized return for Probabilities Fund is 12.6% since inception compared to 6.9% for the S&P 500. Results for the trailing periods ended June 30 are: year-to-date –4.24%; 1 year +1.31%; 3 years +10.28%; 5 years +13.74%; since inception 1/1/2008 +12.59% (returns for periods greater than one year are annualized). Load-adjusted results for the A share class are: year-to-date –9.76%; 1 year –4.71%; since inception 1/16/14 –3.21% (returns for periods greater than one year are annualized).

The performance data quoted here represents past performance. Current performance may be lower or higher than the performance data quoted above. Investment return and principal value will fluctuate, so that shares, when redeemed, may be worth more or less than their original cost. Past performance is no guarantee of future results. The total annual fund operating expenses are Class A 2.33%, Class C 3.08% and Class I 2.08%. The Fund's co-advisors have contractually agreed to reduce their fees and/or absorb expenses of the Fund, at least until January 31, 2016, to ensure that the net annual fund operating expenses will not exceed 2.14% for Class A, 2.89% for Class C and 1.89% for Class I, subject to possible recoupment from the Fund in future years. The maximum sale charge for Class A shares is 5.75%. For performance information current to the most recent month-end, please call toll-free 888-868-9501 or visit our website, www.probabilitiesfund.com.

The Fund utilizes a rules-based, systematic approach to attempt to capitalize on repeating cyclical, seasonal, political, and other long-term historical patterns in the S&P 500 Index. It seeks to identify periods when the S&P 500 is estimated to have the highest and lowest probabilities of capital appreciation and to pinpoint market entry and exit points. This dynamic methodology utilizes strategic rules and tactical signals.

Strategic rules create a calendar blueprint from historical trends and patterns that define the daily biases, either bullish, bearish, or neutral. Daily biases are updated annually as each new year incorporates the previous years' trends and patterns. These strategic rules include:

- Presidential election cycles
- Historical "Best Six Months"
- Historical "Worst Six Months"
- Monthly market patterns
- Quarterly market patterns
- Institutional fund flow patterns

Monday Before March Triple Witching, Dow Up 21 of Last 28

MONDAY

D 66.7
S 52.4
N 52.4

14

Analysts are supposed to be critics of corporations. They often end up being public relations spokesmen for them.
— Ralph Wanger (Chief Investment Officer, Acorn Fund)

FOMC Meeting (2 Days)

TUESDAY

D 61.9
S 61.9
N 47.6

15

A good trader has to have three things: a chronic inability to accept things at face value, to feel continuously unsettled, and to have humility.
— Michael Steinhardt (Financier, philanthropist, political activist, chairman WisdomTree Investments, b. 1940)

Bullish Cluster Highlights March's "Sweet Spot"

WEDNESDAY

D 52.4
S 61.9
N 57.1

16

The less a man knows about the past and the present the more insecure must be his judgment of the future.
— Sigmund Freud (Austrian neurologist, psychiatrist, "Father of Psychoanalysis," 1856–1939)

St. Patrick's Day ♣

THURSDAY

D 66.7
S 71.4
N 61.9

17

Make money and the whole nation will conspire to call you a gentleman.
— George Bernard Shaw (Irish dramatist, 1856–1950)

March Triple Witching Day Mixed Last 28 Years
But, Dow Down 5 of Last 7

FRIDAY

D 61.9
S 47.6
N 61.9

18

I'm very big on having clarified principles. I don't believe in being reactive. You can't do that in the markets effectively. I can't. I need perspective. I need a game plan.
— Ray Dalio (Money manager, founder Bridgewater Associates, *Fortune* 3/16/2009, b. 1949)

SATURDAY

19

SUNDAY

20

Tactical signals are generated from technical or political event-driven decisions used to dial up or down the exposure and predetermined entries and exits. Tactical signals include:

- Technical momentum indicators
- Pre-Fed announcement drift
- Congress in or out of session
- International markets relative to domestic markets
- Special Congressional sessions

In 2015, Jeff joined the Probabilities Fund Management LLC team as a consultant to the firm and an Investment Committee Member. We will be working with them to refine, hone, and improve upon the rules and signals where possible and assist in developing the new Probabilities Tactical Sector Rotation Strategy for mutual funds, ETFs, and separately managed accounts based on much of the seasonal sector work we do.

Probabilities Fund is geared to complement any well-thought-out diversified portfolio. It may serve as a diversifier for traditional and alternative portfolios. With a correlation of 0.42 to the S&P 500 Index since inception, it can act as a separate asset class. Visit www.probabilitiesfund.com for more information.

Disclosure Note: At press time, officers of the Hirsch Holdings Inc., or the accounts they control, held a position in PROTX.

Disclosure included here is information that should be read by prospective investors.

Performance shown before the inception date of the mutual fund, December 12, 2013, is for the Fund's predecessor limited partnership. The prior performance is net of management fee and other expenses, including the effect of the performance fee. The Fund's investment goals, policies, guidelines, and restrictions are similar to the predecessor limited partnership. From its inception date, the predecessor limited partnership was not subject to certain investment restrictions, diversification requirements, and other restrictions of the Investment Company Act of 1940, which if they had been applicable, might have adversely affected its performance. In addition, the predecessor limited partnership was not subject to sales loads that would have adversely affected performance. Performance of the predecessor fund is not an indicator of future results.

There is no guarantee that any investment will achieve its objectives, generate positive returns, or avoid losses.

The indices shown are for informational purposes only and are not reflective of any investment. As it is not possible to invest in the indices, the data shown does not reflect or compare features of an actual investment, such as its objectives, costs and expenses, liquidity, safety, guarantees or insurance, fluctuation of principal or return, or tax features.

Investors should carefully consider the investment objectives, risks, charges, and expenses of the Probabilities Fund. This and other important information about the Fund is contained in the Prospectus, which can be obtained by contacting your financial advisor, or by calling 1.888.868.9501. The Prospectus should be read carefully before investing. Probabilities Fund is distributed by Northern Lights Distributors, LLC member FINRA/SIPC. Princeton Fund Advisors, LLC, Probabilities Fund Management, LLC, and Northern Lights Distributors are not affiliated.

Mutual Funds involve risk including the possible loss of principal.

ETFs are subject to investment advisory and other expenses, which will be indirectly paid by the Fund. As a result, your cost of investing in the Fund will be higher than the cost of investing directly in the ETFs and may be higher than other mutual funds that invest directly in stocks and bonds. Each ETF is subject to specific risks, depending on its investments. Leveraged ETFs employ leverage, which magnifies the changes in the value of the Leveraged ETFs, which could result in significant losses to the Fund. The Fund invests in Leveraged ETFs in an effort to deliver daily performance at twice the rate of the underlying index and if held over long periods of time, particularly in volatile markets, the ETFs may not achieve their objective and may, in fact, perform contrary to expectations. Inverse ETFs are designed to rise in price when stock prices are falling. Inverse ETFs tend to limit the Fund's participation in overall market-wide gains. Accordingly, their performance over longer terms can be very different from underlying assets and benchmarks, and volatile markets can amplify this effect.

The co-advisor's judgments about the attractiveness, value, and potential appreciation of a particular security or derivative in which the Fund invests or sells short may prove to be incorrect and may not produce the desired results. Equity prices can fall rapidly in response to developments affecting a specific company or industry, or to changing economic, political, or market conditions. A higher portfolio turnover may result in higher transactional and brokerage costs. The indices shown are for informational purposes only and are not reflective of any investment. As it is not possible to invest in the indices, the data shown does not reflect or compare features of an actual investment, such as its objectives, costs and expenses, liquidity, safety, guarantees or insurance, fluctuation of principal or return, or tax features. Past performance does not guarantee future results.

The S&P 500 Index is an unmanaged composite of 500 large capitalization companies. This index is widely used by professional investors as a performance benchmark for large-cap stocks.

6279-NLD-7/21/2015

Week After Triple Witching, Dow Down 17 of Last 28, 2000 Up 4.9%, 2007 Up 3.1%, 2009 Up 6.8%, 2011 Up 3.1%, Up 8 of Last 12

MONDAY
D 42.9
S 47.6
N 38.1
21

Over the last 25 years, computer processing capacity has risen more than a millionfold, while communication capacity has risen over a thousandfold.
— Richard Worzel (Futurist, *Facing the Future*, b. 1950)

🐻 TUESDAY
D 47.6
S 38.1
N 57.1
22

Anyone who believes that exponential growth can go on forever in a finite world is either a madman or an economist.
— Kenneth Ewart Boulding (Economist, activist, poet, scientist, philosopher, cofounder General Systems Theory, 1910–1993)

March Historically Weak Later in the Month (Pages 30 and 134)

🐂 WEDNESDAY
D 42.9
S 66.7
N 61.9
23

There's no trick to being a humorist when you have the whole government working for you.
— Will Rogers (American humorist and showman, 1879–1935)

NASDAQ Up 15 Straight Days Before Good Friday

🐂 THURSDAY
D 61.9
S 61.9
N 66.7
24

The greatest good you can do for another is not just to share your riches, but to reveal to him his own.
— Benjamin Disraeli (British prime minister, 1804–1881)

Good Friday *(Market Closed)*

FRIDAY
25

The most important lesson in investing is humility.
— Sir John Templeton (Founder Templeton Funds, philanthropist, 1912–2008)

SATURDAY
26

Easter
April Almanac Investor Sector Seasonalities: See Pages 94, 96, and 98

SUNDAY
27

APRIL ALMANAC

APRIL							MAY						
S	M	T	W	T	F	S	S	M	T	W	T	F	S
					1	2	1	2	3	4	5	6	7
3	4	5	6	7	8	9	8	9	10	11	12	13	14
10	11	12	13	14	15	16	15	16	17	18	19	20	21
17	18	19	20	21	22	23	22	23	24	25	26	27	28
24	25	26	27	28	29	30	29	30	31				

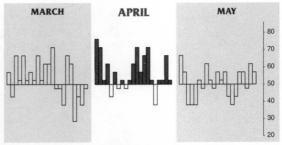

Market Probability Chart above is a graphic representation of the S&P 500 Recent Market Probability Calendar on page 124.

◆ April is still the best Dow month (average 1.9%) since 1950 (page 50) ◆ April 1999, first month ever to gain 1000 Dow points, 856 in 2001, knocked off its high horse in 2002, down 458, 2003 up 488 ◆ Up ten straight, average gain 2.8% ◆ Prone to weakness after mid-month tax deadline ◆ Stocks anticipate great first-quarter earnings by rising sharply before earnings are reported, rather than after ◆ Rarely a dangerous month, recent exceptions are 2002, 2004, and 2005 ◆ "Best Six Months" of the year end with April (page 52) ◆ Presidential election year Aprils weaker since 1950 (Dow 0.9%, S&P 0.7%, NASDAQ 0.2%) ◆ End of April NASDAQ strength (pages 125 & 126).

April Vital Statistics

	DJIA		S&P 500		NASDAQ		Russell 1K		Russell 2K	
Rank	1		3		4		3		4	
Up	44		46		29		25		22	
Down	22		20		16		12		15	
Average % Change	1.9%		1.5%		1.4%		1.6%		1.5%	
Election Year	0.9%		0.7%		−0.2%		0.9%		0.01%	
	Best & Worst April									
	% Change		% Change		% Change		% Change		% Change	
Best	1978	10.6	2009	9.4	2001	15.0	2009	10.0	2009	15.3
Worst	1970	−6.3	1970	−9.0	2000	−15.6	2002	−5.8	2000	−6.1
	Best & Worst April Weeks									
Best	4/11/75	5.7	4/20/00	5.8	4/12/01	14.0	4/20/00	5.9	4/3/09	6.3
Worst	4/14/00	−7.3	4/14/00	−10.5	4/14/00	−25.3	4/14/00	−11.2	4/14/00	−16.4
	Best & Worst April Days									
Best	4/5/01	4.2	4/5/01	4.4	4/5/01	8.9	4/5/01	4.6	4/9/09	5.9
Worst	4/14/00	−5.7	4/14/00	−5.8	4/14/00	−9.7	4/14/00	−6.0	4/14/00	−7.3
	First Trading Day of Expiration Week: 1980–2015									
Record (#Up – #Down)	22–14		20–16		19–17		19–17		16–20	
Current streak	D1		D1		D1		D1		U2	
Avg % Change	0.19		0.11		0.11		0.10		−0.03	
	Options Expiration Day: 1980–2015									
Record (#Up – #Down)	24–12		24–12		21–15		24–12		23–13	
Current streak	D2		D1		D1		D1		D1	
Avg % Change	0.18		0.18		−0.03		0.17		0.20	
	Options Expiration Week: 1980–2015									
Record (#Up – #Down)	28–8		25–11		23–13		23–13		26–10	
Current streak	D1		D1		D1		D1		D1	
Avg % Change	1.05		0.85		0.88		0.83		0.73	
	Week After Options Expiration: 1980–2015									
Record (#Up – #Down)	24–12		24–12		26–10		24–12		24–12	
Current streak	U1		U1		U1		U1		U1	
Avg % Change	0.43		0.43		0.72		0.44		0.84	
	First Trading Day Performance									
% of Time Up	59.1		62.1		46.7		59.5		48.6	
Avg % Change	0.17		0.14		−0.10		0.17		−0.06	
	Last Trading Day Performance									
% of Time Up	51.5		56.1		66.7		56.8		67.6	
Avg % Change	0.08		0.08		0.15		0.06		0.09	

Dow & S&P 1950–April 2015, NASDAQ 1971–April 2015, Russell 1K & 2K 1979–April 2015.

April "Best Month" for Dow since 1950;
Day-before-Good Friday gains are nifty.

Day After Easter, Second Worst Post-Holiday (Page 88)

MONDAY

D 23.8
S 28.6
N 33.3

28

Everything possible today was at one time impossible. Everything impossible today may at some time in the future be possible.
— Edward Lindaman (Apollo space project, president Whitworth College, 1920–1982)

Start Looking for the Dow and S&P MACD SELL Signal (Pages 52 and 54)
Almanac Investor Subscribers Emailed When It Triggers (See Ad Insert)

TUESDAY

D 47.6
S 42.9
N 42.9

29

It is a funny thing about life; if you refuse to accept anything but the best, you very often get it.
— W. Somerset Maugham (British writer, 1874–1965)

WEDNESDAY

D 52.4
S 38.1
N 47.6

30

In my experience, selling a put is much safer than buying a stock.
— Kyle Rosen (Boston Capital Mgmt., *Barron's* 8/23/04)

Last Trading Day of March, Dow Down 16 of Last 27
Russell 2000 Up 15 of Last 21

THURSDAY

D 42.9
S 47.6
N 57.1

31

If banking institutions are protected by the taxpayer and they are given free reign to speculate, I may not live long enough to see the crisis, but my soul is going to come back and haunt you.
— Paul A. Volcker (Fed Chairman 1979–1987, Chair Economic Recovery Advisory Board, 2/2/2010, b. 1927)

First Trading Day in April, Dow Up 16 of Last 21

FRIDAY

D 76.2
S 76.2
N 66.7

1

I went to a restaurant that serves "breakfast at any time." So I ordered French toast during the Renaissance.
— Steven Wright (Comedian, b. 1955)

SATURDAY

2

SUNDAY

3

EIGHTH YEAR OF PRESIDENTIAL TERMS

Prior to President Obama, there have been six previous presidents that served an eighth year in office since 1901; Presidents Wilson (1920), Roosevelt (1940), Eisenhower (1960), Reagan (1988), Clinton (2000), and G.W. Bush (2008). President McKinley was elected to a second term, but was assassinated in his fifth year in office. President Nixon was elected to a second term, but resigned in his sixth year in office. Eighth years are also presidential election years. In the following two charts the one-year seasonal pattern for eighth years is compared to all presidential election years.

Eighth years of presidential terms represent the worst of election years since 1920. In eighth years, DJIA and S&P 500 have suffered average declines of –13.9% and –10.9% respectively. Out of these six full years, only 1988 was positive. As a result, eighth years have vastly differed from the typical election-year pattern. See pages 171 to 173 for additional one-year seasonal pattern charts.

APRIL

🐂 **MONDAY**

D 71.4
S 71.4
N 61.9

4

Charts not only tell what was, they tell what is; and a trend from was to is (projected linearly into the will be) contains better percentages than clumsy guessing.
— Robert A. Levy (Chairman, Cato Institute, founder, CDA Investment Technologies, *The Relative Strength Concept of Common Stock Forecasting*, 1968, b. 1941)

April is the Best Month for the Dow, Average 1.9% Gain Since 1950

TUESDAY

D 42.9
S 52.4
N 66.7

5

Don't put all your eggs in one basket.
— Market maxim

🐂 **WEDNESDAY**

D 66.7
S 61.9
N 57.1

6

The four most expensive words in the English language, "This time it's different."
— Sir John Templeton (Founder Templeton Funds, philanthropist, 1912–2008)

April is 3rd Best Month for S&P, 4th Best for NASDAQ (Since 1971)

THURSDAY

D 38.1
S 42.9
N 33.3

7

Self-discipline is a form of freedom. Freedom from laziness and lethargy, freedom from expectations and demands of others, freedom from weakness and fear—and doubt.
— Harvey A. Dorfman (Sports psychologist, *The Mental ABC's of Pitching*, b. 1935)

FRIDAY

D 52.4
S 57.1
N 61.9

8

The generally accepted view is that markets are always right—that is, market prices tend to discount future developments accurately even when it is unclear what those developments are. I start with the opposite point of view. I believe that market prices are always wrong in the sense that they present a biased view of the future.
— George Soros (1987, Financier, philanthropist, political activist, author and philosopher, b. 1930)

SATURDAY

9

SUNDAY

10

THE SIXTH YEAR OF DECADES

The two losses below were war-related: 1946 (post-WWII top and sell-off) and 1966 (Vietnam bear market). Both losses were midterm years and both bottomed in October. Most "sixth" years delivered genuine buying opportunities. The last four produced solid gains. Election-year 2016 prospects depend heavily on which candidates take an early lead in the polls.

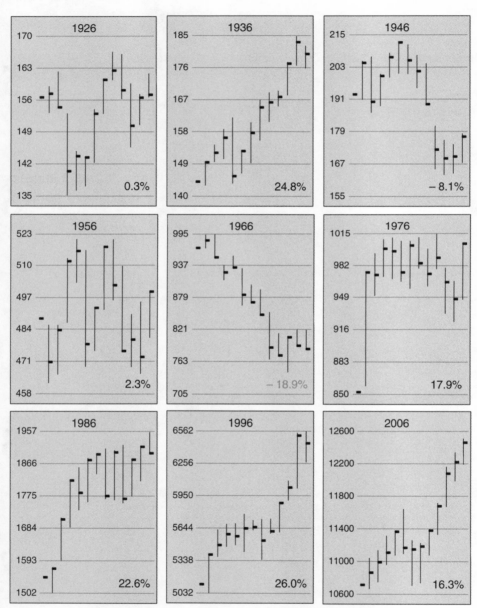

Based on Dow Jones Industrial Average monthly ranges and closing

Monday Before Expiration, Dow Up 18 of Last 27, Though Mixed Last 11 Years

MONDAY

D 52.4
S 47.6
N 47.6

11

There is no one who can replace America. Without American leadership, there is no leadership. That puts a tremendous burden on the American people to do something positive. You can't be tempted by the usual nationalism.
— Lee Hong-koo (South Korean prime minister 1994–1995 and ambassador to U.S. 1998–2000, *NY Times* 2/25/2009, b. 1934)

TUESDAY

D 61.9
S 52.4
N 61.9

12

In the course of evolution and a higher civilization we might be able to get along comfortably without Congress, but without Wall Street, never.
— Henry Clews (American financier and author, 1836–1923)

WEDNESDAY

D 52.4
S 47.6
N 42.9

13

A weak currency is the sign of a weak economy, and a weak economy leads to a weak nation.
— H. Ross Perot (American businessman, *The Dollar Crisis*, 2-time 3rd-party presidential candidate 1992 & 1996, b. 1930)

THURSDAY

D 66.7
S 52.4
N 52.4

14

Another factor contributing to productivity is technology, particularly the rapid introduction of new microcomputers based on single-chip circuits.... The results over the next decade will be a second industrial revolution.
— Yale Hirsch (Creator of *Stock Trader's Almanac*, *Smart Money Newsletter* 9/22/1976, b. 1923)

Income Tax Deadline, *Generally Bullish, Dow Down Only Six Times Since 1981, April Expiration Day Dow Up 14 of Last 19*

FRIDAY

D 66.7
S 61.9
N 47.6

15

If you have an important point to make, don't try to be subtle or clever. Use a pile driver. Hit the point once. Then come back and hit it again. Then hit it a third time—a tremendous whack.
— Winston Churchill (British statesman, 1874–1965)

SATURDAY

16

SUNDAY

17

THE DECEMBER LOW INDICATOR:
A USEFUL PROGNOSTICATING TOOL

When the Dow closes below its December closing low in the first quarter, it is frequently an excellent warning sign. Jeffrey Saut, managing director of investment strategy at Raymond James, brought this to our attention a few years ago. The December Low Indicator was originated by Lucien Hooper, a *Forbes* columnist and Wall Street analyst back in the 1970s. Hooper dismissed the importance of January and January's first week as reliable indicators. He noted that the trend could be random or even manipulated during a holiday-shortened week. Instead, said Hooper, "Pay much more attention to the December low. If that low is violated during the first quarter of the New Year, watch out!"

Nineteen of the 33 occurrences were followed by gains for the rest of the year—and 16 full-year gains—after the low for the year was reached. For perspective, we've included the January Barometer readings for the selected years. Hooper's "Watch Out" warning was absolutely correct, though. All but two of the instances since 1952 experienced further declines, as the Dow fell an additional 10.6% on average when December's low was breached in Q1.

Only three significant drops occurred (not shown) when December's low was not breached in Q1 (1974, 1981, and 1987). Both indicators were wrong only six times, and nine years ended flat. If the December low is not crossed, turn to our January Barometer for guidance. It has been virtually perfect, right nearly 100% of these times (view the complete results at *www.stocktradersalmanac.com*).

YEARS DOW FELL BELOW DECEMBER LOW IN FIRST QUARTER

Year	Previous Dec Low	Date Crossed	Crossing Price	Subseq. Low	% Change Cross-Low	Rest of Year % Change	Full Year % Change	Jan Bar
1952	262.29	2/19/52	261.37	256.35	−1.9%	11.7%	8.4%	1.6%[2]
1953	281.63	2/11/53	281.57	255.49	−9.3	−0.2	−3.8	−0.7[3]
1956	480.72	1/9/56	479.74	462.35	−3.6	4.1	2.3	−3.6[1, 2, 3]
1957	480.61	1/18/57	477.46	419.79	−12.1	−8.7	−12.8	−4.2
1960	661.29	1/12/60	660.43	566.05	−14.3	−6.7	−9.3	−7.1
1962	720.10	1/5/62	714.84	535.76	−25.1	−8.8	−10.8	−3.8
1966	939.53	3/1/66	938.19	744.32	−20.7	−16.3	−18.9	0.5[1]
1968	879.16	1/22/68	871.71	825.13	−5.3	8.3	4.3	−4.4[1, 2, 3]
1969	943.75	1/6/69	936.66	769.93	−17.8	−14.6	−15.2	−0.8
1970	769.93	1/26/70	768.88	631.16	−17.9	9.1	4.8	−7.6[2, 3]
1973	1000.00	1/29/73	996.46	788.31	−20.9	−14.6	−16.6	−1.7
1977	946.64	2/7/77	946.31	800.85	−15.4	−12.2	−17.3	−5.1
1978	806.22	1/5/78	804.92	742.12	−7.8	0.01	−3.1	−6.2[3]
1980	819.62	3/10/80	818.94	759.13	−7.3	17.7	14.9	5.8[2]
1982	868.25	1/5/82	865.30	776.92	−10.2	20.9	19.6	−1.8[1, 2]
1984	1236.79	1/25/84	1231.89	1086.57	−11.8	−1.6	−3.7	−0.9[3]
1990	2687.93	1/15/90	2669.37	2365.10	−11.4	−1.3	−4.3	−6.9[3]
1991	2565.59	1/7/91	2522.77	2470.30	−2.1	25.6	20.3	4.2[2]
1993	3255.18	1/8/93	3251.67	3241.95	−0.3	15.5	13.7	0.7[2]
1994	3697.08	3/30/94	3626.75	3593.35	−0.9	5.7	2.1	3.3[2, 3]
1996	5059.32	1/10/96	5032.94	5032.94	NC	28.1	26.0	3.3[2]
1998	7660.13	1/9/98	7580.42	7539.07	−0.5	21.1	16.1	1.0[2]
2000	10998.39	1/4/00	10997.93	9796.03	−10.9	−1.9	−6.2	−5.1
2001	10318.93	3/12/01	10208.25	8235.81	−19.3	−1.8	−7.1	3.5[1]
2002	9763.96	1/16/02	9712.27	7286.27	−25.0	−14.1	−16.8	−1.6
2003	8303.78	1/24/03	8131.01	7524.06	−7.5	28.6	25.3	−2.7[1, 2]
2005	10440.58	1/21/05	10392.99	10012.36	−3.7	3.1	−0.6	−2.5[3]
2006	10717.50	1/20/06	10667.39	10667.39	NC	16.8	16.3	2.5
2007	12194.13	3/2/07	12114.10	12050.41	−0.5	9.5	6.4	1.4[2]
2008	13167.20	1/2/08	13043.96	7552.29	−42.1	−32.7	−33.8	−6.1
2009	8149.09	1/20/09	7949.09	6547.05	−17.6	31.2	18.8	−8.6[1, 2]
2010	10285.97	1/22/10	10172.98	9686.48	−4.8	13.8	11.0	−3.7[1, 2]
2014	15739.43	1/31/14	15698.85	15372.80	−2.1	13.5	7.5	−3.6[1, 2]
			Average Drop		**−10.6%**			

[1]January Barometer wrong [2]December Low Indicator wrong [3]Year Flat

44

APRIL

MONDAY 18

D 61.9
S 71.4
N 57.1

If a man has no talents, he is unhappy enough; but if he has, envy pursues him in proportion to his ability.
— Leopold Mozart (German musician, to his son Wolfgang Amadeus, 1768, 1719–1787)

April Prone to Weakness After Tax Deadline (Pages 38 and 134)

TUESDAY 19

D 52.4
S 57.1
N 52.4

We will have to pay more and more attention to what the funds are doing. They are the ones who have been contributing to the activity, especially in the high-fliers.
— Humphrey B. Neill (Investor, analyst, author, *NY Times* 6/11/1966, 1895–1977)

WEDNESDAY 20

D 71.4
S 66.7
N 61.9

What's money? A man is a success if he gets up in the morning and goes to bed at night and in between does what he wants to do.
— Bob Dylan (American singer-songwriter, musician, and artist, b. 1941)

April 1999 First Month Ever to Gain 1000 Dow Points

THURSDAY 21

D 66.7
S 71.4
N 66.7

Explosive growth of shadow banking was about the invisible hand having a party, a non-regulated drinking party, with rating agencies handing out fake IDs.
— Paul McCulley (Economist, bond investor, PIMCO, coined "shadow banking" in 2007, *NY Times* 4/26/2010, b. 1957)

FRIDAY 22

D 57.1
S 52.4
N 57.1

I hate to be wrong. That has aborted many a tempting error, but not all of them. But I hate much more to stay wrong.
— Paul A. Samuelson (American economist, 12/23/03 University of Kansas interview, 1915–2009)

Passover

SATURDAY 23

SUNDAY 24

MAY ALMANAC

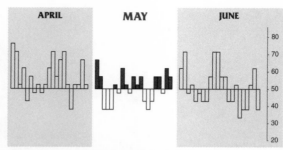

MAY							JUNE					
S	M	T	W	T	F	S	S	M	T	W	T	F	S
				1	2	3							
4	5	6	7				1	2	3	4
8	9	10	11	12	13	14	5	6	7	8	9	10	11
15	16	17	18	19	20	21	12	13	14	15	16	17	18
22	23	24	25	26	27	28	19	20	21	22	23	24	25
29	30	31					26	27	28	29	30

Market Probability Chart above is a graphic representation of the S&P 500 Recent Market Probability Calendar on page 124.

◆ "May/June disaster area" between 1965 and 1984 with S&P down 15 out of 20 Mays ◆ Between 1985 and 1997 May was the best month with 13 straight gains, gaining 3.3% per year on average, up 9, down 8 since ◆ Worst six months of the year begin with May (page 52) ◆ A $10,000 investment compounded to $838,486 for November–April in 65 years compared to a $221 loss for May–October ◆ Dow Memorial Day week record: up 12 years in a row (1984–1995), down 11 of the last 19 years ◆ Since 1950, presidential election year Mays rank poorly: #11 Dow and S&P, and #9 NASDAQ.

May Vital Statistics

	DJIA		S&P 500		NASDAQ		Russell 1K		Russell 2K	
Rank	9		8		5		6		6	
Up	33		37		26		24		23	
Down	32		28		18		12		13	
Average % Change	−0.04%		0.2%		0.8%		0.9%		1.3%	
Election Year	−0.80%		−0.2%		−0.7%		−0.5%		−0.2%	
Best & Worst May										
		% Change		% Change		% Change		% Change		% Change
Best	1990	8.3	1990	9.2	1997	11.1	1990	8.9	1997	11.0
Worst	2010	−7.9	1962	−8.6	2000	−11.9	2010	−8.1	2010	−7.7
Best & Worst May Weeks										
Best	5/29/70	5.8	5/2/97	6.2	5/17/02	8.8	5/2/97	6.4	5/14/10	6.3
Worst	5/25/62	−6.0	5/25/62	−6.8	5/7/10	−8.0	5/7/10	−6.6	5/7/10	−8.9
Best & Worst May Days										
Best	5/27/70	5.1	5/27/70	5.0	5/30/00	7.9	5/10/10	4.4	5/10/10	5.6
Worst	5/28/62	−5.7	5/28/62	−6.7	5/23/00	−5.9	5/20/10	−3.9	5/20/10	−5.1
First Trading Day of Expiration Week: 1980–2014										
Record (#Up – #Down)	22–13		23–12		19–16		21–14		17–18	
Current streak	U1		U2		U2		U1		U1	
Avg % Change	0.18		0.17		0.15		0.15		−0.01	
Options Expiration Day: 1980–2014										
Record (#Up – #Down)	16–19		19–16		17–18		19–16		17–18	
Current streak	U2		U2		U2		U2		U2	
Avg % Change	0.11		−0.11		−0.12		−0.10		−0.02	
Options Expiration Week: 1980–2014										
Record (#Up – #Down)	18–17		17–18		18–17		16–19		18–17	
Current streak	D1		D1		U2		D1		D1	
Avg % Change	0.06		0.02		0.16		0.02		−0.17	
Week After Options Expiration: 1980–2014										
Record (#Up – #Down)	19–16		21–14		23–12		21–14		25–10	
Current streak	U1		U1		U1		U1		U1	
Avg % Change	−0.04		0.11		0.15		0.13		0.28	
First Trading Day Performance										
% of Time Up	56.9		56.9		61.4		55.6		58.3	
Avg % Change	0.20		0.22		0.30		0.24		0.24	
Last Trading Day Performance										
% of Time Up	61.5		63.1		68.2		58.3		66.7	
Avg % Change	0.20		0.28		0.21		0.23		0.34	

Dow & S&P 1950–April 2015, NASDAQ 1971–April 2015, Russell 1K & 2K 1979–April 2015.

May's new pattern, a smile or a frown,
Odd years UP and even years DOWN.

MONDAY

D 42.9
S 38.1
N 57.1

25

I have seen it repeatedly throughout the world: politicians get a country in trouble but swear everything is okay in the face of overwhelming evidence to the contrary.
— Jim Rogers (Financier, *Adventure Capitalist*, b. 1942)

FOMC Meeting (2 Days)

TUESDAY

D 57.1
S 52.4
N 47.6

26

An autobiography must be such that one can sue oneself for libel.
— Thomas Hoving (Museum director, 1931–2009)

WEDNESDAY

D 61.9
S 52.4
N 61.9

27

Successful investing is anticipating the anticipations of others.
— John Maynard Keynes (British economist, 1883–1946)

THURSDAY

D 71.4
S 66.7
N 76.2

28

We always live in an uncertain world. What is certain is that the United States will go forward over time.
— Warren Buffett (CEO Berkshire Hathaway, investor & philanthropist, CNBC 9/22/2010, b. 1930)

End of "Best Six Months" of the Year (Pages 50, 52, 54, and 147)

FRIDAY

D 42.9
S 52.4
N 66.7

29

The "canonical" market bottom typically features below-average valuations, falling interest rates, new lows in some major indices on diminished trading volume...and finally, a quick high-volume reversal in breadth....
— John P. Hussman, Ph.D. (Hussman Funds, 5/22/06)

SATURDAY

30

May Almanac Investor Sector Seasonalities: See Pages 94, 96, and 98

SUNDAY

1

DOWN JANUARYS: A REMARKABLE RECORD

In the first third of the twentieth century, there was no correlation between January markets and the year as a whole. Then, in 1972 Yale Hirsch discovered that the 1933 "lame duck" Amendment to the Constitution changed the political calendar, and the January Barometer was born—its record has been quite accurate (page 16).

Down Januarys are harbingers of trouble ahead, in the economic, political, or military arenas. Eisenhower's heart attack in 1955 cast doubt on whether he could run in 1956—a flat year. Two other election years with down Januarys were also flat (1984 and 1992). Twelve bear markets began, and ten continued into second years with poor Januarys. 1968 started down, as we were mired in Vietnam, but Johnson's "bombing halt" changed the climate. Imminent military action in Iraq held January 2003 down before the market triple-bottomed in March. After Baghdad fell, pre-election and recovery forces fueled 2003 into a banner year. 2005 was flat, registering the narrowest Dow trading range on record. 2008 was the worst January on record and preceded the worst bear market since the Great Depression. A negative reading in 2010 preceded a 16% April–July correction, which was quickly reversed by QE2.

Unfortunately, bull and bear markets do not start conveniently at the beginnings and ends of months or years. Though some years ended higher, **every down January since 1950 was followed by a new or continuing bear market, a 10% correction or a flat year**. Down Januarys were followed by substantial declines averaging *minus* 13.5%, providing excellent buying opportunities later in most years.

FROM DOWN JANUARY S&P CLOSES TO LOW NEXT 11 MONTHS

Year	January Close	% Change	11-Month Low	Date of Low	Jan Close to Low %	% Feb to Dec	Year % Change	
1953	26.38	−0.7%	22.71	14-Sep	−13.9%	−6.0%	−6.6%	bear
1956	43.82	−3.6	43.42	14-Feb	−0.9	6.5	2.6	FLAT/bear
1957	44.72	−4.2	38.98	22-Oct	−12.8	−10.6	−14.3	Cont. bear
1960	55.61	−7.1	52.30	25-Oct	−6.0	4.5	−3.0	bear
1962	68.84	−3.8	52.32	26-Jun	−24.0	−8.3	−11.8	bear
1968	92.24	−4.4	87.72	5-Mar	−4.9	12.6	7.7	−10%/bear
1969	103.01	−0.8	89.20	17-Dec	−13.4	−10.6	−11.4	Cont. bear
1970	85.02	−7.6	69.20	26-May	−18.6	8.4	0.1	Cont. bear/FLAT
1973	116.03	−1.7	92.16	5-Dec	−20.6	−15.9	−17.4	bear
1974	96.57	−1.0	62.28	3-Oct	−35.5	−29.0	−29.7	Cont. bear
1977	102.03	−5.1	90.71	2-Nov	−11.1	−6.8	−11.5	bear
1978	89.25	−6.2	86.90	6-Mar	−2.6	7.7	1.1	Cont. bear/bear
1981	129.55	−4.6	112.77	25-Sep	−13.0	−5.4	−9.7	bear
1982	120.40	−1.8	102.42	12-Aug	−14.9	16.8	14.8	Cont. bear
1984	163.42	−0.9	147.82	24-Jul	−9.5	2.3	1.4	Cont. bear/FLAT
1990	329.07	−6.9	295.46	11-Oct	−10.2	0.4	−6.6	bear
1992	408.79	−2.0	394.50	8-Apr	−3.5	6.6	4.5	FLAT
2000	1394.46	−5.1	1264.74	20-Dec	−9.3	−5.3	−10.1	bear
2002	1130.20	−1.6	776.76	9-Oct	−31.3	−22.2	−23.4	bear
2003	855.70	−2.7	800.73	11-Mar	−6.4	29.9	26.4	Cont. bear
2005	1181.27	−2.5	1137.50	20-Apr	−3.7	5.7	3.0	FLAT
2008	1378.55	−6.1	752.44	20-Nov	−45.4	−34.5	−38.5	Cont. bear
2009	825.88	−8.6	676.53	9-Mar	−18.1	35.0	23.5	Cont. bear
2010	1073.87	−3.7	1022.58	2-Jul	−4.8	17.1	12.8	−10%
2014	1782.59	−3.6	1741.89	3-Feb	−2.3	15.5	11.4	−10% intraday
				Totals	**−334.4%**	**14.4%**	**−84.8%**	
				Average	**−13.5%**	**0.6%**	**−3.4%**	

48

First Trading Day in May, Dow Up 13 of Last 18

MONDAY

D 66.7
S 66.7
N 71.4

2

"Sell in May and go away." However, no one ever said it was the beginning of the month.
— John L. Person (Professional trader, author, speaker, *Commodity Trader's Almanac*, nationalfutures.com, 6/19/2009, b. 1961)

TUESDAY

D 66.7
S 57.1
N 57.1

3

It is tact that is golden, not silence.
— Samuel Butler (English writer, 1600–1680)

WEDNESDAY

D 33.3
S 38.1
N 52.4

4

Every man who knows how to read has it in his power to magnify himself, to multiply the ways in which he exists, to make his life full, significant and interesting.
— Aldous Huxley (English author, *Brave New World*, 1894–1963)

THURSDAY

D 33.3
S 38.1
N 47.6

5

There are three principal means of acquiring knowledge…observation of nature, reflection, and experimentation. Observation collects facts; reflection combines them; experimentation verifies the result of that combination.
— Denis Diderot (French philosopher, edited first modern encyclopedia in 1745, 1713–1784)

Friday Before Mother's Day, Dow Up 14 of Last 21

FRIDAY

D 42.9
S 38.1
N 33.3

6

Fight until death over taxes? Oh, no. Women, country, God, things like that. Taxes? No.
— Daniel Patrick Moynihan (U.S. Senator New York 1977–2001, "Meet The Press" 5/23/1993, 1927–2003)

SATURDAY

7

Mother's Day

SUNDAY

8

TOP PERFORMING MONTHS PAST 65⅓ YEARS: STANDARD & POOR'S 500 AND DOW JONES INDUSTRIALS

Monthly performance of the S&P and the Dow are ranked over the past 65⅓ years. NASDAQ monthly performance is shown on page 58.

April, November, and December still hold the top three positions in both the Dow and the S&P. March has reclaimed the fourth spot on the S&P. Two disastrous Januarys in 2008 and 2009 knocked January into fifth. This, in part, led to our discovery in 1986 of the market's most consistent seasonal pattern. You can divide the year into two sections and have practically all the gains in one six-month section and very little in the other. September is the worst month on both lists. (See "Best Six Months" on page 52.)

MONTHLY % CHANGES (JANUARY 1950–APRIL 2015)

Standard & Poor's 500					Dow Jones Industrials				
Month	Total % Change	Avg. % Change	# Up	# Down	Month	Total % Change	Avg. % Change	# Up	# Down
Jan	67.9%	1.0%	40	26	Jan	63.2	1.0	42	24
Feb	3.5	0.05	37	29	Feb	13.8	0.2	39	27
Mar	76.8	1.2	43	23	Mar	70.6	1.1	43	23
Apr	98.5	1.5	46	20	Apr	127.1	1.9	44	22
May	12.0	0.2	37	28	May	−2.5	−0.04	33	32
Jun	−0.1	−0.001	34	31	Jun	−19.7	−0.3	30	35
Jul	62.5	1.0	35	30	Jul	75.5	1.2	40	25
Aug	0.3	0.004	36	29	Aug	−5.4	−0.1	37	28
Sep*	−31.6	−0.5	29	35	Sep	−48.6	−0.7	26	39
Oct	54.0	0.8	39	26	Oct	34.8	0.5	39	26
Nov	98.9	1.5	43	22	Nov	98.8	1.5	43	22
Dec	108.5	1.7	49	16	Dec	109.5	1.7	46	19
% Rank					**% Rank**				
Dec	108.5%	1.7%	49	16	Apr	127.1	1.9	44	22
Nov	98.9	1.5	43	22	Dec	109.5	1.7	46	19
Apr	98.5	1.5	46	20	Nov	98.8	1.5	43	22
Mar	76.8	1.2	43	23	Jul	75.5	1.2	40	25
Jan	67.9	1.0	40	26	Mar	70.6	1.1	43	23
Jul	62.5	1.0	35	30	Jan	63.2	1.0	42	24
Oct	54.0	0.8	39	26	Oct	34.8	0.5	39	26
May	12.0	0.2	37	28	Feb	13.8	0.2	39	27
Feb	3.5	0.1	37	29	May	−2.5	−0.04	33	32
Aug	0.3	0.004	36	29	Aug	−5.4	−0.1	37	28
Jun	−0.1	−0.001	34	31	Jun	−19.7	−0.3	30	35
Sep*	−31.6	−0.5	29	35	Sep	−48.6	−0.7	26	39
Totals	551.2%	8.5%			**Totals**	517.1%	8.0%		
Average		0.70%			**Average**		0.66%		

*No change 1979

Anticipators, shifts in cultural behavior, and faster information flow have altered seasonality in recent years. Here is how the months ranked over the past 15⅓ years (184 months) using total percentage gains on the S&P 500: April 29.4, March 26.0, October 20.1, December 16.5, November 13.6, July 4.4, May 1.6, August 1.4, February −7.5, January −16.2, June −17.6 and September −18.1.

During the last 15⅓ years front-runners of our Best Six Months may have helped push October into the number-three spot. January has declined in 8 of the last 16 years. Sizeable turnarounds in "bear killing" October were a common occurrence from 1999 to 2007. Recent big Dow losses in the period were: September 2001 (9/11 attack), off 11.1%; September 2002 (Iraq war drums), off 12.4%; June 2008, off 10.2%; October 2008, off 14.1%; and February 2009 (financial crisis), off 11.7%.

MAY

Monday After Mother's Day, Dow Up 15 of Last 21

MONDAY
D 66.7
S 52.4
N 71.4

9

Our firm conviction is that, sooner or later, capitalism will give way to socialism. ... We will bury you.
— Nikita Khrushchev (Soviet leader 1953–1964, 1894–1971)

TUESDAY
D 57.1
S 47.6
N 47.6

10

You have powers you never dreamed of. You can do things you never thought you could do. There are no limitations in what you can do except the limitations in your own mind.
— Darwin P. Kingsley (President New York Life, 1857–1932)

WEDNESDAY
D 71.4
S 61.9
N 47.6

11

A person's greatest virtue is his ability to correct his mistakes and continually make a new person of himself.
— Yang-Ming Wang (Chinese philosopher, 1472–1529)

THURSDAY
D 47.6
S 52.4
N 57.1

12

At a time of war, we need you to work for peace. At a time of inequality, we need you to work for opportunity. At a time of so much cynicism and so much doubt, we need you to make us believe again.
— Barack H. Obama (44th U.S. President, Commencement Wesleyan University 5/28/2008, b. 1961)

FRIDAY
D 57.1
S 47.6
N 42.9

13

It is the growth of total government spending as a percentage of gross national product—not the way it is financed—that crowds out the private sector.
— Paul Craig Roberts (*Business Week*, 1984, b. 1939)

SATURDAY

14

SUNDAY

15

"BEST SIX MONTHS": STILL AN EYE-POPPING STRATEGY

Our Best Six Months Switching Strategy consistently delivers. Investing in the Dow Jones Industrial Average between November 1st and April 30th each year and then switching into fixed income for the other six months has produced reliable returns with reduced risk since 1950.

The chart on page 147 shows November, December, January, March, and April to be the top months since 1950. Add February, and an excellent strategy is born! These six consecutive months gained 17882.70 Dow points in 65 years, while the remaining May-through-October months lost 1066.19 points. The S&P gained 1790.37 points in the same best six months versus 75.51 points in the worst six.

Percentage changes are shown along with a compounding $10,000 investment. The November–April $838,486 gain overshadows May–October's $221 loss. (S&P results were $628,273 to $8,090.) Just three November–April losses were double-digit: April 1970 (Cambodian invasion), 1973 (OPEC oil embargo), and 2008 (financial crisis). Similarly, Iraq muted the Best Six and inflated the Worst Six in 2003. When we discovered this strategy in 1986, November–April outperformed May–October by $88,163 to minus $1,522. Results improved substantially these past 28 years, $740,323 to $1,301. A simple timing indicator triples results (page 54).

SIX-MONTH SWITCHING STRATEGY

	DJIA % Change May 1–Oct 31	Investing $10,000	DJIA % Change Nov 1–Apr 30	Investing $10,000
1950	5.0%	$10,500	15.2%	$11,520
1951	1.2	10,626	−1.8	11,313
1952	4.5	11,104	2.1	11,551
1953	0.4	11,148	15.8	13,376
1954	10.3	12,296	20.9	16,172
1955	6.9	13,144	13.5	18,355
1956	−7.0	12,224	3.0	18,906
1957	−10.8	10,904	3.4	19,549
1958	19.2	12,998	14.8	22,442
1959	3.7	13,479	−6.9	20,894
1960	−3.5	13,007	16.9	24,425
1961	3.7	13,488	−5.5	23,082
1962	−11.4	11,950	21.7	28,091
1963	5.2	12,571	7.4	30,170
1964	7.7	13,539	5.6	31,860
1965	4.2	14,108	−2.8	30,968
1966	−13.6	12,189	11.1	34,405
1967	−1.9	11,957	3.7	35,678
1968	4.4	12,483	−0.2	35,607
1969	−9.9	11,247	−14.0	30,622
1970	2.7	11,551	24.6	38,155
1971	−10.9	10,292	13.7	43,382
1972	0.1	10,302	−3.6	41,820
1973	3.8	10,693	−12.5	36,593
1974	−20.5	8,501	23.4	45,156
1975	1.8	8,654	19.2	53,826
1976	−3.2	8,377	−3.9	51,727
1977	−11.7	7,397	2.3	52,917
1978	−5.4	6,998	7.9	57,097
1979	−4.6	6,676	0.2	57,211
1980	13.1	7,551	7.9	61,731
1981	−14.6	6,449	−0.5	61,422
1982	16.9	7,539	23.6	75,918
1983	−0.1	7,531	−4.4	72,578
1984	3.1	7,764	4.2	75,626
1985	9.2	8,478	29.8	98,163
1986	5.3	8,927	21.8	119,563
1987	−12.8	7,784	1.9	121,835
1988	5.7	8,228	12.6	137,186
1989	9.4	9,001	0.4	137,735
1990	−8.1	8,272	18.2	162,803
1991	6.3	8,793	9.4	178,106
1992	−4.0	8,441	6.2	189,149
1993	7.4	9,066	0.03	189,206
1994	6.2	9,628	10.6	209,262
1995	10.0	10,591	17.1	245,046
1996	8.3	11,470	16.2	284,743
1997	6.2	12,181	21.8	346,817
1998	−5.2	11,548	25.6	435,602
1999	−0.5	11,490	0.04	435,776
2000	2.2	11,743	−2.2	426,189
2001	−15.5	9,923	9.6	467,103
2002	−15.6	8,375	1.0	471,774
2003	15.6	9,682	4.3	492,060
2004	−1.9	9,498	1.6	499,933
2005	2.4	9,726	8.9	544,427
2006	6.3	10,339	8.1	588,526
2007	6.6	11,021	−8.0	541,444
2008	−27.3	8,012	−12.4	474,305
2009	18.9	9,526	13.3	537,388
2010	1.0	9,621	15.2	619,071
2011	−6.7	8,976	10.5	684,073
2012	−0.9	8,895	13.3	775,055
2013	4.8	9,322	6.7	826,984
2014	4.9	$9,779	2.6	$848,486
Average/Gain	0.4%	($221)	7.5%	$838,486
# Up/Down	39/26		51/14	

Monday Before May Expiration, Dow Up 21 of Last 28, Average Gain 0.4%

MONDAY
D 57.1
S 57.1
N 52.4
16

The first human who hurled an insult instead of a stone was the founder of civilization.
— Sigmund Freud (Austrian neurologist, psychiatrist, "father of psychoanalysis," 1856–1939)

TUESDAY
D 47.6
S 52.4
N 52.4
17

The future now belongs to societies that organize themselves for learning. What we know and can do holds the key to economic progress.
— Ray Marshall (b. 1928) and Marc Tucker (b. 1939) (*Thinking for a Living: Education and the Wealth of Nations*, 1992)

WEDNESDAY
D 57.1
S 57.1
N 66.7
18

The world has changed! You can't be an 800-pound gorilla; you need to be an economic gazelle. You've got to be able to change directions quickly.
— Mark Breier (*The 10-Second Internet Manager*)

THURSDAY
D 42.9
S 42.9
N 33.3
19

Politicians use statistics in the same way that a drunk uses lamp-posts—for support rather than illumination.
— Andrew Lang (Scottish writer, literary critic, anthropologist, 1844–1912)

May Expiration Day, Dow Down 14 of Last 26

FRIDAY
D 33.3
S 38.1
N 38.1
20

There is a habitual nature to society and human activity. People's behavior and what they do with their money and time bears upon economics and the stock market.
— Jeffrey A. Hirsch (Editor, *Stock Trader's Almanac*, b. 1966)

SATURDAY
21

SUNDAY
22

MACD-TIMING TRIPLES "BEST SIX MONTHS" RESULTS

Using the simple MACD (Moving Average Convergence Divergence) indicator developed by our friend Gerald Appel to better time entries and exits into and out of the Best Six Months (page 52) period nearly triples the results. Several years ago, Sy Harding enhanced our Best Six Months Switching Strategy with MACD triggers, dubbing it the "best mechanical system ever." In 2006, we improved it even more, achieving similar results with just four trades every four years (page 62).

Our *Almanac Investor eNewsletter* (see ad insert) implements this system with quite a degree of success. Starting October 1, we look to catch the market's first hint of an uptrend after the summer doldrums, and beginning April 1, we prepare to exit these seasonal positions as soon as the market falters.

In up-trending markets, MACD signals get you in earlier and keep you in longer. But if the market is trending down, entries are delayed until the market turns up, and exit points can come a month earlier.

The results are astounding, applying the simple MACD signals. Instead of $10,000 gaining $838,486 over the 65 recent years when invested only during the Best Six Months (page 52), the gain nearly tripled to $2,379,552. The $221 loss during the Worst Six Months expanded to a loss of $6,499.

Impressive results for being invested during only 6.3 months of the year on average! For the rest of the year consider money markets, bonds, puts, bear funds, covered calls, or credit call spreads.

Updated signals are e-mailed to our *Almanac Investor eNewsletter* subscribers as soon as they are triggered. Visit *www.stocktradersalmanac.com,* or see the ad insert for details and a special offer for new subscribers.

BEST SIX-MONTH SWITCHING STRATEGY+TIMING

	DJIA		DJIA	
	% Change	Investing	% Change	Investing
	May 1–Oct 31*	$10,000	Nov 1–Apr 30*	$10,000
1950	7.3%	$10,730	13.3%	$11,330
1951	0.1	10,741	1.9	11,545
1952	1.4	10,891	2.1	11,787
1953	0.2	10,913	17.1	13,803
1954	13.5	12,386	16.3	16,053
1955	7.7	13,340	13.1	18,156
1956	−6.8	12,433	2.8	18,664
1957	−12.3	10,904	4.9	19,579
1958	17.3	12,790	16.7	22,849
1959	1.6	12,995	−3.1	22,141
1960	−4.9	12,358	16.9	25,883
1961	2.9	12,716	−1.5	25,495
1962	−15.3	10,770	22.4	31,206
1963	4.3	11,233	9.6	34,202
1964	6.7	11,986	6.2	36,323
1965	2.6	12,298	−2.5	35,415
1966	−16.4	10,281	14.3	40,479
1967	−2.1	10,065	5.5	42,705
1968	3.4	10,407	0.2	42,790
1969	−11.9	9,169	−6.7	39,923
1970	−1.4	9,041	20.8	48,227
1971	−11.0	8,046	15.4	55,654
1972	−0.6	7,998	−1.4	54,875
1973	−11.0	7,118	0.1	54,930
1974	−22.4	5,524	28.2	70,420
1975	0.1	5,530	18.5	83,448
1976	−3.4	5,342	−3.0	80,945
1977	−11.4	4,733	0.5	81,350
1978	−4.5	4,520	9.3	88,916
1979	−5.3	4,280	7.0	95,140
1980	9.3	4,678	4.7	99,612
1981	−14.6	3,995	0.4	100,010
1982	15.5	4,614	23.5	123,512
1983	2.5	4,729	−7.3	114,496
1984	3.3	4,885	3.9	118,961
1985	7.0	5,227	38.1	164,285
1986	−2.8	5,081	28.2	210,613
1987	−14.9	4,324	3.0	216,931
1988	6.1	4,588	11.8	242,529
1989	9.8	5,038	3.3	250,532
1990	−6.7	4,700	15.8	290,116
1991	4.8	4,926	11.3	322,899
1992	−6.2	4,621	6.6	344,210
1993	5.5	4,875	5.6	363,486
1994	3.7	5,055	13.1	411,103
1995	7.2	5,419	16.7	479,757
1996	9.2	5,918	21.9	584,824
1997	3.6	6,131	18.5	693,016
1998	−12.4	5,371	39.9	969,529
1999	−6.4	5,027	5.1	1,018,975
2000	−6.0	4,725	5.4	1,074,000
2001	−17.3	3,908	15.8	1,243,692
2002	−25.2	2,923	6.0	1,318,314
2003	16.4	3,402	7.8	1,421,142
2004	−0.9	3,371	1.8	1,446,723
2005	−0.5	3,354	7.7	1,558,121
2006	4.7	3,512	14.4	1,782,490
2007	5.6	3,709	−12.7	1,556,114
2008	−24.7	2,793	−14.0	1,338,258
2009	23.8	3,458	10.8	1,482,790
2010	4.6	3,617	7.3	1,591,034
2011	−9.4	3,277	18.7	1,888,557
2012	0.3	3,287	10.0	2,077,413
2013	4.1	3,422	7.1	2,224,909
2014	2.3	3,501	7.4	2,389,552
Average	**−1.1%**		**9.3%**	
# Up	**35**		**56**	
# Down	**30**		**9**	
65-Year Gain (Loss)		**($6,499)**		**$2,379,552**

MACD generated entry and exit points (earlier or later) can lengthen or shorten six-month periods.

54

MONDAY
D 38.1
S 42.9
N 47.6
23

There's a race of men that don't fit in, a race that can't sit still; so they break the hearts of kith and kin, and they roam the world at will. They range the field and rove the flood, And they climb the mountain's crest; theirs is the curse of the gypsy [trader's] blood, and they don't know how to rest.
— Robert W. Service (Bard of the Yukon, "The Men That Don't Fit In", 1874–1958)

TUESDAY
D 52.4
S 57.1
N 42.9
24

If all the economists in the world were laid end to end, they still wouldn't reach a conclusion.
— George Bernard Shaw (Irish dramatist, 1856–1950)

WEDNESDAY
D 52.4
S 57.1
N 52.4
25

A market is the combined behavior of thousands of people responding to information, misinformation and whim.
— Kenneth Chang (*NY Times* journalist)

THURSDAY
D 42.9
S 47.6
N 52.4
26

He who wants to persuade should put his trust not in the right argument, but in the right word. The power of sound has always been greater than the power of sense.
— Joseph Conrad (Polish/British novelist, 1857–1924)

Friday Before Memorial Day Tends to Be Lackluster with Light Trading, Dow Down 8 of Last 15, Average –0.3%

FRIDAY
D 66.7
S 61.9
N 71.4
27

Cooperation is essential to address 21st-century challenges; you can't fire cruise missiles at the global financial crisis.
— Nicholas D. Kristof (*NY Times* columnist, 10/23/2008, b. 1959)

SATURDAY
28

June Almanac Investor Sector Seasonalities: See Pages 94, 96, and 98

SUNDAY
29

JUNE ALMANAC

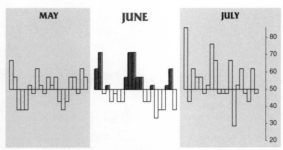

JUNE							JULY						
S	M	T	W	T	F	S	S	M	T	W	T	F	S
			1	2	3	4	31					1	2
5	6	7	8	9	10	11	3	4	5	6	7	8	9
12	13	14	15	16	17	18	10	11	12	13	14	15	16
19	20	21	22	23	24	25	17	18	19	20	21	22	23
26	27	28	29	30			24	25	26	27	28	29	30

Market Probability Chart above is a graphic representation of the S&P 500 Recent Market Probability Calendar on page 124.

◆ The "summer rally" in most years is the weakest rally of all four seasons (page 72) ◆ Week after June Triple-Witching Day Dow down 22 of last 25 (page 78) ◆ RECENT RECORD: S&P up 12, down 9, average loss 0.2%, ranks tenth ◆ Stronger for NASDAQ, average gain 1.1% last 21 years ◆ Watch out for end-of-quarter "portfolio pumping" on last day of June, Dow down 17 of last 24, NASDAQ down 6 of last 10 ◆ Presidential election year Junes: #1 S&P, #4 NASDAQ and Dow ◆ June ends NASDAQ's Best Eight Months.

June Vital Statistics

	DJIA		S&P 500		NASDAQ		Russell 1K		Russell 2K	
Rank	11		11		6		11		8	
Up	30		34		25		21		22	
Down	35		31		19		15		14	
Average % Change	−0.3%		−0.002%		0.8%		0.2%		0.6%	
Election Year	0.9%		1.4%		1.9%		0.8%		1.6%	
Best & Worst June										
	% Change		% Change		% Change		% Change		% Change	
Best	1955	6.2	1955	8.2	2000	16.6	1999	5.1	2000	8.6
Worst	2008	−10.2	2008	−8.6	2002	−9.4	2008	−8.5	2010	−7.9
Best & Worst June Weeks										
Best	6/7/74	6.4	6/2/00	7.2	6/2/00	19.0	6/2/00	8.0	6/2/00	12.2
Worst	6/30/50	−6.8	6/30/50	−7.6	6/15/01	−8.4	6/15/01	−4.2	6/9/06	−4.9
Best & Worst June Days										
Best	6/28/62	3.8	6/28/62	3.4	6/2/00	6.4	6/10/10	3.0	6/2/00	4.2
Worst	6/26/50	−4.7	6/26/50	−5.4	6/29/10	−3.9	6/4/10	−3.5	6/4/10	−5.0
First Trading Day of Expiration Week: 1980–2014										
Record (#Up − #Down)	19–16		21–14		16–19		19–16		14–20	
Current streak	U2		U2		U2		U2		U2	
Avg % Change	0.001		−0.08		−0.24		−0.10		−0.33	
Options Expiration Day: 1980–2014										
Record (#Up − #Down)	22–13		23–12		20–15		23–12		21–14	
Current streak	U5		U6		U1		U6		U6	
Avg % Change	−0.03		0.05		−0.001		0.01		0.02	
Options Expiration Week: 1980–2014										
Record (#Up − #Down)	20–15		18–17		15–20		16–19		16–19	
Current streak	U1		U1		U1		U1		U1	
Avg % Change	−0.07		−0.10		−0.32		−0.17		−0.27	
Week After Options Expiration: 1980–2014										
Record (#Up − #Down)	11–24		17–18		21–14		17–18		18–17	
Current streak	D1		D1		U4		D1		U4	
Avg % Change	−0.44		−0.15		0.18		−0.12		−0.06	
First Trading Day Performance										
% of Time Up	53.8		52.3		56.8		58.3		61.1	
Avg % Change	0.14		0.10		0.11		0.05		0.10	
Last Trading Day Performance										
% of Time Up	52.3		49.2		68.2		50.0		66.7	
Avg % Change	0.03		0.08		0.31		0.01		0.38	

Dow & S&P 1950–April 2015, NASDAQ 1971–April 2015, Russell 1K & 2K 1979–April 2015.

Last Day of June not hot for the Dow;
Down 17 of 24, WOW!

Memorial Day (Market Closed)

Never tell people how to do things. Tell them what to do and they will surprise you with their ingenuity.
— General George S. Patton, Jr. (U.S. Army field commander WWII, 1885–1945)

Day After Memorial Day, Dow Up 21 of Last 29
Memorial Day Week Dow Down 11 of Last 19, Up 12 Straight 1984–1995

TUESDAY
31

D 52.4
S 57.1
N 57.1

The government would not look fondly on Caesar's Palace if it opened a table for wagering on corporate failure.
It should not give greater encouragement for Goldman Sachs [et al.] to do so.
— Roger Lowenstein (Financial journalist and author, *End of Wall Street*, *NY Times* OpEd 4/20/2010, b. 1954)

First Trading Day in June, Dow Up 20 of Last 27
Down 2008/2010 –1.1%, 2011/12 –2.2%

WEDNESDAY
1

D 66.7
S 61.9
N 52.4

Based on my own personal experience—both as an investor in recent years and an expert witness in years
past—rarely do more than three or four variables really count. Everything else is noise.
— Martin J. Whitman (Founder Third Avenue Funds, b. 1924)

Start Looking for NASDAQ MACD Sell Signal on June 1 (Page 60)
Almanac Investor Subscribers Emailed When It Triggers (See Ad Insert)

THURSDAY
2

D 47.6
S 71.4
N 71.4

The riskiest moment is when you are right. That's when you're in the most trouble, because you tend to
overstay the good decisions.
— Peter L. Bernstein (Economist, *Money Magazine* 10/15/2004, 1919–2009)

FRIDAY
3

D 52.4
S 47.6
N 52.4

No profession requires more hard work, intelligence, patience, and mental discipline than successful speculation.
— Robert Rhea (Economist, trader, *The Dow Theory*, 1887–1952)

SATURDAY
4

SUNDAY
5

TOP PERFORMING NASDAQ MONTHS PAST 44¹/₃ YEARS

NASDAQ stocks continue to run away during three consecutive months, November, December, and January, with an average gain of 6.2% despite the slaughter of November 2000, −22.9%, December 2000, −4.9%, December 2002, −9.7%, November 2007, −6.9%, January 2008, −9.9%, November 2008, −10.8%, January 2009, −6.4%, and January 2010, −5.4%. Solid gains in November and December 2004 offset January 2005's 5.2% Iraq-turmoil-fueled drop.

You can see the months graphically on page 148. January by itself is impressive, up 2.7% on average. April, May, and June also shine, creating our NASDAQ Best Eight Months strategy. What appears as a Death Valley abyss occurs during NASDAQ's bleakest four months: July, August, September, and October. NASDAQ's Best Eight Months seasonal strategy using MACD timing is displayed on page 60.

MONTHLY % CHANGES (JANUARY 1971–APRIL 2015)

	NASDAQ Composite*					Dow Jones Industrials			
Month	Total % Change	Avg. % Change	# Up	# Down	Month	Total % Change	Avg. % Change	# Up	# Down
Jan	123.5	2.7	29	16	Jan	53.5	1.2	28	17
Feb	31.8	0.7	25	20	Feb	19.4	0.4	27	18
Mar	34.4	0.8	28	17	Mar	49.4	1.1	30	15
Apr	63.8	1.4	29	16	Apr	96.1	2.1	29	16
May	37.2	0.8	26	18	May	10.9	0.2	23	21
Jun	34.8	0.8	25	19	Jun	−2.5	−0.06	22	22
Jul	6.7	0.2	22	22	Jul	32.0	0.7	24	20
Aug	11.3	0.3	24	20	Aug	−8.1	−0.2	25	19
Sep	−22.9	−0.5	24	20	Sep	−44.7	−1.0	16	28
Oct	27.3	0.6	24	20	Oct	23.4	0.5	27	17
Nov	70.8	1.6	29	15	Nov	54.8	1.2	29	15
Dec	85.7	1.9	26	18	Dec	73.2	1.7	31	13
% Rank					**% Rank**				
Jan	123.5	2.7	29	16	Apr	96.1	2.1	29	16
Dec	85.7	1.9	26	18	Dec	73.2	1.7	31	13
Nov	70.8	1.6	29	15	Nov	54.8	1.2	29	15
Apr	63.8	1.4	29	16	Jan	53.5	1.2	28	17
May	37.2	0.8	26	18	Mar	49.4	1.1	30	15
Jun	34.8	0.8	25	19	Jul	32.0	0.7	24	20
Mar	34.4	0.8	28	17	Oct	23.4	0.5	27	17
Feb	31.8	0.7	25	20	Feb	19.4	0.4	27	18
Oct	27.3	0.6	24	20	May	10.9	0.2	23	21
Aug	11.3	0.3	24	20	Jun	−2.5	−0.06	22	22
Jul	6.7	0.2	22	22	Aug	−8.1	−0.2	25	19
Sep	−22.9	−0.5	24	20	Sep	−44.7	−1.0	16	28
Totals	504.4%	11.3%			**Totals**	357.4%	7.8%		
Average		0.94%			**Average**		0.65%		

Based on NASDAQ composite, prior to Feb. 5, 1971 based on National Quotation Bureau indices

For comparison, Dow figures are shown. During this period, NASDAQ averaged a 0.94% gain per month, 45 percent more than the Dow's 0.65% per month. Between January 1971 and January 1982, NASDAQ's composite index doubled in 12 years, while the Dow stayed flat. But while NASDAQ plummeted 77.9% from its 2000 highs to the 2002 bottom, the Dow only lost 37.8%. The Great Recession and bear market of 2007–2009 spread its carnage equally across Dow and NASDAQ. Recent market moves are increasingly more correlated.

June Ends NASDAQ's "Best Eight Months" (Pages 58, 60, and 148)

MONDAY

D 57.1
S 52.4
N 57.1

6

Stock option plans reward the executive for doing the wrong thing. Instead of asking, "Are we making the right decision?" he asks, "How did we close today?" It is encouragement to loot the corporation.
— Peter Drucker (Austrian-born pioneer management theorist, 1909–2005)

TUESDAY

D 61.9
S 42.9
N 42.9

7

You don't learn to hold your own in the world by standing on guard, but by attacking and getting well hammered yourself.
— George Bernard Shaw (Irish dramatist, 1856–1950)

2008 Second Worst June Ever, Dow –10.2%, S&P –8.6%,
Only 1930 Was Worse, NASDAQ –9.1%, June 2002 –9.4%

WEDNESDAY

D 52.4
S 47.6
N 42.9

8

A president is elected and tries to get rid of the dirty stuff in the economy as quickly as possible, so that by the time the next election comes around, he looks like a hero. The stock market is reacting to what the politicians are doing.
— Yale Hirsch (Creator of *Stock Trader's Almanac*, *NY Times* 10/10/2010, b. 1923)

THURSDAY

D 38.1
S 42.9
N 42.9

9

A realist believes that what is done or left undone in the short run determines the long run.
— Sydney J. Harris (American journalist and author, 1917–1986)

FRIDAY

D 47.6
S 42.9
N 42.9

10

A bank is a place where they lend you an umbrella in fair weather and ask for it back again when it begins to rain.
— Robert Frost (American poet, 1874–1963)

SATURDAY

11

SUNDAY

12

GET MORE OUT OF NASDAQ'S "BEST EIGHT MONTHS" WITH MACD TIMING

NASDAQ's amazing eight-month run from November through June is hard to miss on pages 58 and 148. A $10,000 investment in these eight months since 1971 gained $542,597 versus a loss of $1,655 during the void that is the four-month period July–October (as of May 21, 2015).

Using the same MACD timing indicators on the NASDAQ as is done for the Dow (page 54) has enabled us to capture much of October's improved performance, pumping up NASDAQ's results considerably. Over the 44 years since NASDAQ began, the gain on the same $10,000 leaps to $1,404,013 while the $10,000 during the four-month void shrinks to $6,748. Only four sizeable losses occurred during the favorable period, and the bulk of NASDAQ's bear markets were avoided including the worst of the 2000–2002 bear.

Updated signals are e-mailed to our monthly newsletter subscribers as soon as they are triggered. Visit *www.stocktradersalmanac.com,* or see ad insert for details and a special offer for new subscribers.

BEST EIGHT MONTHS STRATEGY + TIMING

MACD Signal Date	Worst 4 Months July 1–Oct 31* NASDAQ	% Change	Investing $10,000	MACD Signal Date	Best 8 Months Nov 1–June 30* NASDAQ	% Change	Investing $10,000
22-Jul-71	109.54	–3.6	$9,640	4-Nov-71	105.56	24.1	$12,410
7-Jun-72	131.00	–1.8	9,466	23-Oct-72	128.66	–22.7	9,593
25-Jun-73	99.43	–7.2	8,784	7-Dec-73	92.32	–20.2	7,655
3-Jul-74	73.66	–23.2	6,746	7-Oct-74	56.57	47.8	11,314
11-Jun-75	83.60	–9.2	6,125	7-Oct-75	75.88	20.8	13,667
22-Jul-76	91.66	–2.4	5,978	19-Oct-76	89.45	13.2	15,471
27-Jun-77	101.25	–4.0	5,739	4-Nov-77	97.21	26.6	19,586
7-Jun-78	123.10	–6.5	5,366	6-Nov-78	115.08	19.1	23,327
3-Jul-79	137.03	–1.1	5,307	30-Oct-79	135.48	15.5	26,943
20-Jun-80	156.51	26.2	6,697	9-Oct-80	197.53	11.2	29,961
4-Jun-81	219.68	–17.6	5,518	1-Oct-81	181.09	–4.0	28,763
7-Jun-82	173.84	12.5	6,208	7-Oct-82	195.59	57.4	45,273
1-Jun-83	307.95	–10.7	5,544	3-Nov-83	274.86	–14.2	38,844
1-Jun-84	235.90	5.0	5,821	15-Oct-84	247.67	17.3	45,564
3-Jun-85	290.59	–3.0	5,646	1-Oct-85	281.77	39.4	63,516
10-Jun-86	392.83	–10.3	5,064	1-Oct-86	352.34	20.5	76,537
30-Jun-87	424.67	–22.7	3,914	2-Nov-87	328.33	20.1	91,921
8-Jul-88	394.33	–6.6	3,656	29-Nov-88	368.15	22.4	112,511
13-Jul-89	450.73	0.7	3,682	9-Nov-89	454.07	1.9	114,649
11-Jun-90	462.79	–23.0	2,835	2-Oct-90	356.39	39.3	159,706
11-Jun-91	496.62	6.4	3,016	1-Oct-91	528.51	7.4	171,524
11-Jun-92	567.68	1.5	3,061	14-Oct-92	576.22	20.5	206,686
7-Jun-93	694.61	9.9	3,364	1-Oct-93	763.23	–4.4	197,592
17-Jun-94	729.35	5.0	3,532	11-Oct-94	765.57	13.5	224,267
1-Jun-95	868.82	17.2	4,140	13-Oct-95	1018.38	21.6	272,709
3-Jun-96	1238.73	1.0	4,181	7-Oct-96	1250.87	10.3	300,798
4-Jun-97	1379.67	24.4	5,201	3-Oct-97	1715.87	1.8	306,212
1-Jun-98	1746.82	–7.8	4,795	15-Oct-98	1611.01	49.7	458,399
1-Jun-99	2412.03	18.5	5,682	6-Oct-99	2857.21	35.7	622,047
29-Jun-00	3877.23	–18.2	4,648	18-Oct-00	3171.56	–32.2	421,748
1-Jun-01	2149.44	–31.1	3,202	1-Oct-01	1480.46	5.5	444,944
3-Jun-02	1562.56	–24.0	2,434	2-Oct-02	1187.30	38.5	616,247
20-Jun-03	1644.72	15.1	2,802	6-Oct-03	1893.46	4.3	642,746
21-Jun-04	1974.38	–1.6	2,757	1-Oct-04	1942.20	6.1	681,954
8-Jun-05	2060.18	1.5	2,798	19-Oct-05	2091.76	6.1	723,553
1-Jun-06	2219.86	3.9	2,907	5-Oct-06	2306.34	9.5	792,291
7-Jun-07	2541.38	7.9	3,137	1-Oct-07	2740.99	–9.1	724,796
2-Jun-08	2491.53	–31.3	2,155	17-Oct-08	1711.29	6.1	769,009
15-Jun-09	1816.38	17.8	2,539	9-Oct-09	2139.28	1.6	781,313
7-Jun-10	2173.90	18.6	3,011	4-Nov-10	2577.34	7.4	839,130
1-Jun-11	2769.19	–10.5	2,695	7-Oct-11	2479.35	10.8	929,736
1-Jun-12	2747.48	9.6	2,954	6-Nov-12	3011.93	16.2	1,080,376
4-Jun-13	3445.26	10.1	3,252	15-Oct-13	3794.01	15.4	1,227,442
26-Jun-14	4379.05	0.9	3,281	21-Oct-14	4419.48	15.2	1,414,013
21-May-15	5090.79						

As of 5/21/2015, MACD Sell Signal not triggered at press time

44-Year Loss ($6,719)   **44-Year Gain $1,404,013**

MACD-generated entry and exit points (earlier or later) can lengthen or shorten eight-month periods.

Monday of Triple Witching Week, Dow Down 10 of Last 18

MONDAY
13

D 57.1
S 57.1
N 47.6

The market can stay irrational longer than you can stay solvent.
— John Maynard Keynes (British economist, 1883–1946)

FOMC Meeting (2 Days)

TUESDAY
14

D 71.4
S 71.4
N 61.9

To succeed in the markets, it is essential to make your own decisions. Numerous traders cited listening to others as their worst blunder.
— Jack D. Schwager (Investment manager, author, *Stock Market Wizards: Interviews with America's Top Stock Traders*, b. 1948)

Triple Witching Week Often Up in Bull Markets and Down in Bears (Page 78)

WEDNESDAY
15

D 61.9
S 71.4
N 71.4

Give me a stock clerk with a goal and I will give you a man who will make history. Give me a man without a goal, and I will give you a stock clerk.
— James Cash Penney (J.C. Penney founder, 1875–1971)

THURSDAY
16

D 57.1
S 57.1
N 52.4

Good judgment is usually the result of experience and experience frequently is the result of bad judgment.
— Robert Lovell (Quoted by Robert Sobel, *Panic on Wall Street*)

June Triple Witching Day, Dow Up 10 of Last 16
However, Average Loss 0.2%

FRIDAY
17

D 57.1
S 57.1
N 61.9

People somehow think you must buy at the bottom and sell at the top. That's nonsense. The idea is to buy when the probability is greatest that the market is going to advance.
— Martin Zweig (Fund manager, *Winning on Wall Street*, 1943–2013)

SATURDAY
18

Father's Day

SUNDAY
19

TRIPLE RETURNS, LESS TRADES: BEST 6 + 4-YEAR CYCLE

We first introduced this strategy to *Almanac Investor* newsletter subscribers in October 2006. Recurring seasonal stock market patterns and the four-year Presidential Election/Stock Market Cycle (page 130) have been integral to our research since the first Almanac 49 years ago. Yale Hirsch discovered the Best Six Months in 1986 (page 52), and it has been a cornerstone of our seasonal investment analysis and strategies ever since.

Most of the market's gains have occurred during the Best Six Months, and the market generally hits a low point every four years in the first (post-election) or second (midterm) year and exhibits the greatest gains in the third (pre-election) year. This strategy combines the best of these two market phenomena, the Best Six Months and the four-year cycle, timing entries and exits with MACD (pages 54 and 60).

We've gone back to 1949 to include the full four-year cycle that began with post-election year 1949. Only four trades every four years are needed to nearly triple the results of the Best Six Months. Buy and sell during the post-election and midterm years and then hold from the midterm MACD seasonal buy signal sometime after October 1 until the post-election MACD seasonal sell signal sometime after April 1, approximately 2.5 years: better returns, less effort, lower transaction fees, and fewer taxable events.

FOUR TRADES EVERY FOUR YEARS

Year	Worst Six Months May–Oct	Best Six Months Nov–April
Post-election	Sell	Buy
Midterm	Sell	Buy
Pre-election	Hold	Hold
Election	Hold	Hold

BEST SIX MONTHS+TIMING+4-YEAR CYCLE STRATEGY

	DJIA % Change May 1–Oct 31*	Investing $10,000	DJIA % Change Nov 1–Apr 30*	Investing $10,000
1949	3.0%	$10,300	17.5%	$11,750
1950	7.3	11,052	19.7	14,065
1951		11,052		14,065
1952		11,052		14,065
1953	0.2	11,074	17.1	16,470
1954	13.5	12,569	35.7	22,350
1955		12,569		22,350
1956		12,569		22,350
1957	−12.3	11,023	4.9	23,445
1958	17.3	12,930	27.8	29,963
1959		12,930		29,963
1960		12,930		29,963
1961	2.9	13,305	−1.5	29,514
1962	−15.3	11,269	58.5	46,780
1963		11,269		46,780
1964		11,269		46,780
1965	2.6	11,562	−2.5	45,611
1966	−16.4	9,666	22.2	55,737
1967		9,666		55,737
1968		9,666		55,737
1969	−11.9	8,516	−6.7	52,003
1970	−1.4	8,397	21.5	63,184
1971		8,397		63,184
1972		8,397		63,184
1973	−11.0	7,473	0.1	63,247
1974	−22.4	5,799	42.5	90,127
1975		5,799		90,127
1976		5,799		90,127
1977	−11.4	5,138	0.5	90,578
1978	−4.5	4,907	26.8	114,853
1979		4,907		114,853
1980		4,907		114,853
1981	−14.6	4,191	0.4	115,312
1982	15.5	4,841	25.9	145,178
1983		4,841		145,178
1984		4,841		145,178
1985	7.0	5,180	38.1	200,491
1986	−2.8	5,035	33.2	267,054
1987		5,035		267,054
1988		5,035		267,054
1989	9.8	5,528	3.3	275,867
1990	−6.7	5,158	35.1	372,696
1991		5,158		372,696
1992		5,158		372,696
1993	5.5	5,442	5.6	393,455
1994	3.7	5,643	88.2	740,482
1995		5,643		740,482
1996		5,643		740,482
1997	3.6	5,846	18.5	877,471
1998	−12.4	5,121	36.3	1,195,993
1999		5,121		1,195,993
2000		5,121		1,195,993
2001	−17.3	4,235	15.8	1,384,960
2002	−25.2	3,168	34.2	1,858,616
2003		3,168		1,858,616
2004		3,168		1,858,616
2005	−0.5	3,152	7.7	2,001,729
2006	4.7	3,300	−31.7	1,367,181
2007		3,300		1,367,181
2008		3,300		1,367,181
2009	23.8	4,085	10.8	1,514,738
2010	4.6	4,273	27.4	1,929,777
2011		4,273		1,929,777
2012		4,273		1,929,777
2013	4.1	4,448	7.1	2,066,791
2014	2.3	$4,550	7.4	$2,219,733
Average	**−0.8%**		**9.8%**	
# Up	**18**		**30**	
# Down	**16**		**4**	
66-Year Gain (Loss)		**($5,450)**		**$2,209,733**

** MACD and 2.5-year hold lengthen and shorten six-month periods*

MONDAY

D 47.6
S 42.9
N 42.9

20

Between two evils, I always pick the one I never tried before.
— Mae West (American actress and playwright, 1893–1980)

TUESDAY

D 38.1
S 42.9
N 52.4

21

What technology does is make people more productive. It doesn't replace them.
— Michael Bloomberg (Founder Bloomberg L.P., philanthropist, New York Mayor 2002–2013, b. 1942)

Week After June Triple Witching, Dow Down 22 of Last 25
Average Loss Since 1990, 1.1%

WEDNESDAY

D 42.9
S 52.4
N 38.1

22

What investors really get paid for is holding dogs. Small stocks tend to have higher average returns than big stocks, and value stocks tend to have higher average returns than growth stocks.
— Kenneth R. French (Economist, Dartmouth, NBER, b. 1954)

THURSDAY

D 33.3
S 33.3
N 33.3

23

I sold enough papers last year of high school to pay cash for a BMW.
— Michael Dell (Founder Dell Computer, *Forbes*, b. 1965)

FRIDAY

D 33.3
S 38.1
N 38.1

24

We are nowhere near a capitulation point because it's at that point where it's despair, not hope, that reigns supreme, and there was scant evidence of any despair at any of the meetings I gave.
— David Rosenberg (Economist, Merrill Lynch, *Barron's* 4/21/2008)

SATURDAY

25

July Almanac Investor Sector Seasonalities: See Pages 94, 96, and 98

SUNDAY

26

JULY ALMANAC

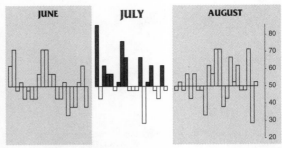

JULY						
S	M	T	W	T	F	S
31					1	2
3	4	5	6	7	8	9
10	11	12	13	14	15	16
17	18	19	20	21	22	23
24	25	26	27	28	29	30

AUGUST						
S	M	T	W	T	F	S
	1	2	3	4	5	6
7	8	9	10	11	12	13
14	15	16	17	18	19	20
21	22	23	24	25	26	27
28	29	30	31			

Market Probability Chart above is a graphic representation of the S&P 500 Recent Market Probability Calendar on page 124.

◆ July is the best month of the third quarter except for NASDAQ (page 66) ◆ Start of 2nd half brings an inflow of retirement funds ◆ First trading day Dow up 21 of last 26 ◆ Graph above shows strength in the first half of July ◆ Huge gain in July usually provides better buying opportunity over next 4 months ◆ Start of NASDAQ's worst four months of the year (page 60) ◆ Presidential election year Julys are ranked #7 Dow (up 8, down 8), #8 S&P (up 7, down 9), and #10 NASDAQ (up 5, down 6).

July Vital Statistics

	DJIA	S&P 500	NASDAQ	Russell 1K	Russell 2K
Rank	4	6	11	8	12
Up	40	35	22	16	17
Down	25	30	22	20	19
Average % Change	1.2%	1.0%	0.2%	0.6%	-0.5%
Election Year	0.3%	0.2%	-1.3%	-0.3%	-0.9%
	Best & Worst July				
	% Change	% Change	% Change	% Change	% Change
Best	1989 9.0	1989 8.8	1997 10.5	1989 8.2	1980 11.0
Worst	1969 -6.6	2002 -7.9	2002 -9.2	2002 -7.5	2002 -15.2
	Best & Worst July Weeks				
Best	7/17/09 7.3	7/17/09 7.0	7/17/09 7.4	7/17/09 7.0	7/17/09 8.0
Worst	7/19/02 -7.7	7/19/02 -8.0	7/28/00 -10.5	7/19/02 -7.4	7/2/10 -7.2
	Best & Worst July Days				
Best	7/24/02 6.4	7/24/02 5.7	7/29/02 5.8	7/24/02 5.6	7/29/02 4.9
Worst	7/19/02 -4.6	7/19/02 -3.8	7/28/00 -4.7	7/19/02 -3.6	7/23/02 -4.1
	First Trading Day of Expiration Week: 1980–2014				
Record (#Up – #Down)	21–14	22–13	23–12	21–14	19–16
Current streak	U2	U2	U2	U2	U2
Avg % Change	0.09	0.02	0.02	-0.01	-0.08
	Options Expiration Day: 1980–2014				
Record (#Up – #Down)	16–17	18–17	15–20	18–17	14–21
Current streak	U1	U2	U1	U2	U2
Avg % Change	-0.25	-0.29	-0.45	-0.31	-0.46
	Options Expiration Week: 1980–2014				
Record (#Up – #Down)	22–13	19–16	18–17	19–16	18–17
Current streak	U3	U3	U1	U3	D1
Avg % Change	0.42	0.09	-0.03	0.04	-0.16
	Week After Options Expiration: 1980–2014				
Record (#Up – #Down)	18–17	17–18	16–19	18–17	13–22
Current streak	D1	U1	U7	U6	D2
Avg % Change	0.01	-0.14	-0.41	-0.15	-0.32
	First Trading Day Performance				
% of Time Up	64.6	70.8	61.4	72.2	63.9
Avg % Change	0.26	0.25	0.12	0.31	0.09
	Last Trading Day Performance				
% of Time Up	50.8	61.5	50.0	58.3	63.9
Avg % Change	0.03	0.07	-0.04	-0.03	-0.04

Dow & S&P 1950–April 2015, NASDAQ 1971–April 2015, Russell 1K & 2K 1979–April 2015.

When Dow and S&P in July are inferior,
NASDAQ days tend to be even drearier.

Studying Market History Can Produce Gains

STOCK TRADER'S ALMANAC

LIKE THESE

- ▶ ProShares UltraShort Crude (SCO) **up 26.1%** in 3 weeks
- ▶ iShares NASDAQ Biotech (IBB) **up 26.5%** in 5 months
- ▶ iShares Russell 2000 (IWM) **up 11.9%** in 7.5 months
- ▶ PowerShares QQQ (QQQ) **up 12.5%** in 7.5 months

AND THESE

- ▶ Avis Budget Group (CAR) **up 164.5%**
- ▶ Hawaiian Holdings (HA) **up 121.1%**
- ▶ JetBlue (JBLU) **up 86.3%**
- ▶ Repligen (RGEN) **up 346.5%**

What do all these big winners have in common? All were undervalued and off Wall Street's radar screen when we selected them. All were chosen by my team of highly-trained veteran market analysts with decades of experience trading and investing in the market with real money. All passed through our multi-disciplined approach that combines our renowned *Stock Trader's Almanac* behavioral finance analysis of the 4-Year Election Cycle, market and sector seasonality in conjunction with our proprietary fundamental stock screening criteria with the entries and exits pinpointed using old-school technical analysis. We refer to our blend of historical rules-based strategy with technical and fundamental tactical signals as DYNAMIC Investing.

Jeffrey A. Hirsch
Editor Stock Trader's Almanac,
Investment Committee Member
Probabilities Fund Management, LLC

My name is Jeffrey A. Hirsch, I am the editor-in chief of the *Stock Trader's Almanac* and I want to introduce you to my **completely revamped eNewsletter ALMANAC INVESTOR**. *ALMANAC INVESTOR* is a unique service that brings you top stocks and top sectors at the right time every week. Subscribe to my highly acclaimed biweekly digital subscription service, *Almanac Investor* eNewsletter, which culminates 50 years of independent market research and publishing and each week you will receive two timely Alerts bringing you actionable trades and investment ideas with clear and specific buy and sell points.

436.5% Gain Since 2001 Vs. 68.5% for S&P 500

Almanac Investor eNewsletter, is the culmination of all we've done with the *Almanac* and newsletters over the years. Our *Almanac Investor* Stock Portfolio currently has a Total Return of 436.5% since inception in 2001 versus a 68.5% return for the S&P 500 over the same timeframe. This includes all of our sold positions.

- ▶ Excludes dividends, fees and any foreign currency gains or losses.
- ▶ No margin or leverage used
- ▶ Long and Short stock trades across Small, Mid and Large-Cap companies
- ▶ Rarely fully invested, maintain cash balance.

Get The *2017 Stock Trader's Almanac* FREE

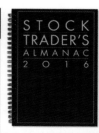

Save 20% Off the regular 1-Year Subscription price of $179.95 and get a **FREE** *Stock Trader's Almanac 2017* (*Retail value $50*). **That's $143.96 for a full 1-Year Subscription** (*Total Savings $86!*): includes, 2 Email Alerts every week, interim buy and sell signal alerts, full access to the website and a **FREE** annual copy of the *Stock Trader's Almanac*. Subscribe today at **www.StockTradersAlmanac.com** click "Subscribe Now" and use Promo Code STA16.

Go to **www.STOCKTRADERSALMANAC.com/STA16**
and click "**Subscribe Now**" or **CALL 845-875-9582**

Those who study market history are bound to profit from it!

"I gladly subscribe because it has made me a very successful trader. In October of 2014 the email newsletter gave me a signal to buy the QQQ index at about 98. Then I patiently waited for the signal to sell which came in early June of 2015. The sell price of about 108 gave me an 11 per cent return or $170,000 profit in just eight months!" – Rick from Arizona

ACT NOW! Visit www.STOCKTRADERSALMANAC.com/STA16
CALL 845-875-9582 or EMAIL info@stocktradersalmanac.com

Almanac Investor Ranked Top 5 Market Timer by Hulbert Past 10 Years

What's even more gratifying is that the independent newsletter watchdog, the *Hulbert Financial Digest*, ranked my *Almanac Investor* among the Top 5 Market Timers in 2014 for the past decade.

Now you can find out what seasonal trends are on schedule and which are not, and how to take advantage of them. What market-moving events are coming up? What are our indicators saying about the next major market move. Every week you will receive timely warnings about good and bad seasonal patterns.

Our digital subscription service, *Almanac Investor*, provides all this plus unusual investing opportunities – exciting small-, mid- and large-cap stocks; seasoned, undervalued equities; timely sector ETF trades and more. Our **Data-Rich and Data-Driven Market Cycle Analysis** is the only investment tool of its kind that helps traders and investors forecast market trends with accuracy and confidence.

YOU RECEIVE 2 EMAIL ALERTS WEEKLY CONTAINING:

- ▶ Opportune ETF and Stock Trading Ideas with Specific Buy and Sell Price Limits
- ▶ Timely Data-Rich and Data-Driven Market Analysis
- ▶ Access to Webinars, Videos, Tools and Resources
- ▶ Market-Tested and Time-Proven Short- and Long-term Trading Strategies
- ▶ Best Six-Months Switching Strategy MACD Timing Signals.

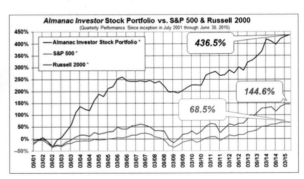

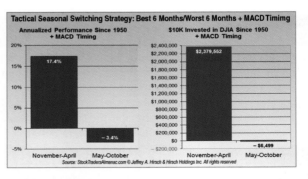

JUNE/JULY

History must repeat itself because we pay such little attention to it the first time.
— Blackie Sherrod (Sportswriter, b. 1919)

I've never been poor, only broke. Being poor is a frame of mind. Being broke is only a temporary situation.
— Mike Todd (Movie Producer, 1903–1958)

The advice of the elders to young men is very apt to be as unreal as a list of the best books.
— Oliver Wendell Holmes Jr. (U.S. Supreme Court Justice 1902–1932, *The Mind and Faith of Justice Holmes*, edited by Max Lerner, 1841–1935)

Last Day of Q2 Bearish for Dow, Down 17 of Last 24
But Bullish for NASDAQ, Up 16 of 23, Although Down 6 of Last 10

Statements by high officials are practically always misleading when they are designed to bolster a falling market.
— Gerald M. Loeb (E.F. Hutton, *The Battle for Investment Survival*, predicted 1929 Crash, 1900–1974)

First Trading Day in July, Dow Up 21 of Last 26, Average Gain 0.5%

640K ought to be enough for anybody.
— William H. Gates (Microsoft founder, 1981, b. 155. Try running Microsoft Vista on less than a Gig)

FIRST MONTH OF QUARTERS IS THE MOST BULLISH

We have observed over the years that the investment calendar reflects the annual, semiannual, and quarterly operations of institutions during January, April, and July. The opening month of the first three quarters produces the greatest gains in the Dow Jones Industrials and the S&P 500. NASDAQ's record differs slightly.

The fourth quarter had behaved quite differently, since it is affected by year-end portfolio adjustments and presidential and congressional elections in even-numbered years. Since 1991, major turnarounds have helped October join the ranks of bullish first months of quarters. October transformed into a bear-killing-turnaround month, posting some mighty gains in 11 of the last 17 years; 2008 was a significant exception. (See pages 152–160.)

After experiencing the most powerful bull market of all time during the 1990s, followed by two ferocious bear markets early in the millennium, we divided the monthly average percentage changes into two groups: before 1991 and after. Comparing the month-by-month quarterly behavior of the three major U.S. averages in the table, you'll see that first months of the first three quarters perform best overall. Nasty sell-offs in April 2000, 2002, 2004, and 2005, and July 2000–2002 and 2004 hit the NASDAQ hardest. The bear market of October 2007–March 2009, which more than cut the markets in half, took a toll on every first month except April. October 2008 was the worst month in a decade. January was also a difficult month in five of the last eight years. (See pages 152–160.)

Between 1950 and 1990, the S&P 500 gained 1.3% (Dow, 1.4%) on average in first months of the first three quarters. Second months barely eked out any gain, while third months, thanks to March, moved up 0.23% (Dow, 0.07%) on average. NASDAQ's first month of the first three quarters averages 1.67% from 1971–1990, with July being a negative drag.

DOW JONES INDUSTRIALS, S&P 500, AND NASDAQ AVERAGE MONTHLY % CHANGES BY QUARTER

	DJIA 1950–1990			S&P 500 1950–1990			NASDAQ 1971–1990		
	1st Mo	2nd Mo	3rd Mo	1st Mo	2nd Mo	3rd Mo	1st Mo	2nd Mo	3rd Mo
1Q	1.5%	−0.01%	1.0%	1.5%	−0.1%	1.1%	3.8%	1.2%	0.9%
2Q	1.6	−0.4	0.1	1.3	−0.1	0.3	1.7	0.8	1.1
3Q	1.1	0.3	−0.9	1.1	0.3	−0.7	−0.5	0.1	−1.6
Tot	4.2%	−0.1%	0.2%	3.9%	0.1%	0.7%	5.0%	2.1%	0.4%
Avg	1.40%	−0.04%	0.07%	1.30%	0.03%	0.23%	1.67%	0.70%	0.13%
4Q	−0.1%	1.4%	1.7%	0.4%	1.7%	1.6%	−1.4%	1.6%	1.4%
	DJIA 1991–April 2015			**S&P 500 1991–April 2015**			**NASDAQ 1991–April 2015**		
1Q	0.1%	0.6%	1.1%	0.3%	0.3%	1.3%	1.9%	0.3%	0.7%
2Q	2.4	0.6	−0.9	1.8	0.7	−0.5	1.2	0.9	0.6
3Q	1.3	−0.7	−0.6	0.7	−0.5	−0.2	0.7	0.4	0.4
Tot	3.8%	0.5%	−0.4%	2.8%	0.5%	0.7%	3.8%	1.6%	1.7%
Avg	1.27%	0.16%	−0.13%	0.93%	0.17%	0.22%	1.27%	0.53%	0.57%
4Q	1.6%	1.7%	1.7%	1.6%	1.3%	1.8%	2.3%	1.6%	2.4%
	DJIA 1950–April 2015			**S&P 500 1950–April 2015**			**NASDAQ 1971–April 2015**		
1Q	1.0%	0.21%	1.1%	1.0%	0.1%	1.2%	2.7%	0.7%	0.8%
2Q	1.9	−0.04	−0.3	1.5	0.2	−0.001	1.4	0.8	0.8
3Q	1.2	−0.1	−0.7	1.0	0.00	−0.5	0.2	0.3	−0.5
Tot	4.1%	0.07%	0.1%	3.5%	0.30%	0.7%	4.3%	1.8%	1.1%
Avg	1.37%	0.02%	0.03%	1.17%	0.10%	0.23%	1.42%	0.59%	0.37%
4Q	0.5%	1.5%	1.7%	0.8%	1.5%	1.7%	0.6%	1.6%	1.9%

Independence Day
(Market Closed)

MONDAY

4

Banking establishments are more dangerous than standing armies; and that the principle of spending money to be paid by posterity, under the name of funding, is but swindling futurity on a large scale.
— Thomas Jefferson (3rd U.S. President, 1816 letter to John Taylor of Caroline, 1743-7/4/1826)

Market Subject to Elevated Volatility After July 4th

D 42.9
S 42.9
N 38.1

TUESDAY

5

Today we deal with 65,000 more pieces of information each day than did our ancestors 100 years ago.
— Dr. Jean Houston (A founder of the Human Potential Movement, b. 1937)

July Begins NASDAQ's "Worst Four Months" (Pages 58, 60, and 148)

WEDNESDAY

D 57.1
S 61.9
N 57.1

6

Writing a book is an adventure. To begin with it is a toy, an amusement; then it is a mistress, and then a master, and then a tyrant.
— Winston Churchill (British statesman, 1874–1965)

THURSDAY

D 57.1
S 57.1
N 61.9

7

As for it being different this time, it is different every time. The question is in what way, and to what extent.
— Tom McClellan (*The McClellan Market Report*)

July Is the Best Performing Dow and S&P Month of the Third Quarter

FRIDAY

D 61.9
S 57.1
N 61.9

8

All there is to investing is picking good stocks at good times and staying with them as long as they remain good companies.
— Warren Buffett (CEO Berkshire Hathaway, investor, and philanthropist, b. 1930)

SATURDAY

9

SUNDAY

10

2014 DAILY DOW POINT CHANGES (DOW JONES INDUSTRIAL AVERAGE)

Week #		Monday**	Tuesday	Wednsday	Thursday	Friday**	Weekly Dow Close	Net Point Change
						2013 Close	16576.66	
1				Holiday	−135.31	28.64	16469.99	−106.67
2	J	−44.89	105.84	−68.20	−17.98	**−7.71**	16437.05	−32.94
3	A	**−179.11**	115.92	108.08	−64.93	41.55	16458.56	21.51
4	N	Holiday	−44.12	−41.10	−175.99	**−318.24**	15879.11	−579.45
5		**−41.23**	90.68	−189.77	109.82	**−149.76**	15698.85	−180.26
6	F	**−326.05**	72.44	−5.01	188.30	165.55	15794.08	95.23
7	E	7.71	192.98	−30.83	63.65	126.80	16154.39	360.31
8	B	Holiday	−23.99	−89.84	92.67	−29.93	16103.30	−51.09
9		103.84	−27.48	18.75	74.24	49.06	16321.71	218.41
10		−153.68	227.85	−35.70	61.71	30.83	16452.72	131.01
11	M	−34.04	−67.43	−11.17	−231.19	−43.22	16065.67	−387.05
12	A	181.55	88.97	−114.02	108.88	**−28.28**	16302.77	237.10
13	R	**−26.08**	91.19	−98.89	−4.76	58.83	16323.06	20.29
14		134.60	74.95	40.39	−0.45	**−159.84**	16412.71	89.65
15	A	**−166.84**	10.27	181.04	−266.96	−143.47	16026.75	−385.96
16	P	146.49	89.32	162.29	−16.31	Holiday	16408.54	381.79
17	R	40.71	65.12	−12.72	0.00	−140.19	16361.46	−47.08
18		87.28	86.63	45.47	−21.97	−45.98	16512.89	151.43
19	M	17.66	−129.53	117.52	32.43	32.37	16583.34	70.45
20	A	112.13	19.97	−101.47	−167.16	44.50	16491.31	−92.03
21	Y	20.55	−137.55	158.75	10.02	63.19	16606.27	114.96
22		Holiday	69.23	−42.32	65.56	18.43	16717.17	110.90
23		26.46	−21.29	15.19	98.58	88.17	16924.28	207.11
24	J	18.82	2.82	−102.04	−109.69	41.55	16775.74	−148.54
25	U	5.27	27.48	98.13	14.84	25.62	16947.08	171.34
26	N	−9.82	−119.13	49.38	−21.38	5.71	16851.84	−95.24
27		−25.24	129.47	20.17	92.02*	Holiday	17068.26	216.42
28	J	−44.05	−117.59	78.99	−70.54	28.74	16943.81	−124.45
29	U	111.61	5.26	77.52	−161.39	123.37	17100.18	156.37
30	L	−48.45	61.81	−26.91	−2.83	−123.23	16960.57	−139.61
31		22.02	−70.48	−31.75	−317.06	−69.93	16493.37	−467.20
32	A	75.91	−139.81	13.87	−75.07	185.66	16553.93	60.56
33	U	16.05	−9.44	91.26	61.78	−50.67	16662.91	108.98
34	G	175.83	80.85	59.54	60.36	−38.27	17001.22	338.31
35		75.65	29.83	15.31	−42.44	18.88	17098.45	97.23
36	S	Holiday	−30.89	10.72	−8.70	67.78	17137.36	38.91
37	E	−25.94	−97.55	54.84	−19.71	−61.49	16987.51	−149.85
38	P	43.63	100.83	24.88	109.14	13.75	17279.74	292.23
39		−107.06	−116.81	154.19	−264.26	167.35	17113.15	−166.59
40		−41.93	−28.32	−238.19	−3.66	208.64	17009.69	−103.46
41	O	−17.78	−272.52	274.83	−334.97	**−115.15**	16544.10	−465.59
42	C	**−223.03**	−5.88	−173.45	−24.50	263.17	16380.41	−163.69
43	T	19.26	215.14	−153.49	216.58	127.51	16805.41	425.00
44		12.53	187.81	−31.44	221.11	195.10	17390.52	585.11
45	N	−24.28	17.60	100.69	69.94	19.46	17573.93	183.41
46	O	39.81	1.16	−2.70	40.59	−18.05	17634.74	60.81
47	V	13.01	40.07	−2.09	33.27	91.06	17810.06	175.32
48		7.84	−2.96	−2.69	Holiday	15.99*	17828.24	18.18
49	D	−51.44	102.75	33.07	−12.52	58.69	17958.79	130.55
50	E	−106.31	−51.28	−268.05	63.19	−315.51	17280.83	−677.96
51	C	**−99.99**	−111.97	288.00	421.28	26.65	17804.80	523.97
52		154.64	64.73	6.04*	Holiday	23.50	18053.71	248.91
53		−15.48	−55.16	−160.00		Year's Close	17823.07	−230.64
TOTALS		**−171.63**	**817.56**	**265.07**	**−337.48**	**672.89**		**1246.41**

Bold Color: Down Friday, Down Monday

* Shortened trading day: Jul 3, Nov 28, Dec 24

** Monday denotes first trading day of week, Friday denotes last trading day of week

Monday Before July Expiration, Dow Up 9 of Last 12

MONDAY
D 47.6
S 47.6
N 57.1
11

If you destroy a free market you create a black market. If you have ten thousand regulations you destroy all respect for the law.
— Winston Churchill (British statesman, 1874–1965)

TUESDAY
D 52.4
S 52.4
N 57.1
12

When everyone starts downgrading a stock, it's usually time to buy.
— Meryl Witmer (General partner, Eagle Capital Partners, Barron's 1/29/07)

WEDNESDAY
D 66.7
S 76.2
N 71.4
13

We spend $500 million a year just in training our people. We've developed some technology that lets us do simulations. Think of Flight Simulation. What we've found is that the retention rate from simulation is about 75%, opposed to 25% from classroom work.
— Joe Forehand (CEO, Accenture, Forbes, 7/7/03)

THURSDAY
D 61.9
S 66.7
N 71.4
14

What people in the Middle East tell you in private is irrelevant. All that matters is what they will defend in public in their language.
— Thomas L. Friedman (*NY Times* Foreign Affairs columnist, "Meet the Press" 12/17/06, b. 1953)

July Expiration Day, Dow Down 9 of Last 15, –4.6% in 2002 and –2.5% in 2010

FRIDAY
D 52.4
S 47.6
N 57.1
15

When a country lives on borrowed time, borrowed money and borrowed energy, it is just begging the markets to discipline it in their own way at their own time. Usually the markets do it in an orderly way— except when they don't.
— Thomas L. Friedman (*NY Times* Foreign Affairs columnist, 2/24/05, b. 1953)

SATURDAY
16

SUNDAY
17

DON'T SELL STOCKS ON MONDAY OR FRIDAY

Since 1989, Monday* and Tuesday have been the most consistently bullish days of the week for the Dow, Thursday and Friday* the most bearish, as traders have become reluctant to stay long going into the weekend. Since 1989 Mondays and Tuesdays gained 13088.44 Dow points, while Thursday and Friday combined for a total gain of 1779.25 points. Also broken out are the last 14 and a third years to illustrate Monday's and Friday's poor performance in bear market years 2001–2002 and 2008–2009. During uncertain market times traders often sell before the weekend and are reluctant to jump in on Monday. See pages 68, 80, and 141–144 for more.

ANNUAL DOW POINT CHANGES FOR DAYS OF THE WEEK SINCE 1953

Year	Monday*	Tuesday	Wednesday	Thursday	Friday*	Year's DJIA Closing	Year's Point Change
1953	−36.16	−7.93	19.63	5.76	7.70	280.90	−11.00
1954	15.68	3.27	24.31	33.96	46.27	404.39	123.49
1955	−48.36	26.38	46.03	−0.66	60.62	488.40	84.01
1956	−27.15	−9.36	−15.41	8.43	64.56	499.47	11.07
1957	−109.50	−7.71	64.12	3.32	−14.01	435.69	−63.78
1958	17.50	23.59	29.10	22.67	55.10	583.65	147.96
1959	−44.48	29.04	4.11	13.60	93.44	679.36	95.71
1960	−111.04	−3.75	−5.62	6.74	50.20	615.89	−63.47
1961	−23.65	10.18	87.51	−5.96	47.17	731.14	115.25
1962	−101.60	26.19	9.97	−7.70	−5.90	652.10	−79.04
1963	−8.88	47.12	16.23	22.39	33.99	762.95	110.85
1964	−0.29	−17.94	39.84	5.52	84.05	874.13	111.18
1965	−73.23	39.65	57.03	3.20	68.48	969.26	95.13
1966	−153.24	−27.73	56.13	−46.19	−12.54	785.69	−183.57
1967	−68.65	31.50	25.42	92.25	38.90	905.11	119.42
1968†	6.41	34.94	25.16	−72.06	44.19	943.75	38.64
1969	−164.17	−36.70	18.33	23.79	15.36	800.36	−143.39
1970	−100.05	−46.09	116.07	−3.48	72.11	838.92	38.56
1971	−2.99	9.56	13.66	8.04	23.01	890.20	51.28
1972	−87.40	−1.23	65.24	8.46	144.75	1020.02	129.82
1973	−174.11	10.52	−5.94	36.67	−36.30	850.86	−169.16
1974	−149.37	47.51	−20.31	−13.70	−98.75	616.24	−234.62
1975	39.46	−109.62	56.93	124.00	125.40	852.41	236.17
1976	70.72	71.76	50.88	−33.70	−7.42	1004.65	152.24
1977	−65.15	−44.89	−79.61	−5.62	21.79	831.17	−173.48
1978	−31.29	−70.84	71.33	−64.67	69.31	805.01	−26.16
1979	−32.52	9.52	−18.84	75.18	0.39	838.74	33.73
1980	−86.51	135.13	137.67	−122.00	60.96	963.99	125.25
1981	−45.68	−49.51	−13.95	−14.67	34.82	875.00	−88.99
1982	5.71	86.20	28.37	−1.47	52.73	1046.54	171.54
1983	30.51	−30.92	149.68	61.16	1.67	1258.64	212.10
1984	−73.80	78.02	−139.24	92.79	−4.84	1211.57	−47.07
1985	80.36	52.70	51.26	46.32	104.46	1546.67	335.10
1986	−39.94	97.63	178.65	29.31	83.63	1895.95	349.28
1987	−559.15	235.83	392.03	139.73	−165.56	1938.83	42.88
1988	268.12	166.44	−60.48	−230.84	86.50	2168.57	229.74
1989	−53.31	143.33	233.25	90.25	171.11	2753.20	584.63
SubTotal	*−1937.20*	*941.79*	*1708.54*	*330.82*	*1417.35*		*2461.30*
1990	219.90	−25.22	47.96	−352.55	−9.63	2633.66	−119.54
1991	191.13	47.97	174.53	254.79	−133.25	3168.83	535.17
1992	237.80	−49.67	3.12	108.74	−167.71	3301.11	132.28
1993	322.82	−37.03	243.87	4.97	−81.65	3754.09	452.98
1994	206.41	−95.33	29.98	−168.87	108.16	3834.44	80.35
1995	262.97	210.06	357.02	140.07	312.56	5117.12	1282.68
1996	626.41	155.55	−34.24	268.52	314.91	6448.27	1331.15
1997	1136.04	1989.17	−590.17	−949.80	−125.26	7908.25	1459.98
1998	649.10	679.95	591.63	−1579.43	931.93	9181.43	1273.18
1999	980.49	−1587.23	826.68	735.94	1359.81	11497.12	2315.69
2000	2265.45	306.47	−1978.34	238.21	−1542.06	10786.85	−710.27
SubTotal	*7098.52*	*1594.69*	*−327.96*	*−1299.41*	*967.81*		*8033.65*
2001	−389.33	336.86	−396.53	976.41	−1292.76	10021.50	−765.35
2002	−1404.94	−823.76	1443.69	−428.12	−466.74	8341.63	−1679.87
2003	978.87	482.11	−425.46	566.22	510.55	10453.92	2112.29
2004	201.12	523.28	358.76	−409.72	−344.35	10783.01	329.09
2005	316.23	−305.62	27.67	−128.75	24.96	10717.50	−65.51
2006	95.74	573.98	1283.87	193.34	−401.28	12463.15	1745.65
2007	278.23	−157.93	1316.74	−766.63	131.26	13264.82	801.67
2008	−1387.20	1704.51	−3073.72	−940.88	−791.14	8776.39	−4488.43
2009	−45.22	161.76	617.56	932.68	−15.12	10428.05	1651.66
2010	1236.88	−421.80	1019.66	−76.73	−608.55	11577.51	1149.46
2011	−571.02	1423.66	−776.05	246.27	317.19	12217.56	640.05
2012	254.59	−49.28	−456.37	847.34	299.30	13104.14	886.58
2013	−79.63	1091.75	170.93	653.64	1635.83	16576.66	3472.52
2014	−171.63	817.56	265.07	−337.48	672.89	17823.07	1246.41
2015 ‡	626.41	−900.95	−387.19	1259.82	−148.60		
Subtotal	*−60.90*	*4456.13*	*988.63*	*2587.41*	*−476.56*		*5789.81*
Totals	**5100.42**	**6992.61**	**2369.21**	**1618.82**	**1908.60**		**16284.76**

* Monday denotes first trading day of week, Friday denotes last trading day of week.
† Most Wednesdays closed last 7 months of 1968. ‡ Partial year through May 16, 2014.

70

MONDAY
D 57.1
S 47.6
N 52.4
18

Even being right 3 or 4 times out of 10 should yield a person a fortune, if he has the sense to cut his losses quickly on the ventures where he has been wrong.
— Bernard Baruch (Financier, speculator, statesman, presidential adviser, 1870–1965)

Week After July Expiration Prone to Wild Swings, Dow Up 9 of Last 13
1998 –4.3%, 2002 +3.1%, 2006 +3.2%, 2007 –4.2%, 2009 +4.0%, 2010 +3.2

TUESDAY
D 52.4
S 47.6
N 57.1
19

The finest thought runs the risk of being irrevocably forgotten if we do not write it down.
— Arthur Schopenhauer (German philosopher, 1788–1860)

WEDNESDAY
D 66.7
S 66.7
N 66.7
20

Experience is helpful, but it is judgment that matters.
— General Colin Powell (Chairman Joint Chiefs 1989–1993, Secretary of State 2001–2005, *NY Times* 10/22/2008, b. 1937)

Beware the "Summer Rally" Hype
Historically the Weakest Rally of All Seasons (Page 72)

THURSDAY
D 23.8
S 28.6
N 23.8
21

When an old man dies, a library burns down.
— African proverb

FRIDAY
D 47.6
S 52.4
N 47.6
22

Regret for the things we did can be tempered by time; it is regret for the things we did not do that is inconsolable.
— Sydney J. Harris (American journalist and author, 1917–1986)

SATURDAY
23

SUNDAY
24

A RALLY FOR ALL SEASONS

Most years, especially when the market sells off during the first half, prospects for the perennial summer rally become the buzz on the street. Parameters for this "rally" were defined by the late Ralph Rotnem as the lowest close in the Dow Jones Industrials in May or June to the highest close in July, August, or September. Such a big deal is made of the "summer rally" that one might get the impression the market puts on its best performance in the summertime. Nothing could be further from the truth! Not only does the market "rally" in every season of the year, but it does so with more gusto in the winter, spring, and fall than in the summer.

Winters in 52 years averaged a 12.9% gain as measured from the low in November or December to the first quarter closing high. Spring rose 11.3% followed by fall with 10.9%. Last and least was the average 9.2% "summer rally." Even 2009's impressive 19.7% "summer rally" was outmatched by spring. Nevertheless, no matter how thick the gloom or grim the outlook, don't despair! There's always a rally for all seasons, statistically.

SEASONAL GAINS IN DOW JONES INDUSTRIALS

	WINTER RALLY Nov/Dec Low to Q1 High	SPRING RALLY Feb/Mar Low to Q2 High	SUMMER RALLY May/Jun Low to Q3 High	FALL RALLY Aug/Sep Low to Q4 High
1964	15.3%	6.2%	9.4%	8.3%
1965	5.7	6.6	11.6	10.3
1966	5.9	4.8	3.5	7.0
1967	11.6	8.7	11.2	4.4
1968	7.0	11.5	5.2	13.3
1969	0.9	7.7	1.9	6.7
1970	5.4	6.2	22.5	19.0
1971	21.6	9.4	5.5	7.4
1972	19.1	7.7	5.2	11.4
1973	8.6	4.8	9.7	15.9
1974	13.1	8.2	1.4	11.0
1975	36.2	24.2	8.2	8.7
1976	23.3	6.4	5.9	4.6
1977	8.2	3.1	2.8	2.1
1978	2.1	16.8	11.8	5.2
1979	11.0	8.9	8.9	6.1
1980	13.5	16.8	21.0	8.5
1981	11.8	9.9	0.4	8.3
1982	4.6	9.3	18.5	37.8
1983	15.7	17.8	6.3	10.7
1984	5.9	4.6	14.1	9.7
1985	11.7	7.1	9.5	19.7
1986	31.1	18.8	9.2	11.4
1987	30.6	13.6	22.9	5.9
1988	18.1	13.5	11.2	9.8
1989	15.1	12.9	16.1	5.7
1990	8.8	14.5	12.4	8.6
1991	21.8	11.2	6.6	9.3
1992	14.9	6.4	3.7	3.3
1993	8.9	7.7	6.3	7.3
1994	9.7	5.2	9.1	5.0
1995	13.6	19.3	11.3	13.9
1996	19.2	7.5	8.7	17.3
1997	17.7	18.4	18.4	7.3
1998	20.3	13.6	8.2	24.3
1999	15.1	21.6	8.2	12.6
2000	10.8	15.2	9.8	3.5
2001	6.4	20.8	1.7	23.1
2002	14.8	7.9	2.8	17.6
2003	6.5	23.9	14.3	15.7
2004	11.6	5.2	4.4	10.6
2005	9.0	2.1	5.6	5.3
2006	8.8	8.3	9.5	13.0
2007	6.7	13.5	6.6	10.3
2008	2.5	11.2	3.8	4.5
2009	19.6	34.4	19.7	15.5
2010	11.6	13.1	11.1	16.0
2011	12.6	10.3	7.0	14.7
2012	18.0	4.5	12.4	5.7
2013	16.2	11.8	6.9	12.2
2014	6.0	10.2	5.5	10.3
2015	7.1	5.3*		
Totals	**671.3%**	**588.6%**	**467.9%**	**555.8%**
Average	**12.9%**	**11.3%**	**9.2%**	**10.9%**

As of 5/15/2015

🐂 MONDAY
D 66.7
S 61.9
N 66.7
25

That's the American way. If little kids don't aspire to make money like I did, what the hell good is this country?
— Lee Iacocca (American industrialist, Former Chrysler CEO, b. 1924)

FOMC Meeting (2 Days)

TUESDAY
D 47.6
S 47.6
N 52.4
26

We like what's familiar, and we dislike change. So, we push the familiar until it starts working against us big-time—a crisis. Then, MAYBE we can accept change.
— Kevin Cameron (Journalist, *Cycle World* April 2013)

WEDNESDAY
D 38.1
S 42.9
N 38.1
27

All great truths begin as blasphemies.
— George Bernard Shaw (Irish dramatist, 1856–1950)

🐂 THURSDAY
D 47.6
S 61.9
N 66.7
28

Short-term volatility is greatest at turning points and diminishes as a trend becomes established.
— George Soros (Financier, philanthropist, political activist, author and philosopher, b. 1930)

Last Trading Day in July, NASDAQ Down 8 of Last 10

FRIDAY
D 38.1
S 47.6
N 42.9
29

Today's generation of young people holds more power than any generation before it to make a positive impact on the world.
— William J. Clinton (42nd U.S. President, Clinton Global Initiative, b. 1946)

SATURDAY
30

August Almanac Investor Sector Seasonalities: See Pages 94, 96, and 98

SUNDAY
31

AUGUST ALMANAC

AUGUST							SEPTEMBER					
S	M	T	W	T	F	S	S	M	T	W	T	F	S
		1	2	3	4	5	6					1	2	3
7	8	9	10	11	12	13	4	5	6	7	8	9	10
14	15	16	17	18	19	20	11	12	13	14	15	16	17
21	22	23	24	25	26	27	18	19	20	21	22	23	24
28	29	30	31				25	26	27	28	29	30	

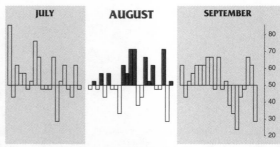

Market Probability Chart above is a graphic representation of the S&P 500 Recent Market Probability Calendar on page 124.

◆ Harvesting made August the best stock market month 1901–1951 ◆ Now that about 2% farm, August is the worst Dow and S&P and second worst NASDAQ (2000 up 11.7%, 2001 down 10.9) month since 1987 ◆ Shortest bear in history (45 days) caused by turmoil in Russia, currency crisis and hedge fund debacle ended here in 1998, 1344.22-point drop in the Dow, second-worst behind October 2008, off 15.1% ◆ Saddam Hussein triggered a 10.0% slide in 1990 ◆ Best Dow gains: 1982 (11.5%) and 1984 (9.8%) as bear markets ended ◆ Next-to-last day S&P up only four times last 19 years ◆ Presidential election year Augusts' rankings #4 S&P, # 5 Dow, and #1 NASDAQ.

August Vital Statistics

	DJIA	S&P 500	NASDAQ	Russell 1K	Russell 2K
Rank	10	10	10	10	9
Up	37	36	24	23	21
Down	28	29	20	13	15
Average % Change	−0.1%	0.005%	0.3%	0.4%	0.4%
Election Year	0.8%	1.0%	2.9%	2.2%	3.5%
Best & Worst August					
	% Change	% Change	% Change	% Change	% Change
Best	1982　11.5	1982　11.6	2000　11.7	1982　11.3	1984　11.5
Worst	1998　−15.1	1998　−14.6	1998　−19.9	1998　−15.1	1998　−19.5
Best & Worst August Weeks					
Best	8/20/82　10.3	8/20/82　8.8	8/3/84　7.4	8/20/82　8.5	8/3/84　7.0
Worst	8/23/74　−6.1	8/5/11　−7.2	8/28/98　−8.8	8/5/11　−7.7	8/5/11　−10.3
Best & Worst August Days					
Best	8/17/82　4.9	8/17/82　4.8	8/9/11　5.3	8/9/11　5.0	8/9/11　6.9
Worst	8/31/98　−6.4	8/31/98　−6.8	8/31/98　−8.6	8/8/11　−6.9	8/8/11　−8.9
First Trading Day of Expiration Week: 1980–2014					
Record (#Up − #Down)	22–13	25–10	26–9	25–10	22–13
Current streak	U1	U1	U5	U1	U2
Avg % Change	0.27	0.28	0.31	0.25	0.26
Options Expiration Day: 1980–2014					
Record (#Up − #Down)	18–17	19–16	20–15	20–15	21–14
Current streak	D2	D2	U1	U2	D2
Avg % Change	−0.06	−0.001	−0.06	0.001	0.11
Options Expiration Week: 1980–2014					
Record (#Up − #Down)	18–17	21–14	20–15	21–14	22–13
Current streak	U1	U1	U1	U1	U1
Avg % Change	0.20	0.39	0.58	0.41	0.61
Week After Options Expiration: 1980–2014					
Record (#Up − #Down)	21–14	23–12	22–13	23–12	22–13
Current streak	U1	U2	U2	U2	U2
Avg % Change	0.29	0.34	0.49	0.33	0.09
First Trading Day Performance					
% of Time Up	47.7	50.8	52.3	47.2	50.0
Avg % Change	0.03	0.06	−0.06	0.12	−0.001
Last Trading Day Performance					
% of Time Up	61.5	64.6	68.2	61.1	72.2
Avg % Change	0.14	0.13	0.06	−0.03	0.06

Dow & S&P 1950–April 2015, NASDAQ 1971–April 2015, Russell 1K & 2K 1979–April 2015.

August's a good month to go on vacation;
Trading stocks will likely lead to frustration.

First Trading Day in August, Dow Down 12 of Last 18
Russell 2000 Up 7 of Last 11

MONDAY

D 38.1
S 47.6
N 47.6

1

The universal line of distinction between the strong and the weak is that one persists, while the other hesitates, falters, trifles and at last collapses or caves in.
— Edwin Percy Whipple (American essayist, 1819–1886)

TUESDAY

D 57.1
S 52.4
N 42.9

2

Laws are like sausages. It's better not to see them being made.
— Otto von Bismarck (German-Prussian politician, 1st Chancellor of Germany, 1815–1898)

First Nine Trading Days of August Are Historically Weak (Pages 74 and 124)

WEDNESDAY

D 47.6
S 47.6
N 42.9

3

Entrepreneurs who believe they're in business to vanquish the competition are less successful than those who believe their goal is to maximize profits or increase their company's value.
— Kaihan Krippendorff (Business consultant, strategist, author, *The Art of the Advantage*, The Strategic Learning Center, b. 1971)

THURSDAY

D 52.4
S 57.1
N 52.4

4

The commodity futures game is a money game—not a game involving the supply-demand of the actual commodity as commonly depicted.
— R. Earl Hadady (*Bullish Consensus, Contrary Opinion*)

August Worst Dow and S&P Month 1988–2014
Harvesting Made August Best Dow Month 1901–1951

FRIDAY

D 52.4
S 42.9
N 38.1

5

We were fairly arrogant, until we realized the Japanese were selling quality products for what it cost us to make them.
— Paul A. Allaire (Former Chairman of Xerox, b. 1938)

SATURDAY

6

SUNDAY

7

BEST INVESTMENT BOOK OF THE YEAR

Fast Forward: The Technologies and Companies Shaping Our Future
By Jim Mellon & Al Chalabi

In April 2015 Jeff journeyed to Europe for a few speaking engagements, including Vince Stanzione's "Financial Trading Day Live," at the world-class QEII Centre. London's largest and arguably finest conference and exhibit space sits in the shadow of Big Ben and across the square from historic Westminster Abbey, the setting for every royal coronation since 1066. For this full-day event, Jeff was the last guest speaker (in a lineup that included the illustrious Marc Faber), so he decided to do some recon and see what the others had to say, enjoy the event, and mingle with the attendees. After some introductory remarks and salient investing oratory from Mr. Stanzione, Jim Mellon took the stage.

Jim blew us away. As soon as his previous book, *Cracking the Code* (Wiley, 2012), was mentioned in his introduction, we were hooked, wishing we had known about Jim and his work before. Had we known about *Cracking the Code*, it probably would have been the Best Investment Book of 2013. It explored the implications of the biotech revolution defining the twenty-first century. Biotech is one of our favorite sectors for the future and will likely be one of the culturally-enabling, paradigm-shifting industries, if not *the* one. It may be the cornerstone of the Next Super Boom and secular bull market that we expect to take the market up at least 500% from the March 2009 lows to Dow 38820 by the year 2025 that was featured in the *Stock Trader's Almanac 2011* (page 36) and in *Super Boom* (Wiley, 2011).

Thankfully, Jim and his colleague and co-author Al Chalabi have now written and published **Fast Forward**. These guys get it, and in *Fast Forward* they lay out the likely roadmap of the technology of the future that will shape the next economic boom. *Fast Forward* is a high-energy read on the fastest-moving trends and innovations in technology and the big ideas likely to shape the future and how our current lives and technology are changing rapidly. Clear guidance on how to profit from these trends and companies in business and investing is central to the book.

In case you are not convinced about the bright future of biotech, consider these highlights from the book and Jim's presentation. The first person who will live to be 150 is alive today. Life sciences are currently the area of greatest change. Disease categories are being knocked down one by one. Longer lifespans will turn cancer into a chronic condition. And we've only just begun to tap into the advances in robotic surgery, stem cell therapy, printing of organs, and gene editing. We agree with Jim and Al that the most significant change *and* opportunity is in life sciences. In addition to biotech or life extension, they cover robotics and automation, the Internet of things, transportation of the future, energy (energy-tech is also one of our pet sectors of the future), payment procession (including Bitcoin), 3D printing, and media.

Fast Forward is smartly designed in 4-color with photos, graphics, and images to scintillate your brain. It's a fun, graduate-level textbook that moves like a spy thriller. So do yourself and your portfolio a favor and take this crash course in investing and profiting from the sectors of the future. *Fast Forward* is the next big thing! Jim Mellon (@JIMMHK) is also a fantastic Twitter follow.

Fruitful Publications, $29.95, www.fastforwardbook.com. **2016 Best Investment Book of the Year.**

AUGUST

I've always preached to my clients that how you do in bad markets is more important than how you do in good markets. Managing your risk is more important than finding avenues to make money.
— Thomas Buck (*Barron's* Top 100 Advisor)

TUESDAY
D 47.6
S 47.6
N 47.6
9

The death of contrarians has been greatly exaggerated. The reason is that the crowd is the market for most of any cycle. You cannot be contrarian all the time, otherwise you end up simply fighting the tape the whole way up (or down), therefore being wildly wrong.
— Barry L. Ritholtz (Founder/CIO Ritholtz Wealth Management, *Bailout Nation, The Big Picture* blog, *Bloomberg View* 12/20/2013, b. 1961)

WEDNESDAY
D 47.6
S 47.6
N 47.6
10

It is not how right or how wrong you are that matters, but how much money you make when right and how much you do not lose when wrong.
— George Soros (Financier, philanthropist, political activist, author, and philosopher, b. 1930)

THURSDAY
D 33.3
S 33.3
N 47.6
11

My best shorts come from research reports where there are recommendations to buy stocks on weakness; also, where a brokerage firm changes its recommendation from a buy to a hold.
— Marc Howard (Hedge fund manager, *New York Magazine* 1976, b. 1941)

Mid-August Stronger Than Beginning and End

FRIDAY
D 66.7
S 61.9
N 61.9
12

The ability to foretell what is going to happen tomorrow, next week, next month, and next year. And to have the ability afterwards to explain why it didn't happen.
— Winston Churchill (British statesman, 1874–1965, when asked what qualities a politician required)

SATURDAY
13

SUNDAY
14

AURA OF THE TRIPLE WITCH—4TH QUARTER MOST BULLISH: DOWN WEEKS TRIGGER MORE WEAKNESS WEEK AFTER

Standard options expire the third Friday of every month, but in March, June, September, and December, a powerful coven gathers. Since the S&P index futures began trading on April 21, 1982, stock options, index options, as well as index futures all expire at the same time four times each year—known as Triple Witching. Traders have long sought to understand and master the magic of this quarterly phenomenon.

The market for single-stock and ETF futures and weekly options continues to grow. However, their impact on the market has thus far been subdued. As their availability continues to expand, trading volumes and market influence are also likely to broaden. Until such time, we do not believe the term "quadruple witching" is applicable just yet.

We have analyzed what the market does prior, during, and following Triple Witching expirations in search of consistent trading patterns. Here are some of our findings of how the Dow Jones Industrials perform around Triple-Witching Week (TWW).

- TWWs have become more bullish since 1990, except in the second quarter.
- Following weeks have become more bearish. Since Q1 2000, only 21 of 60 were up, and 10 occurred in December, 7 in March, 3 in September, 1 in June.
- TWWs have tended to be down in flat periods and dramatically so during bear markets.
- DOWN WEEKS TEND TO FOLLOW DOWN TWWs is a most interesting pattern. Since 1991, of 31 down TWWs, 22 following weeks were also down. This is surprising, inasmuch as the previous decade had an exactly opposite pattern: There were 13 down TWWs then, but 12 up weeks followed them.
- TWWs in the second and third quarter (Worst Six Months May through October) are much weaker, and the weeks following, horrendous. But in the first and fourth quarter (Best Six Months period November through April), only the week after Q1 expiration is negative.

Throughout the *Almanac* you will also see notations on the performance of Mondays and Fridays of TWW, as we place considerable significance on the beginnings and ends of weeks (pages 68, 70, and 141–144).

TRIPLE WITCHING WEEK AND WEEK AFTER DOW POINT CHANGES

	Expiration Week Q1	Week After	Expiration Week Q2	Week After	Expiration Week Q3	Week After	Expiration Week Q4	Week After
1991	−6.93	−89.36	−34.98	−58.81	33.54	−13.19	20.12	167.04
1992	40.48	−44.95	−69.01	−2.94	21.35	−76.73	9.19	12.97
1993	43.76	−31.60	−10.24	−3.88	−8.38	−70.14	10.90	6.15
1994	32.95	−120.92	3.33	−139.84	58.54	−101.60	116.08	26.24
1995	38.04	65.02	86.80	75.05	96.85	−33.42	19.87	−78.76
1996	114.52	51.67	55.78	−50.60	49.94	−15.54	179.53	76.51
1997	−130.67	−64.20	14.47	−108.79	174.30	4.91	−82.01	−76.98
1998	303.91	−110.35	−122.07	231.67	100.16	133.11	81.87	314.36
1999	27.20	−81.31	365.05	−303.00	−224.80	−524.30	32.73	148.33
2000	666.41	517.49	−164.76	−44.55	−293.65	−79.63	−277.95	200.60
2001	−821.21	−318.63	−353.36	−19.05	−1369.70	611.75	224.19	101.65
2002	34.74	−179.56	−220.42	−10.53	−326.67	−284.57	77.61	−207.54
2003	662.26	−376.20	83.63	−211.70	173.27	−331.74	236.06	46.45
2004	−53.48	26.37	6.31	−44.57	−28.61	−237.22	106.70	177.20
2005	−144.69	−186.80	110.44	−325.23	−36.62	−222.35	97.01	7.68
2006	203.31	0.32	122.63	−25.46	168.66	−52.67	138.03	−102.30
2007	−165.91	370.60	215.09	−279.22	377.67	75.44	110.80	−84.78
2008	410.23	−144.92	−464.66	−496.18	−33.55	−245.31	−50.57	−63.56
2009	54.40	497.80	−259.53	−101.34	214.79	−155.01	−142.61	191.21
2010	117.29	108.38	239.57	−306.83	145.08	252.41	81.59	81.58
2011	−185.88	362.07	52.45	−69.78	516.96	−737.61	−317.87	427.61
2012	310.60	−151.89	212.97	−126.39	−13.90	−142.34	55.83	−252.73
2013	117.04	−2.08	−270.78	110.20	75.03	−192.85	465.78	257.27
2014	237.10	20.29	171.34	−95.24	292.23	−166.59	523.97	248.91
2015	378.34	−414.99						
Up	18	10	14	3	15	5	19	17
Down	7	15	10	21	9	19	5	7

AUGUST

Monday Before August Expiration, Dow Up 13 of Last 20, Average Gain 0.4%

MONDAY

D 42.9
S 57.1
N 66.7

15

We can guarantee cash benefits as far out and at whatever size you like, but we cannot guarantee their purchasing power.
— Alan Greenspan (Fed Chairman 1987–2006, on funding Social Security to Senate Banking Committee 2/15/05)

TUESDAY

D 61.9
S 71.4
N 71.4

16

It's not that I am so smart; it's just that I stay with problems longer.
— Albert Einstein (German/American physicist, 1921 Nobel Prize, 1879–1955)

WEDNESDAY

D 66.7
S 71.4
N 66.7

17

Politics ought to be the part-time profession of every citizen who would protect the rights and privileges of free people and who would preserve what is good and fruitful in our national heritage.
— Dwight D. Eisenhower (34th U.S. President, 1890–1969)

THURSDAY

D 42.9
S 38.1
N 38.1

18

The word "crisis" in Chinese is composed of two characters: the first, the symbol of danger; the second, opportunity.
— Anonymous

**August Expiration Day Bullish Lately, Dow Up 8 of Last 12
Up 156 Points (1.7%) in 2009**

FRIDAY

D 33.3
S 42.9
N 38.1

19

People do not change when you tell them they should; they change when they tell themselves they must.
— Michael Mandelbaum (Johns Hopkins foreign policy specialist, *NY Times*, 6/24/2009, b. 1946)

SATURDAY

20

SUNDAY

21

TAKE ADVANTAGE OF DOWN FRIDAY/ DOWN MONDAY WARNING

Fridays and Mondays are the most important days of the week. Friday is the day for squaring positions—trimming longs or covering shorts before taking off for the weekend. Traders want to limit their exposure (particularly to stocks that are not acting well) since there could be unfavorable developments before trading resumes two or more days later.

Monday is important because the market then has the chance to reflect any weekend news, plus what traders think after digesting the previous week's action and the many Monday morning research and strategy comments.

For over 30 years, a down Friday followed by down Monday has frequently corresponded to important market inflection points that exhibit a clearly negative bias, often coinciding with market tops and, on a few climactic occasions, such as in October 2002 and March 2009, near major market bottoms.

One simple way to get a quick reading on which way the market may be heading is to keep track of the performance of the Dow Jones Industrial Average on Fridays and the following Mondays. Since 1995, there have been 200 occurrences of Down Friday/ Down Monday (DF/DM), with 57 falling in the bear market years of 2001, 2002, 2008, and 2011, producing an average decline of 12.8%.

To illustrate how Down Friday/Down Monday can telegraph market inflection points we created the chart below of the Dow Jones Industrials from November 2013 to May 15, 2015 with arrows pointing to occurrences of DF/DM. Use DF/ DM as a warning to examine market conditions carefully. Unprecedented central bank liquidity has tempered subsequent pullbacks, but has not eliminated them.

DOWN FRIDAY/DOWN MONDAY

Year	Total Number Down Friday/ Down Monday	Subsequent Average % Dow Loss*	Average Number of Days it took
1995	8	−1.2%	18
1996	9	−3.0%	28
1997	6	−5.1%	45
1998	9	−6.4%	47
1999	9	−6.4%	39
2000	11	−6.6%	32
2001	13	−13.5%	53
2002	18	−11.9%	54
2003	9	−3.0%	17
2004	9	−3.7%	51
2005	10	−3.0%	37
2006	11	−2.0%	14
2007	8	−6.0%	33
2008	15	−17.0%	53
2009	10	−8.7%	15
2010	7	−3.1%	10
2011	11	−9.0%	53
2012	11	−4.0%	38
2013	7	−2.4%	15
2014	7	−2.5%	8
2015	2	−2.4%	22
Average	**10**	**−5.7%**	**32**

* Over next 3 months, ** Ending May 15, 2015

DOW JONES INDUSTRIALS (NOVEMBER 2013–MAY 15, 2015)

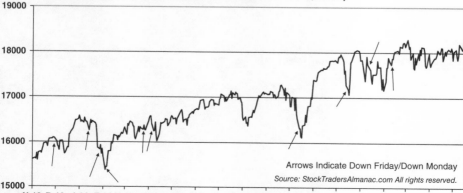

Arrows Indicate Down Friday/Down Monday

N-13 D-13 J-14 F-14 M-14 A-14 M-14 J-14 J-14 A-14 S-14 O-14 N-14 D-14 J-15 F-15 M-15 A-15 M-15

AUGUST

MONDAY

D 61.9
S 66.7
N 76.2 **22**

Good luck is what happens when preparation meets opportunity, bad luck is what happens when lack of preparation meets a challenge.
— Paul Krugman (Economist, *NY Times* 3/3/2006, b. 1953)

TUESDAY

D 52.4
S 52.4
N 57.1 **23**

Age is a question of mind over matter. If you don't mind, it doesn't matter.
— Leroy Robert "Satchel" Paige (Hall of Fame Negro League and Major League pitcher, 1906–1982)

Week After August Expiration Mixed, Dow Down 6 of Last 10

WEDNESDAY

D 57.1
S 61.9
N 52.4 **24**

The fear of capitalism has compelled socialism to widen freedom, and the fear of socialism has compelled capitalism to increase equality.
— Will and Ariel Durant

THURSDAY

D 47.6
S 47.6
N 57.1 **25**

...those inquirers who desire an exact knowledge of the past as an aid to the interpretation of the future...
— Thucydides (Greek aristocrat and historian, *The Peloponnesian War*, 460–400 BC)

FRIDAY

D 42.9
S 47.6
N 42.9 **26**

The real difference between men is energy. A strong will, a settled purpose, an invincible determination, can accomplish almost anything; and in this lies the distinction between great men and little men.
— Buckminster Fuller (*American architect, author*, 1895–1983)

SATURDAY

27

September Almanac Investor Sector Seasonalities: See Pages 94, 96, and 98

SUNDAY

28

SEPTEMBER ALMANAC

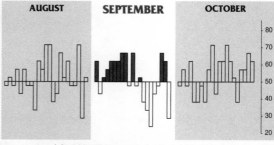

SEPTEMBER						
S	M	T	W	T	F	S
					1	2	3
4	5	6	7	8	9	10
11	12	13	14	15	16	17
18	19	20	21	22	23	24
25	26	27	28	29	30	

OCTOBER						
S	M	T	W	T	F	S
30	31					1
2	3	4	5	6	7	8
9	10	11	12	13	14	15
16	17	18	19	20	21	22
23	24	25	26	27	28	29

Market Probability Chart above is a graphic representation of the S&P 500 Recent Market Probability Calendar on page 124.

◆ Start of business year, end of vacations, and back to school made September a leading barometer month in first 60 years of 20th century, now portfolio managers back after Labor Day tend to clean house ◆ Biggest % loser on the S&P, Dow, and NASDAQ since 1950 (pages 50 & 58) ◆ Streak of four great Dow Septembers averaging 4.2% gains ended in 1999 with six losers in a row averaging –5.9% (see page 152), up three straight 2005– 2007, down 6% in 2008 and 2011 ◆ Day after Labor Day Dow up 14 of last 21 ◆ S&P opened strong 13 of last 20 years but tends to close weak due to end-of-quarter mutual fund portfolio restructuring, last trading day: S&P down 16 of past 22 ◆ September Triple-Witching Week can be dangerous, week after is pitiful (see page 78).

September Vital Statistics

	DJIA		S&P 500		NASDAQ		Russell 1K		Russell 2K	
Rank	12		12		12		12		11	
Up	26		29		24		18		20	
Down	39		35		20		18		16	
Average % Change	–0.7%		–0.5%		–0.5%		–0.6%		–0.4%	
Election Year	–0.4%		–0.2%		–0.2%		0.2%		0.7%	
Best & Worst September										
	% Change		% Change		% Change		% Change		% Change	
Best	2010	7.7	2010	8.8	1998	13.0	2010	9.0	2010	12.3
Worst	2002	–12.4	1974	–11.9	2001	–17.0	2002	–10.9	2001	–13.6
Best & Worst September Weeks										
Best	9/28/01	7.4	9/28/01	7.8	9/16/11	6.3	9/28/01	7.6	9/28/01	6.9
Worst	9/21/01	–14.3	9/21/01	–11.6	9/21/01	–16.1	9/21/01	–11.7	9/21/01	–14.0
Best & Worst September Days										
Best	9/8/98	5.0	9/30/08	5.4	9/8/98	6.0	9/30/08	5.3	9/18/08	7.0
Worst	9/17/01	–7.1	9/29/08	–8.8	9/29/08	–9.1	9/29/08	–8.7	9/29/08	–6.7
First Trading Day of Expiration Week: 1980–2014										
Record (#Up – #Down)	23–12		19–16		13–22		19–16		14–21	
Current streak	U2		D1		D3		D1		D1	
Avg % Change	–0.08		–0.12		–0.34		–0.15		–0.25	
Options Expiration Day: 1980–2014										
Record (#Up – #Down)	18–17		19–16		23–12		20–15		23–12	
Current streak	U1		D3		D2		D2		D2	
Avg % Change	0.01		0.14		0.15		0.12		0.17	
Options Expiration Week: 1980–2014										
Record (#Up – #Down)	19–16		21–14		20–15		21–14		18–17	
Current streak	U2		U2		U2		U2		D1	
Avg % Change	–0.21		0.03		0.05		0.02		0.11	
Week After Options Expiration: 1980–2014										
Record (#Up – #Down)	12–23		10–25		15–20		10–24		12–23	
Current streak	D4		D4		D1		D4		D1	
Avg % Change	–0.75		–0.79		–0.87		–0.80		–1.36	
First Trading Day Performance										
% of Time Up	60.0		61.5		56.8		52.8		52.8	
Avg % Change	0.04		0.02		0.02		–0.01		0.07	
Last Trading Day Performance										
% of Time Up	36.9		40.0		45.5		44.4		58.3	
Avg % Change	–0.15		–0.09		–0.06		–0.02		0.21	

Dow & S&P 1950–April 2015, NASDAQ 1971–April 2015, Russell 1K & 2K 1979–April 2015.

September is when leaves and stocks tend to fall;
On Wall Street it's the worst month of all.

MONDAY
D 71.4
S 71.4
N 71.4
29

New indicator: CFO Magazine gave Excellence awards to WorldCom's Scott Sullivan (1998), Enron's Andrew Fastow (1999), and to Tyco's Mark Swartz (2000). All were subsequently indicted.
— Roger Lowenstein (Financial journalist and author, *Origins Of The Crash*, b. 1954)

August's Next-to-Last Trading Day, S&P Down 15 of Last 19 Years

TUESDAY
D 28.6
S 28.6
N 52.4
30

Taxes are what we pay for civilized society.
— Oliver Wendell Holmes Jr. (U.S. Supreme Court Justice 1902–1932, "The Great Dissenter," inscribed above IRS HQ entrance, 1841–1935)

WEDNESDAY
D 52.4
S 52.4
N 57.1
31

Throughout the centuries there were men who took first steps down new roads armed with nothing but their own vision.
— Ayn Rand (Russian-born American novelist and philosopher, *The Fountainhead*, 1957, 1905–1982)

First Trading Day in September, S&P Up 13 of Last 20, But Down 5 of Last 7

THURSDAY
D 57.1
S 61.9
N 61.9
1

If you are ready to give up everything else to study the whole history of the market as carefully as a medical student studies anatomy and you have the cool nerves of a great gambler, the sixth sense of a clairvoyant, and the courage of a lion, you have a ghost of a chance.
— Bernard Baruch (Financier, speculator, statesman, presidential adviser, 1870–1965)

FRIDAY
D 66.7
S 42.9
N 52.4
2

Your chances for success in any undertaking can be measured by your belief in yourself.
— Robert Collier (Direct marketing copywriter and author, 1885–1950)

SATURDAY
3

SUNDAY
4

A CORRECTION FOR ALL SEASONS

While there's a rally for every season (page 72), almost always there's a decline or correction, too. Fortunately, corrections tend to be smaller than rallies, and that's what gives the stock market its long-term upward bias. In each season the average bounce outdoes the average setback. On average, the net gain between the rally and the correction is smallest in summer and fall.

The summer setback tends to be slightly outdone by the average correction in the fall. Tax selling and portfolio cleaning are the usual explanations—individuals sell to register a tax loss, and institutions like to get rid of their losers before preparing year-end statements. The October jinx also plays a major part. Since 1964, there have been 18 fall declines of over 10%, and in 10 of them (1966, 1974, 1978, 1979, 1987, 1990, 1997, 2000, 2002, and 2008) much damage was done in October, where so many bear markets end. Recent October lows were also seen in 1998, 1999, 2004, 2005, and 2011. Most often, it has paid to buy after fourth quarter or late third quarter "waterfall declines" for a rally that may continue into January or even beyond. Anticipation of war in Iraq put the market down in 2003 Q1. Quick success rallied stocks through Q3. Financial crisis affected the pattern in 2008–2009, producing the worst winter decline since 1932. Easy monetary policy and strong corporate earnings spared Q1 2011 and 2012 from a seasonal slump.

SEASONAL CORRECTIONS IN DOW JONES INDUSTRIALS

	WINTER SLUMP Nov/Dec High to Q1 Low	SPRING SLUMP Feb/Mar High to Q2 Low	SUMMER SLUMP May/Jun High to Q3 Low	FALL SLUMP Aug/Sep High to Q4 Low
1964	−0.1%	−2.4%	−1.0%	−2.1%
1965	−2.5	−7.3	−8.3	−0.9
1966	−6.0	−13.2	−17.7	−12.7
1967	−4.2	−3.9	−5.5	−9.9
1968	−8.8	−0.3	−5.5	+0.4
1969	−8.7	−8.7	−17.2	−8.1
1970	−13.8	−20.2	−8.8	−2.5
1971	−1.4	−4.8	−10.7	−13.4
1972	−0.5	−2.6	−6.3	−5.3
1973	−11.0	−12.8	−10.9	−17.3
1974	−15.3	−10.8	−29.8	−27.6
1975	−6.3	−5.5	−9.9	−6.7
1976	−0.2	−5.1	−4.7	−8.9
1977	−8.5	−7.2	−11.5	−10.2
1978	−12.3	−4.0	−7.0	−13.5
1979	−2.5	−5.8	−3.7	−10.9
1980	−10.0	−16.0	−1.7	−6.8
1981	−6.9	−5.1	−18.6	−12.9
1982	−10.9	−7.5	−10.6	−3.3
1983	−4.1	−2.8	−6.8	−3.6
1984	−11.9	−10.5	−8.4	−6.2
1985	−4.8	−4.4	−2.8	−2.3
1986	−3.3	−4.7	−7.3	−7.6
1987	−1.4	−6.6	−1.7	−36.1
1988	−6.7	−7.0	−7.6	−4.5
1989	−1.7	−2.4	−3.1	−6.6
1990	−7.9	−4.0	−17.3	−18.4
1991	−6.3	−3.6	−4.5	−6.3
1992	+0.1	−3.3	−5.4	−7.6
1993	−2.7	−3.1	−3.0	−2.0
1994	−4.4	−9.6	−4.4	−7.1
1995	−0.8	−0.1	−0.2	−2.0
1996	−3.5	−4.6	−7.5	+0.2
1997	−1.8	−9.8	−2.2	−13.3
1998	−7.0	−3.1	−18.2	−13.1
1999	−2.7	−1.7	−8.0	−11.5
2000	−14.8	−7.4	−4.1	−11.8
2001	−14.5	−13.6	−27.4	−16.2
2002	−5.1	−14.2	−26.7	−19.5
2003	−15.8	−5.3	−3.1	−2.1
2004	−3.9	−7.7	−6.3	−5.7
2005	−4.5	−8.5	−3.3	−4.5
2006	−2.4	−5.4	−7.8	−0.4
2007	−3.7	−3.2	−6.1	−8.4
2008	−14.5	−11.0	−20.6	−35.9
2009	−32.0	−6.3	−7.4	−3.5
2010	−6.1	−10.4	−13.1	−1.0
2011	+0.2	−4.0	−16.3	−12.2
2012	+0.5	−8.7	−5.3	−7.8
2013	−0.2	−0.3	−4.1	−5.7
2014	−7.3	−2.6	−3.4	−6.7
2015	−4.9	−3.2*		
Totals	**−329.8%**	**−336.3%**	**−452.8%**	**−461.9%**
Average	**−6.3%**	**−6.5%**	**−8.9%**	**−9.1%**

* As of 5/15/2015

SEPTEMBER

Labor Day *(Market Closed)*

MONDAY

5

Take care of your employees and they'll take care of your customers.
— John W. Marriott (Founder Marriott International, 1900–1985)

Day After Labor Day, Dow Up 14 of Last 21, 1997 Up 3.4%, 1998 Up 5.0%

D 52.4
S 52.4
N 52.4

TUESDAY

6

Man's mind, once stretched by a new idea, never regains its original dimensions.
— Oliver Wendell Holmes (American author, poet, and physician, 1809–1894)

WEDNESDAY

D 42.9
S 57.1
N 61.9

7

There is no great mystery to satisfying your customers. Build them a quality product and treat them with respect. It's that simple.
— Lee Iacocca (American industrialist, Former Chrysler CEO, b. 1924)

THURSDAY

D 66.7
S 61.9
N 66.7

8

A successful man is one who can lay a firm foundation with the bricks that others throw at him.
— Sidney Greenberg (Rabbi, author, 1918–2003)

FRIDAY

D 52.4
S 61.9
N 61.9

9

The four horsemen of the Investment Apocalypse are fear, greed, hope and ignorance. Only one is not an emotion – ignorance. These four things have accounted for more losses in the market than any recession or depression, and they will never change. Even if you correct ignorance, the other three will get you every time.
— James P. O'Shaughnessy (Chairman and CEO at O'Shaughnessy Asset Management, b. 1960)

SATURDAY

10

2001 4-Day Market Closing, Longest Since 9-Day Banking Moratorium in March 1933

SUNDAY

11

"In Memory"

FIRST-TRADING-DAY-OF-THE-MONTH PHENOMENON: DOW GAINS MORE ONE DAY THAN ALL OTHER DAYS

Over the last 18 years the Dow Jones Industrial Average has gained more points on the first trading days of all months than all other days combined. While the Dow has gained 10650.14 points between September 2, 1997 (7622.42) and May 15, 2015 (18272.56), it is incredible that 5317.02 points were gained on the first trading days of these 213 months. The remaining 4242 trading days combined gained 5333.12 points during the period. This averages out to gains of 24.96 points on first days, in contrast to just 1.26 points on all others.

Note September 1997 through October 2000 racked up a total gain of 2632.39 Dow points on the first trading days of these 38 months (winners except for seven occasions). But between November 2000 and September 2002, when the 2000–2002 bear markets did the bulk of their damage, frightened investors switched from pouring money into the market on that day to pulling it out, fourteen months out of twenty-three, netting a 404.80 Dow point loss. The 2007–2009 bear market lopped off 964.14 Dow points on first days in 17 months November 2007–March 2009. First days had their worst year in 2014, declining eight times for a total loss of 820.86 Dow points.

First days of June have performed worst. Triple-digit declines in four of the last seven years have resulted in the biggest net losses. Due to persistent weakness, December is a net loser as well. In rising market trends, first days tend to perform much better, as institutions are likely anticipating strong performance at each month's outset. S&P 500 first days differ slightly from Dow's pattern as October is a loser. NASDAQ first days are not as strong with weakness in April, June, August, and October.

DOW POINTS GAINED FIRST DAY OF MONTH
SEPT 1997–MAY 15, 2015

	Jan	Feb	Mar	Apr	May	Jun	Jul	Aug	Sep	Oct	Nov	Dec	Totals
1997									257.36	70.24	232.31	189.98	749.89
1998	56.79	201.28	4.73	68.51	83.70	22.42	96.65	−96.55	288.36	−210.09	114.05	16.99	646.84
1999	2.84	−13.13	18.20	46.35	225.65	36.52	95.62	−9.19	108.60	−63.95	−81.35	120.58	486.74
2000	−139.61	100.52	9.62	300.01	77.87	129.87	112.78	84.97	23.68	49.21	−71.67	−40.95	636.30
2001	−140.70	96.27	−45.14	−100.85	163.37	78.47	91.32	−12.80	47.74	−10.73	188.76	−87.60	268.11
2002	51.90	−12.74	262.73	−41.24	113.41	−215.46	−133.47	−229.97	−355.45	346.86	120.61	−33.52	−126.34
2003	265.89	56.01	−53.22	77.73	−25.84	47.55	55.51	−79.83	107.45	194.14	57.34	116.59	819.32
2004	−44.07	11.11	94.22	15.63	88.43	14.20	−101.32	39.45	−5.46	112.38	26.92	162.20	413.69
2005	−53.58	62.00	63.77	−99.46	59.19	82.39	28.47	−17.76	−21.97	−33.22	−33.30	106.70	143.23
2006	129.91	89.09	60.12	35.62	−23.85	91.97	77.80	−59.95	83.00	−8.72	−49.71	−27.80	397.48
2007	11.37	51.99	−34.29	27.95	73.23	40.47	126.81	150.38	91.12	191.92	−362.14	−57.15	311.66
2008	−220.86	92.83	−7.49	391.47	189.87	−134.50	32.25	−51.70	−26.63	−19.59	−5.18	−679.95	−439.48
2009	258.30	−64.03	−299.64	152.68	44.29	221.11	57.06	114.95	−185.68	−203.00	76.71	126.74	299.49
2010	155.91	118.20	78.53	70.44	143.22	−112.61	−41.49	208.44	254.75	41.63	6.13	249.76	1172.91
2011	93.24	148.23	−168.32	56.99	−3.18	−279.65	168.43	−10.75	−119.96	−258.08	−297.05	−25.65	−695.75
2012	179.82	83.55	28.23	52.45	65.69	−274.88	−8.70	−37.62	−54.90	77.98	136.16	−59.98	187.80
2013	308.41	149.21	35.17	−5.69	−138.85	138.46	65.36	128.48	23.65	62.03	69.80	−77.64	758.39
2014	−135.31	−326.05	−153.68	74.95	−21.97	26.46	129.47	−69.93	−30.89	−238.19	−24.28	−51.44	−820.86
2015	9.92	196.09	155.93	−77.94	185.54								
Totals	790.17	1040.43	49.47	1045.60	1299.77	−87.21	852.55	50.62	484.77	100.82	104.11	−52.14	5209.42

SUMMARY FIRST DAYS VS. OTHER DAYS OF MONTH

	# of Days	Total Points Gained	Average Daily Point Gain
First days	213	5317.02	24.96
Other days	4242	5333.12	1.26

Monday Before September Triple Witching,
Russell 2000 Down 10 of Last 16

🐻 **MONDAY**

D 61.9
S 61.9
N 52.4

12

One machine can do the work of fifty ordinary men. No machine can do the work of one extraordinary man.
— Elbert Hubbard (American author, *A Message To Garcia*, 1856–1915)

🐂 **TUESDAY**

D 61.9
S 66.7
N 71.4

13

If the market prefers a system that looks inefficient that's a good sign that its more efficient than it looks.
— Matt Levine (*Bloomberg View* columnist, former investment banker, lawyer, high school Latin teacher)

Expiration Week 2001, Dow Lost 1370 Points (14.3%)
2nd Worst Weekly Point Loss Ever, 5th Worst Week Overall

🐂 **WEDNESDAY**

D 57.1
S 66.7
N 81.0

14

But how do we know when irrational exuberance has unduly escalated asset values, which then become
subject to unexpected and prolonged contractions as they have in Japan over the past decade?
— Alan Greenspan (Fed Chairman 1987–2006, 12/5/96 speech to American Enterprise Institute, b. 1926)

THURSDAY

D 52.4
S 47.6
N 33.3

15

If investing is entertaining, if you're having fun, you're probably not making any money. Good investing is boring.
— George Soros (Financier, philanthropist, political activist, author, and philosopher, b. 1930)

September Triple Witching, Dow Up 10 of Last 13

🐻 🐂🐂🐂 **FRIDAY**

D 66.7
S 66.7
N 71.4

16

When you get to the end of your rope, tie a knot and hang on.
— Franklin D. Roosevelt (32nd U.S. President, 1882–1945)

SATURDAY

17

SUNDAY

18

MARKET BEHAVIOR THREE DAYS BEFORE AND THREE DAYS AFTER HOLIDAYS

The *Stock Trader's Almanac* has tracked holiday seasonality annually since the first edition in 1968. Stocks used to rise on the day before holidays and sell off the day after, but nowadays, each holiday moves to its own rhythm. Eight holidays are separated into seven groups. Average percentage changes for the Dow, S&P 500, NASDAQ, and Russell 2000 are shown.

The Dow and S&P consist of blue chips and the largest cap stocks, whereas NASDAQ and the Russell 2000 would be more representative of smaller-cap stocks. This is evident on the last day of the year with NASDAQ and the Russell 2000 having a field day, while their larger brethren in the Dow and S&P are showing losses on average.

Thanks to the Santa Claus Rally, the three days before and after New Year's Day and Christmas are best. NASDAQ and the Russell 2000 average gains of 1.3% to 1.7% over the six-day spans. However, trading around the first day of the year has been mixed. Traders have been selling more the first trading day of the year recently, pushing gains and losses into the New Year.

Bullishness before Labor Day and after Memorial Day is affected by strength the first day of September and June. The second worst day after a holiday is the day after Easter. Surprisingly, the following day is one of the best second days after a holiday, right up there with the second day after New Year's Day.

Presidents' Day is the least bullish of all the holidays, bearish the day before and three days after. NASDAQ has dropped 19 of the last 26 days before Presidents' Day (Dow, 16 of 26; S&P, 18 of 26; Russell 2000, 14 of 26).

HOLIDAYS: 3 DAYS BEFORE, 3 DAYS AFTER (Average % change 1980–April 2015)

	−3	−2	−1	Mixed	+1	+2	+3
S&P 500	0.02	0.23	−0.10	New Year's	0.23	0.28	0.03
DJIA	−0.02	0.18	−0.17	Day	0.34	0.29	0.14
NASDAQ	0.08	0.27	0.21	*1/1/16*	0.23	0.57	0.15
Russell 2K	0.08	0.39	0.45		0.07	0.19	0.09
S&P 500	0.34	0.06	−0.20	Negative Before & After	−0.21	−0.08	−0.12
DJIA	0.32	0.05	−0.13	Presidents'	−0.13	−0.12	−0.15
NASDAQ	0.54	0.31	−0.35	Day	−0.54	−0.08	−0.05
Russell 2K	0.41	0.22	−0.10	*2/15/16*	−0.39	−0.19	−0.03
S&P 500	0.19	−0.04	0.39	Positive Before &	−0.20	0.30	0.10
DJIA	0.15	−0.07	0.30	Negative After	−0.13	0.30	0.10
NASDAQ	0.40	0.24	0.49	Good Friday	−0.31	0.33	0.20
Russell 2K	0.21	0.11	0.52	*3/25/16*	−0.32	0.19	0.13
S&P 500	0.04	0.05	0.001	Positive After	0.36	0.09	0.26
DJIA	0.02	0.01	−0.06	Memorial	0.42	0.10	0.16
NASDAQ	0.09	0.24	0.03	Day	0.30	−0.05	0.49
Russell 2K	−0.06	0.33	0.11	*5/30/16*	0.32	−0.003	0.42
S&P 500	0.14	0.08	0.07	Negative After	−0.14	0.03	0.08
DJIA	0.11	0.07	0.08	Independence	−0.07	0.07	0.06
NASDAQ	0.29	0.10	0.07	Day	−0.15	−0.12	0.23
Russell 2K	0.29	−0.003	−0.01	*7/4/16*	−0.23	−0.04	0.05
S&P 500	0.16	−0.22	0.18	Positive Day Before	0.05	0.10	−0.08
DJIA	0.14	−0.27	0.18	Labor	0.07	0.16	−0.17
NASDAQ	0.37	0.001	0.18	Day	−0.02	−0.04	0.07
Russell 2K	0.51	0.04	0.12	*9/5/16*	0.06	0.15	0.03
S&P 500	0.14	0.01	0.27	Positive Before & After	0.19	−0.43	0.29
DJIA	0.14	0.01	0.27	Thanksgiving	0.16	−0.37	0.30
NASDAQ	0.09	−0.21	0.42	*11/24/16*	0.46	−0.44	0.11
Russell 2K	0.16	−0.10	0.38		0.29	−0.51	0.27
S&P 500	0.18	0.19	0.22	Christmas	0.15	−0.01	0.29
DJIA	0.27	0.22	0.28	*12/26/16*	0.19	−0.01	0.25
NASDAQ	−0.06	0.42	0.41		0.12	0.04	0.34
Russell 2K	0.25	0.36	0.36		0.21	0.05	0.47

SEPTEMBER

Week After Sepetmber Triple Witching Dow Down 20 of Last 25
Average Loss Since 1990, 1.2%

MONDAY
D 42.9
S 47.6
N 52.4
19

Benjamin Graham was correct in suggesting that while the stock market in the short run may be a voting mechanism, in the long run it is a weighing mechanism. True value will win out in the end.
— Burton G. Malkiel (Economist, April 2003 Princeton Paper, *A Random Walk Down Wall Street*, b. 1932)

FOMC Meeting (2 Days)

TUESDAY
D 57.1
S 52.4
N 61.9
20

The two most abundant elements in the universe are Hydrogen and Stupidity.
— Harlan Ellison (Science fiction writer, b. 1934)

WEDNESDAY
D 47.6
S 38.1
N 42.9
21

Only those who will risk going too far can possibly find out how far one can go.
— T.S. Eliot (English poet, essayist, and critic, "The Waste Land," 1888–1965)

THURSDAY
D 33.3
S 33.3
N 33.3
22

Welch's genius was the capacity to energize and inspire hundreds of thousands of people across a range of businesses and countries.
— Warren G. Bennis (USC Business professor, *Business Week*, 9/10/01, referring to retiring CEO Jack Welch of General Electric)

End of September Prone to Weakness
From End-of-Q3 Institutional Portfolio Restructuring

FRIDAY
D 28.6
S 23.8
N 38.1
23

Inflation is the modern way that governments default on their debt.
— Mike Epstein (MTA, MIT/Sloan Lab for Financial Engineering)

SATURDAY
24

SUNDAY
25

OCTOBER ALMANAC

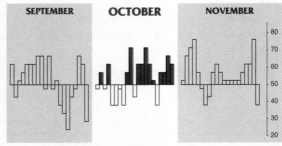

OCTOBER							NOVEMBER						
S	M	T	W	T	F	S	S	M	T	W	T	F	S
30	31					1							1 2 3 4 5
2	3	4	5	6	7	8	6	7	8	9	10	11	12
9	10	11	12	13	14	15	13	14	15	16	17	18	19
16	17	18	19	20	21	22	20	21	22	23	24	25	26
23	24	25	26	27	28	29	27	28	29	30			

Market Probability Chart above is a graphic representation of the S&P 500 Recent Market Probability Calendar on page 124.

◆ Known as the jinx month because of crashes in 1929 and 1987, the 554-point drop on October 27, 1997, back-to-back massacres in 1978 and 1979, Friday the 13th in 1989, and the meltdown in 2008 ◆ Yet October is a "bear killer" and turned the tide in 12 post–WWII bear markets: 1946, 1957, 1960, 1962, 1966, 1974, 1987, 1990, 1998, 2001, 2002, and 2011 ◆ First October Dow top in 2007, 20-year 1987 Crash anniversary −2.6% ◆ Worst six months of the year ends with October (page 52) ◆ No longer worst month (pages 50 & 58) ◆ Best Dow, S&P, and NASDAQ month from 1993 to 2007 ◆ Worst month of presidential election years since: Dow −0.8%, S&P −0.7%, NASDAQ −2.1% ◆ October is a great time to buy ◆ Big October gains five years 1999–2003 after atrocious Septembers ◆ Can get into Best Six Months earlier using MACD (page 52) ◆ October 2011, second month to gain 1000 Dow points.

October Vital Statistics

	DJIA		S&P 500		NASDAQ		Russell 1K		Russell 2K	
Rank	7		7		9		7		10	
Up	39		39		24		23		20	
Down	26		26		20		13		16	
Average % Change	0.5%		0.8%		0.6%		0.9%		−0.3%	
Election Year	−0.8%		−0.7%		−2.1%		−1.4%		−2.6%	
Best & Worst October										
	% Change		% Change		% Change		% Change		% Change	
Best	1982	10.7	1974	16.3	1974	17.2	1982	11.3	2011	15.0
Worst	1987	−23.2	1987	−21.8	1987	−27.2	1987	−21.9	1987	−30.8
Best & Worst October Weeks										
Best	10/11/74	12.6	10/11/74	14.1	10/31/08	10.9	10/31/08	10.8	10/31/08	14.1
Worst	10/10/08	−18.2	10/10/08	−18.2	10/23/87	−19.2	10/10/08	−18.2	10/23/87	−20.4
Best & Worst October Days										
Best	10/13/08	11.1	10/13/08	11.6	10/13/08	11.8	10/13/08	11.7	10/13/08	9.3
Worst	10/19/87	−22.6	10/19/87	−20.5	10/19/87	−11.4	10/19/87	−19.0	10/19/87	−12.5
First Trading Day of Expiration Week: 1980–2014										
Record (#Up – #Down)	28–7		26–9		21–11		27–8		26–9	
Current streak	D1		D1		D1		D1		D1	
Avg % Change	0.75		0.72		0.57		0.69		0.42	
Options Expiration Day: 1980–2014										
Record (#Up – #Down)	16–19		18–17		19–16		18–17		15–20	
Current streak	U2		U2		U2		U2		D1	
Avg % Change	−0.17		−0.24		−0.12		−0.22		−0.19	
Options Expiration Week: 1980–2014										
Record (#Up – #Down)	24–11		24–11		19–16		24–11		21–14	
Current streak	D1		D1		D1		D1		U2	
Avg % Change	0.60		0.65		0.69		0.65		0.43	
Week After Options Expiration: 1980–2014										
Record (#Up – #Down)	16–19		15–20		18–17		15–20		16–19	
Current streak	U2		U2		U2		U2		U2	
Avg % Change	−0.39		−0.38		−0.39		−0.40		−0.58	
First Trading Day Performance										
% of Time Up	49.2		49.2		47.7		52.8		50.0	
Avg % Change	0.06		0.05		−0.15		0.22		−0.25	
Last Trading Day Performance										
% of Time Up	53.8		55.4		65.9		63.9		72.2	
Avg % Change	0.07		0.15		0.51		0.36		0.63	

Dow & S&P 1950–April 2015, NASDAQ 1971–April 2015, Russell 1K & 2K 1979–April 2015.

October has killed many a bear;
Buy techs and small caps and soon wear a grin ear to ear.

MONDAY

D 42.9
S 42.9
N 42.9

26

One of the more prolonged and extreme periods favoring large-cap stocks was 1994–1999. The tide turned in 2000. A cycle has begun of investors favoring small-cap stocks, which is likely to continue through the next several years.
— Jim Oberweis (*The Oberweis Report*, February 2001)

TUESDAY

D 52.4
S 47.6
N 42.9

27

Over time, you weed out luck.
— Billy Beane (American baseball player and general manager, b. 1962)

WEDNESDAY

D 61.9
S 66.7
N 47.6

28

When new money is created on a grand scale, it must go somewhere and have some major consequences. One of these will be greatly increased volatility and instability in the economy and financial system.
— J. Anthony Boeckh, Ph.D (Chairman Bank Credit Analyst 1968–2002, *The Great Reflation, Boeckh Investment Letter*)

Start Looking for MACD BUY Signals on October 1 (Pages 54, 60, and 62)
Almanac Investor Subscribers Emailed When It Triggers (See Ad Insert)

THURSDAY

D 57.1
S 61.9
N 47.6

29

Let us have the courage to stop borrowing to meet the continuing deficits. Stop the deficits.
— Franklin D. Roosevelt (32nd U.S. President, 1932, 1882–1945)

Last Day of Q3, Dow Down 14 of Last 18, Massive 4.7% Rally in 2008

FRIDAY

D 28.6
S 28.6
N 28.6

30

So much hangs on the decisions of a small number of poorly educated people. That's Democracy. A terrible way to run a country, but every other system is worse.
— Kenneth Martin Follett (Welsh author, *Fall of Giants*, b. 1949)

SATURDAY

1

October Almanac Investor Sector Seasonalities: See Pages 94, 96, and 98

SUNDAY

2

MARKET GAINS MORE ON SUPER-8 DAYS EACH MONTH THAN ON ALL 13 REMAINING DAYS COMBINED

For many years, the last day plus the first four days were the best days of the month. The market currently exhibits greater bullish bias from the last three trading days of the previous month through the first two days of the current month, and now shows significant bullishness during the middle three trading days, 9 to 11, due to 401(k) cash inflows (see pages 145 and 146). This pattern was not as pronounced during the boom years of the 1990s, with market strength all month long. It returned in 2000 with monthly bullishness at the ends, beginnings, and middles of months versus weakness during the rest of the month. "Super Eight" performance in 2015, was on track as were other seasonal patterns and indicators.

SUPER-8 DAYS* DOW % CHANGES VS. REST OF MONTH

	Super 8 Days	Rest of Month	Super 8 Days	Rest of Month	Super 8 Days	Rest of Month
	2007		**2008**		**2009**	
Jan	0.68%	−0.04%	−4.76%	−4.11%	3.16%	−6.92%
Feb	3.02	−1.72	1.83	0.65	−6.05	−4.39
Mar	−5.51	3.64	−4.85	2.92	−4.37	12.84
Apr	2.66	2.82	−0.27	4.09	1.52	−0.24
May	2.21	0.95	2.19	−4.81	2.64	2.98
Jun	3.84	−5.00	0.37	−6.30	1.71	−1.64
Jul	2.59	−1.47	−3.80	−1.99	2.30	5.03
Aug	−2.94	−0.26	1.53	1.06	0.04	4.91
Sep	4.36	1.18	−2.23	−1.19	−0.81	2.21
Oct	1.28	−1.05	−3.39	−13.70	−0.05	2.40
Nov	−0.59	−5.63	6.07	−11.90	0.00	5.57
Dec	−0.04	4.62	−2.54	3.49	0.62	0.46
Totals	**11.56%**	**−1.96%**	**−9.85%**	**−31.79%**	**0.71%**	**23.21%**
Average	**0.96%**	**−0.163%**	**−0.82%**	**−2.649%**	**0.06%**	**1.93%**
	2010		**2011**		**2012**	
Jan	0.66%	−3.92%	1.70%	1.80%	1.90%	1.66%
Feb	3.31	−2.38	0.45	0.57	−0.39	2.33
Mar	1.91	3.51	−1.40	2.21	2.22	−0.55
Apr	1.13	0.18	2.30	0.95	1.00	−1.80
May	−3.08	−5.75	1.03	−2.61	−0.38	−4.52
Jun	4.33	−3.26	−1.64	−1.19	−1.30	2.08
Jul	−7.07	11.34	3.52	0.31	5.11	−2.22
Aug	0.20	−5.49	2.04	−11.39	−0.40	2.09
Sep	3.83	4.22	3.24	−3.96	−0.24	2.98
Oct	−0.18	3.47	−4.47	10.71	0.77	−3.60
Nov	−1.20	1.37	1.42	−6.66	−2.01	0.55
Dec	1.98	1.45	5.74	3.58	0.49	1.35
Totals	**5.82%**	**4.74%**	**13.93%**	**−5.68%**	**6.77%**	**0.35%**
Average	**0.49%**	**0.40%**	**1.16%**	**−0.47%**	**0.56%**	**0.03%**
	2013		**2014**		**2015**	
Jan	2.28%	3.47%	0.92%	−4.26%	−3.64%	−0.07%
Feb	−0.27	−0.41	−1.99	3.66	2.65	2.00
Mar	2.93	1.82	0.77	−0.21	1.91	−4.78
Apr	0.11	1.65	2.44	−1.82	1.20	0.83
May	1.93	2.81	−0.56	2.50		
Jun	−0.27	−3.96	−0.09	1.24		
Jul	1.11	4.23	1.79	−1.10		
Aug	−1.35	−3.75	−1.81	2.61		
Sep	2.55	0.83	0.32	−1.26		
Oct	−0.64	2.60	−3.28	3.82		
Nov	1.79	1.41	2.42	2.28		
Dec	−0.72	3.30	−1.66	3.14		
Totals	**9.45%**	**14.00%**	**−0.73%**	**10.60%**	**2.12%**	**−2.02%**
Average	**0.79%**	**1.17%**	**−0.06%**	**0.88%**	**0.53%**	**−0.51%**

	Super Eight Days		Rest of Month (13 days)	
100	Net % Changes	39.78%	Net % Changes	11.46%
Month	Average Period	0.40%	Average Period	0.11%
Totals	Average Day	0.05%	Average Day	0.009%

* Super-8 Days = Last 3 + First 2 + Middle 3

OCTOBER

Rosh Hashanah

First Trading Day in October, Dow Down 6 of Last 10, Off 2.4% in 2011

MONDAY

D 52.4
S 47.6
N 38.1

3

When you're one step ahead of the crowd, you're a genius. When you're two steps ahead, you're a crackpot.
— Shlomo Riskin (Rabbi, author, b. 1940)

October Ends Dow and S&P "Worst Six Months" (Pages 50, 52, 54, and 147)
And NASDAQ "Worst Four Months" (Pages 58, 60, and 148)

TUESDAY

D 47.6
S 57.1
N 57.1

4

Oil has fostered massive corruption in almost every country that has been "blessed" with it, and the expectation that oil wealth will transform economies has lead to disastrous policy choices.
— Ted Tyson (Chief Investment Officer, Mastholm Asset Management)

WEDNESDAY

D 47.6
S 47.6
N 57.1

5

Those that forget the past are condemned to repeat its mistakes, and those that mis-state the past should be condemned.
— Eugene D. Cohen (*Financial Times* Letter to the Editor 10/30/06)

Dow Lost 1874 Points (18.2%) on the Week Ending 10/10/08
Worst Dow Week in the History of Wall Street

THURSDAY

D 66.7
S 61.9
N 61.9

6

If the market does not rally, as it should during bullish seasonal periods, it is a sign that other forces are stronger and that when the seasonal period ends those forces will really have their say.
— Edson Gould (Stock market analyst, *Findings & Forecasts*, 1902–1987)

FRIDAY

D 38.1
S 38.1
N 47.6

7

When investment decisions need to consider the speed of light, something is seriously wrong.
— Frank M. Bifulco (Senior Portfolio Manager Alcott Capital Management, *Barron's* Letters to the Editor, 5/24/2010)

SATURDAY

8

SUNDAY

9

SECTOR SEASONALITY: SELECTED PERCENTAGE PLAYS

Sector seasonality was featured in the first 1968 *Almanac*. A Merrill Lynch study showed that buying seven sectors around September or October and selling in the first few months of 1954–1964 tripled the gains of holding them for 10 years. Over the years we have honed this strategy significantly and now devote a large portion of our time and resources to investing and trading during positive and negative seasonal periods for different sectors with Exchange Traded Funds (ETFs).

Updated seasonalities appear in the table below. We specify whether the seasonality starts or finishes in the beginning third (B), middle third (M), or last third (E) of the month. These selected percentage plays are geared to take advantage of the bulk of seasonal sector strength or weakness.

By design, entry points are in advance of the major seasonal moves, providing traders ample opportunity to accumulate positions at favorable prices. Conversely, exit points have been selected to capture the majority of the move.

From the major seasonalities in the table below, we created the Sector Index Seasonality Strategy Calendar on pages 96 and 98. Note the concentration of bullish sector seasonalities during the Best Six Months, November to April, and bearish sector seasonalities during the Worst Six Months, May to October.

Almanac Investor newsletter subscribers receive specific entry and exit points for highly correlated ETFs and detailed analysis in ETF Trades Alerts. Visit *www.stocktradersalmanac.com,* or see the ad insert for additional details and a special offer for new subscribers.

SECTOR INDEX SEASONALITY TABLE

Ticker	Sector Index	Type	Start		Finish		15-Year	10-Year	5-Year
							Average % Return†		
XCI	Computer Tech	Short	January	B	March	B	−7.5	−4.9	1.9
XNG	Natural Gas	Long	February	E	June	B	15.1	11.8	3.4
MSH	High-Tech	Long	March	M	July	B	7.0	7.1	0.9
UTY	Utilities	Long	March	M	October	B	9.9	8.2	6.1
XCI	Computer Tech	Long	April	M	July	M	7.1	6.9	4.4
BKX	Banking	Short	May	B	July	B	−7.6	−10.1	−6.1
XAU	Gold & Silver	Short	May	M	June	E	−6.6	−6.2	−5.1
S5MATR	Materials	Short	May	M	October	M	−7.2	−5.2	−2.3
XNG	Natural Gas	Short	June	M	July	E	−7.4	−3.8	−0.8
XAU	Gold & Silver	Long	July	E	December	E	11.8	6.6	−0.5
DJT	Transports	Short	July	M	October	M	−6.6	−5.1	−3.9
BTK	Biotech	Long	August	B	March	B	16.0	20.0	31.3
MSH	High-Tech	Long	August	M	January	M	10.8	9.5	16.1
SOX	Semiconductor	Short	August	M	October	E	−10.4	−7.2	−1.3
XOI	Oil	Short	September	B	November	E	−5.6	−6.0	−2.8
BKX	Banking	Long	October	B	May	B	12.3	11.6	18.9
XBD	Broker/Dealer	Long	October	B	April	M	15.8	15.7	24.7
XCI	Computer Tech	Long	October	B	January	B	12.2	8.8	9.3
S5COND	Consumer Discretionary	Long	October	B	June	B	14.1	13.4	21.0
S5CONS	Consumer Staples	Long	October	B	June	B	8.4	9.0	12.3
S5HLTH	Healthcare	Long	October	B	May	B	8.9	10.5	18.3
S5MATR	Materials	Long	October	B	May	B	18.1	17.7	18.1
DRG	Pharmaceutical	Long	October	M	January	B	6.9	7.1	7.1
RMZ	Real Estate	Long	October	E	May	B	13.2	12.5	13.0
SOX	Semiconductor	Long	October	E	December	B	12.7	8.7	10.2
XTC	Telecom	Long	October	M	December	E	7.2	4.9	4.4
DJT	Transports	Long	October	B	May	B	19.3	20.5	23.1
XOI	Oil	Long	December	M	July	B	11.9	11.6	7.5

† *Average % Return based on full seasonality completion through May 29, 2015.*

Columbus Day *(Bond Market Closed)*
Monday Before October Expiration, Dow Up 28 of 35

MONDAY
D 38.1
S 38.1
N 52.4
10

The authority of a thousand is not worth the humble reasoning of a single individual.
— Galileo Galilei (Italian physicist and astronomer, 1564–1642)

TUESDAY
D 47.6
S 47.6
N 52.4
11

Being uneducated is sometimes beneficial. Then you don't know what can't be done.
— Michael Ott (Venture capitalist)

Yom Kippur
October 2011, Second Dow Month to Gain 1000 Points

WEDNESDAY
D 38.1
S 38.1
N 52.4
12

Six words that spell business success: create concept, communicate concept, sustain momentum.
— Yale Hirsch (Creator of *Stock Trader's Almanac*, b. 1923)

THURSDAY
D 52.4
S 57.1
N 66.7
13

I'd be a bum on the street with a tin cup, if the markets were always efficient.
— Warren Buffett (CEO Berkshire Hathaway, investor, philanthropist, b. 1930)

FRIDAY
D 76.2
S 71.4
N 71.4
14

I'm not better than the next trader, just quicker at admitting my mistakes and moving on to the next opportunity.
— George Soros (Financier, philanthropist, political activist, author, and philosopher, b. 1930)

SATURDAY
15

SUNDAY
16

SECTOR INDEX SEASONALITY STRATEGY CALENDAR*

* Graphic representation of the Sector Index Seasonality Percentage Plays on page 94.
L = Long Trade, S = Short Trade, ——➤ = Start of Trade

(continued on page 98)

96

MONDAY

D 47.6
S 42.9
N 42.9

17

The Stone Age didn't end for lack of stone, and the oil age will end long before the world runs out of oil.
— Sheik Ahmed Zaki Yamani (Saudi oil minister 1962–1986, b. 1930)

TUESDAY

D 52.4
S 61.9
N 52.4

18

What is conservatism? Is it not adherence to the old and tried, against the new and untried?
— Abraham Lincoln (16th U.S. President, 1809–1865)

Crash of October 19, 1987, Dow down 22.6% in One Day

WEDNESDAY

D 47.6
S 61.9
N 47.6

19

Executives owe it to the organization and to their fellow workers not to tolerate nonperforming individuals in important jobs.
— Peter Drucker (Austria-born pioneer management theorist, 1909–2005)

Late October Is Time to Buy Depressed Stocks
Especially Techs and Small Caps

THURSDAY

D 66.7
S 71.4
N 71.4

20

I'm not nearly so concerned about the return on my capital as I am the return of my capital.
— Will Rogers (American humorist and showman, 1879–1935)

October Expiration Day, Dow Down 6 Straight 2005–2010 and 8 of Last 12

FRIDAY

D 52.4
S 61.9
N 57.1

21

Any human anywhere will blossom in a hundred unexpected talents and capacities simply by being given the opportunity to do so.
— Doris Lessing (British novelist, born in Persia, 1919–2013)

SATURDAY

22

SUNDAY

23

(continued from page 96)

SECTOR INDEX SEASONALITY STRATEGY CALENDAR*

Index	Jan	Feb	Mar	Apr	May	Jun	Jul	Aug	Sep	Oct	Nov	Dec
S5MATR L/S												
SOX L/S												
UTY L/S												
XAU L/S												
XBD L/S												
XCI L/S												
XNG L/S												
XOI L/S												
XTC L/S												

* Graphic representation of the Sector Index Seasonality Percentage Plays on page 94.
L = Long Trade, S = Short Trade, ⟶ = Start of Trade

MONDAY

D 47.6
S 52.4
N 42.9

24

If you don't profit from your investment mistakes, someone else will.
— Yale Hirsch (Creator of *Stock Trader's Almanac*, b. 1923)

TUESDAY

D 38.1
S 38.1
N 38.1

25

Don't fritter away your time. Create, act, take a place wherever you are and be somebody.
— Theodore Roosevelt (26th U.S. President, 1858–1919)

WEDNESDAY

D 57.1
S 57.1
N 52.4

26

Whatever method you use to pick stocks…, your ultimate success or failure will depend
on your ability to ignore the worries of the world long enough to allow your investments to succeed.
It isn't the head but the stomach that determines the fate of the stockpicker.
— Peter Lynch (Fidelity Investments, *Beating the Street*, 1994, b. 1944)

THURSDAY

D 66.7
S 57.1
N 57.1

27

We prefer to cut back exposure on what's going against us and add exposure where it's more favorable to
our portfolio. This way, we're always attempting to tilt the odds in our favor. This is the exact opposite of
a long investor that would average down. Averaging down is a very dangerous practice.
— John Del Vecchio & Brad Lamensdorf (Portfolio managers Active Bear ETF, 5/10/12 *Almanac*
Investor interview)

85th Anniversary of 1929 Crash, Dow Down 23.0% in Two Days,
October 28 and 29

FRIDAY

D 66.7
S 66.7
N 66.7

28

What lies behind us and what lies before us are tiny matters, compared to what lies within us.
— Ralph Waldo Emerson (American author, poet, and philosopher, *Self-Reliance*, 1803–1882)

SATURDAY

29

November Almanac Investor Sector Seasonalities: See Pages 94, 96, and 98

SUNDAY

30

NOVEMBER ALMANAC

NOVEMBER							DECEMBER						
S	M	T	W	T	F	S	S	M	T	W	T	F	S
		1	2	3	4	5			1	2	3	4	5
6	7	8	9	10	11	12	4	5	6	7	8	9	10
13	14	15	16	17	18	19	11	12	13	14	15	16	17
20	21	22	23	24	25	26	18	19	20	21	22	23	24
27	28	29	30				25	26	27	28	29	30	31

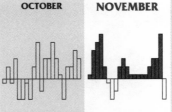

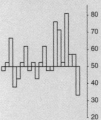

Market Probability Chart above is a graphic representation of the S&P 500 Recent Market Probability Calendar on page 124.

◆ #2 S&P and #3 Dow month since 1950, #3 on NASDAQ since 1971 (pages 50 & 58) ◆ Start of the "Best Six Months" of the year (page 52), NASDAQ's Best Eight Months and Best Three (pages 147 & 148) ◆ Simple timing indicator almost triples "Best Six Months" strategy (page 54), doubles NASDAQ's Best Eight (page 60) ◆ Day before and after Thanksgiving Day combined, only 13 losses in 63 years (page 104) ◆ Week before Thanksgiving Dow up 17 of last 22 ◆ Presidential election year Novembers rank #1 Dow, #2 S&P, and #1 NASDAQ.

November Vital Statistics

	DJIA		S&P 500		NASDAQ		Russell 1K		Russell 2K	
Rank	3		2		3		1		2	
Up	43		43		29		26		23	
Down	22		22		15		10		13	
Average % Change	1.5%		1.5%		1.6%		1.7%		1.8%	
Election Year	1.5%		1.3%		−0.6%		0.5%		−0.2%	
Best & Worst November										
	% Change		% Change		% Change		% Change		% Change	
Best	1962	10.1	1980	10.2	2001	14.2	1980	10.1	2002	8.8
Worst	1973	−14.0	1973	−11.4	2000	−22.9	2000	−9.3	2008	−12.0
Best & Worst November Weeks										
Best	11/28/08	9.7	11/28/08	12.0	11/28/08	10.9	11/28/08	12.5	11/28/08	16.4
Worst	11/21/08	−5.3	11/21/08	−8.4	11/10/00	−12.2	11/21/08	−8.8	11/21/08	−11.0
Best & Worst November Days										
Best	11/13/08	6.7	11/13/08	6.9	11/13/08	6.5	11/13/08	7.0	11/13/08	8.5
Worst	11/20/08	−5.6	11/20/08	−6.7	11/19/08	−6.5	11/20/08	−6.9	11/19/08	−7.9
First Trading Day of Expiration Week: 1980–2014										
Record (#Up – #Down)	18–17		16–19		13–22		17–18		15–20	
Current streak	U2		U3		D1		U3		D1	
Avg % Change	−0.04		−0.08		−0.16		−0.09		−0.12	
Options Expiration Day: 1980–2014										
Record (#Up – #Down)	23–12		21–14		19–16		21–14		18–16	
Current streak	U5		U3		U3		U3		U5	
Avg % Change	0.24		0.18		0.03		0.17		0.12	
Options Expiration Week: 1980–2014										
Record (#Up – #Down)	23–12		21–14		18–17		20–15		17–18	
Current streak	U2		U2		U2		U2		D1	
Avg % Change	0.27		0.03		−0.04		0.001		−0.31	
Week After Options Expiration: 1980–2014										
Record (#Up – #Down)	21–14		22–13		23–12		22–13		21–14	
Current streak	U3		U3		U3		U3		U3	
Avg % Change	0.70		0.68		0.79		0.67		0.76	
First Trading Day Performance										
% of Time Up	63.1		63.1		65.9		72.2		61.1	
Avg % Change	0.27		0.29		0.28		0.38		0.18	
Last Trading Day Performance										
% of Time Up	55.4		53.8		65.9		47.2		69.4	
Avg % Change	0.11		0.14		−0.07		0.02		0.17	

Dow & S&P 1950–April 2015, NASDAQ 1971–April 2015, Russell 1K & 2K 1979–April 2015.

Astute investors always smile and remember,
When stocks seasonally start soaring, and salute November.

Halloween 🎃

MONDAY
D 57.1
S 61.9
N 66.7
31

We are all born originals; why is it so many die copies?
— Edward Young (English poet, 1683–1765)

First Trading Day in November, Dow Up 4 of Last 6
FOMC Meeting (2 Days)

TUESDAY
D 52.4
S 52.4
N 66.7
1

Financial markets will find and exploit hidden flaws, particularly in untested new innovations—and do so at a time that will inflict the most damage to the most people.
— Raymond F. DeVoe, Jr. (Market strategist Jesup & Lamont, *The DeVoe Report*, 3/30/07)

WEDNESDAY
D 57.1
S 66.7
N 61.9
2

The whole secret to our success is being able to con ourselves into believing that we're going to change the world [even though] we are unlikely to do it.
— Tom Peters (American writer, *In Search of Excellence*, Fortune, 11/13/2000, b. 1942)

November Begins Dow and S&P "Best Six Months" (Pages 50, 52, 54, and 147)
And NASDAQ "Best Eight Months" (Pages 58, 60, and 148)

THURSDAY
D 71.4
S 71.4
N 76.2
3

The bigger a man's head gets, the easier it is to fill his shoes.
— Anonymous

FRIDAY
D 76.2
S 76.2
N 66.7
4

There are ways for the individual investor to make money in the securities markets. Buying value and holding long term while collecting dividends has been proven over and over again.
— Robert M. Sharp (Author, *The Lore and Legends of Wall Street*)

SATURDAY
5

Daylight Saving Time Ends

SUNDAY
6

FOURTH QUARTER MARKET MAGIC

Examining market performance on a quarterly basis reveals several intriguing and helpful patterns. Fourth-quarter market gains have been magical, providing the greatest and most consistent gains over the years. First-quarter performance runs a respectable second. This should not be surprising, as cash inflows, trading volume, and buying bias are generally elevated during these two quarters.

Positive market psychology hits a fever pitch as the holiday season approaches, and does not begin to wane until spring. Professionals drive the market higher, as they make portfolio adjustments to maximize year-end numbers. Bonuses are paid and invested around the turn of the year.

The market's sweet spot of the four-year cycle begins in the fourth quarter of the midterm year. The best two-quarter span runs from the fourth quarter of the midterm year through the first quarter of the pre-election year, averaging 14.6% for the Dow, 15.4% for the S&P 500, and an amazing 22.0% for NASDAQ. Pre-election Q2 is smoking, too, the third best quarter of the cycle, creating a three-quarter sweet spot from midterm Q4 to pre-election Q2. Only NASDAQ's Q1 is a notable standout in election years.

Quarterly strength fades in the latter half of the pre-election year, but stays impressively positive through the election year. Losses dominate the first quarter of post-election years and the second and third quarters of midterm years.

QUARTERLY % CHANGES

	Q1	Q2	Q3	Q4	Year	Q2–Q3	Q4–Q1
Dow Jones Industrials (1949–March 2015)							
Average	**2.2%**	**1.5%**	**0.5%**	**3.9%**	**8.5%**	**2.1%**	**6.4%**
Post-Election	−0.4%	1.6%	0.3%	3.8%	5.7%	2.0%	5.4%
Midterm	1.4%	−1.5%	−0.4%	7.1%	6.7%	−1.8%	14.6%
Pre-Election	7.1%	5.3%	1.6%	2.3%	16.9%	6.8%	3.2%
Election	0.8%	1.0%	0.6%	2.0%	4.8%	1.7%	1.7%
S&P 500 (1949–March 2015)							
Average	**2.2%**	**1.6%**	**0.7%**	**4.1%**	**9.1%**	**2.3%**	**6.7%**
Post-Election	−0.6%	2.2%	0.7%	3.5%	6.2%	3.0%	4.7%
Midterm	1.0%	−2.4%	0.1%	7.8%	6.7%	−2.2%	15.4%
Pre-Election	7.1%	5.2%	1.1%	3.0%	17.1%	6.3%	4.6%
Election	1.4%	1.8%	0.9%	1.9%	6.6%	2.8%	1.6%
NASDAQ Composite (1971–March 2015)							
Average	**4.4%**	**3.1%**	**0.1%**	**4.4%**	**12.6%**	**3.4%**	**9.0%**
Post-Election	−2.2%	6.6%	2.2%	4.8%	11.1%	8.7%	6.7%
Midterm	2.0%	−2.7%	−4.5%	8.6%	2.8%	−6.7%	22.0%
Pre-Election	12.9%	8.0%	1.7%	5.1%	30.9%	9.8%	9.7%
Election	3.9%	0.8%	1.1%	−0.8%	5.8%	2.2%	−2.4%

NOVEMBER

MONDAY
D 57.1
S 57.1
N 52.4
7

When everbody thinks alike, everyone is likely to be wrong.
— Humphrey B. Neill (Investor, analyst, author, *Art of Contrary Thinking* 1954, 1895–1977)

Election Day

TUESDAY
D 52.4
S 47.6
N 57.1
8

A senior European diplomat said he was convinced that the choice of starting a war this spring was made for political as well as military reasons. [The President] clearly does not want to have a war raging on the eve of his presumed reelection campaign.
— Reported by Steven R. Weisman (*NY Times* 3/14/03)

WEDNESDAY
D 47.6
S 38.1
N 42.9
9

There have been three great inventions since the beginning of time: Fire, the wheel, and central banking.
— Will Rogers (American humorist and showman, 1879–1935)

THURSDAY
D 42.9
S 42.9
N 52.4
10

The principles of successful stock speculation are based on the supposition that people will continue in the future to make the mistakes that they have made in the past.
— Thomas F. Woodlock (*Wall Street Journal* editor and columnist, 1866–1945, quoted in *Reminiscences of a Stock Operator*)

Veterans' Day *(Bond Market Closed)*

FRIDAY
D 66.7
S 57.1
N 61.9
11

On [TV financial news programs], if the stock is near its high, 90% of the guests like it, if it is near its lows, 90% of the guests hate it.
— Michael L. Burke (*Investors Intelligence*, May 2002, Army 101st Airborne, 1935–2014)

SATURDAY
12

SUNDAY
13

TRADING THE THANKSGIVING MARKET

For 35 years, the "holiday spirit" gave the Wednesday before Thanksgiving and the Friday after a great track record, except for two occasions. Publishing it in the 1987 *Almanac* was the kiss of death. Wednesday, Friday, and Monday were all crushed, down 6.6% over the three days in 1987. Since 1988, Wednesday–Friday gained 17 of 27 times, with a total Dow point-gain of 699.28 versus Monday's total Dow point-loss of 790.46, down 12 of 17 since 1998. The best strategy appears to be coming into the week long and exiting into strength Friday.

DOW JONES INDUSTRIALS BEFORE AND AFTER THANKSGIVING

	Tuesday Before	Wednesday Before		Friday After	Total Gain Dow Points	Dow Close	Next Monday
1952	−0.18	1.54		1.22	2.76	283.66	0.04
1953	1.71	0.65		2.45	3.10	280.23	1.14
1954	3.27	1.89		3.16	5.05	387.79	0.72
1955	4.61	0.71		0.26	0.97	482.88	−1.92
1956	−4.49	−2.16		4.65	2.49	472.56	−2.27
1957	−9.04	10.69		3.84	14.53	449.87	−2.96
1958	−4.37	8.63		8.31	16.94	557.46	2.61
1959	2.94	1.41		1.42	2.83	652.52	6.66
1960	−3.44	1.37		4.00	5.37	606.47	−1.04
1961	−0.77	1.10		2.18	3.28	732.60	−0.61
1962	6.73	4.31		7.62	11.93	644.87	−2.81
1963	32.03	−2.52	T	9.52	7.00	750.52	1.39
1964	−1.68	−5.21		−0.28	−5.49	882.12	−6.69
1965	2.56	N/C	H	−0.78	−0.78	948.16	−1.23
1966	−3.18	1.84		6.52	8.36	803.34	−2.18
1967	13.17	3.07	A	3.58	6.65	877.60	4.51
1968	8.14	−3.17		8.76	5.59	985.08	−1.74
1969	−5.61	3.23	N	1.78	5.01	812.30	−7.26
1970	5.21	1.98		6.64	8.62	781.35	12.74
1971	−5.18	0.66	K	17.96	18.62	816.59	13.14
1972	8.21	7.29		4.67	11.96	1025.21	−7.45
1973	−17.76	10.08	S	−0.98	9.10	854.00	−29.05
1974	5.32	2.03		−0.63	1.40	618.66	−15.64
1975	9.76	3.15	G	2.12	5.27	860.67	−4.33
1976	−6.57	1.66		5.66	7.32	956.62	−6.57
1977	6.41	0.78	I	1.12	1.90	844.42	−4.85
1978	−1.56	2.95		3.12	6.07	810.12	3.72
1979	−6.05	−1.80	V	4.35	2.55	811.77	16.98
1980	3.93	7.00		3.66	10.66	993.34	−23.89
1981	18.45	7.90	I	7.80	15.70	885.94	3.04
1982	−9.01	9.01		7.36	16.37	1007.36	−4.51
1983	7.01	−0.20	N	1.83	1.63	1277.44	−7.62
1984	9.83	6.40		18.78	25.18	1220.30	−7.95
1985	0.12	18.92	G	−3.56	15.36	1472.13	−14.22
1986	6.05	4.64		−2.53	2.11	1914.23	−1.55
1987	40.45	−16.58		−36.47	−53.05	1910.48	−76.93
1988	11.73	14.58		−17.60	−3.02	2074.68	6.76
1989	7.25	17.49		18.77	36.26	2675.55	19.42
1990	−35.15	9.16		−12.13	−2.97	2527.23	5.94
1991	14.08	−16.10	G	−5.36	−21.46	2894.68	40.70
1992	25.66	17.56		15.94	33.50	3282.20	22.96
1993	3.92	13.41		−3.63	9.78	3683.95	−6.15
1994	−91.52	−3.36		33.64	30.28	3708.27	31.29
1995	40.46	18.06		7.23*	25.29	5048.84	22.04
1996	−19.38	−29.07	D	22.36*	−6.71	6521.70	N/C
1997	41.03	−14.17		28.35*	14.18	7823.13	189.98
1998	−73.12	13.13	A	18.80*	31.93	9333.08	−216.53
1999	−93.89	12.54		−19.26*	−6.72	10988.91	−40.99
2000	31.85	−95.18	Y	70.91*	−24.27	10470.23	75.84
2001	−75.08	−66.70		125.03*	58.33	9959.71	23.04
2002	−172.98	255.26		−35.59*	219.67	8896.09	−33.52
2003	16.15	15.63		2.89*	18.52	9782.46	116.59
2004	3.18	27.71		1.92*	29.63	10522.23	−46.33
2005	51.15	44.66		15.53*	60.19	10931.62	−40.90
2006	5.05	5.36		−46.78*	−41.42	12280.17	−158.46
2007	51.70	−211.10		181.84*	−29.26	12980.88	−237.44
2008	36.08	247.14		102.43*	349.57	8829.04	−679.95
2009	−17.24	30.69		−154.48*	−123.79	10309.92	34.92
2010	−142.21	150.91		−95.28*	55.63	11092.00	−39.51
2011	−53.59	−236.17		−25.77*	−261.94	11231.78	291.23
2012	−7.45	48.38		172.79*	221.17	13009.68	−42.31
2013	0.26	24.53		−10.92*	13.61	16086.41	−77.64
2014	−2.96	− 2.69		15.99*	13.30	17828.24	−51.44

104   *Shortened trading day*

Monday Before November Expiration, Dow Down 9 of Last 16

MONDAY
D 61.9
S 61.9
N 57.1
14

Never mind telling me what *stocks to buy; tell me* when *to buy them.*
— Humphrey B. Neill (Investor, analyst, author, *Neill Letters of Contrary Opinion*, 1895–1977)

TUESDAY
D 66.7
S 57.1
N 47.6
15

I really do inhabit a system in which words are capable of shaking the entire structure of government, where words can prove mightier than ten military divisions.
— Vaclav Havel (Czech dramatist, essayist, political leader, and president, 1936–2011)

Week Before Thanksgiving, Dow Up 17 of Last 22,
2003 –1.4%, 2004 –0.8%, 2008 –5.3%, 2011 –2.9%, 2012 –1.8%

WEDNESDAY
D 47.6
S 52.4
N 52.4
16

If you spend more than 14 minutes a year worrying about the market, you've wasted 12 minutes.
— Peter Lynch (Fidelity Investments, *One Up On Wall Street*, b. 1944)

THURSDAY
D 47.6
S 52.4
N 47.6
17

There is a perfect inverse correlation between inflation rates and price/earnings ratios... When inflation has been very high…P/E has been [low].
— Liz Ann Sonders (Chief Investment Strategist Charles Schwab, June 2006)

November Expiration Day, Dow Up 11 of Last 13
Dow Surged in 2008, Up 494 Points (6.5%)

FRIDAY
D 52.4
S 52.4
N 57.1
18

Government is like fire—useful when used legitimately, but dangerous when not.
— David Brooks (*NY Times* columnist, 10/5/07, b. 1961)

SATURDAY
19

SUNDAY
20

MOST OF THE SO-CALLED "JANUARY EFFECT" TAKES PLACE IN THE LAST HALF OF DECEMBER

Over the years we have reported annually on the fascinating January Effect, showing that small-cap stocks handily outperformed large-cap stocks during January 40 out of 43 years between 1953 and 1995. Readers saw that "Cats and Dogs" on average quadrupled the returns of blue chips in this period. Then, the January Effect disappeared over the next four years.

Looking at the graph on page 110, comparing the Russell 1000 index of large-capitalization stocks to the Russell 2000 smaller-capitalization stocks, shows small-cap stocks beginning to outperform the blue chips in mid-December. Narrowing the comparison down to half-month segments was an inspiration and proved to be quite revealing, as you can see in the table below.

28-YEAR AVERAGE RATES OF RETURN (DEC 1987 – FEB 2015)

From	Russell 1000		Russell 2000	
mid-Dec*	Change	Annualized	Change	Annualized
12/15–12/31	1.9%	53.9%	3.5%	119.9%
12/15–01/15	2.3	29.8	4.0	56.7
12/15–01/31	2.4	21.3	4.1	38.6
12/15–02/15	3.5	22.9	5.9	41.1
12/15–02/28	2.8	14.9	5.7	32.2
end-Dec*				
12/31–01/15	0.4	8.7	0.5	11.0
12/31–01/31	0.5	6.2	0.6	7.4
12/31–02/15	1.5	12.4	2.3	19.6
12/31–02/28	0.9	5.8	2.1	14.0

36-YEAR AVERAGE RATES OF RETURN (DEC 1979 – FEB 2015)

From	Russell 1000		Russell 2000	
mid-Dec*	Change	Annualized	Change	Annualized
12/15–12/31	1.7%	47.1%	3.1%	101.3%
12/15–01/15	2.4	31.2	4.4	63.8
12/15–01/31	2.6	23.2	4.6	44.1
12/15–02/15	3.6	23.6	6.2	43.5
12/15–02/28	3.2	16.8	6.1	34.0
end-Dec*				
12/31–01/15	0.7	15.8	1.2	28.5
12/31–01/31	1.0	12.7	1.5	19.6
12/31–02/15	1.9	16.0	3.1	27.2
12/31–02/28	1.5	9.8	3.0	20.5

Mid-month dates are the 11th trading day of the month; month end dates are monthly closes.

Small-cap strength in the last half of December became even more magnified after the 1987 market crash. Note the dramatic shift in gains in the last half of December during the 28-year period starting in 1987, versus the 36 years from 1979 to 2015. With all the beaten-down small stocks being dumped for tax loss purposes, it generally pays to get a head start on the January Effect in mid-December. You don't have to wait until December either; the small-cap sector often begins to turn around toward the end of October and November.

Trading Thanksgiving Market: Long into Weakness Prior,
Exit into Strength After (Page 104)

MONDAY
D 52.4
S 52.4
N 47.6
21

I would rather be positioned as a petrified bull rather than a penniless bear.
— John L. Person (Professional trader, author, speaker, *Commodity Trader's Almanac*,
nationalfutures.com, 11/3/2010, b. 1961)

TUESDAY
D 61.9
S 52.4
N 61.9
22

What's the difference between when you pray in church or at your screen?
When you pray at your screen you really mean it!
— Vince Stanzione (British entrepreneur, trader, author, b. 1968)

WEDNESDAY
D 61.9
S 57.1
N 61.9
23

If you torture the data long enough, it will confess to anything.
— Darrell Huff (*How to Lie With Statistics*, 1954, 1913–2001)

Thanksgiving *(Market Closed)*

THURSDAY
24

The pursuit of gain is the only way in which people can serve the needs of others whom they do not know.
— Friedrich von Hayek (*Counterrevolution of Science*, 1899–1992)

(Shortened Trading Day)

FRIDAY
D 66.7
S 61.9
N 57.1
25

Today's Ponzi-style acute fragility and speculative dynamics dictate that he who panics first panics best.
— Doug Noland (Prudent Bear Funds, *Credit Bubble Bulletin*, 10/26/07)

SATURDAY
26

December Almanac Investor Sector Seasonalities: See Pages 94, 96, and 98

SUNDAY
27

DECEMBER ALMANAC

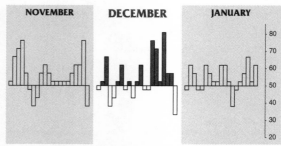

DECEMBER	JANUARY
S M T W T F S	S M T W T F S
1 2 3	1 2 3 4 5 6 7
4 5 6 7 8 9 10	8 9 10 11 12 13 14
11 12 13 14 15 16 17	15 16 17 18 19 20 21
18 19 20 21 22 23 24	22 23 24 25 26 27 28
25 26 27 28 29 30 31	29 30 31

Market Probability Chart above is a graphic representation of the S&P 500 Recent Market Probability Calendar on page 124.

◆ #1 S&P (+1.7%) and #2 Dow (+1.7%) month since 1950 (page 50), #2 NASDAQ 1.9% since 1971 ◆ 2002 worst December since 1931, down over 6% Dow and S&P, −9.7% on NASDAQ (pages 152, 155, & 157) ◆ "Free lunch" served on Wall Street before Christmas (page 112) ◆ Small caps start to outperform larger caps near middle of month (pages 106 & 110) ◆ "Santa Claus Rally" visible in graph above and on page 114 ◆ In 1998 was part of best fourth quarter since 1928 (page 167) ◆ Fourth quarter expiration week most bullish triple witching week, Dow up 19 of last 24 (page 78) ◆ Presidential election year Decembers rankings: #2 Dow, #3 S&P, #2 and #5 NASDAQ.

December Vital Statistics

	DJIA	S&P 500	NASDAQ	Russell 1K	Russell 2K
Rank	2	1	2	2	1
Up	46	49	26	28	29
Down	19	16	18	8	7
Average % Change	1.7%	1.7%	1.9%	1.6%	2.8%
Election Year	1.3%	1.2%	1.4%	0.7%	3.0%
Best & Worst December					
	% Change	% Change	% Change	% Change	% Change
Best	1991 9.5	1991 11.2	1999 22.0	1991 11.2	1999 11.2
Worst	2002 −6.2	2002 −6.0	2002 −9.7	2002 −5.8	2002 −5.7
Best & Worst December Weeks					
Best	12/2/11 7.0	12/2/11 7.4	12/8/00 10.3	12/2/11 7.4	12/2/11 10.3
Worst	12/4/87 −7.5	12/6/74 −7.1	12/15/00 −9.1	12/4/87 −7.0	12/12/80 −6.5
Best & Worst December Days					
Best	12/16/08 4.2	12/16/08 5.1	12/5/00 10.5	12/16/08 5.2	12/16/08 6.7
Worst	12/1/08 −7.7	12/1/08 −8.9	12/1/08 −9.0	12/1/08 −9.1	12/1/08 −11.9
First Trading Day of Expiration Week: 1980–2014					
Record (#Up – #Down)	20–15	21–14	15–20	21–14	16–19
Current streak	D1	D1	D1	D1	D1
Avg % Change	0.17	0.13	−0.06	0.10	−0.15
Options Expiration Day: 1980–2014					
Record (#Up – #Down)	23–12	26–9	25–10	26–9	23–12
Current streak	U2	U2	U2	U2	U2
Avg % Change	0.33	0.39	0.37	0.38	0.45
Options Expiration Week: 1980–2014					
Record (#Up – #Down)	27–8	26–9	21–14	25–10	19–16
Current streak	U3	U3	U3	U3	U3
Avg % Change	0.78	0.81	0.30	0.75	0.70
Week After Options Expiration: 1980–2014					
Record (#Up – #Down)	24–10	21–14	22–13	21–14	24–11
Current streak	U2	U2	U2	U2	U2
Avg % Change	0.75	0.48	0.65	0.51	0.82
First Trading Day Performance					
% of Time Up	46.2	49.2	59.1	50.0	50.0
Avg % Change	−0.07	−0.05	0.11	−0.07	−0.16
Last Trading Day Performance					
% of Time Up	53.8	61.5	72.7	52.8	69.4
Avg % Change	0.07	0.11	0.35	−0.05	0.45

Dow & S&P 1950–April 2015, NASDAQ 1971–April 2015, Russell 1K & 2K 1979–April 2015.

*If Santa Claus should fail to call,
Bears may come to Broad and Wall.*

MONDAY

D 61.9
S 61.9
N 61.9

28

If I had eight hours to chop down a tree, I'd spend six sharpening my axe.
— Abraham Lincoln (16th U.S. President, 1809–1865)

TUESDAY

D 57.1
S 76.2
N 71.4

29

If there is something you really want to do, make your plan and do it. Otherwise, you'll just regret it forever.
— Richard Rocco (PostNet franchisee, *Entrepreneur Magazine* 12/2006, b. 1946)

Last Trading Day of November, S&P Up 6 of Last 9

WEDNESDAY

D 52.4
S 38.1
N 47.6

30

Bear markets don't act like a medicine ball rolling down a smooth hill. Instead, they behave like a basketball bouncing down a rock-strewn mountainside; there's lots of movement up and sideways before the bottom is reached.
— Daniel Turov (*Turov on Timing, Barron's* May 21, 2001, b. 1947)

First Trading Day in December, NASDAQ Up 19 of 28
Down 6 of Last 9

THURSDAY

D 42.9
S 47.6
N 57.1

1

The inherent vice of capitalism is the unequal sharing of blessings; the inherent virtue of socialism is the equal sharing of miseries.
— Winston Churchill (British statesman, 1874–1965)

FRIDAY

D 47.6
S 52.4
N 61.9

2

I do not rule Russia; ten thousand clerks do.
— Nicholas I (1795–1855)

SATURDAY

3

SUNDAY

4

JANUARY EFFECT NOW STARTS IN MID-DECEMBER

Small-cap stocks tend to outperform big caps in January. Known as the "January Effect," the tendency is clearly revealed by the graph below. Thirty-six years of daily data for the Russell 2000 index of smaller companies are divided by the Russell 1000 index of largest companies, and then compressed into a single year to show an idealized yearly pattern. When the graph is descending, big blue chips are outperforming smaller companies; when the graph is rising, smaller companies are moving up faster than their larger brethren.

In a typical year, the smaller fry stay on the sidelines while the big boys are on the field. Then, around late November, small stocks begin to wake up, and in mid-December they take off. Anticipated year-end dividends, payouts, and bonuses could be a factor. Other major moves are quite evident just before Labor Day—possibly because individual investors are back from vacations. Small caps hold the lead through the beginning of May, though the bulk of the move is complete by early March.

RUSSELL 2000/RUSSELL 1000 ONE-YEAR SEASONAL PATTERN

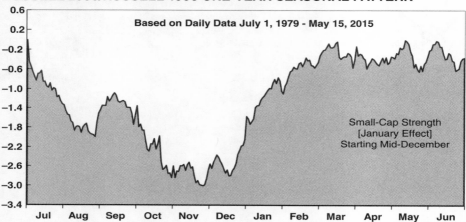

The bottom graph shows the actual ratio of the Russell 2000 divided by the Russell 1000 from 1979. Smaller companies had the upper hand for five years into 1983, as the last major bear trend wound to a close and the nascent bull market logged its first year. After falling behind for about eight years, they came back after the Persian Gulf War bottom in 1990, moving up until 1994, when big caps ruled the latter stages of the millennial bull. For six years, the picture was bleak for small fry, as the blue chips and tech stocks moved to stratospheric PE ratios. Small caps spiked in late 1999 and early 2000 and reached a peak in early 2006, as the four-year-old bull entered its final year. Note how the small-cap advantage has waned during major bull moves and intensified during weak market times.

RUSSELL 2000/RUSSELL 1000 (1979–APRIL 2015)

MONDAY

D 66.7
S 66.7
N 61.9

5

Ideas are easy; it's execution that's hard.
— Jeff Bezos (Amazon.com, b. 1964)

TUESDAY

D 52.4
S 38.1
N 52.4

6

In most admired companies, key priorities are teamwork, customer focus, fair treatment of employees, initiative, and innovation. In average companies the top priorities are minimizing risk, respecting the chain of command, supporting the boss, and making budget.
— Bruce Pfau (*Fortune*)

Small Cap Strength Starts in Mid-December (Page 106)

WEDNESDAY

D 47.6
S 42.9
N 38.1

7

We're not believers that the government is bigger than the business cycle.
— David Rosenberg (Economist, Merrill Lynch, *Barron's* 4/21/2008)

THURSDAY

D 47.6
S 52.4
N 57.1

8

At the end of the day, the most important thing is how good are you at risk control. Ninety-percent of any great trader is going to be the risk control.
— Paul Tudor Jones II (Founder Tudor Investment Corporation, b. 1954)

FRIDAY

D 57.1
S 61.9
N 61.9

9

The monuments of wit survive the monuments of power.
— Francis Bacon (English philosopher, essayist, statesman, 1561–1626)

SATURDAY

10

SUNDAY

11

WALL STREET'S ONLY "FREE LUNCH" SERVED BEFORE CHRISTMAS

Investors tend to get rid of their losers near year-end for tax purposes, often hammering these stocks down to bargain levels. Over the years, the *Almanac* has shown that NYSE stocks selling at their lows on December 15 will usually outperform the market by February 15 in the following year. Preferred stocks, closed-end funds, splits, and new issues are eliminated. When there are a huge number of new lows, stocks down the most are selected, even though there are usually good reasons why some stocks have been battered.

BARGAIN STOCKS VS. THE MARKET*

Short Span* Late Dec–Jan/Feb	New Lows Late Dec	% Change Jan/Feb	% Change NYSE Composite	Bargain Stocks Advantage
1974–75	112	48.9%	22.1%	26.8%
1975–76	21	34.9	14.9	20.0
1976–77	2	1.3	–3.3	4.6
1977–78	15	2.8	–4.5	7.3
1978–79	43	11.8	3.9	7.9
1979–80	5	9.3	6.1	3.2
1980–81	14	7.1	–2.0	9.1
1981–82	21	–2.6	–7.4	4.8
1982–83	4	33.0	9.7	23.3
1983–84	13	–3.2	–3.8	0.6
1984–85	32	19.0	12.1	6.9
1985–86	4	–22.5	3.9	–26.4
1986–87	22	9.3	12.5	–3.2
1987–88	23	13.2	6.8	6.4
1988–89	14	30.0	6.4	23.6
1989–90	25	–3.1	–4.8	1.7
1990–91	18	18.8	12.6	6.2
1991–92	23	51.1	7.7	43.4
1992–93	9	8.7	0.6	8.1
1993–94	10	–1.4	2.0	–3.4
1994–95	25	14.6	5.7	8.9
1995–96	5	–11.3	4.5	–15.8
1996–97	16	13.9	11.2	2.7
1997–98	29	9.9	5.7	4.2
1998–99	40	–2.8	4.3	–7.1
1999–00	26	8.9	–5.4	14.3
2000–01	51	44.4	0.1	44.3
2001–02	12	31.4	–2.3	33.7
2002–03	33	28.7	3.9	24.8
2003–04	15	16.7	2.3	14.4
2004–05	36	6.8	–2.8	9.6
2005–06	71	12.0	2.6	9.4
2006–07	43	5.1	–0.5	5.6
2007–08	71	–3.2	–9.4	6.2
2008–09	88	11.4	–2.4	13.8
2009–10	25	1.8	–3.0	4.8
2010–11	20	8.3	3.4	4.9
2011–12	65	18.1	6.1	12.0
2012–13	17	20.9	3.4	17.5
2013–14	18	25.7	1.7	24.0
2014-15	17	0.2%	–0.4%	0.6%
41-Year Totals		**527.9%**	**124.2%**	**403.7%**
Average		**12.9%**	**3.0%**	**9.8%**

* Dec 15–Feb 15 (1974–1999), Dec 1999–2015 based on actual newsletter portfolio

In response to changing market conditions, we tweaked the strategy the last 16 years, adding selections from NASDAQ and AMEX, and selling in mid-January some years. We e-mail the list of stocks to our *Almanac Investor* newsletter subscribers. Visit *www.stocktradersalmanac.com,* or see the ad insert for additional details and a special offer for new subscribers.

We have come to the conclusion that the most prudent course of action is to compile our list from the stocks making new lows on Triple-Witching Friday before Christmas, capitalizing on the Santa Claus Rally (page 114). This also gives us the weekend to evaluate the issues in greater depth and weed out any glaringly problematic stocks. Subscribers will receive the list of stocks selected from the new lows made on December 18, 2015 and December 16, 2016 via e-mail.

This "Free Lunch" strategy is an extremely short-term strategy reserved for the nimblest traders. It has performed better after market corrections and when there are more new lows to choose from. The object is to buy bargain stocks near their 52-week lows and sell any quick, generous gains, as these issues can often be real dogs.

Monday Before December Triple Witching S&P Up 10 of Last 15

MONDAY

D 42.9
S 47.6
N 42.9

12

I had an unshakable faith. I had it in my head that if I had to, I'd crawl over broken glass. I'd live in a tent—it was gonna happen. And I think when you have that kind of steely determination…people get out of the way.
— Rick Newcombe (Syndicator, *Investor's Business Daily*)

FOMC Meeting (2 Days)

TUESDAY

D 47.6
S 52.4
N 47.6

13

People have difficulty cutting losses, admitting an error, and moving on. I am rather frequently—and on occasion, quite spectacularly—wrong. However, if we expect to be wrong, then there should be no ego tied up in admitting the error, honoring the stop loss, selling the loser—and preserving your capital.
— Barry L. Ritholtz (Founder/CIO Ritholtz Wealth Management, *Bailout Nation*, The Big Picture blog, 8/12/2010, b. 1961)

December Triple Witching Week, S&P Up 25 of Last 31

WEDNESDAY

D 52.4
S 42.9
N 42.9

14

It is better to be out wishing you were in, than in wishing you were out.
— Albert W. Thomas (Trader, investor, *Over My Shoulder*, mutualfundmagic.com, *If It Doesn't Go Up, Don't Buy It!*, b. 1927)

THURSDAY

D 52.4
S 52.4
N 47.6

15

You have to keep digging, keep asking questions, because otherwise you'll be seduced or brainwashed into the idea that it's somehow a great privilege, an honor, to report the lies they've been feeding you.
— David Halberstam (Amercian writer, war reporter, 1964 Pulitzer Prize, 1934–2007)

December Triple Witching, S&P Up 24 of 33, Average Gain 0.4%

FRIDAY

D 57.1
S 61.9
N 52.4

16

If you can buy more of your best idea, why put [the money] into your 10th-best idea or your 20th-best idea? The more positions you have, the more average you are.
— Bruce Berkowitz (Fairholme Fund, *Barron's* 3/17/08, b. 1958)

SATURDAY

17

SUNDAY

18

IF SANTA CLAUS SHOULD FAIL TO CALL, BEARS MAY COME TO BROAD AND WALL

Santa Claus tends to come to Wall Street nearly every year, bringing a short, sweet, respectable rally within the last five days of the year and the first two in January. This has been good for an average 1.4% gain since 1969 (1.4% since 1950). Santa's failure to show tends to precede bear markets, or times stocks could be purchased later in the year at much lower prices. We discovered this phenomenon in 1972.

DAILY % CHANGE IN S&P 500 AT YEAR END

	Trading Days Before Year End						First Days in January			Rally %
	6	5	4	3	2	1	1	2	3	Change
1969	−0.4	1.1	0.8	−0.7	0.4	0.5	1.0	0.5	−0.7	3.6
1970	0.1	0.6	0.5	1.1	0.2	−0.1	−1.1	0.7	0.6	1.9
1971	−0.4	0.2	1.0	0.3	−0.4	0.3	−0.4	0.4	1.0	1.3
1972	−0.3	−0.7	0.6	0.4	0.5	1.0	0.9	0.4	−0.1	3.1
1973	−1.1	−0.7	3.1	2.1	−0.2	0.01	0.1	2.2	−0.9	6.7
1974	−1.4	1.4	0.8	−0.4	0.03	2.1	2.4	0.7	0.5	7.2
1975	0.7	0.8	0.9	−0.1	−0.4	0.5	0.8	1.8	1.0	4.3
1976	0.1	1.2	0.7	−0.4	0.5	0.5	−0.4	−1.2	−0.9	0.8
1977	0.8	0.9	N/C	0.1	0.2	0.2	−1.3	−0.3	−0.8	−0.3
1978	0.03	1.7	1.3	−0.9	−0.4	−0.2	0.6	1.1	0.8	3.3
1979	−0.6	0.1	0.1	0.2	−0.1	0.1	−2.0	−0.5	1.2	−2.2
1980	−0.4	0.4	0.5	−1.1	0.2	0.3	0.4	1.2	0.1	2.0
1981	−0.5	0.2	−0.2	−0.5	0.5	0.2	0.2	−2.2	−0.7	−1.8
1982	0.6	1.8	−1.0	0.3	−0.7	0.2	−1.6	2.2	0.4	1.2
1983	−0.2	−0.03	0.9	0.3	−0.2	0.05	−0.5	1.7	1.2	2.1
1984	−0.5	0.8	−0.2	−0.4	0.3	0.6	−1.1	−0.5	−0.5	−0.6
1985	−1.1	−0.7	0.2	0.9	0.5	0.3	−0.8	0.6	−0.1	1.1
1986	−1.0	0.2	0.1	−0.9	−0.5	−0.5	1.8	2.3	0.2	2.4
1987	1.3	−0.5	−2.6	−0.4	1.3	−0.3	3.6	1.1	0.1	2.2
1988	−0.2	0.3	−0.4	0.1	0.8	−0.6	−0.9	1.5	0.2	0.9
1989	0.6	0.8	−0.2	0.6	0.5	0.8	1.8	−0.3	−0.9	4.1
1990	0.5	−0.6	0.3	−0.8	0.1	0.5	−1.1	−1.4	−0.3	−3.0
1991	2.5	0.6	1.4	0.4	2.1	0.5	0.04	0.5	−0.3	5.7
1992	−0.3	0.2	−0.1	−0.3	0.2	−0.7	−0.1	−0.2	0.04	−1.1
1993	0.01	0.7	0.1	−0.1	−0.4	−0.5	−0.2	0.3	0.1	−0.1
1994	0.01	0.2	0.4	−0.3	0.1	−0.4	−0.03	0.3	−0.1	0.2
1995	0.8	0.2	0.4	0.04	−0.1	0.3	0.8	0.1	−0.6	1.8
1996	−0.3	0.5	0.6	0.1	−0.4	−1.7	−0.5	1.5	−0.1	0.1
1997	−1.5	−0.7	0.4	1.8	1.8	−0.04	0.5	0.2	−1.1	4.0
1998	2.1	−0.2	−0.1	1.3	−0.8	−0.2	−0.1	1.4	2.2	1.3
1999	1.6	−0.1	0.04	0.4	0.1	0.3	−1.0	−3.8	0.2	−4.0
2000	0.8	2.4	0.7	1.0	0.4	−1.0	−2.8	5.0	−1.1	5.7
2001	0.4	−0.02	0.4	0.7	0.3	−1.1	0.6	0.9	0.6	1.8
2002	0.2	−0.5	−0.3	−1.6	0.5	0.05	3.3	−0.05	2.2	1.2
2003	0.3	−0.2	0.2	1.2	0.01	0.2	−0.3	1.2	0.1	2.4
2004	0.1	−0.4	0.7	−0.01	0.01	−0.1	−0.8	−1.2	−0.4	−1.8
2005	0.4	0.04	−1.0	0.1	−0.3	−0.5	1.6	0.4	0.002	0.4
2006	−0.4	−0.5	0.4	0.7	−0.1	−0.5	−0.1	0.1	−0.6	0.003
2007	1.7	0.8	0.1	−1.4	0.1	−0.7	−1.4	N/C	−2.5	−2.5
2008	−1.0	0.6	0.5	−0.4	2.4	1.4	3.2	−0.5	0.8	7.4
2009	0.2	0.5	0.1	−0.1	0.02	−1.0	1.6	0.3	0.05	1.4
2010	−0.2	0.1	0.1	0.1	−0.2	−0.02	1.1	−0.1	0.5	1.1
2011	0.8	0.9	0.01	−1.3	1.1	−0.4	1.6	0.02	0.3	1.9
2012	−0.9	−0.2	−0.5	−0.1	−1.1	1.7	2.5	−0.2	0.5	2.0
2013	0.5	0.3	0.5	−0.03	−0.02	0.4	−0.9	−0.03	−0.3	0.2
2014	0.2	−0.01	0.3	0.10	−0.50	−1.0	−0.03	−1.8	−0.9	−3.0
Avg	0.10	0.31	0.27	0.05	0.18	0.03	0.24	0.35	0.02	1.4

The couplet above was certainly on the mark in 1999, as the period suffered a horrendous 4.0% loss. On January 14, 2000, the Dow started its 33-month 37.8% slide to the October 2002 midterm election year bottom. NASDAQ cracked eight weeks later, falling 37.3% in 10 weeks, eventually dropping 77.9% by October 2002. Saddam Hussein cancelled Christmas by invading Kuwait in 1990. Energy prices and Middle East terror woes may have grounded Santa in 2004. In 2007, the third worst reading since 1950 was recorded, as a full-blown financial crisis led to the second worst bear market in history. In 2015, the period was clobbered as rate hike fears prompted profit taking.

DECEMBER

The Only FREE LUNCH on Wall Street is Served (Page 112)
Almanac Investors Emailed Alert Before the Open, Monday (See ad Insert)

MONDAY

D 42.9
S 47.6
N 38.1

19

A.I. (artificial intelligence) is the science of how to get machines to do the things they do in the movies.
— Dr. Astro Teller (Carnegie Mellon University, b. 1970)

TUESDAY

D 47.6
S 47.6
N 52.4

20

The first panacea for a mismanaged nation is inflation of the currency; the second is war. Both bring a temporary prosperity; both bring a permanent ruin. But both are the refuge of political and economic opportunists.
— Ernest Hemingway (American writer, 1954 Nobel Prize winner, 1899–1961)

WEDNESDAY

D 76.2
S 76.2
N 61.9

21

It doesn't pay to anticipate the correction; there are already plenty who have been carried out on their shields trying to do that. Rather, we will wait for some confirmed sell signals before altering our still-bullish view.
— Lawrence G. McMillan (Professional trader, author, Registered Investment Advisor, speaker, educator, OptionStrategist.com, b. 1946)

Watch for the Santa Claus Rally (Page 112)

THURSDAY

D 76.2
S 71.4
N 66.7

22

The heights by great men reached and kept, were not attained by sudden flight, but they, while their companions slept, were toiling upward in the night.
— Henry Wadsworth Longfellow (American poet and educator, 1807–1882)

Last Trading Day Before Christmas, Dow Up 7 of Last 8 Years

FRIDAY

D 52.4
S 52.4
N 61.9

23

Markets are constantly in a state of uncertainty and flux and money is made by discounting the obvious and betting on the unexpected.
— George Soros (Financier, philanthropist, political activist, author and philosopher, b. 1930)

SATURDAY

24

Christmas Day
Chanukah

SUNDAY

25

YEAR'S TOP INVESTMENT BOOKS

Fast Forward: The Technologies and Companies Shaping Our Future, Jim Mellon and Al Chalabi, Fruitful Publications, $29.95, www.fastforwardbook.com. 2016 Best Investment Book of the Year. See page 76.

Doug Kass on the Market: A Life on TheStreet, Douglas A. Kass, Wiley, $29.95. A trip down memory lane with venerable trader, hedge fund manager, market pundit, and renowned short seller. Dougie's tales from the crypt teach many lessons learned from trials and tribulations, winners and losers, and rubbing elbows with the titans of Wall Street and financial media for more than four decades. It's a comprehensive account of his talent and techniques, including a scorecard of his lists of "Surprises" for the past dozen years.

I'll Give You Exactly Five Minutes, Peter Danish, Motivational Press, $19.95. One of our favorite quotations in the *Almanac* is Shakespeare's "Brevity is the soul of Wit." *I'll Give You Exactly Five Minutes* embodies this brilliant sentiment with bells on. Peter Danish is an award-winning author, educator, and marketing communications expert with a novel, a play, and a musical to his credit. For the past two decades, Danish has been coaching and speechwriting for C-level executives. It is from this experience that this book and his ORSON System TM of presenting evolved. It's short, to the point, and funny, too!

The High-Speed Company: Creating Urgency and Growth in a Nanosecond Culture, Jason Jennings, Portfolio/Penguin, $27.95. This bestselling author, keynote speaker, and consultant, who specializes in business leadership, sales, management, and customer satisfaction, has spent the past decade interviewing 11,000 business owners, CEOs, and high-ranking executives. They all said what they needed most was for everyone in their companies to be faster and to act with a greater sense of urgency about the need for growth, to speed everything up. *The High-Speed Company* is chockfull of strategies, tactics, and information for achieving stellar performance.

A Wealth of Common Sense: Why Simplicity Trumps Complexity in Any Investment Plan, Ben Carlson, Wiley/Bloomberg Press, $40.00. Our buddy Downtown Josh Brown, The Reformed Broker, says it best: "Ben Carlson seemingly came out of nowhere and took the financial commentariat by storm with his straightforward, insightful blog posts. True investing wisdom—born out of experience and success—cannot be faked; it must be earned. This is precisely the type of wisdom that comes oozing out of every chapter."

Frontier: Exploring the Top Ten Emerging Markets of Tomorrow, Gavin Serkin, Bloomberg Financial, $50.00. With an introduction from the eminent emerging market fund manager Mark Mobius, you know this book delivers the goods. As head of the emerging markets international desk at Bloomberg News in London, Gavin Serkin is in the foreign market catbird seat. Serkin traveled alongside top money managers and found an exotic collection of countries and markets that goes beyond the emerging into the realm of frontier markets.

Beat the Crowd: How You Can Out-Invest the Herd by Thinking Differently, Kenneth L. Fisher with Elisabeth Dellinger, Wiley, $29.95. Fisher does it again! Being a contrarian investor is not just going against the crowd; it means behaving independently, but not necessarily opposite. With his usual wit and style, bestselling author Ken Fisher ventures away from the herd and the opposition and finds "true contrary" by debunking conventional wisdom and shows you how to think and invest for yourself.

The Energy World Is Flat: Opportunities from the End of Peak Oil, Daniel Lacalle with Diego Parrilla, Wiley, $40.00. With fresh perspectives and a novel comparison to the Internet revolution and Dot-com bubble, energy market and financial expert Daniel Lacalle offers a concise history and up-to-date analysis of energy markets and the economic implications of the planet's unwavering pursuit of affordable, abundant, and clean energy, including actionable investment tactics.

Investing Psychology: The Effects of Behavioral Finance on Investment Choice and Bias, Tim Richards, Wiley, $65.00. Behavioral investment expert Tim Richards explains the essential mindset for effective investing and the preservation of capital, and how to handle our worst investing enemy: our brain. Right out of the *Almanac* playbook (page 189), Richard emphasizes how crucial it is to always track your results and shows the pitfalls of trading tired, hungry, or emotional and competing with institutions. Check your biases at the door and rigorously challenge your own ideas.

The 52-Week Low Formula: A Contrarian Strategy That Lowers Risk, Beats the Market, and Overcomes Human Emotion, Luke L. Wiley, Wiley, $34.95. The key to improving the results of our "Free Lunch" strategy of buying new 52-week lows in late December has been weeding out the wheat from the chaff. Top financial advisor Luke Wiley presents his method for finding solid companies in out-of-favor shares. It's no magic formula, but it is an excellent screening and filtering process.

Christmas Day *(observed) (Market Closed)*

MONDAY

26

An economist is someone who sees something happen, and then wonders if it would work in theory.
— Ronald Reagan (40th U.S. President, 1911–2004)

TUESDAY

D 81.0
S 81.0
N 71.4

27

I've learned that only through focus can you do world-class things, no matter how capable you are.
— William H. Gates (Microsoft founder, *Fortune*, 7/8/02, b. 1955)

WEDNESDAY

D 47.6
S 57.1
N 47.6

28

There are two kinds of people who lose money: those who know nothing and those who know everything.
— Henry Kaufman (German-American economist, b. 1927, in *Forbes* 10/19/98 to Robert Lenzner, who added, "With two Nobel Prize winners in the house, Long-Term Capital clearly fits the second case.")

THURSDAY

D 42.9
S 57.1
N 42.9

29

Don't be the last bear or last bull standing, let history guide you, be contrary to the crowd, and let the tape tell you when to act.
— Jeffrey A. Hirsch (Editor, *Stock Trader's Almanac*, b. 1966)

Last Trading Day of the Year, NASDAQ Down 12 of last 15
NASDAQ Was Up 29 Years in a Row 1971–1999

FRIDAY

D 42.9
S 33.3
N 42.9

30

Your emotions are often a reverse indicator of what you ought to be doing.
— John F. Hindelong (Dillon, Reed)

SATURDAY

31

New Years Day
January Almanac Investor Sector Seasonalities: See Pages 94, 96, and 98

SUNDAY

1

2017 STRATEGY CALENDAR

(Option expiration dates circled)

	MONDAY	TUESDAY	WEDNESDAY	THURSDAY	FRIDAY	SATURDAY	SUNDAY
	26	27	28	29	30	31	1 JANUARY New Year's Day
JANUARY	2	3	4	5	6	7	8
	9	10	11	12	13	14	15
	16 Martin Luther King Day	17	18	19	⑳	21	22
	23	24	25	26	27	28	29
	30	31	1 FEBRUARY	2	3	4	5
FEBRUARY	6	7	8	9	10	11	12
	13	14 ♥	15	16	⑰	18	19
	20 President's Day	21	22	23	24	25	26
	27	28	1 MARCH Ash Wednesday	2	3	4	5
MARCH	6	7	8	9	10	11	12 Daylight Saving Time Begins
	13	14	15	16	⑰ ♣ St. Patrick's Day	18	19
	20	21	22	23	24	25	26
	27	28	29	30	31	1 APRIL	2
APRIL	3	4	5	6	7	8	9
	10	11 Passover	12	13	14 Good Friday	15	16 Easter
	17	18	19	20	㉑	22	23
	24	25	26	27	28	29	30
MAY	1 MAY	2	3	4	5	6	7
	8	9	10	11	12	13	14 Mother's Day
	15	16	17	18	⑲	20	21
	22	23	24	25	26	27	28
	29 Memorial Day	30	31	1 JUNE	2	3	4
JUNE	5	6	7	8	9	10	11
	12	13	14	15	⑯	17	18 Father's Day
	19	20	21	22	23	24	25
	26	27	28	29	30	1 JULY	2

Market closed on shaded weekdays; closes early when half-shaded.

2017 STRATEGY CALENDAR

(Option expiration dates circled)

MONDAY	TUESDAY	WEDNESDAY	THURSDAY	FRIDAY	SATURDAY	SUNDAY	
3	4 Independence Day	5	6	7	8	9	JULY
10	11	12	13	14	15	16	
17	18	19	20	(21)	22	23	
24	25	26	27	28	29	30	
31	1 AUGUST	2	3	4	5	6	AUGUST
7	8	9	10	11	12	13	
14	15	16	17	(18)	19	20	
21	22	23	24	25	26	27	
28	29	30	31	1 SEPTEMBER	2	3	SEPTEMBER
4 Labor Day	5	6	7	8	9	10	
11	12	13	14	(15)	16	17	
18	19	20	21 Rosh Hashanah	22	23	24	
25	26	27	28	29	30 Yom Kippur	1 OCTOBER	OCTOBER
2	3	4	5	6	7	8	
9 Columbus Day	10	11	12	13	14	15	
16	17	18	19	(20)	21	22	
23	24	25	26	27	28	29	
30	31 🎃	1 NOVEMBER	2	3	4	5 Daylight Saving Time Ends	NOVEMBER
6	7 Election Day	8	9	10	11 Veterans' Day	12	
13	14	15	16	(17)	18	19	
20	21	22	23 Thanksgiving Day	24	25	26	
27	28	29	30	1 DECEMBER	2	3	DECEMBER
4	5	6	7	8	9	10	
11	12	13 Chanukah	14	(15)	16	17	
18	19	20	21	22	23	24	
25 Christmas	26	27	28	29	30	31	

DIRECTORY OF TRADING PATTERNS AND DATABANK

CONTENTS

DOW JONES INDUSTRIALS MARKET PROBABILITY CALENDAR 2016

THE % CHANCE OF THE MARKET RISING ON ANY TRADING DAY OF THE YEAR*
(Based on the number of times the DJIA rose on a particular trading day during **January 1954–December 2014**)

Date	Jan	Feb	Mar	Apr	May	Jun	Jul	Aug	Sep	Oct	Nov	Dec
1	H	59.0	63.9	60.7	S	57.4	63.9	44.3	57.4	S	60.7	44.3
2	S	54.1	63.9	S	55.7	50.8	S	47.5	59.0	S	52.5	52.5
3	S	39.3	59.0	S	63.9	52.5	S	49.2	S	47.5	67.2	S
4	57.4	55.7	49.2	60.7	50.8	S	H	50.8	S	55.7	60.7	S
5	72.1	49.2	S	52.5	47.5	S	59.0	54.1	H	52.5	S	63.9
6	49.2	S	S	57.4	45.9	59.0	60.7	S	59.0	62.3	S	57.4
7	55.7	S	47.5	50.8	S	52.5	55.7	S	45.9	44.3	47.5	49.2
8	45.9	44.3	54.1	59.0	S	45.9	62.3	47.5	47.5	S	60.7	45.9
9	S	47.5	59.0	S	52.5	37.7	S	47.5	44.3	S	52.5	54.1
10	S	60.7	54.1	S	49.2	55.7	S	47.5	S	50.8	57.4	S
11	49.2	45.9	55.7	63.9	54.1	S	55.7	45.9	S	42.6	49.2	S
12	47.5	49.2	S	63.9	45.9	S	49.2	63.9	59.0	39.3	S	55.7
13	49.2	S	S	54.1	52.5	59.0	42.6	S	59.0	52.5	S	44.3
14	57.4	S	52.5	70.5	S	59.0	65.6	S	47.5	59.0	49.2	52.5
15	57.4	H	59.0	65.6	S	52.5	50.8	55.7	54.1	S	57.4	45.9
16	S	54.1	60.7	S	54.1	49.2	S	52.5	55.7	S	50.8	55.7
17	S	41.0	59.0	S	44.3	50.8	S	49.2	S	50.8	49.2	S
18	H	49.2	54.1	57.4	54.1	S	45.9	54.1	S	50.8	50.8	S
19	59.0	49.2	S	54.1	42.6	S	50.8	42.6	41.0	42.6	S	49.2
20	41.0	S	S	55.7	41.0	44.3	52.5	S	50.8	62.3	S	55.7
21	36.1	S	41.0	52.5	S	50.8	41.0	S	45.9	42.6	57.4	60.7
22	41.0	54.1	50.8	52.5	S	45.9	45.9	59.0	41.0	S	67.2	52.5
23	S	37.7	37.7	S	34.4	41.0	S	49.2	37.7	S	59.0	60.7
24	S	42.6	50.8	S	52.5	36.1	S	54.1	S	49.2	H	S
25	57.4	59.0	H	50.8	45.9	S	60.7	49.2	S	29.5	63.9	S
26	57.4	49.2	S	57.4	45.9	52.5	45.9	S	50.8	54.1	S	H
27	50.8	S	S	55.7	57.4	49.2	44.3	S	52.5	54.1	S	72.1
28	57.4	S	44.3	50.8	S	45.9	59.0	S	52.5	60.7	59.0	47.5
29	57.4	52.5	54.1	52.5	S	55.7	49.2	60.7	49.2	S	52.5	55.7
30	S		44.3	S	H	50.8	S	41.0	37.7	S	52.5	54.1
31	S		44.3		59.0		S	62.3		54.1		S

* See new trends developing on pages 70, 92, 141–146.

121

RECENT DOW JONES INDUSTRIALS MARKET PROBABILITY CALENDAR 2016

THE % CHANCE OF THE MARKET RISING ON ANY TRADING DAY OF THE YEAR*
(Based on the number of times the DJIA rose on a particular trading day during **January 1994–December 2014****)

Date	Jan	Feb	Mar	Apr	May	Jun	Jul	Aug	Sep	Oct	Nov	Dec
1	H	71.4	57.1	76.2	S	66.7	81.0	38.1	57.1	S	52.4	42.9
2	S	47.6	47.6	S	66.7	47.6	S	57.1	66.7	S	57.1	47.6
3	S	42.9	57.1	S	66.7	52.4	S	47.6	S	52.4	71.4	S
4	66.7	52.4	47.6	71.4	33.3	S	H	52.4	S	47.6	76.2	S
5	71.4	57.1	S	42.9	33.3	S	42.9	52.4	H	47.6	S	66.7
6	52.4	S	S	66.7	42.9	57.1	57.1	S	52.4	66.7	S	52.4
7	52.4	S	66.7	38.1	S	61.9	57.1	S	42.9	38.1	57.1	47.6
8	38.1	47.6	47.6	52.4	S	52.4	61.9	47.6	66.7	S	52.4	47.6
9	S	57.1	61.9	S	66.7	38.1	S	47.6	52.4	S	47.6	57.1
10	S	57.1	61.9	S	57.1	47.6	S	47.6	S	38.1	42.9	S
11	52.4	61.9	52.4	52.4	71.4	S	47.6	33.3	S	47.6	66.7	S
12	47.6	47.6	S	61.9	47.6	S	52.4	66.7	61.9	38.1	S	42.9
13	57.1	S	S	52.4	57.1	57.1	66.7	S	61.9	52.4	S	47.6
14	52.4	S	66.7	66.7	S	71.4	61.9	S	57.1	76.2	61.9	52.4
15	61.9	H	61.9	66.7	S	61.9	52.4	42.9	52.4	S	66.7	52.4
16	S	66.7	52.4	S	57.1	57.1	S	61.9	66.7	S	47.6	57.1
17	S	47.6	66.7	S	47.6	57.1	S	66.7	S	47.6	47.6	S
18	H	38.1	61.9	61.9	57.1	S	57.1	42.9	S	52.4	52.4	S
19	52.4	47.6	S	52.4	42.9	S	52.4	33.3	42.9	47.6	S	42.9
20	38.1	S	S	71.4	33.3	47.6	66.7	S	57.1	66.7	S	47.6
21	33.3	S	42.9	66.7	S	38.1	23.8	S	47.6	52.4	52.4	76.2
22	33.3	52.4	47.6	57.1	S	42.9	47.6	61.9	33.3	S	61.9	76.2
23	S	57.1	42.9	S	38.1	33.3	S	52.4	28.6	S	61.9	52.4
24	S	33.3	61.9	S	52.4	33.3	S	57.1	S	47.6	H	S
25	57.1	42.9	H	42.9	52.4	S	66.7	47.6	S	38.1	66.7	S
26	61.9	47.6	S	57.1	42.9	S	47.6	42.9	42.9	57.1	S	H
27	61.9	S	S	61.9	66.7	47.6	38.1	S	52.4	66.7	S	81.0
28	47.6	S	23.8	71.4	S	52.4	47.6	S	61.9	66.7	61.9	47.6
29	57.1	42.9	47.6	42.9	S	52.4	38.1	71.4	57.1	S	57.1	42.9
30	S		52.4	S	H	33.3	S	28.6	28.6	S	52.4	42.9
31	S		42.9		52.4		S	52.4		57.1		S

*See new trends developing on pages 70, 92, 141–146.   ** Based on most recent 21-year period.*

S&P 500 MARKET PROBABILITY CALENDAR 2016

THE % CHANCE OF THE MARKET RISING ON ANY TRADING DAY OF THE YEAR*

(Based on the number of times the S&P 500 rose on a particular trading day during **January 1954–December 2014**)

Date	Jan	Feb	Mar	Apr	May	Jun	Jul	Aug	Sep	Oct	Nov	Dec
1	H	60.7	60.7	65.6	S	55.7	70.5	47.5	60.7	S	60.7	45.9
2	S	57.4	59.0	S	55.7	60.7	S	45.9	52.5	S	57.4	52.5
3	S	47.5	62.3	S	67.2	52.5	S	49.2	S	47.5	68.9	S
4	49.2	50.8	47.5	60.7	55.7	S	H	50.8	S	65.6	57.4	S
5	68.9	52.5	S	54.1	44.3	S	55.7	54.1	H	54.1	S	62.3
6	54.1	S	S	54.1	44.3	57.4	55.7	S	59.0	62.3	S	55.7
7	50.8	S	49.2	52.5	S	45.9	59.0	S	47.5	45.9	47.5	44.3
8	44.3	45.9	57.4	60.7	S	44.3	60.7	47.5	49.2	S	59.0	50.8
9	S	41.0	59.0	S	50.8	41.0	S	54.1	52.5	S	59.0	55.7
10	S	62.3	50.8	S	49.2	55.7	S	45.9	S	49.2	57.4	S
11	52.5	54.1	62.3	63.9	54.1	S	55.7	47.5	S	41.0	49.2	S
12	54.1	45.9	S	55.7	45.9	S	50.8	63.9	59.0	44.3	S	49.2
13	54.1	S	S	49.2	49.2	62.3	50.8	S	63.9	52.5	S	49.2
14	59.0	S	45.9	60.7	S	59.0	70.5	S	52.5	54.1	50.8	44.3
15	63.9	H	60.7	63.9	S	59.0	54.1	62.3	52.5	S	49.2	45.9
16	S	54.1	62.3	S	54.1	47.5	S	55.7	55.7	S	50.8	57.4
17	S	37.7	57.4	S	49.2	55.7	S	55.7	S	50.8	52.5	S
18	H	52.5	50.8	60.7	55.7	S	42.6	52.5	S	55.7	54.1	S
19	55.7	42.6	S	52.5	39.3	S	45.9	45.9	47.5	42.6	S	45.9
20	50.8	S	S	55.7	49.2	41.0	52.5	S	52.5	67.2	S	47.5
21	45.9	S	44.3	55.7	S	50.8	41.0	S	47.5	42.6	55.7	57.4
22	47.5	47.5	44.3	45.9	S	50.8	45.9	62.3	45.9	S	63.9	49.2
23	S	42.6	52.5	S	44.3	42.6	S	47.5	36.1	S	59.0	60.7
24	S	37.7	45.9	S	52.5	36.1	S	52.5	S	44.3	H	S
25	54.1	57.4	H	47.5	50.8	S	57.4	47.5	S	32.8	65.6	S
26	52.5	52.5	S	57.4	47.5	S	52.5	45.9	49.2	60.7	S	H
27	47.5	S	S	49.2	57.4	42.6	47.5	S	49.2	57.4	S	73.8
28	60.7	S	45.9	47.5	S	50.8	63.9	S	59.0	60.7	60.7	52.5
29	62.3	59.0	54.1	59.0	S	59.0	60.7	60.7	49.2	S	59.0	62.3
30	S		37.7	S	H	49.2	S	44.3	41.0	S	50.8	62.3
31	S		42.6		60.7		S	65.6		55.7		S

* See new trends developing on pages 70, 92, 141–146.

RECENT S&P 500 MARKET PROBABILITY CALENDAR 2016

THE % CHANCE OF THE MARKET RISING ON ANY TRADING DAY OF THE YEAR*
(Based on the number of times the S&P 500 rose on a particular trading day during January 1994–December 2014**)

Date	Jan	Feb	Mar	Apr	May	Jun	Jul	Aug	Sep	Oct	Nov	Dec
1	H	71.4	57.1	76.2	S	61.9	85.7	47.6	61.9	S	52.4	47.6
2	S	52.4	42.9	S	66.7	71.4	S	52.4	42.9	S	66.7	52.4
3	S	42.9	66.7	S	57.1	47.6	S	47.6	S	47.6	71.4	S
4	47.6	52.4	52.4	71.4	38.1	S	H	57.1	S	57.1	76.2	S
5	61.9	57.1	S	52.4	38.1	S	42.9	42.9	H	47.6	S	66.7
6	57.1	S	S	61.9	38.1	52.4	61.9	S	52.4	61.9	S	38.1
7	47.6	S	66.7	42.9	S	42.9	57.1	S	57.1	38.1	57.1	42.9
8	47.6	61.9	52.4	57.1	S	47.6	57.1	57.1	61.9	S	47.6	52.4
9	S	47.6	57.1	S	52.4	42.9	S	47.6	61.9	S	38.1	61.9
10	S	66.7	52.4	S	47.6	42.9	S	47.6	S	38.1	42.9	S
11	61.9	71.4	66.7	47.6	61.9	S	47.6	33.3	S	47.6	57.1	S
12	57.1	47.6	S	52.4	52.4	S	52.4	61.9	61.9	38.1	S	47.6
13	52.4	S	S	47.6	47.6	57.1	76.2	S	66.7	57.1	S	52.4
14	52.4	S	52.4	52.4	S	71.4	66.7	S	66.7	71.4	61.9	42.9
15	61.9	H	61.9	61.9	S	71.4	47.6	57.1	47.6	S	57.1	52.4
16	S	71.4	61.9	S	57.1	57.1	S	71.4	66.7	S	52.4	61.9
17	S	42.9	71.4	S	52.4	57.1	S	71.4	S	42.9	52.4	S
18	H	42.9	47.6	71.4	57.1	S	47.6	38.1	S	61.9	52.4	S
19	61.9	42.9	S	57.1	42.9	S	47.6	42.9	47.6	61.9	S	47.6
20	52.4	S	S	66.7	38.1	42.9	66.7	S	52.4	71.4	S	47.6
21	38.1	S	47.6	71.4	S	42.9	28.6	S	38.1	61.9	52.4	76.2
22	47.6	47.6	38.1	52.4	S	52.4	52.4	66.7	33.3	S	52.4	71.4
23	S	61.9	66.7	S	42.9	33.3	S	52.4	23.8	S	57.1	52.4
24	S	38.1	61.9	S	57.1	38.1	S	61.9	S	52.4	H	S
25	52.4	47.6	H	38.1	57.1	S	61.9	47.6	S	38.1	61.9	S
26	57.1	57.1	S	52.4	47.6	S	47.6	47.6	42.9	57.1	S	H
27	66.7	S	S	52.4	61.9	38.1	42.9	S	47.6	57.1	S	81.0
28	52.4	S	28.6	66.7	S	52.4	61.9	S	66.7	66.7	61.9	57.1
29	61.9	47.6	42.9	52.4	S	61.9	47.6	71.4	61.9	S	76.2	57.1
30	S		38.1	S	H	38.1	S	28.6	28.6	S	38.1	33.3
31	S		47.6		57.1		S	52.4		61.9		S

* See new trends developing on pages 70, 92, 141–146.   ** Based on most recent 21-year period.

NASDAQ COMPOSITE MARKET PROBABILITY CALENDAR 2016

THE % CHANCE OF THE MARKET RISING ON ANY TRADING DAY OF THE YEAR*

(Based on the number of times the NASDAQ rose on a particular trading day during **January 1972–December 2014**)

Date	Jan	Feb	Mar	Apr	May	Jun	Jul	Aug	Sep	Oct	Nov	Dec
1	H	69.8	60.5	46.5	S	55.8	60.5	51.2	55.8	S	67.4	58.1
2	S	67.4	55.8	S	62.8	72.1	S	44.2	58.1	S	55.8	62.8
3	S	55.8	67.4	S	69.8	55.8	S	51.2	S	46.5	69.8	S
4	55.8	62.8	48.8	62.8	60.5	S	H	58.1	S	60.5	58.1	S
5	67.4	58.1	S	62.8	53.5	S	46.5	53.5	H	55.8	S	65.1
6	58.1	S	S	53.5	53.5	60.5	46.5	S	58.1	62.8	S	58.1
7	62.8	S	51.2	44.2	S	48.8	51.2	S	58.1	55.8	48.8	41.9
8	53.5	53.5	55.8	60.5	S	46.5	60.5	41.9	55.8	S	55.8	53.5
9	S	48.8	55.8	S	62.8	44.2	S	53.5	51.2	S	58.1	48.8
10	S	62.8	51.2	S	53.5	51.2	S	48.8	S	60.5	65.1	S
11	60.5	60.5	69.8	62.8	41.9	S	62.8	55.8	S	48.8	55.8	S
12	58.1	62.8	S	62.8	55.8	S	58.1	58.1	53.5	48.8	S	41.9
13	60.5	S	S	51.2	53.5	60.5	72.1	S	62.8	74.4	S	41.9
14	62.8	S	51.2	58.1	S	67.4	74.4	S	62.8	65.1	53.5	41.9
15	65.1	H	51.2	53.5	S	60.5	65.1	58.1	34.9	S	41.9	44.2
16	S	58.1	60.5	S	55.8	46.5	S	51.2	53.5	S	46.5	55.8
17	S	48.8	58.1	S	55.8	53.5	S	60.5	S	51.2	51.2	S
18	H	55.8	62.8	60.5	53.5	S	48.8	51.2	S	53.5	55.8	S
19	69.8	37.2	S	55.8	39.5	S	55.8	37.2	53.5	41.9	S	48.8
20	60.5	S	S	55.8	46.5	46.5	58.1	S	65.1	72.1	S	53.5
21	39.5	S	41.9	58.1	S	60.5	39.5	S	51.2	46.5	51.2	60.5
22	46.5	39.5	58.1	53.5	S	46.5	51.2	69.8	48.8	S	69.8	65.1
23	S	51.2	55.8	S	48.8	46.5	S	53.5	46.5	S	60.5	69.8
24	S	51.2	51.2	S	53.5	41.9	S	53.5	S	44.2	H	S
25	46.5	62.8	H	51.2	55.8	S	58.1	53.5	S	34.9	58.1	S
26	67.4	55.8	S	46.5	58.1	S	48.8	53.5	53.5	46.5	S	H
27	62.8	S	S	67.4	58.1	48.8	44.2	S	44.2	58.1	S	72.1
28	53.5	S	41.9	65.1	S	60.5	58.1	48.8	48.8	60.5	67.4	48.8
29	62.8	51.2	51.2	69.8	S	67.4	51.2	62.8	46.5	S	65.1	62.8
30	S		53.5	S	H	67.4	S	60.5	44.2	S	65.1	72.1
31	S		65.1		67.4		S	69.8		65.1		S

* See new trends developing on pages 70, 92, 141–146.
Based on NASDAQ composite, prior to Feb. 5, 1971; based on National Quotation Bureau indices.

125

RECENT NASDAQ COMPOSITE MARKET PROBABILITY CALENDAR 2016

THE % CHANCE OF THE MARKET RISING ON ANY TRADING DAY OF THE YEAR*
(Based on the number of times the NASDAQ rose on a particular trading day during January 1994–December 2014**)

Date	Jan	Feb	Mar	Apr	May	Jun	Jul	Aug	Sep	Oct	Nov	Dec
1	H	76.2	52.4	66.7	S	52.4	76.2	47.6	61.9	S	66.7	57.1
2	S	57.1	38.1	S	71.4	71.4	S	42.9	52.4	S	61.9	61.9
3	S	42.9	71.4	S	57.1	52.4	S	42.9	S	38.1	76.2	S
4	66.7	52.4	38.1	61.9	52.4	S	H	52.4	S	57.1	66.7	S
5	57.1	61.9	S	66.7	47.6	S	38.1	38.1	H	57.1	S	61.9
6	52.4	S	S	57.1	33.3	57.1	57.1	S	52.4	61.9	S	52.4
7	57.1	S	47.6	33.3	S	42.9	61.9	S	61.9	47.6	52.4	38.1
8	57.1	66.7	47.6	61.9	S	42.9	61.9	38.1	66.7	S	57.1	57.1
9	S	47.6	47.6	S	71.4	42.9	S	47.6	61.9	S	42.9	61.9
10	S	52.4	47.6	S	47.6	42.9	S	47.6	S	52.4	52.4	S
11	66.7	61.9	66.7	47.6	47.6	S	57.1	47.6	S	52.4	61.9	S
12	61.9	66.7	S	61.9	57.1	S	57.1	61.9	52.4	52.4	S	42.9
13	57.1	S	S	42.9	42.9	47.6	71.4	S	71.4	66.7	S	47.6
14	52.4	S	52.4	52.4	S	61.9	71.4	S	81.0	71.4	57.1	42.9
15	47.6	H	47.6	47.6	S	71.4	57.1	66.7	33.3	S	47.6	47.6
16	S	57.1	57.1	S	52.4	52.4	S	71.4	71.4	S	52.4	52.4
17	S	42.9	61.9	S	52.4	61.9	S	66.7	S	42.9	47.6	S
18	H	42.9	61.9	57.1	66.7	S	52.4	38.1	S	52.4	57.1	S
19	71.4	33.3	S	52.4	33.3	S	57.1	38.1	52.4	47.6	S	38.1
20	66.7	S	S	61.9	38.1	42.9	66.7	S	61.9	71.4	S	52.4
21	28.6	S	38.1	66.7	S	52.4	23.8	S	42.9	57.1	47.6	61.9
22	38.1	38.1	57.1	57.1	S	38.1	47.6	76.2	33.3	S	61.9	66.7
23	S	66.7	61.9	S	47.6	33.3	S	57.1	38.1	S	61.9	61.9
24	S	52.4	66.7	S	42.9	38.1	S	52.4	S	42.9	H	S
25	42.9	52.4	H	57.1	52.4	S	66.7	57.1	S	38.1	57.1	S
26	76.2	52.4	S	47.6	52.4	S	52.4	42.9	42.9	52.4	S	H
27	71.4	S	S	61.9	71.4	47.6	38.1	S	42.9	57.1	S	71.4
28	47.6	S	33.3	76.2	S	66.7	66.7	S	47.6	66.7	61.9	47.6
29	57.1	33.3	42.9	66.7	S	71.4	42.9	71.4	47.6	S	71.4	42.9
30	S		47.6	S	H	66.7	S	52.4	28.6	S	47.6	42.9
31	S		57.1		57.1		S	57.1		66.7		S

* See new trends developing on pages 70, 92, 141–146. ** Based on most recent 21-year period.

RUSSELL 1000 INDEX MARKET PROBABILITY CALENDAR 2016

THE % CHANCE OF THE MARKET RISING ON ANY TRADING DAY OF THE YEAR*
(Based on the number of times the RUSSELL 1000 rose on a particular trading day during **January 1980–December 2014**)

Date	Jan	Feb	Mar	Apr	May	Jun	Jul	Aug	Sep	Oct	Nov	Dec
1	H	65.7	57.1	62.9	S	57.1	74.3	45.7	54.3	S	71.4	51.4
2	S	60.0	48.6	S	57.1	57.1	S	42.9	48.6	S	57.1	54.3
3	S	57.1	60.0	S	62.9	48.6	S	48.6	S	54.3	62.9	S
4	42.9	51.4	42.9	62.9	54.3	S	H	45.7	S	57.1	62.9	S
5	57.1	62.9	S	51.4	40.0	S	40.0	51.4	H	51.4	S	62.9
6	60.0	S	S	54.3	42.9	57.1	45.7	S	51.4	60.0	S	40.0
7	51.4	S	45.7	45.7	S	34.3	57.1	S	42.9	40.0	48.6	45.7
8	51.4	51.4	57.1	65.7	S	42.9	57.1	57.1	48.6	S	54.3	48.6
9	S	40.0	54.3	S	54.3	40.0	S	48.6	57.1	S	48.6	54.3
10	S	68.6	45.7	S	57.1	48.6	S	45.7	S	54.3	57.1	S
11	62.9	65.7	60.0	57.1	54.3	S	51.4	42.9	S	37.1	60.0	S
12	57.1	45.7	S	54.3	54.3	S	57.1	60.0	62.9	40.0	S	42.9
13	57.1	S	S	45.7	51.4	57.1	68.6	S	65.7	65.7	S	45.7
14	57.1	S	45.7	57.1	S	62.9	80.0	S	60.0	68.6	54.3	42.9
15	71.4	H	57.1	68.6	S	62.9	48.6	62.9	51.4	S	48.6	51.4
16	S	62.9	60.0	S	54.3	51.4	S	62.9	51.4	S	48.6	60.0
17	S	37.1	57.1	S	54.3	62.9	S	65.7	S	57.1	60.0	S
18	H	45.7	51.4	60.0	57.1	S	51.4	62.9	S	54.3	51.4	S
19	65.7	40.0	S	48.6	45.7	S	48.6	48.6	45.7	42.9	S	51.4
20	42.9	S	S	54.3	48.6	37.1	62.9	S	48.6	74.3	S	45.7
21	34.3	S	42.9	54.3	S	48.6	37.1	S	40.0	48.6	51.4	71.4
22	48.6	42.9	45.7	54.3	S	51.4	40.0	71.4	42.9	S	62.9	60.0
23	S	48.6	48.6	S	42.9	40.0	S	51.4	37.1	S	60.0	62.9
24	S	42.9	57.1	S	60.0	34.3	S	57.1	S	40.0	H	S
25	51.4	60.0	H	45.7	62.9	S	74.3	42.9	S	34.3	65.7	S
26	62.9	60.0	S	54.3	57.1	S	51.4	54.3	42.9	57.1	S	H
27	60.0	S	S	57.1	57.1	42.9	42.9	S	45.7	54.3	S	71.4
28	57.1	S	34.3	57.1	S	51.4	65.7	S	65.7	65.7	71.4	57.1
29	60.0	57.1	48.6	60.0	S	60.0	57.1	57.1	54.3	S	65.7	65.7
30	S		42.9	S	H	48.6	S	45.7	45.7	S	48.6	51.4
31	S		51.4		57.1		S	60.0		65.7		S

* See new trends developing on pages 70, 92, 141–146.

RUSSELL 2000 INDEX MARKET PROBABILITY CALENDAR 2016

THE % CHANCE OF THE MARKET RISING ON ANY TRADING DAY OF THE YEAR*
(Based on the number of times the RUSSELL 2000 rose on a particular trading day during **January 1980–December 2014**)

Date	Jan	Feb	Mar	Apr	May	Jun	Jul	Aug	Sep	Oct	Nov	Dec
1	H	68.6	62.9	51.4	S	60.0	65.7	48.6	54.3	S	60.0	51.4
2	S	62.9	60.0	S	57.1	65.7	S	45.7	60.0	S	68.6	62.9
3	S	54.3	65.7	S	65.7	51.4	S	48.6	S	51.4	68.6	S
4	45.7	68.6	54.3	60.0	60.0	S	H	48.6	S	48.6	60.0	S
5	62.9	65.7	S	45.7	57.1	S	48.6	45.7	H	48.6	S	65.7
6	60.0	S	S	51.4	54.3	57.1	42.9	S	54.3	68.6	S	60.0
7	60.0	S	60.0	40.0	S	54.3	51.4	S	65.7	40.0	54.3	45.7
8	57.1	62.9	51.4	60.0	S	37.1	51.4	45.7	54.3	S	54.3	54.3
9	S	42.9	54.3	S	54.3	45.7	S	57.1	60.0	S	51.4	48.6
10	S	71.4	40.0	S	60.0	51.4	S	48.6	S	48.6	68.6	S
11	65.7	62.9	60.0	60.0	51.4	S	60.0	45.7	S	45.7	51.4	S
12	57.1	65.7	S	62.9	54.3	S	51.4	71.4	60.0	54.3	S	45.7
13	65.7	S	S	48.6	48.6	57.1	62.9	S	65.7	68.6	S	40.0
14	62.9	S	54.3	57.1	S	68.6	65.7	S	57.1	62.9	48.6	42.9
15	68.6	H	48.6	62.9	S	60.0	54.3	60.0	34.3	S	45.7	37.1
16	S	54.3	57.1	S	45.7	51.4	S	62.9	51.4	S	22.9	57.1
17	S	51.4	65.7	S	54.3	42.9	S	60.0	S	60.0	57.1	S
18	H	42.9	57.1	57.1	54.3	S	48.6	48.6	S	45.7	48.6	S
19	71.4	37.1	S	48.6	51.4	S	51.4	48.6	42.9	45.7	S	62.9
20	71.4	S	S	60.0	45.7	40.0	51.4	S	42.9	71.4	S	60.0
21	34.3	S	48.6	65.7	S	51.4	37.1	S	45.7	48.6	34.3	65.7
22	48.6	37.1	60.0	51.4	S	42.9	45.7	65.7	48.6	S	62.9	68.6
23	S	54.3	48.6	S	54.3	45.7	S	48.6	40.0	S	60.0	77.1
24	S	54.3	54.3	S	57.1	40.0	S	62.9	S	42.9	H	S
25	45.7	60.0	H	51.4	54.3	S	62.9	57.1	S	34.3	60.0	S
26	68.6	65.7	S	60.0	68.6	S	60.0	60.0	48.6	40.0	S	H
27	62.9	S	S	62.9	68.6	51.4	45.7	S	31.4	54.3	S	68.6
28	54.3	S	40.0	62.9	S	57.1	57.1	S	54.3	57.1	62.9	54.3
29	77.1	60.0	51.4	71.4	S	71.4	62.9	62.9	57.1	S	68.6	60.0
30	S		51.4	S	H	65.7	S	60.0	60.0	S	68.6	68.6
31	S		82.9		68.6		S	71.4		74.3		S

See new trends developing on pages 70, 92, 141–146.

128

DECENNIAL CYCLE: A MARKET PHENOMENON

By arranging each year's market gain or loss so that the first and succeeding years of each decade fall into the same column, certain interesting patterns emerge—strong fifth and eighth years; weak first, seventh, and zero years.

This fascinating phenomenon was first presented by Edgar Lawrence Smith in *Common Stocks and Business Cycles* (William-Frederick Press, 1959). Anthony Gaubis co-pioneered the decennial pattern with Smith.

When Smith first cut graphs of market prices into 10-year segments and placed them above one another, he observed that each decade tended to have three bull market cycles and that the longest and strongest bull markets seem to favor the middle years of a decade.

Don't place too much emphasis on the decennial cycle nowadays, other than the extraordinary fifth and zero years, as the stock market is more influenced by the quadrennial presidential election cycle, shown on page 130. Also, the last half-century, which has been the most prosperous in U.S. history, has distributed the returns among most years of the decade. Interestingly, NASDAQ suffered its worst bear market ever in a zero year.

Sixth years of decades are generally bullish, up eight of the last thirteen, but are only fifth-best by average percent change. 2016 is an election year, the second-best year of the 4-year cycle, so odds are favorable for a solid advance, especially if 2015 ends with sub-par gains.

THE 10-YEAR STOCK MARKET CYCLE
Annual % Change in Dow Jones Industrial Average
Year of Decade

DECADES	1st	2nd	3rd	4th	5th	6th	7th	8th	9th	10th
1881–1890	3.0%	−2.9%	−8.5%	−18.8%	20.1%	12.4%	−8.4%	4.8%	5.5%	−14.1%
1891–1900	17.6	−6.6	−24.6	−0.6	2.3	−1.7	21.3	22.5	9.2	7.0
1901–1910	−8.7	−0.4	−23.6	41.7	38.2	−1.9	−37.7	46.6	15.0	−17.9
1911–1920	0.4	7.6	−10.3	−5.4	81.7	−4.2	−21.7	10.5	30.5	−32.9
1921–1930	12.7	21.7	−3.3	26.2	30.0	0.3	28.8	48.2	−17.2	−33.8
1931–1940	−52.7	−23.1	66.7	4.1	38.5	24.8	−32.8	28.1	−2.9	−12.7
1941–1950	−15.4	7.6	13.8	12.1	26.6	−8.1	2.2	−2.1	12.9	17.6
1951–1960	14.4	8.4	−3.8	44.0	20.8	2.3	−12.8	34.0	16.4	−9.3
1961–1970	18.7	−10.8	17.0	14.6	10.9	−18.9	15.2	4.3	−15.2	4.8
1971–1980	6.1	14.6	−16.6	−27.6	38.3	17.9	−17.3	−3.1	4.2	14.9
1981–1990	−9.2	19.6	20.3	−3.7	27.7	22.6	2.3	11.8	27.0	−4.3
1991–2000	20.3	4.2	13.7	2.1	33.5	26.0	22.6	16.1	25.2	−6.2
2001–2010	−7.1	−16.8	25.3	3.1	−0.6	16.3	6.4	−33.8	18.8	11.0
2011–2020	5.5	7.3	26.5	7.5						
Total % Change	5.6%	30.4%	92.6%	99.3%	368.0%	87.3%	−31.9%	187.9%	129.4%	−75.9%
Avg % Change	0.4%	2.2%	6.6%	7.1%	28.3%	6.8%	−2.5%	14.5%	10.0%	−5.8%
Up Years	9	8	7	9	12	8	7	10	10	5
Down Years	5	6	7	5	1	5	6	3	3	8

Based on annual close; Cowles indices 1881–1885; 12 Mixed Stocks, 10 Rails, 2 Inds 1886–1889;

20 Mixed Stocks, 18 Rails, 2 Inds 1890–1896; Railroad average 1897 (First industrial average published May 26, 1896).

PRESIDENTIAL ELECTION/STOCK MARKET CYCLE: THE 182-YEAR SAGA CONTINUES

It is no mere coincidence that the last two years (pre-election year and election year) of the 45 administrations since 1833 produced a total net market gain of 731.3%, dwarfing the 299.6% gain of the first two years of these administrations.

Presidential elections every four years have a profound impact on the economy and the stock market. Wars, recessions, and bear markets tend to start or occur in the first half of the term; prosperous times and bull markets, in the latter half. After nine straight annual Dow gains during the millennial bull, the four-year election cycle reasserted its overarching domination of market behavior until 2008. Recovery from the worst recession since the Great Depression has produced six straight annual gains.

STOCK MARKET ACTION SINCE 1833
Annual % Change in Dow Jones Industrial Average[1]

4-Year Cycle Beginning	Elected President	Post-Election Year	Mid-Term Year	Pre-Election Year	Election Year
1833	Jackson (D)	−0.9	13.0	3.1	−11.7
1837	Van Buren (D)	−11.5	1.6	−12.3	5.5
1841*	W.H. Harrison (W)**	−13.3	−18.1	45.0	15.5
1845*	Polk (D)	8.1	−14.5	1.2	−3.6
1849*	Taylor (W)	N/C	18.7	−3.2	19.6
1853*	Pierce (D)	−12.7	−30.2	1.5	4.4
1857	Buchanan (D)	−31.0	14.3	−10.7	14.0
1861*	Lincoln (R)	−1.8	55.4	38.0	6.4
1865	Lincoln (R)**	−8.5	3.6	1.6	10.8
1869	Grant (R)	1.7	5.6	7.3	6.8
1873	Grant (R)	−12.7	2.8	−4.1	−17.9
1877	Hayes (R)	−9.4	6.1	43.0	18.7
1881	Garfield (R)**	3.0	−2.9	−8.5	−18.8
1885*	Cleveland (D)	20.1	12.4	−8.4	4.8
1889*	B. Harrison (R)	5.5	−14.1	17.6	−6.6
1893*	Cleveland (D)	−24.6	−0.6	2.3	−1.7
1897*	McKinley (R)	21.3	22.5	9.2	7.0
1901	McKinley (R)**	−8.7	−0.4	−23.6	41.7
1905	T. Roosevelt (R)	38.2	−1.9	−37.7	46.6
1909	Taft (R)	15.0	−17.9	0.4	7.6
1913*	Wilson (D)	−10.3	−5.4	81.7	−4.2
1917	Wilson (D)	−21.7	10.5	30.5	−32.9
1921*	Harding (R)**	12.7	21.7	−3.3	26.2
1925	Coolidge (R)	30.0	0.3	28.8	48.2
1929	Hoover (R)	−17.2	−33.8	−52.7	−23.1
1933*	F. Roosevelt (D)	66.7	4.1	38.5	24.8
1937	F. Roosevelt (D)	−32.8	28.1	−2.9	−12.7
1941	F. Roosevelt (D)	−15.4	7.6	13.8	12.1
1945	F. Roosevelt (D)**	26.6	−8.1	2.2	−2.1
1949	Truman (D)	12.9	17.6	14.4	8.4
1953*	Eisenhower (R)	−3.8	44.0	20.8	2.3
1957	Eisenhower (R)	−12.8	34.0	16.4	−9.3
1961*	Kennedy (D)**	18.7	−10.8	17.0	14.6
1965	Johnson (D)	10.9	−18.9	15.2	4.3
1969*	Nixon (R)	−15.2	4.8	6.1	14.6
1973	Nixon (R)***	−16.6	−27.6	38.3	17.9
1977*	Carter (D)	−17.3	−3.1	4.2	14.9
1981*	Reagan (R)	−9.2	19.6	20.3	−3.7
1985	Reagan (R)	27.7	22.6	2.3	11.8
1989	G. H. W. Bush (R)	27.0	−4.3	20.3	4.2
1993*	Clinton (D)	13.7	2.1	33.5	26.0
1997	Clinton (D)	22.6	16.1	25.2	−6.2
2001*	G. W. Bush (R)	−7.1	−16.8	25.3	3.1
2005	G. W. Bush (R)	−0.6	16.3	6.4	−33.8
2009*	Obama (D)	18.8	11.0	5.5	7.3
2013	Obama (D)	26.5	7.5		
Total % Gain		**112.6%**	**194.5%**	**469.5%**	**261.8%**
Average % Gain		**2.5%**	**4.2%**	**10.4%**	**5.8%**
# Up		21	28	34	30
# Down		24	18	11	15

*Party in power ousted   **Death in office   ***Resigned   **D**–Democrat, **W**–Whig, **R**–Republican
[1] Based on annual close; Prior to 1886 based on Cowles and other indices; 12 Mixed Stocks, 10 Rails, 2 Inds 1886–1889; 20 Mixed Stocks, 18 Rails, 2 Inds 1890–1896; Railroad average 1897 (First industrial average published May 26, 1896).

DOW JONES INDUSTRIALS BULL AND BEAR MARKETS SINCE 1900

Bear markets begin at the end of one bull market and end at the start of the next bull market (7/17/90 to 10/11/90 as an example). The high at Dow 3978.36 on 1/31/94, was followed by a 9.7 percent correction. A 10.3 percent correction occurred between the 5/22/96 closing high of 5778 and the intraday low on 7/16/96. The longest bull market on record ended on 7/17/98, and the shortest bear market on record ended on 8/31/98, when the new bull market began. The greatest bull super cycle in history that began 8/12/82 ended in 2000 after the Dow gained 1409% and NASDAQ climbed 3072%. The Dow gained only 497% in the eight-year super bull from 1921 to the top in 1929. NASDAQ suffered its worst loss ever from the 2000 top to the 2002 bottom, down 77.9%, nearly as much as the 89.2% drop in the Dow from the 1929 top to the 1932 bottom. The third-longest Dow bull since 1900 that began 10/9/02 ended on its fifth anniversary. The ensuing bear market was the second worst bear market since 1900, slashing the Dow 53.8%. European debt concerns in 2011 triggered a 16.8% Dow slide, ending the recovery bull shortly after its second anniversary. At press time, the current bull market was alive and well, making new all-time Dow highs. (See page 132 for S&P 500 and NASDAQ bulls and bears.)

DOW JONES INDUSTRIALS BULL AND BEAR MARKETS SINCE 1900

— Beginning —		— Ending —		Bull		Bear	
Date	DJIA	Date	DJIA	% Gain	Days	% Change	Days
9/24/00	38.80	6/17/01	57.33	47.8%	266	−46.1%	875
11/9/03	30.88	1/19/06	75.45	144.3	802	−48.5	665
11/15/07	38.83	11/19/09	73.64	89.6	735	−27.4	675
9/25/11	53.43	9/30/12	68.97	29.1	371	−24.1	668
7/30/14	52.32	11/21/16	110.15	110.5	845	−40.1	393
12/19/17	65.95	11/3/19	119.62	81.4	684	−46.6	660
8/24/21	63.90	3/20/23	105.38	64.9	573	−18.6	221
10/27/23	85.76	9/3/29	381.17	344.5	2138	−47.9	71
11/13/29	198.69	4/17/30	294.07	48.0	155	−86.0	813
7/8/32	41.22	9/7/32	79.93	93.9	61	−37.2	173
2/27/33	50.16	2/5/34	110.74	120.8	343	−22.8	171
7/26/34	85.51	3/10/37	194.40	127.3	958	−49.1	386
3/31/38	98.95	11/12/38	158.41	60.1	226	−23.3	147
4/8/39	121.44	9/12/39	155.92	28.4	157	−40.4	959
4/28/42	92.92	5/29/46	212.50	128.7	1492	−23.2	353
5/17/47	163.21	6/15/48	193.16	18.4	395	−16.3	363
6/13/49	161.60	1/5/53	293.79	81.8	1302	−13.0	252
9/14/53	255.49	4/6/56	521.05	103.9	935	−19.4	564
10/22/57	419.79	1/5/60	685.47	63.3	805	−17.4	294
10/25/60	566.05	12/13/61	734.91	29.8	414	−27.1	195
6/26/62	535.76	2/9/66	995.15	85.7	1324	−25.2	240
10/7/66	744.32	12/3/68	985.21	32.4	788	−35.9	539
5/26/70	631.16	4/28/71	950.82	50.6	337	−16.1	209
11/23/71	797.97	1/11/73	1051.70	31.8	415	−45.1	694
12/6/74	577.60	9/21/76	1014.79	75.7	655	−26.9	525
2/28/78	742.12	9/8/78	907.74	22.3	192	−16.4	591
4/21/80	759.13	4/27/81	1024.05	34.9	371	−24.1	472
8/12/82	776.92	11/29/83	1287.20	65.7	474	−15.6	238
7/24/84	1086.57	8/25/87	2722.42	150.6	1127	−36.1	55
10/19/87	1738.74	7/17/90	2999.75	72.5	1002	−21.2	86
10/11/90	2365.10	7/17/98	9337.97	294.8	2836	−19.3	45
8/31/98	7539.07	1/14/00	11722.98	55.5	501	−29.7	616
9/21/01	8235.81	3/19/02	10635.25	29.1	179	−31.5	204
10/9/02	7286.27	10/9/07	14164.53	94.4	1826	−53.8	517
3/9/09	6547.05	4/29/11	12810.54	95.7	781	−16.8	157
10/3/11	10655.30	3/2/15	18288.63	71.6*	1246*	*As of May 6, 2015 – not in averages	
		Average		**86.0%**	**756**	**−31.1%**	**402**

Based on Dow Jones Industrial Average.
The NYSE was closed from 7/31/1914 to 12/11/1914 due to World War I.
DJIA figures were then adjusted back to reflect the composition change from 12 to 20 stocks in September 1916.

1900–2000 Data: Ned Davis Research

STANDARD & POOR'S 500 BULL AND BEAR MARKETS SINCE 1929
NASDAQ COMPOSITE SINCE 1971

A constant debate of the definition and timing of bull and bear markets permeates Wall Street like the bell that signals the open and close of every trading day. We have relied on the Ned Davis Research parameters for years to track bulls and bears on the Dow (see page 131). Standard & Poor's 500 index has been a stalwart indicator for decades and at times marched to a different beat than the Dow. The moves of the S&P 500 and NASDAQ have been correlated to the bull and bear dates on page 131. Many dates line up for the three indices, but you will notice quite a lag or lead on several occasions, including NASDAQ's independent cadence from 1975 to 1980.

STANDARD & POOR'S 500 BULL AND BEAR MARKETS

— Beginning —		— Ending —		Bull		Bear	
Date	S&P 500	Date	S&P 500	% Gain	Days	% Change	Days
11/13/29	17.66	4/10/30	25.92	46.8%	148	−83.0%	783
6/1/32	4.40	9/7/32	9.31	111.6	98	−40.6	173
2/27/33	5.53	2/6/34	11.82	113.7	344	−31.8	401
3/14/35	8.06	3/6/37	18.68	131.8	723	−49.0	390
3/31/38	8.50	11/9/38	13.79	62.2	223	−26.2	150
4/8/39	10.18	10/25/39	13.21	29.8	200	−43.5	916
4/28/42	7.47	5/29/46	19.25	157.7	1492	−28.8	353
5/17/47	13.71	6/15/48	17.06	24.4	395	−20.6	363
6/13/49	13.55	1/5/53	26.66	96.8	1302	−14.8	252
9/14/53	22.71	8/2/56	49.74	119.0	1053	−21.6	446
10/22/57	38.98	8/3/59	60.71	55.7	650	−13.9	449
10/25/60	52.30	12/12/61	72.64	38.9	413	−28.0	196
6/26/62	52.32	2/9/66	94.06	79.8	1324	−22.2	240
10/7/66	73.20	11/29/68	108.37	48.0	784	−36.1	543
5/26/70	69.29	4/28/71	104.77	51.2	337	−13.9	209
11/23/71	90.16	1/11/73	120.24	33.4	415	−48.2	630
10/3/74	62.28	9/21/76	107.83	73.1	719	−19.4	531
3/6/78	86.90	9/12/78	106.99	23.1	190	−8.2	562
3/27/80	98.22	11/28/80	140.52	43.1	246	−27.1	622
8/12/82	102.42	10/10/83	172.65	68.6	424	−14.4	288
7/24/84	147.82	8/25/87	336.77	127.8	1127	−33.5	101
12/4/87	223.92	7/16/90	368.95	64.8	955	−19.9	87
10/11/90	295.46	7/17/98	1186.75	301.7	2836	−19.3	45
8/31/98	957.28	3/24/00	1527.46	59.6	571	−36.8	546
9/21/01	965.80	1/4/02	1172.51	21.4	105	−33.8	278
10/9/02	776.76	10/9/07	1565.15	101.5	1826	−56.8	517
3/9/09	676.53	4/29/11	1363.61	101.6	781	−19.4	157
10/3/11	1099.23	4/24/15	2117.69	92.7*	1299*	*As of May 6, 2015 – not in averages	
		Average		**81.0%**	**729**	**−30.2%**	**379**

NASDAQ COMPOSITE BULL AND BEAR MARKETS

— Beginning —		— Ending —		Bull		Bear	
Date	NASDAQ	Date	NASDAQ	% Gain	Days	% Change	Days
11/23/71	100.31	1/11/73	136.84	36.4%	415	−59.9%	630
10/3/74	54.87	7/15/75	88.00	60.4	285	−16.2	63
9/16/75	73.78	9/13/78	139.25	88.7	1093	−20.4	62
11/14/78	110.88	2/8/80	165.25	49.0	451	−24.9	48
3/27/80	124.09	5/29/81	223.47	80.1	428	−28.8	441
8/13/82	159.14	6/24/83	328.91	106.7	315	−31.5	397
7/25/84	225.30	8/26/87	455.26	102.1	1127	−35.9	63
10/28/87	291.88	10/9/89	485.73	66.4	712	−33.0	372
10/16/90	325.44	7/20/98	2014.25	518.9	2834	−29.5	80
10/8/98	1419.12	3/10/00	5048.62	255.8	519	−71.8	560
9/21/01	1423.19	1/4/02	2059.38	44.7	105	−45.9	278
10/9/02	1114.11	10/31/07	2859.12	156.6	1848	−55.6	495
3/9/09	1268.64	4/29/11	2873.54	126.5	781	−18.7	157
10/3/11	2335.83	4/24/15	5092.08	118.0*	1299*	*As of May 6, 2015 – not in averages	
		Average		**130.2%**	**839**	**−36.3%**	**280**

JANUARY DAILY POINT CHANGES DOW JONES INDUSTRIALS

Previous Month	2006	2007	2008	2009	2010	2011	2012	2013	2014	2015
Close	10717.50	12463.15	13264.82	8776.39	10428.05	11577.51	12217.56	13104.14	16576.66	17823.07
1	S	H	H	H	H	S	S	H	H	H
2	H	H*	−220.86	258.30	S	S	H	308.41	−135.31	9.92
3	129.91	11.37	12.76	S	S	93.24	179.82	−21.19	28.64	S
4	32.74	6.17	−256.54	S	155.91	20.43	21.04	43.85	S	S
5	2.00	−82.68	S	−81.80	−11.94	31.71	−2.72	S	S	−331.34
6	77.16	S	S	62.21	1.66	−25.58	−55.78	S	−44.89	−130.01
7	S	S	27.31	−245.40	33.18	−22.55	S	−50.92	105.84	212.88
8	S	25.48	−238.42	−27.24	11.33	S	S	−55.44	−68.20	323.35
9	52.59	−6.89	146.24	−143.28	S	S	32.77	61.66	−17.98	−170.50
10	−0.32	25.56	117.78	S	S	−37.31	69.78	80.71	−7.71	S
11	31.86	72.82	−246.79	S	45.80	34.43	−13.02	17.21	S	S
12	−81.08	41.10	S	−125.21	−36.73	83.56	21.57	S	S	−96.53
13	−2.49	S	S	−25.41	53.51	−23.54	−48.96	S	−179.11	−27.16
14	S	S	171.85	−248.42	29.78	55.48	S	18.89	115.92	−186.59
15	S	H	−277.04	12.35	−100.90	S	S	27.57	108.08	−106.38
16	H	26.51	−34.95	68.73	S	S	H	−23.66	−64.93	190.86
17	−63.55	−5.44	−306.95	S	S	H	60.01	84.79	41.55	S
18	−41.46	−9.22	−59.91	S	H	50.55	96.88	53.68	S	S
19	25.85	−2.40	S	H	115.78	−12.64	45.03	S	S	H
20	−213.32	S	S	−332.13	−122.28	−2.49	96.50	S	S	3.66
21	S	S	H	279.01	−213.27	49.04	S	H	−44.12	39.05
22	S	−88.37	−128.11	−105.30	−216.90	S	S	62.51	−41.10	259.70
23	21.38	56.64	298.98	−45.24	S	S	−11.66	67.12	−175.99	−141.38
24	23.45	87.97	108.44	S	S	108.68	−33.07	46.00	−318.24	S
25	−2.48	−119.21	−171.44	S	23.88	−3.33	81.21	70.65	S	S
26	99.73	−15.54	S	38.47	−2.57	8.25	−22.33	S	S	6.10
27	97.74	S	S	58.70	41.87	4.39	−74.17	S	−41.23	−291.49
28	S	S	176.72	200.72	−115.70	−166.13	S	−14.05	90.68	−195.84
29	S	3.76	96.41	−226.44	−53.13	S	S	72.49	−189.77	225.48
30	−7.29	32.53	−37.47	−148.15	S	S	−6.74	−44.00	109.82	−251.90
31	−35.06	98.38	207.53	S	S	68.23	−20.81	−49.84	−149.76	S
Close	10864.86	12621.69	12650.36	8000.86	10067.33	11891.93	12632.91	13860.58	15698.85	17164.95
Change	147.36	158.54	−614.46	−775.53	−360.72	314.42	415.35	756.44	−877.81	−658.12

* Ford funeral

FEBRUARY DAILY POINT CHANGES DOW JONES INDUSTRIALS

Previous Month	2006	2007	2008	2009	2010	2011	2012	2013	2014	2015
Close	10864.86	12621.69	12650.36	8000.86	10067.33	11891.93	12632.91	13860.58	15698.85	17164.95
1	89.09	51.99	92.83	S	118.20	148.23	83.55	149.21	S	S
2	−101.97	−20.19	S	−64.03	111.32	1.81	−11.05	S	S	196.09
3	−58.36	S	S	141.53	−26.30	20.29	156.82	S	−326.05	305.36
4	S	S	−108.03	−121.70	−268.37	29.89	S	−129.71	72.44	6.62
5	S	8.25	−370.03	106.41	10.05	S	S	99.22	−5.01	211.86
6	4.65	4.57	−65.03	217.52	S	S	−17.10	7.22	188.30	−60.59
7	−48.51	0.56	46.90	S	S	69.48	33.07	−42.47	165.55	S
8	108.86	−29.24	−64.87	S	−103.84	71.52	5.75	48.92	S	S
9	24.73	−56.80	S	−9.72	150.25	6.74	6.51	S	S	−95.08
10	35.70	S	S	−381.99	−20.26	−10.60	−89.23	S	7.71	139.55
11	S	S	57.88	50.65	105.81	43.97	S	−21.73	192.98	−6.62
12	S	−28.28	133.40	−6.77	−45.05	S	S	47.46	−30.83	110.24
13	−26.73	102.30	178.83	−82.35	S	S	72.81	−35.79	63.65	46.97
14	136.07	87.01	−175.26	S	S	−5.07	4.24	−9.52	126.80	S
15	30.58	23.15	−28.77	S	H	−41.55	−97.33	8.37	S	S
16	61.71	2.56	S	H	169.67	61.53	123.13	S	S	H
17	−5.36	S	S	−297.81	40.43	29.97	45.79	S	H	28.23
18	S	S		3.03	83.66	73.11	S	S	−23.99	−17.73
19	S	H	−10.99	−89.68	9.45	S	S	53.91	−89.84	−44.08
20	H	19.07	90.04	−100.28	S	S	H	−108.13	92.67	154.67
21	−46.26	−48.23	−142.96	S	S	H	15.82	−46.92	−29.93	S
22	68.11	−52.39	96.72	S	−18.97	−178.46	−27.02	119.95	S	S
23	−67.95	−38.54	S	−250.89	−100.97	−107.01	46.02	S	S	−23.60
24	−7.37	S	S	236.16	91.75	−37.28	−1.74	S	103.84	92.35
25	S	S	189.20	−80.05	−53.13	61.95	S	−216.40	−27.48	15.38
26	S	−15.22	114.70	−88.81	4.23	S	S	115.96	18.75	−10.15
27	35.70	−416.02	9.36	−119.15	S	S	−1.44	175.24	74.24	−81.72
28	−104.14	52.39	−112.10	S	S	95.89	23.61	−20.88	49.06	S
29	—	—	−315.79	S	S	—	−53.05	—	—	—
Close	10993.41	12268.63	12266.39	7062.93	10325.26	12226.34	12952.07	14054.49	16321.71	18132.70
Change	128.55	−353.06	−383.97	−937.93	257.93	334.41	319.16	193.91	622.86	967.75

MARCH DAILY POINT CHANGES DOW JONES INDUSTRIALS

	2006	2007	2008	2009	2010	2011	2012	2013	2014	2015
Previous Month Close	10993.41	12268.63	12266.39	7062.93	10325.26	12226.34	12952.07	14054.49	16321.71	18132.70
1	60.12	-34.29	S	S	78.53	-168.32	28.23	35.17	S	S
2	-28.02	-120.24	S	-299.64	2.19	8.78	-2.73	S	S	155.93
3	-3.92	S	-7.49	-37.27	-9.22	191.40	S	S	-153.68	-85.26
4	S	S	-45.10	149.82	47.38	-88.32	S	38.16	227.85	-106.47
5	S	-63.69	41.19	-281.40	122.06	S	-14.76	125.95	-35.70	38.82
6	-63.00	157.18	-214.60	32.50	S	S	-203.66	42.47	61.71	-278.94
7	22.10	-15.14	-146.70	S	S	-79.85	78.18	33.25	30.83	S
8	25.05	68.25	S	S	-13.68	124.35	70.61	67.58	S	S
9	-33.46	15.62	S	-79.89	11.86	-1.29	14.08	S	S	138.94
10	104.06	S	-153.54	379.44	2.95	-228.48	S	S	-34.04	-332.78
11	S	S	416.66	3.91	44.51	59.79	S	50.22	-67.43	-27.55
12	S	42.30	-46.57	239.66	12.85	S	37.69	2.77	-11.17	259.83
13	-0.32	-242.66	35.50	53.92	S	S	217.97	5.22	-231.19	-145.91
14	75.32	57.44	-194.65	S	S	-51.24	16.42	83.86	-43.22	S
15	58.43	26.28	S	S	17.46	-137.74	58.66	-25.03	S	S
16	43.47	-49.27	S	-7.01	43.83	-242.12	-20.14	S	S	228.11
17	26.41	S	21.16	178.73	47.69	161.29	S	S	181.55	-128.34
18	S	S	420.41	90.88	45.50	83.93	S	-62.05	88.97	227.11
19	S	115.76	-293.00	-85.78	-37.19	S	6.51	3.76	-114.02	-117.16
20	-5.12	61.93	261.66	-122.42	S	S	-68.94	55.91	108.88	168.62
21	-39.06	159.42	H	S	S	178.01	-45.57	-90.24	-28.28	S
22	81.96	13.62	S	S	43.91	-17.90	-78.48	90.54	S	S
23	-47.14	19.87	S	497.48	102.94	67.39	34.59	S	S	-11.61
24	9.68	S	187.32	-115.89	-52.68	84.54	S	S	-26.08	-104.90
25	S	S	-16.04	89.84	5.06	50.03	S	-64.28	91.19	-292.60
26	S	-11.94	-109.74	174.75	9.15	S	160.90	111.90	-98.89	-40.31
27	-29.86	-71.78	-120.40	-148.38	S	S	-43.90	-33.49	-4.76	34.43
28	-95.57	-96.93	-86.06	S	S	-22.71	-71.52	52.38	58.83	S
29	61.16	48.39	S	S	45.50	81.13	19.61	H	S	S
30	-65.00	5.60	S	-254.16	11.56	71.60	66.22	S	S	263.65
31	-41.38	S	46.49	86.90	-50.79	-30.88	S	S	134.60	-200.19
Close	11109.32	12354.35	12262.89	7608.92	10856.63	12319.73	13212.04	14578.54	16457.66	17776.12
Change	115.91	85.72	-3.50	545.99	531.37	93.39	259.97	524.05	135.95	-356.58

APRIL DAILY POINT CHANGES DOW JONES INDUSTRIALS

	2006	2007	2008	2009	2010	2011	2012	2013	2014	2015
Previous Month Close	11109.32	12354.35	12262.89	7608.92	10856.63	12319.73	13212.04	14578.54	16457.66	17776.12
1	S	S	391.47	152.68	70.44	56.99	S	-5.69	74.95	-77.94
2	S	27.95	-48.53	216.48	H	S	52.45	89.16	40.39	65.06
3	35.62	128.00	20.20	39.51	S	S	-64.94	-111.66	-0.45	H
4	58.91	19.75	-16.61	S	S	23.31	-124.80	55.76	-159.84	S
5	35.70	30.15	S	S	46.48	-6.13	-14.61	-40.86	S	S
6	-23.05	H	S	-41.74	-3.56	32.85	H	S	S	117.61
7	-96.46	S	3.01	-186.29	-72.47	-17.26	S	S	-166.84	-5.43
8	S	S	-35.99	47.55	29.55	-29.44	S	48.23	10.27	27.09
9	S	8.94	-49.18	246.27	70.28	S	-130.55	59.98	181.04	56.22
10	21.29	4.71	54.72	H	S	S	-213.66	128.78	-266.96	98.92
11	-51.70	-89.23	-256.56	S	S	1.06	89.46	62.90	-143.47	S
12	40.34	68.34	S	S	8.62	-117.53	181.19	-0.08	S	S
13	7.68	59.17	S	-25.57	13.45	7.41	-136.99	S	S	-80.61
14	H	S	-23.36	-137.63	103.69	14.16	S	S	146.49	59.66
15	S	S	60.41	109.44	21.46	56.68	S	-265.86	89.32	75.91
16	S	108.33	256.80	95.81	-125.91	S	71.82	157.58	162.29	-6.84
17	-63.87	52.58	1.22	5.90	S	S	194.13	-138.19	-16.31	-279.47
18	194.99	30.80	228.87	S	S	-140.24	-82.79	-81.45	H	S
19	10.00	4.79	S	S	73.39	65.16	-68.65	10.37	S	S
20	64.12	153.35	S	-289.60	25.01	186.79	65.16	S	S	208.63
21	4.56	S	-24.34	127.83	7.86	52.45	S	S	40.71	-85.34
22	S	S	-104.79	-82.99	9.37	H	S	19.66	65.12	88.68
23	S	-42.58	42.99	70.49	69.99	S	-102.09	152.29	-12.72	20.42
24	-11.13	34.54	85.73	119.23	S	S	74.39	-43.16	0.00	21.45
25	-53.07	135.95	42.91	S	S	-26.11	89.16	24.50	-140.19	S
26	71.24	15.61	S	S	0.75	115.49	113.90	11.75	S	S
27	28.02	15.44	S	-51.29	-213.04	95.59	23.69	S	S	-42.17
28	-15.37	S	-20.11	-8.05	53.28	72.35	S	S	87.28	72.17
29	S	S	-39.81	168.78	122.05	47.23	S	106.20	86.63	-74.61
30	S	-58.03	-11.81	-17.61	-158.71	S	-14.68	21.05	45.47	-195.01
Close	11367.14	13062.91	12820.13	8168.12	11008.61	12810.54	13213.63	14839.80	16580.84	17840.52
Change	257.82	708.56	557.24	559.20	151.98	490.81	1.59	261.26	123.18	64.40

134

MAY DAILY POINT CHANGES DOW JONES INDUSTRIALS

Previous Month	2005	2006	2007	2008	2009	2010	2011	2012	2013	2014
Close	10192.51	11367.14	13062.91	12820.13	8168.12	11008.61	12810.54	13213.63	14839.80	16580.84
1	S	−23.85	73.23	189.87	44.29	S	S	65.69	−138.85	−21.97
2	59.19	73.16	75.74	48.20	S	S	−3.18	−10.75	130.63	−45.98
3	5.25	−16.17	29.50	S	S	143.22	0.15	−61.98	142.38	S
4	127.69	38.58	23.24	S	214.33	−225.06	−83.93	−168.32	S	S
5	−44.26	138.88	S	−88.66	−16.09	−58.65	−139.41	S	S	17.66
6	5.02	S	S	51.29	101.63	−347.80	54.57	S	−5.07	−129.53
7	S	S	48.35	−206.48	−102.43	−139.89	S	−29.74	87.31	117.52
8	S	6.80	−3.90	52.43	164.80	S	S	−76.44	48.92	32.43
9	38.94	55.23	53.80	−120.90	S	S	45.94	−97.03	−22.50	32.37
10	−103.23	2.88	−147.74	S	S	404.71	75.68	19.98	35.87	S
11	19.14	−141.92	111.09	S	−155.88	−36.88	−130.33	−34.44	S	S
12	−110.77	−119.74	S	130.43	50.34	148.65	65.89	S	S	112.13
13	−49.36	S	S	−44.13	−184.22	−113.96	−100.17	S	−26.81	19.97
14	S	S	20.56	66.20	46.43	−162.79	S	−125.25	123.57	−101.47
15	S	47.78	37.06	94.28	−62.68	S	S	−63.35	60.44	−167.16
16	112.17	−8.88	103.69	−5.86	S	S	−47.38	−33.45	−42.47	44.50
17	79.59	−214.28	−10.81	S	S	5.67	−68.79	−156.06	121.18	S
18	132.57	−77.32	79.81	S	235.44	−114.88	80.60	−73.11	S	S
19	28.74	15.77	S	41.36	−29.23	−66.58	45.14	S	S	20.55
20	−21.28	S	S	−199.48	−52.81	−376.36	−93.28	S	−19.12	−137.55
21	S	S	−13.65	−227.49	−129.91	125.38	S	135.10	52.30	158.75
22	S	−18.73	−2.93	24.43	−14.81	S	S	−1.67	−80.41	10.02
23	51.65	−26.98	−14.30	−145.99	S	S	−130.78	−6.66	−12.67	63.19
24	−19.88	18.97	−84.52	S	S	−126.82	−25.05	33.60	8.60	S
25	−45.88	93.73	66.15	S	H	−22.82	38.45	−74.92	S	S
26	79.80	67.56	S	H	196.17	−69.30	8.10	S	S	H
27	4.95	S	S	68.72	−173.47	284.54	38.82	S	H	69.23
28	S	S	H	45.68	103.78	−122.36	S	H	106.29	−42.32
29	S	H	14.06	52.19	96.53	S	S	125.86	−106.59	65.56
30	H	−184.18	111.74	−7.90	S	S	H	−160.83	21.73	18.43
31	−75.07	73.88	−5.44	S	S	H	128.21	−26.41	−208.96	S
Close	10467.48	11168.31	13627.64	12638.32	8500.33	10136.63	12569.79	12393.45	15115.57	16717.17
Change	274.97	−198.83	564.73	−181.81	332.21	−871.98	−240.75	−820.18	275.77	136.33

JUNE DAILY POINT CHANGES DOW JONES INDUSTRIALS

Previous Month	2005	2006	2007	2008	2009	2010	2011	2012	2013	2014
Close	10467.48	11168.31	13627.64	12638.32	8500.33	10136.63	12569.79	12393.45	15115.57	16717.17
1	82.39	91.97	40.47	S	221.11	−112.61	−279.65	−274.88	S	S
2	3.62	−12.41	S	−134.50	19.43	225.52	−41.59	S	S	26.46
3	−92.52	S	S	−100.97	−65.59	5.74	−97.29	S	138.46	−21.29
4	S	S	8.21	−12.37	74.96	−323.31	S	−17.11	−76.49	15.19
5	S	−199.15	−80.86	213.97	12.89	S	S	26.49	−216.95	98.58
6	6.06	−46.58	−129.79	−394.64	S	S	−61.30	286.84	80.03	88.17
7	16.04	−71.24	−198.94	S	S	−115.48	−19.15	46.17	207.50	S
8	−6.21	7.92	157.66	S	1.36	123.49	−21.87	93.24	S	S
9	26.16	−46.90	S	70.51	−1.43	−40.73	75.42	S	S	18.82
10	9.61	S	S	9.44	−24.04	273.28	−172.45	S	−9.53	2.82
11	S	S	0.57	−205.99	31.90	38.54	S	−142.97	−116.57	−102.04
12	S	−99.34	−129.95	57.81	28.34	S	S	162.57	−126.79	−109.69
13	9.93	−86.44	187.34	165.77	S	S	1.06	−77.42	180.85	41.55
14	25.01	110.78	71.37	S	S	−20.18	123.14	155.53	−105.90	S
15	18.80	198.27	85.76	S	−187.13	213.88	−178.84	115.26	S	S
16	12.28	−0.64	S	−38.27	−107.46	4.69	64.25	S	S	5.27
17	44.42	S	S	−108.78	−7.49	24.71	42.84	S	109.67	27.48
18	S	S	−26.50	−131.24	58.42	16.47	S	−25.35	138.38	98.13
19	S	−72.44	22.44	34.03	−15.87	S	S	95.51	−206.04	14.84
20	−13.96	32.73	−146.00	−220.40	S	S	76.02	−12.94	−353.87	25.62
21	−9.44	104.62	56.42	S	S	−8.23	109.63	−250.82	41.08	S
22	−11.74	−60.35	−185.58	S	−200.72	−148.89	−80.34	67.21	S	S
23	−166.49	−30.02	S	−0.33	−16.10	4.92	−59.67	S	S	−9.82
24	−123.60	S	S	−34.93	−23.05	−145.64	−115.42	S	−139.84	−119.13
25	S	S	−8.21	4.40	172.54	−8.99	S	−138.12	100.75	49.38
26	S	56.19	−14.39	−358.41	−34.01	S	S	32.01	149.83	−21.38
27	−7.06	−120.54	90.07	−106.91	S	S	108.98	92.34	114.35	5.71
28	114.85	48.82	−5.45	S	S	−5.29	145.13	−24.75	−114.89	S
29	−31.15	217.24	−13.66	S	90.99	−268.22	72.73	277.83	S	S
30	−99.51	−40.58	S	3.50	−82.38	−96.28	152.92	S	S	−25.24
Close	10274.97	11150.22	13408.62	11350.01	8447.00	9774.02	12414.34	12880.09	14909.60	16826.60
Change	−192.51	−18.09	−219.02	−1288.31	−53.33	−362.61	−155.45	486.64	−205.97	109.43

JULY DAILY POINT CHANGES DOW JONES INDUSTRIALS

Previous Month	2005	2006	2007	2008	2009	2010	2011	2012	2013	2014
Close	10274.97	11150.22	13408.62	11350.01	8447.00	9774.02	12414.34	12880.09	14909.60	16826.60
1	28.47	S	S	32.25	57.06	-41.49	168.43	S	65.36	129.47
2	S	S	126.81	-166.75	-223.32	-46.05	S	-8.70	-42.55	20.17
3	S	77.80*	41.87*	73.03*	H	S	S	72.43*	56.14*	92.02
4	H	H	H	H	S	S	H	H	H	H
5	68.36	-76.20	-11.46	S	S	H	-12.90	-47.15	147.29	S
6	-101.12	73.48	45.84	S	44.13	57.14	56.15	-124.20	S	S
7	31.61	-134.63	S	-56.58	-161.27	274.66	93.47	S	S	-44.05
8	146.85	S	S	152.25	14.81	120.71	-62.29	S	88.85	-117.59
9	S	S	38.29	-236.77	4.76	59.04	S	-36.18	75.65	78.99
10	S	12.88	-148.27	81.58	-36.65	S	S	-83.17	-8.68	-70.54
11	70.58	31.22	76.17	-128.48	S	S	-151.44	-48.59	169.26	28.74
12	-5.83	-121.59	283.86	S	S	18.24	-58.88	-31.26	3.38	S
13	43.50	-166.89	45.52	S	185.16	146.75	44.73	203.82	S	S
14	71.50	-106.94	S	-45.35	27.81	3.70	-54.49	S	S	111.61
15	11.94	S	S	-92.65	256.72	-7.41	42.61	S	19.96	5.26
16	S	S	43.73	276.74	95.61	-261.41	S	-49.88	-32.41	77.52
17	S	8.01	20.57	207.38	32.12	S	S	78.33	18.67	-161.39
18	-65.84	51.87	-53.33	49.91	S	S	-94.57	103.16	78.02	123.37
19	71.57	212.19	82.19	S	S	56.53	202.26	34.66	-4.80	S
20	42.59	-83.32	-149.33	S	104.21	75.53	-15.51	-120.79	S	S
21	-61.38	-59.72	S	-29.23	67.79	-109.43	152.50	S	S	-48.45
22	23.41	S	S	135.16	-34.68	201.77	-43.25	S	1.81	61.81
23	S	S	92.34	29.88	188.03	102.32	S	-101.11	22.19	-26.91
24	S	182.67	-226.47	-283.10	23.95	S	S	-104.14	-25.50	-2.83
25	-54.70	52.66	68.12	21.41	S	S	-88.36	58.73	13.37	-123.23
26	-16.71	-1.20	-311.50	S	S	100.81	-91.50	211.88	3.22	S
27	57.32	-2.08	-208.10	S	15.27	12.26	-198.75	187.73	S	S
28	68.46	119.27	S	-239.61	-11.79	-39.81	-62.44	S	S	22.02
29	-64.64	S	S	266.48	-26.00	-30.72	-96.87	S	-36.86	-70.48
30	S	S	92.84	186.13	83.74	-1.22	S	-2.65	-1.38	-31.75
31	S	-34.02	-146.32	-205.67	17.15	S	S	-64.33	-21.05	-317.06
Close	10640.91	11185.68	13211.99	11378.02	9171.61	10465.94	12143.24	13008.68	15499.54	16563.30
Change	365.94	35.46	-196.63	28.01	724.61	691.92	-271.10	128.59	589.94	-263.30

* Shortened trading day

AUGUST DAILY POINT CHANGES DOW JONES INDUSTRIALS

Previous Month	2005	2006	2007	2008	2009	2010	2011	2012	2013	2014
Close	10640.91	11185.68	13211.99	11378.02	9171.61	10465.94	12143.24	13008.68	15499.54	16563.30
1	-17.76	-59.95	150.38	-51.70	S	S	-10.75	-37.62	128.48	-69.93
2	60.59	74.20	100.96	S	S	208.44	-265.87	-92.18	30.34	S
3	13.85	42.66	-281.42	S	114.95	-38.00	29.82	217.29	S	S
4	-87.49	-2.24	S	-42.17	33.63	44.05	-512.76	S	S	75.91
5	-52.07	S	S	331.62	-39.22	-5.45	60.93	S	-46.23	-139.81
6	S	S	286.87	40.30	-24.71	-21.42	S	21.34	-93.39	13.87
7	S	-20.97	35.52	-224.64	113.81	S	S	51.09	-48.07	-75.07
8	-21.10	-45.79	153.56	302.89	S	S	-634.76	7.04	27.65	185.66
9	78.74	-97.41	-387.18	S	S	45.19	429.92	-10.45	-72.81	S
10	-21.26	48.19	-31.14	S	-32.12	-54.50	-519.83	42.76	S	S
11	91.48	-36.34	S	48.03	-96.50	-265.42	423.37	S	S	16.05
12	-85.58	S	S	-139.88	120.16	-58.88	125.71	S	-5.83	-9.44
13	S	S	-3.01	-109.51	36.58	-16.80	S	-38.52	31.33	91.26
14	S	9.84	-207.61	82.97	-76.79	S	S	2.71	-113.35	61.78
15	34.07	132.39	-167.45	43.97	S	S	213.88	-7.36	-225.47	-50.67
16	-120.93	96.86	-15.69	S	S	-1.14	-76.97	85.33	-30.72	S
17	37.26	7.84	233.30	S	-186.06	103.84	4.28	25.09	S	S
18	4.22	46.51	S	-180.51	82.60	9.69	-419.63	S	S	175.83
19	4.30	S	S	-130.84	61.22	-144.33	-172.93	S	-70.73	80.85
20	S	S	42.27	68.88	70.89	-57.59	S	-3.56	-7.75	59.54
21	S	-36.42	-30.49	12.78	155.91	S	S	-68.06	-105.44	60.36
22	10.66	-5.21	145.27	197.85	S	S	37.00	-30.82	66.19	-38.27
23	-50.31	-41.94	-0.25	S	S	-39.21	322.11	-115.30	46.77	S
24	-84.71	6.56	142.99	S	3.32	-133.96	143.95	100.51	S	S
25	15.76	-20.41	S	-241.81	30.01	19.61	-170.89	S	S	75.65
26	-53.34	S	S	26.62	4.23	-74.25	134.72	S	-64.05	29.83
27	S	S	-56.74	89.64	37.11	164.84	S	-33.30	-170.33	15.31
28	S	67.96	-280.28	212.67	-36.43	S	S	-21.68	48.38	-42.44
29	65.76	17.93	247.44	-171.63	S	S	254.71	4.49	16.44	18.88
30	-50.23	12.97	-50.56	S	S	-140.92	20.70	-106.77	-30.64	S
31	68.78	-1.76	119.01	S	-47.92	4.99	53.58	90.13	S	S
Close	10481.60	11381.15	13357.74	11543.55	9496.28	10014.72	11613.53	13090.84	14810.31	17098.45
Change	-159.31	195.47	145.75	165.53	324.67	-451.22	-529.71	82.16	-689.23	535.15

Previous Month Close	2005	2006	2007	2008	2009	2010	2011	2012	2013	2014
	10481.60	11381.15	13357.74	11543.55	9496.28	10014.72	11613.53	13090.84	14810.31	17098.45
1	−21.97	83.00	S	H	−185.68	254.75	−119.96	S	S	H
2	−12.26	S	S	−26.63	−29.93	50.63	−253.31	S	H	−30.89
3	S	S	H	15.96	63.94	157.83	S	H	23.65	10.72
4	S	H	91.12	−344.65	96.66	S	S	−54.90	96.91	−8.70
5	H	5.13	−143.39	32.73	S	S	H	11.54	6.61	67.78
6	141.87	−63.08	57.88	S	S	H	−100.96	244.52	−14.98	S
7	44.26	−74.76	−249.97	S	H	−137.24	275.56	14.64	S	S
8	−37.57	60.67	S	289.78	56.07	46.32	−119.05	S	S	−25.94
9	82.63	S	S	−280.01	49.88	28.23	−303.68	S	140.62	−97.55
10	S	S	14.47	38.19	80.26	47.53	S	−52.35	127.94	54.84
11	S	4.73	180.54	164.79	−22.07	S	S	69.07	135.54	−19.71
12	4.38	101.25	−16.74	−11.72	S	S	68.99	9.99	−25.96	−61.49
13	−85.50	45.23	133.23	S	S	81.36	44.73	206.51	75.42	S
14	−52.54	−15.93	17.64	S	21.39	−17.64	140.88	53.51	S	S
15	13.85	33.38	S	−504.48	56.61	46.24	186.45	S	S	43.63
16	83.19	S	S	141.51	108.30	22.10	75.91	S	118.72	100.83
17	S	S	−39.10	−449.36	−7.79	13.02	S	−40.27	34.95	24.88
18	S	−5.77	335.97	410.03	36.28	S	S	11.54	147.21	109.14
19	−84.31	−14.09	76.17	368.75	S	S	−108.08	13.32	−40.39	13.75
20	−76.11	72.28	−48.86	S	S	145.77	7.65	18.97	−185.46	S
21	−103.49	−79.96	53.49	S	−41.34	7.41	−283.82	−17.46	S	S
22	44.02	−25.13	S	−372.75	51.01	−21.72	−391.01	S	S	−107.06
23	−2.46	S	S	−161.52	−81.32	−76.89	37.65	S	−49.71	−116.81
24	S	S	−61.13	−29.00	−41.11	197.84	S	−20.55	−66.79	154.19
25	S	67.71	19.59	196.89	−42.25	S	S	−101.37	−61.33	−264.26
26	24.04	93.58	99.50	121.07	S	S	272.38	−44.04	55.04	167.35
27	12.58	19.85	34.79	S	S	−48.22	146.83	72.46	−70.06	S
28	16.88	29.21	−17.31	S	124.17	46.10	−179.79	−48.84	S	S
29	79.69	−39.38	S	−777.68	−47.16	−22.86	143.08	S	S	−41.93
30	15.92	S	S	485.21	−29.92	−47.23	−240.60	S	−128.57	−28.32
Close	10568.70	11679.07	13895.63	10850.66	9712.28	10788.05	10913.38	13437.13	15129.67	17042.90
Change	87.10	297.92	537.89	−692.89	216.00	773.33	−700.15	346.29	319.36	−55.55

Previous Month Close	2005	2006	2007	2008	2009	2010	2011	2012	2013	2014
	10568.70	11679.07	13895.63	10850.66	9712.28	10788.05	10913.38	13437.13	15129.67	17042.90
1	S	S	191.92	−19.59	−203.00	41.63	S	77.98	62.03	−238.19
2	S	−8.72	−40.24	−348.22	−21.61	S	S	−32.75	−58.56	−3.66
3	−33.22	56.99	−79.26	−157.47	S	S	−258.08	12.25	−136.66	208.64
4	−94.37	123.27	6.26	S	S	−78.41	153.41	80.75	76.10	S
5	−123.75	16.08	91.70	S	112.08	193.45	131.24	34.79	S	S
6	−30.26	−16.48	S	−369.88	131.50	22.93	183.38	S	S	−17.78
7	5.21	S	S	−508.39	−5.67	−19.07	−20.21	S	−136.34	−272.52
8	S	S	−22.28	−189.01	61.29	57.90	S	−26.50	−159.71	274.83
9	S	7.60	120.80	−678.91	78.07	S	S	−110.12	26.45	−334.97
10	−53.55	9.36	−85.84	−128.00	S	S	330.06	−128.56	323.09	−115.15
11	14.41	−15.04	−63.57	S	S	3.86	−16.88	−18.58	111.04	S
12	−36.26	95.57	77.96	S	20.86	10.06	102.55	2.46	S	S
13	−0.32	12.81	S	936.42	−14.74	75.68	−40.72	S	S	−223.03
14	70.75	S	S	−76.62	144.80	−1.51	166.36	S	64.15	−5.88
15	S	S	−108.28	−733.08	47.08	−31.79	S	95.38	−133.25	−173.45
16	S	20.09	−71.86	401.35	−67.03	S	S	127.55	205.82	−24.50
17	60.76	−30.58	−20.40	−127.04	S	S	−247.49	5.22	−2.18	263.17
18	−62.84	42.66	−3.58	S	S	80.91	180.05	−8.06	28.00	S
19	128.87	19.05	−366.94	S	96.28	−165.07	−72.43	−205.43	S	S
20	−133.03	−9.36	S	413.21	−50.71	129.35	37.16	S	S	19.26
21	−65.88	S	S	−231.77	−92.12	38.60	267.01	S	−7.45	215.14
22	S	S	44.95	−514.45	131.95	−14.01	S	2.38	75.46	−153.49
23	S	114.54	109.26	172.04	−109.13	S	S	−243.36	−54.33	216.58
24	169.78	10.97	−0.98	−312.30	S	S	104.83	−25.19	95.88	127.51
25	−7.13	6.80	−3.33	S	S	31.49	−207.00	26.34	61.07	S
26	−32.89	28.98	134.78	S	−104.22	5.41	162.42	3.53	S	S
27	−115.03	−73.40	S	−203.18	14.21	−43.18	339.51	S	S	12.53
28	172.82	S	S	889.35	−119.48	−12.33	22.56	S	−1.35	187.81
29	S	S	63.56	−74.16	199.89	4.54	S	H*	111.42	−31.44
30	S	−3.76	−77.79	189.73	−249.85	S	S	H*	−61.59	221.11
31	37.30	−5.77	137.54	144.32	S	S	−276.10	−10.75	−73.01	195.10
Close	10440.07	12080.73	13930.01	9325.01	9712.73	11118.49	11955.01	13096.46	15545.75	17390.52
Change	−128.63	401.66	34.38	−1525.65	0.45	330.44	1041.63	−340.67	416.08	347.62

* Hurricane Sandy

NOVEMBER DAILY POINT CHANGES DOW JONES INDUSTRIALS

Previous Month	2005	2006	2007	2008	2009	2010	2011	2012	2013	2014
Close	10440.07	12080.73	13930.01	9325.01	9712.73	11118.49	11955.01	13096.46	15545.75	17390.52
1	−33.30	−49.71	−362.14	S	S	6.13	−297.05	136.16	69.80	S
2	65.96	−12.48	27.23	S	76.71	64.10	178.08	−139.46	S	S
3	49.86	−32.50	S	−5.18	−17.53	26.41	208.43	S	S	−24.28
4	8.17	S	S	305.45	30.23	219.71	−61.23	S	23.57	17.60
5	S	S	−51.70	−486.01	203.82	9.24	S	19.28	−20.90	100.69
6	S	119.51	117.54	−443.48	17.46	S	S	133.24	128.66	69.94
7	55.47	51.22	−360.92	248.02	S	S	85.15	−312.95	−152.90	19.46
8	−46.51	19.77	−33.73	S	S	−37.24	101.79	−121.41	167.80	S
9	6.49	−73.24	−223.55	S	203.52	−60.09	−389.24	4.07	S	S
10	93.89	5.13	S	−73.27	20.03	10.29	112.85	S	S	39.81
11	45.94	S	S	−176.58	44.29	−73.94	259.89	S	21.32	1.16
12	S	S	−55.19	−411.30	−93.79	−90.52	S	−0.31	−32.43	−2.70
13	S	23.45	319.54	552.59	73.00	S	S	−58.90	70.96	40.59
14	11.13	86.13	−76.08	−337.94	S	S	−74.70	−185.23	54.59	−18.05
15	−10.73	33.70	−120.96	S	S	9.39	17.18	−28.57	85.48	S
16	−11.68	54.11	66.74	S	136.49	−178.47	−190.57	45.93	S	S
17	45.46	36.74	S	−223.73	30.46	−15.62	−134.86	S	S	13.01
18	46.11	S	S	151.17	−11.11	173.35	25.43	S	14.32	40.07
19	S	S	−218.35	−427.47	−93.87	22.32	S	207.65	−8.99	−2.09
20	S	−26.02	51.70	−444.99	−14.28	S	S	−7.45	−66.21	33.27
21	53.95	5.05	−211.10	494.13	S	S	−248.85	48.38	109.17	91.06
22	51.15	5.36	H	S	S	−24.97	−53.59	H	54.78	S
23	44.66	H	181.84*	S	132.79	−142.21	−236.17	172.79*	S	S
24	H	−46.78*	S	396.97	−17.24	150.91	H	S	S	7.84
25	15.53*	S	S	36.08	30.69	H	−25.77*	S	7.77	−2.96
26	S	S	−237.44	247.14	H	−95.28*	S	−42.31	0.26	−2.69
27	S	−158.46	215.00	H	−154.48*	S	S	−89.24	24.53	H
28	−40.90	14.74	331.01	102.43*	S	S	291.23	S	S	15.99*
29	−2.56	90.28	22.28	S	S	−39.51	32.62	36.71	−10.92*	S
30	−82.29	−4.80	59.99	S	34.92	−46.47	490.05	3.76	S	S
Close	10805.87	12221.93	13371.72	8829.04	10344.84	11006.02	12045.68	13025.58	16086.41	17828.24
Change	365.80	141.20	−558.29	−495.97	632.11	−112.47	90.67	−70.88	540.66	437.72

* Shortened trading day

DECEMBER DAILY POINT CHANGES DOW JONES INDUSTRIALS

Previous Month	2005	2006	2007	2008	2009	2010	2011	2012	2013	2014
Close	10805.87	12221.93	13371.72	8829.04	10344.84	11006.02	12045.68	13025.58	16086.41	17828.24
1	106.70	−27.80	S	−679.95	126.74	249.76	−25.65	S	S	−51.44
2	−35.06	S	S	270.00	−18.90	106.63	−0.61	S	−77.64	102.75
3	S	S	−57.15	172.60	−86.53	19.68	S	−59.98	−94.15	33.07
4	S	89.72	−65.84	−215.45	22.75	S	S	−13.82	−24.85	−12.52
5	−42.50	47.75	196.23	259.18	S	S	78.41	82.71	−68.26	58.69
6	21.85	−22.35	174.93	S	S	−19.90	52.30	39.55	198.69	S
7	−45.95	−30.84	5.69	S	1.21	−3.03	46.24	81.09	S	S
8	−55.79	29.08	S	298.76	−104.14	13.32	−198.67	S	S	−106.31
9	23.46	S	S	−242.85	51.08	−2.42	186.56	S	5.33	−51.28
10	S	S	101.45	70.09	68.78	40.26	S	14.75	−52.40	−268.05
11	S	20.99	−294.26	−196.33	65.67	S	S	78.56	−129.60	63.19
12	−10.81	−12.90	41.13	64.59	S	S	−162.87	−2.99	−104.10	−315.51
13	55.95	1.92	44.06	S	S	18.24	−66.45	−74.73	15.93	S
14	59.79	99.26	−178.11	S	29.55	47.98	−131.46	−35.71	S	S
15	−1.84	28.76	S	−65.15	−49.05	−19.07	45.33	S	S	−99.99
16	−6.08	S	S	359.61	−10.88	41.78	−2.42	S	129.21	−111.97
17	S	S	−172.65	−99.80	−132.86	−7.34	S	100.38	−9.31	288.00
18	S	−4.25	65.27	−219.35	20.63	S	S	115.57	292.71	421.28
19	−39.06	30.05	−25.20	−25.88	S	S	−100.13	−98.99	11.11	26.65
20	−30.98	−7.45	38.37	S	S	−13.78	337.32	59.75	42.06	S
21	28.18	−42.62	205.01	S	85.25	55.03	4.16	−120.88	S	S
22	55.71	−78.03	S	−59.34	50.79	26.33	61.91	S	S	154.64
23	−6.17	S	S	−100.28	1.51	14.00	124.35	S	73.47	64.73
24	S	S	98.68*	48.99*	53.66*	H	S	−51.76*	62.94*	6.04*
25	S	H	H	H	H	H	H	H	H	H
26	H	64.41	2.36	47.07	S	S	H	−24.49	122.33	23.50
27	−105.50	102.94	−192.08	S	S	−18.46	−2.65	−18.28	−1.47	S
28	18.49	−9.05	6.26	S	26.98	20.51	−139.94	−158.20	S	S
29	−11.44	−38.37	S	−31.62	−1.67	9.84	135.63	S	S	−15.48
30	−67.32	S	S	184.46	3.10	−15.67	−69.48	S	25.88	−55.16
31	S	S	−101.05	108.00	−120.46	7.80	S	166.03	72.37	−160.00
Close	10717.50	12463.15	13264.82	8776.39	10428.05	11577.51	12217.56	13104.14	16576.66	17823.07
Change	−88.37	241.22	−106.90	−52.65	83.21	571.49	171.88	78.56	490.25	−5.17

* Shortened trading day

A TYPICAL DAY IN THE MARKET

Half-hourly data became available for the Dow Jones Industrial Average starting in January 1987. The NYSE switched 10:00 a.m. openings to 9:30 a.m. in October 1985. Below is the comparison between half-hourly performance from January 1987 to May 1, 2015, and hourly performance from November 1963 to June 1985. Stronger openings and closings in a more bullish climate are evident. Morning and afternoon weaknesses appear an hour earlier.

MARKET % PERFORMANCE EACH HALF-HOUR OF THE DAY
(January 1987–May 1, 2015)

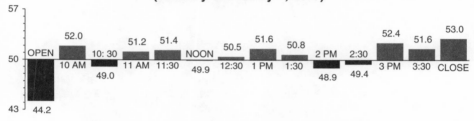

Based on the number of times the Dow Jones Industrial Average increased over previous half-hour.

MARKET % PERFORMANCE EACH HOUR OF THE DAY
(November 1963–June 1985)

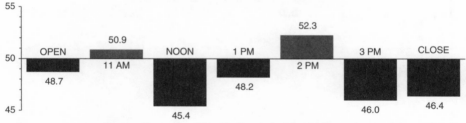

Based on the number of times the Dow Jones Industrial Average increased over previous hour.

On the next page, half-hourly movements since January 1987 are separated by day of the week. From 1953 to 1989, Monday was the worst day of the week, especially during long bear markets, but times changed. Monday reversed positions and became the best day of the week and on the plus side eleven years in a row from 1990 to 2000.

During the last 14 years (2001–May 1, 2015) Monday and Friday are net losers. Tuesday through Thursday are solid gainers, Tuesday the best (page 70). On all days, stocks do tend to firm up near the close with weakness in the early morning and from 2 to 2:30 frequently.

THROUGH THE WEEK ON A HALF-HOURLY BASIS

From the chart showing the percentage of times the Dow Jones Industrial Average rose over the preceding half-hour (January 1987 to May 1, 2015*), the typical week unfolds.

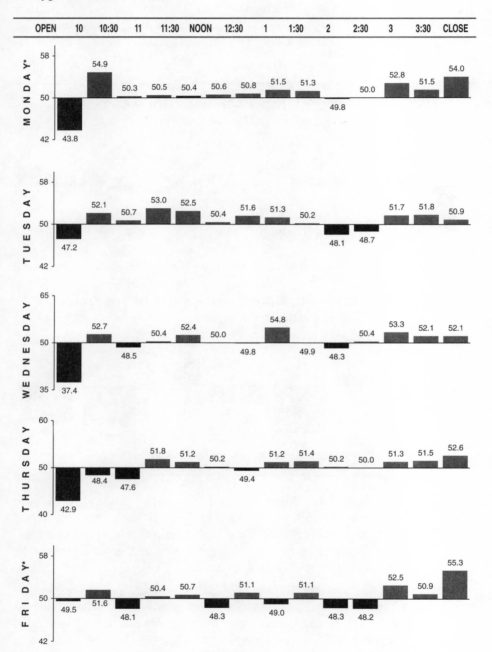

*Monday denotes first trading day of the week, Friday denotes last trading day of the week.

TUESDAY MOST PROFITABLE DAY OF WEEK

Between 1952 and 1989, Monday was the worst trading day of the week. The first trading day of the week (including Tuesday, when Monday is a holiday) rose only 44.3% of the time, while the other trading days closed higher 54.8% of the time. (NYSE Saturday trading was discontinued June 1952.)

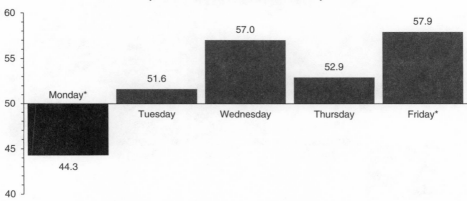

MARKET % PERFORMANCE EACH DAY OF THE WEEK
(June 1952–December 1989)

A dramatic reversal occurred in 1990—Monday became the most powerful day of the week. However, during the last 14 and a third years, Tuesday has produced the most gains. Since the top in 2000, traders have not been inclined to stay long over the weekend nor buy up equities at the outset of the week. This is not uncommon during uncertain market times. Monday was the worst day during the 2007–2009 bear, and only Tuesday was a net gainer. Since the March 2009 bottom, Tuesday and Thursday are best. See pages 70 and 143.

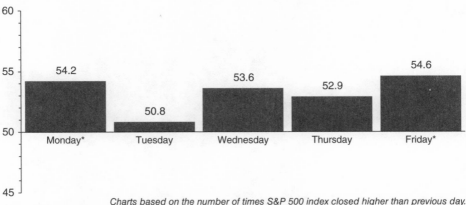

MARKET % PERFORMANCE EACH DAY OF THE WEEK
(January 1990–May 1, 2015)

Charts based on the number of times S&P 500 index closed higher than previous day.
*Monday denotes first trading day of the week, Friday denotes last trading day of the week.

NASDAQ STRONGEST LAST 3 DAYS OF WEEK

Despite 20 years less data, daily trading patterns on NASDAQ through 1989 appear to be fairly similar to the S&P on page 141, except for more bullishness on Thursdays. During the mostly flat markets of the 1970s and early 1980s, it would appear that apprehensive investors decided to throw in the towel over weekends and sell on Mondays and Tuesdays.

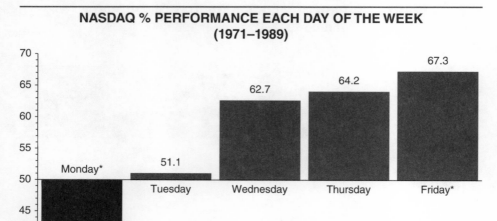

**NASDAQ % PERFORMANCE EACH DAY OF THE WEEK
(1971–1989)**

Notice the vast difference in the daily trading pattern between NASDAQ and S&P from January 1, 1990, to recent times. The reason for so much more bullishness is that NASDAQ moved up 1010%, over three times as much during the 1990 to 2000 period. The gain for the S&P was 332% and for the Dow Jones industrials, 326%. NASDAQ's weekly patterns are beginning to move in step with the rest of the market. Notice the similarities to the S&P since 2001 on pages 143 and 144—Monday and Friday weakness, midweek strength.

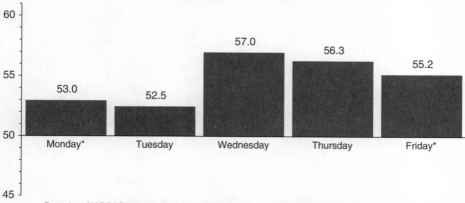

**NASDAQ % PERFORMANCE EACH DAY OF THE WEEK
(1990–May 1, 2015)**

*Based on NASDAQ composite, prior to February 5, 1971, based on National Quotation Bureau indices.
Monday denotes first trading day of the week, Friday denotes last trading day of the week.

S&P DAILY PERFORMANCE EACH YEAR SINCE 1952

To determine if market trend alters performance of different days of the week, we separated 22 bear years—1953, '56, '57, '60, '62, '66, '69, '70, '73, '74, '77, '78, '81, '84, '87, '90, '94, 2000, 2001, 2002, 2008, and 2011—from 41 bull market years. While Tuesday and Thursday did not vary much between bull and bear years, Mondays and Fridays were sharply affected. There was a swing of 10.6 percentage points in Monday's and 9.5 in Friday's performance. Tuesday is the best day of the week based upon total points gained. See page 70.

PERCENTAGE OF TIMES MARKET CLOSED HIGHER THAN PREVIOUS DAY
(JUNE 1952–MAY 1, 2015)

	Monday*	Tuesday	Wednesday	Thursday	Friday*
1952	48.4%	55.6%	58.1%	51.9%	66.7%
1953	32.7	50.0	54.9	57.5	56.6
1954	50.0	57.5	63.5	59.2	73.1
1955	50.0	45.7	63.5	60.0	78.9
1956	36.5	39.6	46.9	50.0	59.6
1957	25.0	54.0	66.7	48.9	44.2
1958	59.6	52.0	59.6	68.1	72.6
1959	42.3	53.1	55.8	48.9	69.8
1960	34.6	50.0	44.2	54.0	59.6
1961	52.9	54.4	64.7	56.0	67.3
1962	28.3	52.1	54.0	51.0	50.0
1963	46.2	63.3	51.0	57.5	69.2
1964	40.4	48.0	61.5	58.7	77.4
1965	44.2	57.5	55.8	51.0	71.2
1966	36.5	47.8	53.9	42.0	57.7
1967	38.5	50.0	60.8	64.0	69.2
1968†	49.1	57.5	64.3	42.6	54.9
1969	30.8	45.8	50.0	67.4	50.0
1970	38.5	46.0	63.5	48.9	52.8
1971	44.2	64.6	57.7	55.1	51.9
1972	38.5	60.9	57.7	51.0	67.3
1973	32.1	51.1	52.9	44.9	44.2
1974	32.7	57.1	51.0	36.7	30.8
1975	53.9	38.8	61.5	56.3	55.8
1976	55.8	55.3	55.8	40.8	58.5
1977	40.4	40.4	46.2	53.1	53.9
1978	51.9	43.5	59.6	54.0	48.1
1979	54.7	53.2	58.8	66.0	44.2
1980	55.8	54.2	71.7	35.4	59.6
1981	44.2	38.8	55.8	53.2	47.2
1982	46.2	39.6	44.2	44.9	50.0
1983	55.8	46.8	61.5	52.0	55.8
1984	39.6	63.8	31.4	46.0	44.2
1985	44.2	61.2	54.9	56.3	53.9
1986	51.9	44.9	67.3	58.3	55.8
1987	51.9	57.1	63.5	61.7	49.1
1988	51.9	61.7	51.9	48.0	59.6
1989	51.9	47.8	69.2	58.0	69.2
1990	67.9	53.2	52.9	40.0	51.9
1991	44.2	46.9	52.9	49.0	51.9
1992	51.9	49.0	53.9	56.3	45.3
1993	65.4	41.7	55.8	44.9	48.1
1994	55.8	46.8	52.9	48.0	59.6
1995	63.5	56.5	63.5	62.0	63.5
1996	54.7	44.9	51.0	57.1	63.5
1997	67.3	67.4	42.3	41.7	57.7
1998	57.7	62.5	57.7	38.3	60.4
1999	46.2	29.8	67.3	53.1	57.7
2000	51.9	43.5	40.4	56.0	46.2
2001	45.3	51.1	44.0	59.2	43.1
2002	40.4	37.5	56.9	38.8	48.1
2003	59.6	62.5	42.3	58.3	50.0
2004	51.9	61.7	59.6	52.1	52.8
2005	59.6	47.8	59.6	56.0	55.8
2006	55.8	55.6	67.3	52.0	48.1
2007	47.2	50.0	64.0	50.0	61.5
2008	42.3	50.0	41.5	60.4	55.8
2009	53.9	50.0	57.7	63.8	52.8
2010	61.5	57.5	55.8	53.1	57.7
2011	48.1	56.5	55.8	56.0	57.7
2012	52.8	48.9	50.0	58.0	53.9
2013	51.9	60.4	54.9	59.2	65.4
2014	53.9	56.3	57.7	56.3	61.5
2015‡	58.8	33.3	35.3	56.3	50.0
Average	**48.1%**	**51.6%**	**55.9%**	**52.8%**	**56.7%**
41 Bull Years	**51.8%**	**53.0%**	**58.1%**	**53.7%**	**60.0%**
22 Bear Years	**41.2%**	**48.9%**	**51.8%**	**51.3%**	**50.5%**

Based on S&P 500

† Most Wednesdays closed last 7 months of 1968   ‡ Through 5/1/2015 only, not included in averages
*Monday denotes first trading day of the week, Friday denotes last trading day of the week.

NASDAQ DAILY PERFORMANCE EACH YEAR SINCE 1971

After dropping a hefty 77.9% from its 2000 high (versus −37.8% on the Dow and −49.1% on the S&P 500), NASDAQ tech stocks still outpace the blue chips and big caps—but not by nearly as much as they did. From January 1, 1971 through May 1, 2015, NASDAQ, moved up an impressive 5486%. The Dow (up 2048%) and the S&P (up 2188%) gained less than half as much.

Monday's performance on NASDAQ was lackluster during the three-year bear market of 2000–2002. As NASDAQ rebounded (up 50% in 2003), strength returned to Monday during 2003–2006. During the bear market from late 2007 to early 2009, weakness was most consistent on Monday and Friday.

PERCENTAGE OF TIMES NASDAQ CLOSED HIGHER THAN PREVIOUS DAY (1971–MAY 1, 2015)

	Monday*	Tuesday	Wednesday	Thursday	Friday*
1971	51.9%	52.1%	59.6%	65.3%	71.2%
1972	30.8	60.9	63.5	57.1	78.9
1973	34.0	48.9	52.9	53.1	48.1
1974	30.8	44.9	52.9	51.0	42.3
1975	44.2	42.9	63.5	64.6	63.5
1976	50.0	63.8	67.3	59.2	58.5
1977	51.9	40.4	53.9	63.3	73.1
1978	48.1	47.8	73.1	72.0	84.6
1979	45.3	53.2	64.7	86.0	82.7
1980	46.2	64.6	84.9	52.1	73.1
1981	42.3	32.7	67.3	76.6	69.8
1982	34.6	47.9	59.6	51.0	63.5
1983	42.3	44.7	67.3	68.0	73.1
1984	22.6	53.2	35.3	52.0	51.9
1985	36.5	59.2	62.8	68.8	66.0
1986	38.5	55.1	65.4	72.9	75.0
1987	42.3	49.0	65.4	68.1	66.0
1988	50.0	55.3	61.5	66.0	63.5
1989	38.5	54.4	71.2	72.0	75.0
1990	54.7	42.6	60.8	46.0	55.8
1991	51.9	59.2	66.7	65.3	51.9
1992	44.2	53.1	59.6	60.4	45.3
1993	55.8	56.3	69.2	57.1	67.3
1994	51.9	46.8	54.9	52.0	55.8
1995	50.0	52.2	63.5	64.0	63.5
1996	50.9	57.1	64.7	61.2	63.5
1997	65.4	59.2	53.9	52.1	55.8
1998	59.6	58.3	65.4	44.7	58.5
1999	61.5	40.4	63.5	57.1	65.4
2000	40.4	41.3	42.3	60.0	57.7
2001	41.5	57.8	52.0	55.1	47.1
2002	44.2	37.5	56.9	46.9	46.2
2003	57.7	60.4	40.4	60.4	46.2
2004	57.7	59.6	53.9	50.0	50.9
2005	61.5	47.8	51.9	48.0	59.6
2006	55.8	51.1	65.4	50.0	44.2
2007	47.2	63.0	66.0	56.0	57.7
2008	34.6	52.1	49.1	54.2	42.3
2009	51.9	54.2	63.5	63.8	50.9
2010	61.5	53.2	61.5	55.1	61.5
2011	50.0	56.5	50.0	64.0	53.9
2012	49.1	53.3	50.0	54.0	51.9
2013	57.7	60.4	52.9	59.2	67.3
2014	57.7	58.3	57.7	52.1	59.6
2015†	64.7	33.3	47.1	75.0	55.6
Average	**47.6%**	**52.3%**	**59.7%**	**59.3%**	**60.4%**
32 Bull Years	**50.6%**	**53.7%**	**61.7%**	**60.7%**	**63.0%**
12 Bear Years	**40.8%**	**46.9%**	**53.3%**	**56.6%**	**53.1%**

Based on NASDAQ composite; prior to February 5, 1971, based on National Quotation Bureau indices.
† Through 5/1/2015 only, not included in averages.
*Monday denotes first trading day of the week, Friday denotes last trading day of the week.

MONTHLY CASH INFLOWS INTO S&P STOCKS

For many years, the last trading day of the month, plus the first four of the following month, were the best market days of the month. This pattern is quite clear in the first chart, showing these five consecutive trading days towering above the other 16 trading days of the average month in the 1953–1981 period. The rationale was that individuals and institutions tended to operate similarly, causing a massive flow of cash into stocks near beginnings of months.

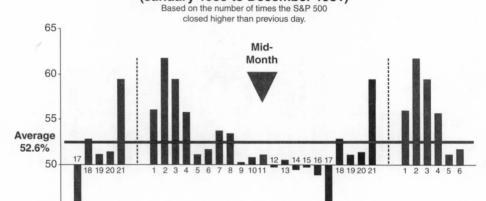

MARKET % PERFORMANCE EACH DAY OF THE MONTH
(January 1953 to December 1981)
Based on the number of times the S&P 500
closed higher than previous day.

Clearly, "front-running" traders took advantage of this phenomenon, drastically altering the previous pattern. The second chart from 1982 onward shows the trading shift caused by these "anticipators" to the last three trading days of the month, plus the first two. Another astonishing development shows the ninth, tenth, and eleventh trading days rising strongly as well. Growth of 401(k) retirement plans, IRAs, and similar plans (participants' salaries are usually paid twice monthly) is responsible for this mid-month bulge. First trading days of the month have produced the greatest gains in recent years (see page 86).

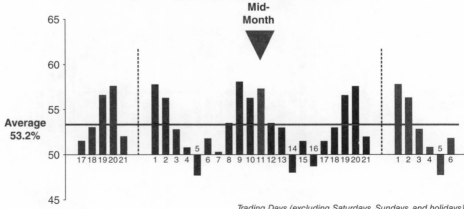

MARKET % PERFORMANCE EACH DAY OF THE MONTH
(January 1982 to December 2014)

Trading Days (excluding Saturdays, Sundays, and holidays).

145

MONTHLY CASH INFLOWS INTO NASDAQ STOCKS

NASDAQ stocks moved up 58.1% of the time through 1981 compared to 52.6% for the S&P on page 145. Ends and beginnings of the month are fairly similar, specifically the last plus the first four trading days. But notice how investors piled into NASDAQ stocks until mid-month. NASDAQ rose 118.6% from January 1, 1971, to December 31, 1981, compared to 33.0% for the S&P.

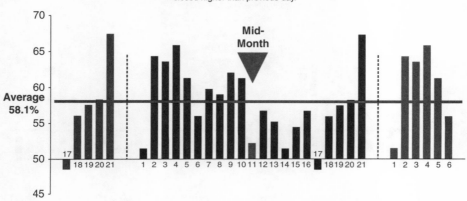

NASDAQ % PERFORMANCE EACH DAY OF THE MONTH
(January 1971 to December 1981)
Based on the number of times the NASDAQ composite closed higher than previous day.

After the air was let out of the tech market 2000–2002, S&P's 1580% gain over the last 33 years is more evenly matched with NASDAQ's 2318% gain. Last three, first four, and middle ninth and tenth days rose the most. Where the S&P has three days of the month that go down more often than up, NASDAQ has none. NASDAQ exhibits the most strength on the last trading day of the month; however, over the past 17 years, last days have weakened considerably, down more often than not.

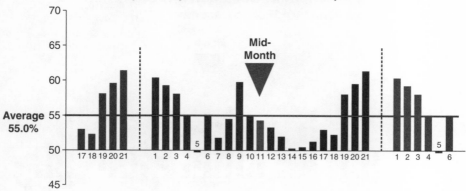

NASDAQ % PERFORMANCE EACH DAY OF THE MONTH
(January 1982 to December 2014)

Trading Days (excluding Saturdays, Sundays, and holidays).
Based on NASDAQ composite, prior to February 5, 1971, based on National Quotation Bureau indices.

146

NOVEMBER, DECEMBER, AND JANUARY: YEAR'S BEST THREE-MONTH SPAN

The most important observation to be made from a chart showing the average monthly percent change in market prices since 1950 is that institutions (mutual funds, pension funds, banks, etc.) determine the trading patterns in today's market.

The "investment calendar" reflects the annual, semi-annual, and quarterly operations of institutions during January, April, and July. October, besides being the last campaign month before elections, is also the time when most bear markets seem to end, as in 1946, 1957, 1960, 1966, 1974, 1987, 1990, 1998, and 2002. (August and September tend to combine to make the worst consecutive two-month period.)

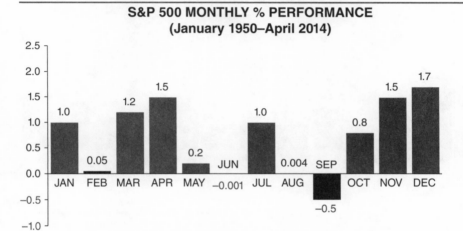

S&P 500 MONTHLY % PERFORMANCE
(January 1950–April 2014)

Average month-to-month % change in S&P 500
(Based on monthly closing prices.)

Unusual year-end strength comes from corporate and private pension funds, producing a 4.2% gain on average between November 1 and January 31. In 2007–2008, these three months were all down for the fourth time since 1930; previously in 1931–1932, 1940–1941, and 1969–1970, also bear markets. September's dismal performance makes it the worst month of the year. However, in the last 11 years, it has been up 8 times after being down five in a row 1999–2003.

In election years since 1952, the best three months are June +1.4% (13–3), November +1.3% (9–7), and December +1.2% (13–3). January, February, March, April, July, and August are winners, while May, September, and October are losers. October is the worst, –0.7% (7–9).

See page 50 for monthly performance tables for the S&P 500 and the Dow Jones industrials. See pages 52, 54, and 62 for unique switching strategies.

On page 66, you can see how the first month of the first three quarters far outperforms the second and the third months since 1950, and note the improvement in May's and October's performance since 1991.

NOVEMBER THROUGH JUNE: NASDAQ'S EIGHT-MONTH RUN

The two-and-a-half-year plunge of 77.9% in NASDAQ stocks, between March 10, 2000, and October 9, 2002, brought several horrendous monthly losses (the two greatest were November 2000, −22.9%, and February 2001, −22.4%), which trimmed average monthly performance over the $44^1/_3$-year period. Ample Octobers in 12 of the last 17 years, including three huge turnarounds in 2001 (+12.8%), 2002 (+13.5%), and 2011 (+11.1%) have put bear-killing October in the number one spot since 1998. January's 2.7% average gain is still awesome, and more than twice S&P's 1.2% January average since 1971.

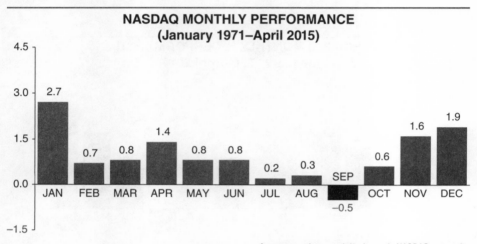

NASDAQ MONTHLY PERFORMANCE
(January 1971–April 2015)

Average month-to-month % change in NASDAQ composite, prior to February 5, 1971, based on National Quotation Bureau indices. (Based on monthly closing prices.)

Bear in mind, when comparing NASDAQ to the S&P on page 147, that there are 22 fewer years of data here. During this $44^1/_3$-year (1971–April 2015) period, NASDAQ gained 5414%, while the S&P and the Dow rose only 2163% and 2027%, respectively. On page 58, you can see a statistical monthly comparison between NASDAQ and the Dow.

Year-end strength is even more pronounced in NASDAQ, producing a 6.2% gain on average between November 1 and January 31—nearly 1.5 times greater than that of the S&P 500 on page 147. September is the worst month of the year for the over-the-counter index as well, posting an average loss of −0.5%. These extremes underscore NASDAQ's higher volatility—and moves of greater magnitude.

In election years since 1972, the best three months are August +2.9% (7−4), February +2.8% (7−4), and January +2.6% (8−3). June and December also produce average gains. March, April, May, July, September, October, and November are all net losers. October is the worst, averaging −2.1% (4−7).

DOW JONES INDUSTRIALS ANNUAL HIGHS, LOWS, & CLOSES SINCE 1901

YEAR	HIGH DATE	HIGH CLOSE	LOW DATE	LOW CLOSE	YEAR CLOSE	YEAR	HIGH DATE	HIGH CLOSE	LOW DATE	LOW CLOSE	YEAR CLOSE
1901	6/17	57.33	12/24	45.07	47.29	1959	12/31	679.36	2/9	574.46	679.36
1902	4/24	50.14	12/15	43.64	47.10	1960	1/5	685.47	10/25	566.05	615.89
1903	2/16	49.59	11/9	30.88	35.98	1961	12/13	734.91	1/3	610.25	731.14
1904	12/5	53.65	3/12	34.00	50.99	1962	1/3	726.01	6/26	535.76	652.10
1905	12/29	70.74	1/25	50.37	70.47	1963	12/18	767.21	1/2	646.79	762.95
1906	1/19	75.45	7/13	62.40	69.12	1964	11/18	891.71	1/2	766.08	874.13
1907	1/7	70.60	11/15	38.83	43.04	1965	12/31	969.26	6/28	840.59	969.26
1908	11/13	64.74	2/13	42.94	63.11	1966	2/9	995.15	10/7	744.32	785.69
1909	11/19	73.64	2/23	58.54	72.56	1967	9/25	943.08	1/3	786.41	905.11
1910	1/3	72.04	7/26	53.93	59.60	1968	12/3	985.21	3/21	825.13	943.75
1911	6/19	63.78	9/25	53.43	59.84	1969	5/14	968.85	12/17	769.93	800.36
1912	9/30	68.97	2/10	58.72	64.37	1970	12/29	842.00	5/26	631.16	838.92
1913	1/9	64.88	6/11	52.83	57.71	1971	4/28	950.82	11/23	797.97	890.20
1914	3/20	61.12	7/30	52.32	54.58	1972	12/11	1036.27	1/26	889.15	1020.02
1915	12/27	99.21	2/24	54.22	99.15	1973	1/11	1051.70	12/5	788.31	850.86
1916	11/21	110.15	4/22	84.96	95.00	1974	3/13	891.66	12/6	577.60	616.24
1917	1/3	99.18	12/19	65.95	74.38	1975	7/15	881.81	1/2	632.04	852.41
1918	10/18	89.07	1/15	73.38	82.20	1976	9/21	1014.79	1/2	858.71	1004.65
1919	11/3	119.62	2/8	79.15	107.23	1977	1/3	999.75	11/2	800.85	831.17
1920	1/3	109.88	12/21	66.75	71.95	1978	9/8	907.74	2/28	742.12	805.01
1921	12/15	81.50	8/24	63.90	81.10	1979	10/5	897.61	11/7	796.67	838.74
1922	10/14	103.43	1/10	78.59	98.73	1980	11/20	1000.17	4/21	759.13	963.99
1923	3/20	105.38	10/27	85.76	95.52	1981	4/27	1024.05	9/25	824.01	875.00
1924	12/31	120.51	5/20	88.33	120.51	1982	12/27	1070.55	8/12	776.92	1046.54
1925	11/6	159.39	3/30	115.00	156.66	1983	11/29	1287.20	1/3	1027.04	1258.64
1926	8/14	166.64	3/30	135.20	157.20	1984	1/6	1286.64	7/24	1086.57	1211.57
1927	12/31	202.40	1/25	152.73	202.40	1985	12/16	1553.10	1/4	1184.96	1546.67
1928	12/31	300.00	2/20	191.33	300.00	1986	12/2	1955.57	1/22	1502.29	1895.95
1929	9/3	381.17	11/13	198.69	248.48	1987	8/25	2722.42	10/19	1738.74	1938.83
1930	4/17	294.07	12/16	157.51	164.58	1988	10/21	2183.50	1/20	1879.14	2168.57
1931	2/24	194.36	12/17	73.79	77.90	1989	10/9	2791.41	1/3	2144.64	2753.20
1932	3/8	88.78	7/8	41.22	59.93	1990	7/17	2999.75	10/11	2365.10	2633.66
1933	7/18	108.67	2/27	50.16	99.90	1991	12/31	3168.83	1/9	2470.30	3168.83
1934	2/5	110.74	7/26	85.51	104.04	1992	6/1	3413.21	10/9	3136.58	3301.11
1935	11/19	148.44	3/14	96.71	144.13	1993	12/29	3794.33	1/20	3241.95	3754.09
1936	11/17	184.90	1/6	143.11	179.90	1994	1/31	3978.36	4/4	3593.35	3834.44
1937	3/10	194.40	11/24	113.64	120.85	1995	12/13	5216.47	1/30	3832.08	5117.12
1938	11/12	158.41	3/31	98.95	154.76	1996	12/27	6560.91	1/10	5032.94	6448.27
1939	9/12	155.92	4/8	121.44	150.24	1997	8/6	8259.31	4/11	6391.69	7908.25
1940	1/3	152.80	6/10	111.84	131.13	1998	11/23	9374.27	8/31	7539.07	9181.43
1941	1/10	133.59	12/23	106.34	110.96	1999	12/31	11497.12	1/22	9120.67	11497.12
1942	12/26	119.71	4/28	92.92	119.40	2000	1/14	11722.98	3/7	9796.03	10786.85
1943	7/14	145.82	1/8	119.26	135.89	2001	5/21	11337.92	9/21	8235.81	10021.50
1944	12/16	152.53	2/7	134.22	152.32	2002	3/19	10635.25	10/9	7286.27	8341.63
1945	12/11	195.82	1/24	151.35	192.91	2003	12/31	10453.92	3/11	7524.06	10453.92
1946	5/29	212.50	10/9	163.12	177.20	2004	12/28	10854.54	10/25	9749.99	10783.01
1947	7/24	186.85	5/17	163.21	181.16	2005	3/4	10940.55	4/20	10012.36	10717.50
1948	6/15	193.16	3/16	165.39	177.30	2006	12/27	12510.57	1/20	10667.39	12463.15
1949	12/30	200.52	6/13	161.60	200.13	2007	10/9	14164.53	3/5	12050.41	13264.82
1950	11/24	235.47	1/13	196.81	235.41	2008	5/2	13058.20	11/20	7552.29	8776.39
1951	9/13	276.37	1/3	238.99	269.23	2009	12/30	10548.51	3/9	6547.05	10428.05
1952	12/30	292.00	5/1	256.35	291.90	2010	12/29	11585.38	7/2	9686.48	11577.51
1953	1/5	293.79	9/14	255.49	280.90	2011	4/29	12810.54	10/3	10655.30	12217.56
1954	12/31	404.39	1/11	279.87	404.39	2012	10/5	13610.15	6/4	12101.46	13104.14
1955	12/30	488.40	1/17	388.20	488.40	2013	12/31	16576.66	1/8	13328.85	16576.66
1956	4/6	521.05	1/23	462.35	499.47	2014	12/26	18053.71	2/3	15372.80	17823.07
1957	7/12	520.77	10/22	419.79	435.69	2015*	3/2	18288.63	1/30	17164.95	At Press-time
1958	12/31	583.65	2/25	436.89	583.65						

*Through May 1, 2015

149

S&P 500 ANNUAL HIGHS, LOWS, & CLOSES SINCE 1930

YEAR	HIGH DATE	HIGH CLOSE	LOW DATE	LOW CLOSE	YEAR CLOSE	YEAR	HIGH DATE	HIGH CLOSE	LOW DATE	LOW CLOSE	YEAR CLOSE
1930	4/10	25.92	12/16	14.44	15.34	1973	1/11	120.24	12/5	92.16	97.55
1931	2/24	18.17	12/17	7.72	8.12	1974	1/3	99.80	10/3	62.28	68.56
1932	9/7	9.31	6/1	4.40	6.89	1975	7/15	95.61	1/8	70.04	90.19
1933	7/18	12.20	2/27	5.53	10.10	1976	9/21	107.83	1/2	90.90	107.46
1934	2/6	11.82	7/26	8.36	9.50	1977	1/3	107.00	11/2	90.71	95.10
1935	11/19	13.46	3/14	8.06	13.43	1978	9/12	106.99	3/6	86.90	96.11
1936	11/9	17.69	1/2	13.40	17.18	1979	10/5	111.27	2/27	96.13	107.94
1937	3/6	18.68	11/24	10.17	10.55	1980	11/28	140.52	3/27	98.22	135.76
1938	11/9	13.79	3/31	8.50	13.21	1981	1/6	138.12	9/25	112.77	122.55
1939	1/4	13.23	4/8	10.18	12.49	1982	11/9	143.02	8/12	102.42	140.64
1940	1/3	12.77	6/10	8.99	10.58	1983	10/10	172.65	1/3	138.34	164.93
1941	1/10	10.86	12/29	8.37	8.69	1984	11/6	170.41	7/24	147.82	167.24
1942	12/31	9.77	4/28	7.47	9.77	1985	12/16	212.02	1/4	163.68	211.28
1943	7/14	12.64	1/2	9.84	11.67	1986	12/2	254.00	1/22	203.49	242.17
1944	12/16	13.29	2/7	11.56	13.28	1987	8/25	336.77	12/4	223.92	247.08
1945	12/10	17.68	1/23	13.21	17.36	1988	10/21	283.66	1/20	242.63	277.72
1946	5/29	19.25	10/9	14.12	15.30	1989	10/9	359.80	1/3	275.31	353.40
1947	2/8	16.20	5/17	13.71	15.30	1990	7/16	368.95	10/11	295.46	330.22
1948	6/15	17.06	2/14	13.84	15.20	1991	12/31	417.09	1/9	311.49	417.09
1949	12/30	16.79	6/13	13.55	16.76	1992	12/18	441.28	4/8	394.50	435.71
1950	12/29	20.43	1/14	16.65	20.41	1993	12/28	470.94	1/8	429.05	466.45
1951	10/15	23.85	1/3	20.69	23.77	1994	2/2	482.00	4/4	438.92	459.27
1952	12/30	26.59	2/20	23.09	26.57	1995	12/13	621.69	1/3	459.11	615.93
1953	1/5	26.66	9/14	22.71	24.81	1996	11/25	757.03	1/10	598.48	740.74
1954	12/31	35.98	1/11	24.80	35.98	1997	12/5	983.79	1/2	737.01	970.43
1955	11/14	46.41	1/17	34.58	45.48	1998	12/29	1241.81	1/9	927.69	1229.23
1956	8/2	49.74	1/23	43.11	46.67	1999	12/31	1469.25	1/14	1212.19	1469.25
1957	7/15	49.13	10/22	38.98	39.99	2000	3/24	1527.46	12/20	1264.74	1320.28
1958	12/31	55.21	1/2	40.33	55.21	2001	2/1	1373.47	9/21	965.80	1148.08
1959	8/3	60.71	2/9	53.58	59.89	2002	1/4	1172.51	10/9	776.76	879.82
1960	1/5	60.39	10/25	52.30	58.11	2003	12/31	1111.92	3/11	800.73	1111.92
1961	12/12	72.64	1/3	57.57	71.55	2004	12/30	1213.55	8/12	1063.23	1211.92
1962	1/3	71.13	6/26	52.32	63.10	2005	12/14	1272.74	4/20	1137.50	1248.29
1963	12/31	75.02	1/2	62.69	75.02	2006	12/15	1427.09	6/13	1223.69	1418.30
1964	11/20	86.28	1/2	75.43	84.75	2007	10/9	1565.15	3/5	1374.12	1468.36
1965	11/15	92.63	6/28	81.60	92.43	2008	1/2	1447.16	11/20	752.44	903.25
1966	2/9	94.06	10/7	73.20	80.33	2009	12/28	1127.78	3/9	676.53	1115.10
1967	9/25	97.59	1/3	80.38	96.47	2010	12/29	1259.78	7/2	1022.58	1257.64
1968	11/29	108.37	3/5	87.72	103.86	2011	4/29	1363.61	10/3	1099.23	1257.60
1969	5/14	106.16	12/17	89.20	92.06	2012	9/14	1465.77	1/3	1277.06	1426.19
1970	1/5	93.46	5/26	69.29	92.15	2013	12/31	1848.36	1/8	1457.15	1848.36
1971	4/28	104.77	11/23	90.16	102.09	2014	12/29	2090.57	2/3	1741.89	2058.90
1972	12/11	119.12	1/3	101.67	118.05	2015*	4/24	2117.69	1/15	1992.67	At Press-time

*Through May 1, 2015

NASDAQ ANNUAL HIGHS, LOWS, & CLOSES SINCE 1971

YEAR	DATE	HIGH CLOSE	DATE	LOW CLOSE	YEAR CLOSE	YEAR	DATE	HIGH CLOSE	DATE	LOW CLOSE	YEAR CLOSE
1971	12/31	114.12	1/5	89.06	114.12	1994	3/18	803.93	6/24	693.79	751.96
1972	12/8	135.15	1/3	113.65	133.73	1995	12/4	1069.79	1/3	743.58	1052.13
1973	1/11	136.84	12/24	88.67	92.19	1996	12/9	1316.27	1/15	988.57	1291.03
1974	3/15	96.53	10/3	54.87	59.82	1997	10/9	1745.85	4/2	1201.00	1570.35
1975	7/15	88.00	1/2	60.70	77.62	1998	12/31	2192.69	10/8	1419.12	2192.69
1976	12/31	97.88	1/2	78.06	97.88	1999	12/31	4069.31	1/4	2208.05	4069.31
1977	12/30	105.05	4/5	93.66	105.05	2000	3/10	5048.62	12/20	2332.78	2470.52
1978	9/13	139.25	1/11	99.09	117.98	2001	1/24	2859.15	9/21	1423.19	1950.40
1979	10/5	152.29	1/2	117.84	151.14	2002	1/4	2059.38	10/9	1114.11	1335.51
1980	11/28	208.15	3/27	124.09	202.34	2003	12/30	2009.88	3/11	1271.47	2003.37
1981	5/29	223.47	9/28	175.03	195.84	2004	12/30	2178.34	8/12	1752.49	2175.44
1982	12/8	240.70	8/13	159.14	232.41	2005	12/2	2273.37	4/28	1904.18	2205.32
1983	6/24	328.91	1/3	230.59	278.60	2006	11/22	2465.98	7/21	2020.39	2415.29
1984	1/6	287.90	7/25	225.30	247.35	2007	10/31	2859.12	3/5	2340.68	2652.28
1985	12/16	325.16	1/2	245.91	324.93	2008	1/2	2609.63	11/20	1316.12	1577.03
1986	7/3	411.16	1/9	323.01	349.33	2009	12/30	2291.28	3/9	1268.64	2269.15
1987	8/26	455.26	10/28	291.88	330.47	2010	12/22	2671.48	7/2	2091.79	2652.87
1988	7/5	396.11	1/12	331.97	381.38	2011	4/29	2873.54	10/3	2335.83	2605.15
1989	10/9	485.73	1/3	378.56	454.82	2012	9/14	3183.95	1/4	2648.36	3019.51
1990	7/16	469.60	10/16	325.44	373.84	2013	12/31	4176.59	1/8	3091.81	4176.59
1991	12/31	586.34	1/14	355.75	586.34	2014	12/29	4806.91	2/3	3996.96	4736.05
1992	12/31	676.95	6/26	547.84	676.95	2015*	4/24	5092.08	1/15	4570.82	At Press-time
1993	10/15	787.42	4/26	645.87	776.80						

RUSSELL 1000 ANNUAL HIGHS, LOWS, & CLOSES SINCE 1979

YEAR	DATE	HIGH CLOSE	DATE	LOW CLOSE	YEAR CLOSE	YEAR	DATE	HIGH CLOSE	DATE	LOW CLOSE	YEAR CLOSE
1979	10/5	61.18	2/27	51.83	59.87	1998	12/29	645.36	1/9	490.26	642.87
1980	11/28	78.26	3/27	53.68	75.20	1999	12/31	767.97	2/9	632.53	767.97
1981	1/6	76.34	9/25	62.03	67.93	2000	9/1	813.71	12/20	668.75	700.09
1982	11/9	78.47	8/12	55.98	77.24	2001	1/30	727.35	9/21	507.98	604.94
1983	10/10	95.07	1/3	76.04	90.38	2002	3/19	618.74	10/9	410.52	466.18
1984	1/6	92.80	7/24	79.49	90.31	2003	12/31	594.56	3/11	425.31	594.56
1985	12/16	114.97	1/4	88.61	114.39	2004	12/30	651.76	8/13	566.06	650.99
1986	7/2	137.87	1/22	111.14	130.00	2005	12/14	692.09	4/20	613.37	679.42
1987	8/25	176.22	12/4	117.65	130.02	2006	12/15	775.08	6/13	665.81	770.08
1988	10/21	149.94	1/20	128.35	146.99	2007	10/9	852.32	3/5	749.85	799.82
1989	10/9	189.93	1/3	145.78	185.11	2008	1/2	788.62	11/20	402.91	487.77
1990	7/16	191.56	10/11	152.36	171.22	2009	12/28	619.22	3/9	367.55	612.01
1991	12/31	220.61	1/9	161.94	220.61	2010	12/29	698.11	7/2	562.58	696.90
1992	12/18	235.06	4/8	208.87	233.59	2011	4/29	758.45	10/3	604.42	693.36
1993	10/15	252.77	1/8	229.91	250.71	2012	9/14	809.01	1/4	703.72	789.90
1994	2/1	258.31	4/4	235.38	244.65	2013	12/31	1030.36	1/8	807.95	1030.36
1995	12/13	331.18	1/3	244.41	328.89	2014	12/29	1161.45	2/3	972.95	1144.37
1996	12/2	401.21	1/10	318.24	393.75	2015*	4/24	1183.20	1/15	1108.32	At Press-time
1997	12/5	519.72	4/11	389.03	513.79						

RUSSELL 2000 ANNUAL HIGHS, LOWS, & CLOSES SINCE 1979

YEAR	DATE	HIGH CLOSE	DATE	LOW CLOSE	YEAR CLOSE	YEAR	DATE	HIGH CLOSE	DATE	LOW CLOSE	YEAR CLOSE
1979	12/31	55.91	1/2	40.81	55.91	1998	4/21	491.41	10/8	310.28	421.96
1980	11/28	77.70	3/27	45.36	74.80	1999	12/31	504.75	3/23	383.37	504.75
1981	6/15	85.16	9/25	65.37	73.67	2000	3/9	606.05	12/20	443.80	483.53
1982	12/8	91.01	8/12	60.33	88.90	2001	5/22	517.23	9/21	378.89	488.50
1983	6/24	126.99	1/3	88.29	112.27	2002	4/16	522.95	10/9	327.04	383.09
1984	1/12	116.69	7/25	93.95	101.49	2003	12/30	565.47	3/12	345.94	556.91
1985	12/31	129.87	1/2	101.21	129.87	2004	12/28	654.57	8/12	517.10	651.57
1986	7/3	155.30	1/9	128.23	135.00	2005	12/2	690.57	4/28	575.02	673.22
1987	8/25	174.44	10/28	106.08	120.42	2006	12/27	797.73	7/21	671.94	787.66
1988	7/15	151.42	1/12	121.23	147.37	2007	7/13	855.77	11/26	735.07	766.03
1989	10/9	180.78	1/3	146.79	168.30	2008	6/5	763.27	11/20	385.31	499.45
1990	6/15	170.90	10/30	118.82	132.16	2009	12/24	634.07	3/9	343.26	625.39
1991	12/31	189.94	1/15	125.25	189.94	2010	12/27	792.35	2/8	586.49	783.65
1992	12/31	221.01	7/8	185.81	221.01	2011	4/29	865.29	10/3	609.49	740.92
1993	11/2	260.17	2/23	217.55	258.59	2012	9/14	864.70	6/4	737.24	849.35
1994	3/18	271.08	12/9	235.16	250.36	2013	12/31	1163.64	1/3	872.60	1163.64
1995	9/14	316.12	1/30	246.56	315.97	2014	12/29	1219.11	10/13	1049.30	1204.70
1996	5/22	364.61	1/16	301.75	362.61	2015*	4/15	1275.35	1/15	1154.71	At Press-time
1997	10/13	465.21	4/25	335.85	437.02						

*Through May 1, 2015

	Jan	Feb	Mar	Apr	May	Jun	Jul	Aug	Sep	Oct	Nov	Dec	Year's Change
1950	0.8	0.8	1.3	4.0	4.2	-6.4	0.1	3.6	4.4	-0.6	1.2	3.4	17.6
1951	5.7	1.3	-1.6	4.5	-3.7	-2.8	6.3	4.8	0.3	-3.2	-0.4	3.0	14.4
1952	0.5	-3.9	3.6	-4.4	2.1	4.3	1.9	-1.6	-1.6	-0.5	5.4	2.9	8.4
1953	-0.7	-1.9	-1.5	-1.8	-0.9	-1.5	2.7	-5.1	1.1	4.5	2.0	-0.2	-3.8
1954	4.1	0.7	3.0	5.2	2.6	1.8	4.3	-3.5	7.3	-2.3	9.8	4.6	44.0
1955	1.1	0.7	-0.5	3.9	-0.2	6.2	3.2	0.5	-0.3	-2.5	6.2	1.1	20.8
1956	-3.6	2.7	5.8	0.8	-7.4	3.1	5.1	-3.0	-5.3	1.0	-1.5	5.6	2.3
1957	-4.1	-3.0	2.2	4.1	2.1	-0.3	1.0	-4.8	-5.8	-3.3	2.0	-3.2	-12.8
1958	3.3	-2.2	1.6	2.0	1.5	3.3	5.2	1.1	4.6	2.1	2.6	4.7	34.0
1959	1.8	1.6	-0.3	3.7	3.2	-0.03	4.9	-1.6	-4.9	2.4	1.9	3.1	16.4
1960	-8.4	1.2	-2.1	-2.4	4.0	2.4	-3.7	1.5	-7.3	0.04	2.9	3.1	-9.3
1961	5.2	2.1	2.2	0.3	2.7	-1.8	3.1	2.1	-2.6	0.4	2.5	1.3	18.7
1962	-4.3	1.1	-0.2	-5.9	-7.8	-8.5	6.5	1.9	-5.0	1.9	10.1	0.4	-10.8
1963	4.7	-2.9	3.0	5.2	1.3	-2.8	-1.6	4.9	0.5	3.1	-0.6	1.7	17.0
1964	2.9	1.9	1.6	-0.3	1.2	1.3	1.2	-0.3	4.4	-0.3	0.3	-0.1	14.6
1965	3.3	0.1	-1.6	3.7	-0.5	-5.4	1.6	1.3	4.2	3.2	-1.5	2.4	10.9
1966	1.5	-3.2	-2.8	1.0	-5.3	-1.6	-2.6	-7.0	-1.8	4.2	-1.9	-0.7	-18.9
1967	8.2	-1.2	3.2	3.6	-5.0	0.9	5.1	-0.3	2.8	-5.1	-0.4	3.3	15.2
1968	-5.5	-1.7	0.02	8.5	-1.4	-0.1	-1.6	1.5	4.4	1.8	3.4	-4.2	4.3
1969	0.2	-4.3	3.3	1.6	-1.3	-6.9	-6.6	2.6	-2.8	5.3	-5.1	-1.5	-15.2
1970	-7.0	4.5	1.0	-6.3	-4.8	-2.4	7.4	4.1	-0.5	-0.7	5.1	5.6	4.8
1971	3.5	1.2	2.9	4.1	-3.6	-1.8	-3.7	4.6	-1.2	-5.4	-0.9	7.1	6.1
1972	1.3	2.9	1.4	1.4	0.7	-3.3	-0.5	4.2	-1.1	0.2	6.6	0.2	14.6
1973	-2.1	-4.4	-0.4	-3.1	-2.2	-1.1	3.9	-4.2	6.7	1.0	-14.0	3.5	-16.6
1974	0.6	0.6	-1.6	-1.2	-4.1	0.03	-5.6	-10.4	-10.4	9.5	-7.0	-0.4	-27.6
1975	14.2	5.0	3.9	6.9	1.3	5.6	-5.4	0.5	-5.0	5.3	2.9	-1.0	38.3
1976	14.4	-0.3	2.8	-0.3	-2.2	2.8	-1.8	-1.1	1.7	-2.6	-1.8	6.1	17.9
1977	-5.0	-1.9	-1.8	0.8	-3.0	2.0	-2.9	-3.2	-1.7	-3.4	1.4	0.2	-17.3
1978	-7.4	-3.6	2.1	10.6	0.4	-2.6	5.3	1.7	-1.3	-8.5	0.8	0.7	-3.1
1979	4.2	-3.6	6.6	-0.8	-3.8	2.4	0.5	4.9	-1.0	-7.2	0.8	2.0	4.2
1980	4.4	-1.5	-9.0	4.0	4.1	2.0	7.8	-0.3	-0.02	-0.9	7.4	-3.0	14.9
1981	-1.7	2.9	3.0	-0.6	-0.6	-1.5	-2.5	-7.4	-3.6	0.3	4.3	-1.6	-9.2
1982	-0.4	-5.4	-0.2	3.1	-3.4	-0.9	-0.4	11.5	-0.6	10.7	4.8	0.7	19.6
1983	2.8	3.4	1.6	8.5	-2.1	1.8	-1.9	1.4	1.4	-0.6	4.1	-1.4	20.3
1984	-3.0	-5.4	0.9	0.5	-5.6	2.5	-1.5	9.8	-1.4	0.1	-1.5	1.9	-3.7
1985	6.2	-0.2	-1.3	-0.7	4.6	1.5	0.9	-1.0	-0.4	3.4	7.1	5.1	27.7
1986	1.6	8.8	6.4	-1.9	5.2	0.9	-6.2	6.9	-6.9	6.2	1.9	-1.0	22.6
1987	13.8	3.1	3.6	-0.8	0.2	5.5	6.3	3.5	-2.5	-23.2	-8.0	5.7	2.3
1988	1.0	5.8	-4.0	2.2	-0.1	5.4	-0.6	-4.6	4.0	1.7	-1.6	2.6	11.8
1989	8.0	-3.6	1.6	5.5	2.5	-1.6	9.0	2.9	-1.6	-1.8	2.3	1.7	27.0
1990	-5.9	1.4	3.0	-1.9	8.3	0.1	0.9	-10.0	-6.2	-0.4	4.8	2.9	-4.3
1991	3.9	5.3	1.1	-0.9	4.8	-4.0	4.1	0.6	-0.9	1.7	-5.7	9.5	20.3
1992	1.7	1.4	-1.0	3.8	1.1	-2.3	2.3	-4.0	0.4	-1.4	2.4	-0.1	4.2
1993	0.3	1.8	1.9	-0.2	2.9	-0.3	0.7	3.2	-2.6	3.5	0.1	1.9	13.7
1994	6.0	-3.7	-5.1	1.3	2.1	-3.5	3.8	4.0	-1.8	1.7	-4.3	2.5	2.1
1995	0.2	4.3	3.7	3.9	3.3	2.0	3.3	-2.1	3.9	-0.7	6.7	0.8	33.5
1996	5.4	1.7	1.9	-0.3	1.3	0.2	-2.2	1.6	4.7	2.5	8.2	-1.1	26.0
1997	5.7	0.9	-4.3	6.5	4.6	4.7	7.2	-7.3	4.2	-6.3	5.1	1.1	22.6
1998	-0.02	8.1	3.0	3.0	-1.8	0.6	-0.8	-15.1	4.0	9.6	6.1	0.7	16.1
1999	1.9	-0.6	5.2	10.2	-2.1	3.9	-2.9	1.6	-4.5	3.8	1.4	5.7	25.2
2000	-4.8	-7.4	7.8	-1.7	-2.0	-0.7	0.7	6.6	-5.0	3.0	-5.1	3.6	-6.2
2001	0.9	-3.6	-5.9	8.7	1.6	-3.8	0.2	-5.4	-11.1	2.6	8.6	1.7	-7.1
2002	-1.0	1.9	2.9	-4.4	-0.2	-6.9	-5.5	-0.8	-12.4	10.6	5.9	-6.2	-16.8
2003	-3.5	-2.0	1.3	6.1	4.4	1.5	2.8	2.0	-1.5	5.7	-0.2	6.9	25.3
2004	0.3	0.9	-2.1	-1.3	-0.4	2.4	-2.8	0.3	-0.9	-0.5	4.0	3.4	3.1
2005	-2.7	2.6	-2.4	-3.0	2.7	-1.8	3.6	-1.5	0.8	-1.2	3.5	-0.8	-0.6
2006	1.4	1.2	1.1	2.3	-1.7	-0.2	0.3	1.7	2.6	3.4	1.2	2.0	16.3
2007	1.3	-2.8	0.7	5.7	4.3	-1.6	-1.5	1.1	4.0	0.2	-4.0	-0.8	6.4
2008	-4.6	-3.0	-0.03	4.5	-1.4	-10.2	0.2	1.5	-6.0	-14.1	-5.3	-0.6	-33.8
2009	-8.8	-11.7	7.7	7.3	4.1	-0.6	8.6	3.5	2.3	0.005	6.5	0.8	18.8
2010	-3.5	2.6	5.1	1.4	-7.9	-3.6	7.1	-4.3	7.7	3.1	-1.0	5.2	11.0
2011	2.7	2.8	0.8	4.0	-1.9	-1.2	-2.2	-4.4	-6.0	9.5	0.8	1.4	5.5
2012	3.4	2.5	2.0	0.01	-6.2	3.9	1.0	0.6	2.6	-2.5	-0.5	0.6	7.3
2013	5.8	1.4	3.7	1.8	1.9	-1.4	4.0	-4.4	2.2	2.8	3.5	3.0	26.5
2014	-5.3	4.0	0.8	0.7	0.8	0.7	-1.6	3.2	-0.3	2.0	2.5	-0.03	7.5
2015	-3.7	5.6	-2.0	0.4									
TOTALS	63.2	13.8	70.6	127.1	-2.5	-19.7	75.5	-5.4	-48.6	34.8	98.8	109.5	
AVG.	1.0	0.2	1.1	1.9	-0.04	-0.3	1.2	-0.1	-0.7	0.5	1.5	1.7	
# Up	42	39	43	44	33	30	40	37	26	39	43	46	
# Down	24	27	23	22	32	35	25	28	39	26	22	19	

DOW JONES INDUSTRIALS MONTHLY POINT CHANGES SINCE 1950

	Jan	Feb	Mar	Apr	May	Jun	Jul	Aug	Sep	Oct	Nov	Dec	Year's Close
1950	1.66	1.65	2.61	8.28	9.09	−14.31	0.29	7.47	9.49	−1.35	2.59	7.81	235.41
1951	13.42	3.22	−4.11	11.19	−9.48	−7.01	15.22	12.39	0.91	−8.81	−1.08	7.96	269.23
1952	1.46	−10.61	9.38	−11.83	5.31	11.32	5.30	−4.52	−4.43	−1.38	14.43	8.24	291.90
1953	−2.13	−5.50	−4.40	−5.12	−2.47	−4.02	7.12	−14.16	2.82	11.77	5.56	−0.47	280.90
1954	11.49	2.15	8.97	15.82	8.16	6.04	14.39	−12.12	24.66	−8.32	34.63	17.62	404.39
1955	4.44	3.04	−2.17	15.95	−0.79	26.52	14.47	2.33	−1.56	−11.75	28.39	5.14	488.40
1956	−17.66	12.91	28.14	4.33	−38.07	14.73	25.03	−15.77	−26.79	4.60	−7.07	26.69	499.47
1957	−20.31	−14.54	10.19	19.55	10.57	−1.64	5.23	−24.17	−28.05	−15.26	8.83	−14.18	435.69
1958	14.33	−10.10	6.84	9.10	6.84	15.48	24.81	5.64	23.46	11.13	14.24	26.19	583.65
1959	10.31	9.54	−1.79	22.04	20.04	−0.19	31.28	−10.47	−32.73	14.92	12.58	20.18	679.36
1960	−56.74	7.50	−13.53	−14.89	23.80	15.12	−23.89	9.26	−45.85	0.22	16.86	18.67	615.89
1961	32.31	13.88	14.55	2.08	18.01	−12.76	21.41	14.57	−18.73	2.71	17.68	9.54	731.14
1962	−31.14	8.05	−1.10	−41.62	−51.97	−52.08	36.65	11.25	−30.20	10.79	59.53	2.80	652.10
1963	30.75	−19.91	19.58	35.18	9.26	−20.08	−11.45	33.89	3.47	22.44	−4.71	12.43	762.95
1964	22.39	14.80	13.15	−2.52	9.79	10.94	9.60	−2.62	36.89	−2.29	2.35	−1.30	874.13
1965	28.73	0.62	−14.43	33.26	−4.27	−50.01	13.71	11.36	37.48	30.24	−14.11	22.55	969.26
1966	14.25	−31.62	−27.12	8.91	−49.61	−13.97	−22.72	−58.97	−14.19	32.85	−15.48	−5.90	785.69
1967	64.20	−10.52	26.61	31.07	−44.49	7.70	43.98	−2.95	25.37	−46.92	−3.93	29.30	905.11
1968	−49.64	−14.97	0.17	71.55	−13.22	−1.20	−14.80	13.01	39.78	16.60	32.69	−41.33	943.75
1969	2.30	−40.84	30.27	14.70	−12.62	−64.37	−57.72	21.25	−23.63	42.90	−43.69	−11.94	800.36
1970	−56.30	33.53	7.98	−49.50	−35.63	−16.91	50.59	30.46	−3.90	−5.07	38.48	44.83	838.92
1971	29.58	10.33	25.54	37.38	−33.94	−16.67	−32.71	39.64	−10.88	−48.19	−7.66	58.86	890.20
1972	11.97	25.96	12.57	13.47	6.55	−31.69	−4.29	38.99	−10.46	2.25	62.69	1.81	1020.02
1973	−21.00	−43.95	−4.06	−29.58	−20.02	−9.70	34.69	−38.83	59.53	9.48	−134.33	28.61	850.86
1974	4.69	4.98	−13.85	−9.93	−34.58	0.24	−44.98	−78.85	−70.71	57.65	−46.86	−2.42	616.24
1975	87.45	35.36	29.10	53.19	10.95	46.70	−47.48	3.83	−41.46	42.16	24.63	−8.26	852.41
1976	122.87	−2.67	26.84	−2.60	−21.62	27.55	−18.14	−10.90	16.45	−25.26	−17.71	57.43	1004.65
1977	−50.28	−17.95	−17.29	7.77	−28.24	17.64	−26.23	−28.58	−14.38	−28.76	11.35	1.47	831.17
1978	−61.25	−27.80	15.24	79.96	3.29	−21.66	43.32	14.55	−11.00	−73.37	6.58	5.98	805.01
1979	34.21	−30.40	53.36	−7.28	−32.57	19.65	4.44	41.21	−9.05	−62.88	6.65	16.39	838.74
1980	37.11	−12.71	−77.39	31.31	33.79	17.07	67.40	−2.73	−0.17	−7.93	68.85	−29.35	963.99
1981	−16.72	27.31	29.29	−6.12	−6.00	−14.87	−24.54	−70.87	−31.49	2.57	36.43	−13.98	875.00
1982	−3.90	−46.71	−1.62	25.59	−28.82	−7.61	−3.33	92.71	−5.06	95.47	47.56	7.26	1046.54
1983	29.16	36.92	17.41	96.17	−26.22	21.98	−22.74	16.94	16.97	−7.93	50.82	−17.38	1258.64
1984	−38.06	−65.95	10.26	5.86	−65.90	27.55	−17.12	109.10	−17.67	0.67	−18.44	22.63	1211.57
1985	75.20	−2.76	−17.23	−8.72	57.35	20.05	11.99	−13.44	−5.38	45.68	97.82	74.54	1546.67
1986	24.32	138.07	109.55	−34.63	92.73	16.01	−117.41	123.03	−130.76	110.23	36.42	−18.28	1895.95
1987	262.09	65.95	80.70	−18.33	5.21	126.96	153.54	90.88	−66.67	−602.75	−159.98	105.28	1938.83
1988	19.39	113.40	−83.56	44.27	−1.21	110.59	−12.98	−97.08	81.26	35.74	−34.14	54.06	2168.57
1989	173.75	−83.93	35.23	125.18	61.35	−40.09	220.60	76.61	−44.45	−47.74	61.19	46.93	2753.20
1990	−162.66	36.71	79.96	−50.45	219.90	4.03	24.51	−290.84	−161.88	−10.15	117.32	74.01	2633.66
1991	102.73	145.79	31.68	−25.99	139.63	−120.75	118.07	18.78	−26.83	52.33	−174.42	274.15	3168.83
1992	54.56	44.28	−32.20	123.65	37.76	−78.36	75.26	−136.43	14.31	−45.38	78.88	−4.05	3301.11
1993	8.92	60.78	64.30	−7.56	99.88	−11.35	23.39	111.78	−96.13	125.47	3.36	70.14	3754.09
1994	224.27	−146.34	−196.06	45.73	76.68	−133.41	139.54	148.92	−70.23	64.93	−168.89	95.21	3834.44
1995	9.42	167.19	146.64	163.58	143.87	90.96	152.37	−97.91	178.52	−33.60	319.01	42.63	5117.12
1996	278.18	90.32	101.52	−18.06	74.10	11.45	−125.72	87.30	265.96	147.21	492.32	−73.43	6448.27
1997	364.82	64.65	−294.26	425.51	322.05	341.75	549.82	−600.19	322.84	−503.18	381.05	85.12	7908.25
1998	−1.75	639.22	254.09	263.56	−163.42	52.07	−68.73	−1344.22	303.55	749.48	524.45	64.88	9181.43
1999	177.40	−52.25	479.58	1002.88	−229.30	411.06	−315.65	174.13	−492.33	392.91	147.95	619.31	11497.12
2000	−556.59	−812.22	793.61	−188.01	−211.58	−74.44	74.09	693.12	−564.18	320.22	−556.65	372.36	10786.85
2001	100.51	−392.08	−616.50	856.19	176.97	−409.54	20.41	−573.06	−1102.19	227.58	776.42	169.94	10021.50
2002	−101.50	186.13	297.81	−457.72	−20.97	−681.99	−506.67	−73.09	−1071.57	805.10	499.06	−554.46	8341.63
2003	−287.82	−162.73	101.05	487.96	370.17	135.18	248.36	182.02	−140.76	526.06	−18.66	671.46	10453.92
2004	34.15	95.85	−226.22	−132.13	−37.12	247.03	−295.77	34.21	−93.65	−52.80	400.55	354.99	10783.01
2005	−293.07	276.29	−262.47	−311.25	274.97	−192.51	365.94	−159.31	87.10	−128.63	365.80	−88.37	10717.50
2006	147.36	128.55	115.91	257.82	−198.83	−18.09	35.46	195.47	297.92	401.66	141.20	241.22	12463.15
2007	158.54	−353.06	85.72	708.56	564.73	−219.02	−196.63	145.75	537.89	34.38	−558.29	−106.90	13264.82
2008	−614.46	−383.97	−3.50	557.24	−181.81	−1288.31	28.01	165.53	−692.89	−1525.65	−495.97	−52.65	8776.39
2009	−775.53	−937.93	545.99	559.20	332.21	−53.33	724.61	324.67	216.00	6.83	632.11	83.21	10428.05
2010	−360.72	257.93	531.37	151.98	−871.98	−362.61	691.92	−451.22	773.33	330.44	−112.47	571.49	11577.51
2011	314.42	334.41	93.39	490.81	−240.75	−155.45	−271.10	−529.71	−700.15	1041.63	90.67	171.88	12217.56
2012	415.35	319.16	259.97	1.59	−820.18	486.64	128.59	82.16	346.29	−340.67	−70.88	78.56	13104.14
2013	756.44	193.91	524.05	261.26	275.77	−205.97	589.94	−689.23	319.36	416.08	540.66	490.25	16576.66
2014	−877.81	622.86	135.95	123.18	136.33	109.43	−263.30	535.15	−55.55	347.62	437.72	−5.17	17823.07
2015	−658.12	967.75	−356.58	64.40									
TOTALS	−804.26	1466.93	2994.68	5934.42	99.43	−1956.53	2299.25	−1712.88	−1926.38	2940.60	4082.94	4222.19	
# Up	42	39	43	44	33	30	40	37	26	39	43	46	
# Down	24	27	23	22	32	35	25	28	39	26	22	19	

153

DOW JONES INDUSTRIALS MONTHLY CLOSING PRICES SINCE 1950

	Jan	Feb	Mar	Apr	May	Jun	Jul	Aug	Sep	Oct	Nov	Dec
1950	201.79	203.44	206.05	214.33	223.42	209.11	209.40	216.87	226.36	225.01	227.60	235.41
1951	248.83	252.05	247.94	259.13	249.65	242.64	257.86	270.25	271.16	262.35	261.27	269.23
1952	270.69	260.08	269.46	257.63	262.94	274.26	279.56	275.04	270.61	269.23	283.66	291.90
1953	289.77	284.27	279.87	274.75	272.28	268.26	275.38	261.22	264.04	275.81	281.37	280.90
1954	292.39	294.54	303.51	319.33	327.49	333.53	347.92	335.80	360.46	352.14	386.77	404.39
1955	408.83	411.87	409.70	425.65	424.86	451.38	465.85	468.18	466.62	454.87	483.26	488.40
1956	470.74	483.65	511.79	516.12	478.05	492.78	517.81	502.04	475.25	479.85	472.78	499.47
1957	479.16	464.62	474.81	494.36	504.93	503.29	508.52	484.35	456.30	441.04	449.87	435.69
1958	450.02	439.92	446.76	455.86	462.70	478.18	502.99	508.63	532.09	543.22	557.46	583.65
1959	593.96	603.50	601.71	623.75	643.79	643.60	674.88	664.41	631.68	646.60	659.18	679.36
1960	622.62	630.12	616.59	601.70	625.50	640.62	616.73	625.99	580.14	580.36	597.22	615.89
1961	648.20	662.08	676.63	678.71	696.72	683.96	705.37	719.94	701.21	703.92	721.60	731.14
1962	700.00	708.05	706.95	665.33	613.36	561.28	597.93	609.18	578.98	589.77	649.30	652.10
1963	682.85	662.94	682.52	717.70	726.96	706.88	695.43	729.32	732.79	755.23	750.52	762.95
1964	785.34	800.14	813.29	810.77	820.56	831.50	841.10	838.48	875.37	873.08	875.43	874.13
1965	902.86	903.48	889.05	922.31	918.04	868.03	881.74	893.10	930.58	960.82	946.71	969.26
1966	983.51	951.89	924.77	933.68	884.07	870.10	847.38	788.41	774.22	807.07	791.59	785.69
1967	849.89	839.37	865.98	897.05	852.56	860.26	904.24	901.29	926.66	879.74	875.81	905.11
1968	855.47	840.50	840.67	912.22	899.00	897.80	883.00	896.01	935.79	952.39	985.08	943.75
1969	946.05	905.21	935.48	950.18	937.56	873.19	815.47	836.72	813.09	855.99	812.30	800.36
1970	744.06	777.59	785.57	736.07	700.44	683.53	734.12	764.58	760.68	755.61	794.09	838.92
1971	868.50	878.83	904.37	941.75	907.81	891.14	858.43	898.07	887.19	839.00	831.34	890.20
1972	902.17	928.13	940.70	954.17	960.72	929.03	924.74	963.73	953.27	955.52	1018.21	1020.02
1973	999.02	955.07	951.01	921.43	901.41	891.71	926.40	887.57	947.10	956.58	822.25	850.86
1974	855.55	860.53	846.68	836.75	802.17	802.41	757.43	678.58	607.87	665.52	618.66	616.24
1975	703.69	739.05	768.15	821.34	832.29	878.99	831.51	835.34	793.88	836.04	860.67	852.41
1976	975.28	972.61	999.45	996.85	975.23	1002.78	984.64	973.74	990.19	964.93	947.22	1004.65
1977	954.37	936.42	919.13	926.90	898.66	916.30	890.07	861.49	847.11	818.35	829.70	831.17
1978	769.92	742.12	757.36	837.32	840.61	818.95	862.27	876.82	865.82	792.45	799.03	805.01
1979	839.22	808.82	862.18	854.90	822.33	841.98	846.42	887.63	878.58	815.70	822.35	838.74
1980	875.85	863.14	785.75	817.06	850.85	867.92	935.32	932.59	932.42	924.49	993.34	963.99
1981	947.27	974.58	1003.87	997.75	991.75	976.88	952.34	881.47	849.98	852.55	888.98	875.00
1982	871.10	824.39	822.77	848.36	819.54	811.93	808.60	901.31	896.25	991.72	1039.28	1046.54
1983	1075.70	1112.62	1130.03	1226.20	1199.98	1221.96	1199.22	1216.16	1233.13	1225.20	1276.02	1258.64
1984	1220.58	1154.63	1164.89	1170.75	1104.85	1132.40	1115.28	1224.38	1206.71	1207.38	1188.94	1211.57
1985	1286.77	1284.01	1266.78	1258.06	1315.41	1335.46	1347.45	1334.01	1328.63	1374.31	1472.13	1546.67
1986	1570.99	1709.06	1818.61	1783.98	1876.71	1892.72	1775.31	1898.34	1767.58	1877.81	1914.23	1895.95
1987	2158.04	2223.99	2304.69	2286.36	2291.57	2418.53	2572.07	2662.95	2596.28	1993.53	1833.55	1938.83
1988	1958.22	2071.62	1988.06	2032.33	2031.12	2141.71	2128.73	2031.65	2112.91	2148.65	2114.51	2168.57
1989	2342.32	2258.39	2293.62	2418.80	2480.15	2440.06	2660.66	2737.27	2692.82	2645.08	2706.27	2753.20
1990	2590.54	2627.25	2707.21	2656.76	2876.66	2880.69	2905.20	2614.36	2452.48	2442.33	2559.65	2633.66
1991	2736.39	2882.18	2913.86	2887.87	3027.50	2906.75	3024.82	3043.60	3016.77	3069.10	2894.68	3168.83
1992	3223.39	3267.67	3235.47	3359.12	3396.88	3318.52	3393.78	3257.35	3271.66	3226.28	3305.16	3301.11
1993	3310.03	3370.81	3435.11	3427.55	3527.43	3516.08	3539.47	3651.25	3555.12	3680.59	3683.95	3754.09
1994	3978.36	3832.02	3635.96	3681.69	3758.37	3624.96	3764.50	3913.42	3843.19	3908.12	3739.23	3834.44
1995	3843.86	4011.05	4157.69	4321.27	4465.14	4556.10	4708.47	4610.56	4789.08	4755.48	5074.49	5117.12
1996	5395.30	5485.62	5587.14	5569.08	5643.18	5654.63	5528.91	5616.21	5882.17	6029.38	6521.70	6448.27
1997	6813.09	6877.74	6583.48	7008.99	7331.04	7672.79	8222.61	7622.42	7945.26	7442.08	7823.13	7908.25
1998	7906.50	8545.72	8799.81	9063.37	8899.95	8952.02	8883.29	7539.07	7842.62	8592.10	9116.55	9181.43
1999	9358.83	9306.58	9786.16	10789.04	10559.74	10970.80	10655.15	10829.28	10336.95	10729.86	10877.81	11497.12
2000	10940.53	10128.31	10921.92	10733.91	10522.33	10447.89	10521.98	11215.10	10650.92	10971.14	10414.49	10786.85
2001	10887.36	10495.28	9878.78	10734.97	10911.94	10502.40	10522.81	9949.75	8847.56	9075.14	9851.56	10021.50
2002	9920.00	10106.13	10403.94	9946.22	9925.25	9243.26	8736.59	8663.50	7591.93	8397.03	8896.09	8341.63
2003	8053.81	7891.08	7992.13	8480.09	8850.26	8985.44	9233.80	9415.82	9275.06	9801.12	9782.46	10453.92
2004	10488.07	10583.92	10357.70	10225.57	10188.45	10435.48	10139.71	10173.92	10080.27	10027.47	10428.02	10783.01
2005	10489.94	10766.23	10503.76	10192.51	10467.48	10274.97	10640.91	10481.60	10568.70	10440.07	10805.87	10717.50
2006	10864.86	10993.41	11109.32	11367.14	11168.31	11150.22	11185.68	11381.15	11679.07	12080.73	12221.93	12463.15
2007	12621.69	12268.63	12354.35	13062.91	13627.64	13408.62	13211.99	13357.74	13895.63	13930.01	13371.72	13264.82
2008	12650.36	12266.39	12262.89	12820.13	12638.32	11350.01	11378.02	11543.55	10850.66	9325.01	8829.04	8776.39
2009	8000.86	7062.93	7608.92	8168.12	8500.33	8447.00	9171.61	9496.28	9712.28	9712.73	10344.84	10428.05
2010	10067.33	10325.26	10856.63	11008.61	10136.63	9774.02	10465.94	10014.72	10788.05	11118.49	11006.02	11577.51
2011	11891.93	12226.34	12319.73	12810.54	12569.79	12414.34	12143.24	11613.53	10913.38	11955.01	12045.68	12217.56
2012	12632.91	12952.07	13212.04	13213.63	12393.45	12880.09	13008.68	13090.84	13437.13	13096.46	13025.58	13104.14
2013	13860.58	14054.49	14578.54	14839.80	15115.57	14909.60	15499.54	14810.31	15129.67	15545.75	16086.41	16576.66
2014	15698.85	16321.71	16457.66	16580.84	16717.17	16826.60	16563.30	17098.45	17042.90	17390.52	17828.24	17823.07
2015	17164.95	18132.70	17776.12	17840.52								

154

STANDARD & POOR'S 500 MONTHLY PERCENT CHANGES SINCE 1950

	Jan	Feb	Mar	Apr	May	Jun	Jul	Aug	Sep	Oct	Nov	Dec	Year's Change
1950	1.7	1.0	0.4	4.5	3.9	−5.8	0.8	3.3	5.6	0.4	−0.1	4.6	21.8
1951	6.1	0.6	−1.8	4.8	−4.1	−2.6	6.9	3.9	−0.1	−1.4	−0.3	3.9	16.5
1952	1.6	−3.6	4.8	−4.3	2.3	4.6	1.8	−1.5	−2.0	−0.1	4.6	3.5	11.8
1953	−0.7	−1.8	−2.4	−2.6	−0.3	−1.6	2.5	−5.8	0.1	5.1	0.9	0.2	−6.6
1954	5.1	0.3	3.0	4.9	3.3	0.1	5.7	−3.4	8.3	−1.9	8.1	5.1	45.0
1955	1.8	0.4	−0.5	3.8	−0.1	8.2	6.1	−0.8	1.1	−3.0	7.5	−0.1	26.4
1956	−3.6	3.5	6.9	−0.2	−6.6	3.9	5.2	−3.8	−4.5	0.5	−1.1	3.5	2.6
1957	−4.2	−3.3	2.0	3.7	3.7	−0.1	1.1	−5.6	−6.2	−3.2	1.6	−4.1	−14.3
1958	4.3	−2.1	3.1	3.2	1.5	2.6	4.3	1.2	4.8	2.5	2.2	5.2	38.1
1959	0.4	−0.02	0.1	3.9	1.9	−0.4	3.5	−1.5	−4.6	1.1	1.3	2.8	8.5
1960	−7.1	0.9	−1.4	−1.8	2.7	2.0	−2.5	2.6	−6.0	−0.2	4.0	4.6	−3.0
1961	6.3	2.7	2.6	0.4	1.9	−2.9	3.3	2.0	−2.0	2.8	3.9	0.3	23.1
1962	−3.8	1.6	−0.6	−6.2	−8.6	−8.2	6.4	1.5	−4.8	0.4	10.2	1.3	−11.8
1963	4.9	−2.9	3.5	4.9	1.4	−2.0	−0.3	4.9	−1.1	3.2	−1.1	2.4	18.9
1964	2.7	1.0	1.5	0.6	1.1	1.6	1.8	−1.6	2.9	0.8	−0.5	0.4	13.0
1965	3.3	−0.1	−1.5	3.4	−0.8	−4.9	1.3	2.3	3.2	2.7	−0.9	0.9	9.1
1966	0.5	−1.8	−2.2	2.1	−5.4	−1.6	−1.3	−7.8	−0.7	4.8	0.3	−0.1	−13.1
1967	7.8	0.2	3.9	4.2	−5.2	1.8	4.5	−1.2	3.3	−2.9	0.1	2.6	20.1
1968	−4.4	−3.1	0.9	8.2	1.1	0.9	−1.8	1.1	3.9	0.7	4.8	−4.2	7.7
1969	−0.8	−4.7	3.4	2.1	−0.2	−5.6	−6.0	4.0	−2.5	4.4	−3.5	−1.9	−11.4
1970	−7.6	5.3	0.1	−9.0	−6.1	−5.0	7.3	4.4	3.3	−1.1	4.7	5.7	0.1
1971	4.0	0.9	3.7	3.6	−4.2	0.1	−4.1	3.6	−0.7	−4.2	−0.3	8.6	10.8
1972	1.8	2.5	0.6	0.4	1.7	−2.2	0.2	3.4	−0.5	0.9	4.6	1.2	15.6
1973	−1.7	−3.7	−0.1	−4.1	−1.9	−0.7	3.8	−3.7	4.0	−0.1	−11.4	1.7	−17.4
1974	−1.0	−0.4	−2.3	−3.9	−3.4	−1.5	−7.8	−9.0	−11.9	16.3	−5.3	−2.0	−29.7
1975	12.3	6.0	2.2	4.7	4.4	4.4	−6.8	−2.1	−3.5	6.2	2.5	−1.2	31.5
1976	11.8	−1.1	3.1	−1.1	−1.4	4.1	−0.8	−0.5	2.3	−2.2	−0.8	5.2	19.1
1977	−5.1	−2.2	−1.4	0.02	−2.4	4.5	−1.6	−2.1	−0.2	−4.3	2.7	0.3	−11.5
1978	−6.2	−2.5	2.5	8.5	0.4	−1.8	5.4	2.6	−0.7	−9.2	1.7	1.5	1.1
1979	4.0	−3.7	5.5	0.2	−2.6	3.9	0.9	5.3	N/C	−6.9	4.3	1.7	12.3
1980	5.8	−0.4	−10.2	4.1	4.7	2.7	6.5	0.6	2.5	1.6	10.2	−3.4	25.8
1981	−4.6	1.3	3.6	−2.3	−0.2	−1.0	−0.2	−6.2	−5.4	4.9	3.7	−3.0	−9.7
1982	−1.8	−6.1	−1.0	4.0	−3.9	−2.0	−2.3	11.6	0.8	11.0	3.6	1.5	14.8
1983	3.3	1.9	3.3	7.5	−1.2	3.5	−3.3	1.1	1.0	−1.5	1.7	−0.9	17.3
1984	−0.9	−3.9	1.3	0.5	−5.9	1.7	−1.6	10.6	−0.3	−0.01	−1.5	2.2	1.4
1985	7.4	0.9	−0.3	−0.5	5.4	1.2	−0.5	−1.2	−3.5	4.3	6.5	4.5	26.3
1986	0.2	7.1	5.3	−1.4	5.0	1.4	−5.9	7.1	−8.5	5.5	2.1	−2.8	14.6
1987	13.2	3.7	2.6	−1.1	0.6	4.8	4.8	3.5	−2.4	−21.8	−8.5	7.3	2.0
1988	4.0	4.2	−3.3	0.9	0.3	4.3	−0.5	−3.9	4.0	2.6	−1.9	1.5	12.4
1989	7.1	−2.9	2.1	5.0	3.5	−0.8	8.8	1.6	−0.7	−2.5	1.7	2.1	27.3
1990	−6.9	0.9	2.4	−2.7	9.2	−0.9	−0.5	−9.4	−5.1	−0.7	6.0	2.5	−6.6
1991	4.2	6.7	2.2	0.03	3.9	−4.8	4.5	2.0	−1.9	1.2	−4.4	11.2	26.3
1992	−2.0	1.0	−2.2	2.8	0.1	−1.7	3.9	−2.4	0.9	0.2	3.0	1.0	4.5
1993	0.7	1.0	1.9	−2.5	2.3	0.1	−0.5	3.4	−1.0	1.9	−1.3	1.0	7.1
1994	3.3	−3.0	−4.6	1.2	1.2	−2.7	3.1	3.8	−2.7	2.1	−4.0	1.2	−1.5
1995	2.4	3.6	2.7	2.8	3.6	2.1	3.2	−0.03	4.0	−0.5	4.1	1.7	34.1
1996	3.3	0.7	0.8	1.3	2.3	0.2	−4.6	1.9	5.4	2.6	7.3	−2.2	20.3
1997	6.1	0.6	−4.3	5.8	5.9	4.3	7.8	−5.7	5.3	−3.4	4.5	1.6	31.0
1998	1.0	7.0	5.0	0.9	−1.9	3.9	−1.2	−14.6	6.2	8.0	5.9	5.6	26.7
1999	4.1	−3.2	3.9	3.8	−2.5	5.4	−3.2	−0.6	−2.9	6.3	1.9	5.8	19.5
2000	−5.1	−2.0	9.7	−3.1	−2.2	2.4	−1.6	6.1	−5.3	−0.5	−8.0	0.4	−10.1
2001	3.5	−9.2	−6.4	7.7	0.5	−2.5	−1.1	−6.4	−8.2	1.8	7.5	0.8	−13.0
2002	−1.6	−2.1	3.7	−6.1	−0.9	−7.2	−7.9	0.5	−11.0	8.6	5.7	−6.0	−23.4
2003	−2.7	−1.7	1.0	8.0	5.1	1.1	1.6	1.8	−1.2	5.5	0.7	5.1	26.4
2004	1.7	1.2	−1.6	−1.7	1.2	1.8	−3.4	0.2	0.9	1.4	3.9	3.2	9.0
2005	−2.5	1.9	−1.9	−2.0	3.0	−0.01	3.6	−1.1	0.7	−1.8	3.5	−0.1	3.0
2006	2.5	0.05	1.1	1.2	−3.1	0.01	0.5	2.1	2.5	3.2	1.6	1.3	13.6
2007	1.4	−2.2	1.0	4.3	3.3	−1.8	−3.2	1.3	3.6	1.5	−4.4	−0.9	3.5
2008	−6.1	−3.5	−0.6	4.8	1.1	−8.6	−1.0	1.2	−9.1	−16.9	−7.5	0.8	−38.5
2009	−8.6	−11.0	8.5	9.4	5.3	0.02	7.4	3.4	3.6	−2.0	5.7	1.8	23.5
2010	−3.7	2.9	5.9	1.5	−8.2	−5.4	6.9	−4.7	8.8	3.7	−0.2	6.5	12.8
2011	2.3	3.2	−0.1	2.8	−1.4	−1.8	−2.1	−5.7	−7.2	10.8	−0.5	0.9	−0.003
2012	4.4	4.1	3.1	−0.7	−6.3	4.0	1.3	2.0	2.4	−2.0	0.3	0.7	13.4
2013	5.0	1.1	3.6	1.8	2.1	−1.5	4.9	−3.1	3.0	4.5	2.8	2.4	29.6
2014	−3.6	4.3	0.7	0.6	2.1	1.9	−1.5	3.8	−1.6	2.3	2.5	−0.4	11.4
2015	−3.1	5.5	−1.7	0.9									
TOTALS	67.9	3.5	76.8	98.5	12.0	−0.1	62.5	0.3	−31.6	54.0	98.9	108.5	
AVG.	1.0	0.05	1.2	1.5	0.2	−0.001	1.0	0.004	−0.5	0.8	1.5	1.7	
# Up	40	37	43	46	37	34	35	36	29	39	43	49	
# Down	26	29	23	20	28	31	30	29	35	26	22	16	

155

STANDARD & POOR'S 500 MONTHLY CLOSING PRICES SINCE 1950

	Jan	Feb	Mar	Apr	May	Jun	Jul	Aug	Sep	Oct	Nov	Dec
1950	17.05	17.22	17.29	18.07	18.78	17.69	17.84	18.42	19.45	19.53	19.51	20.41
1951	21.66	21.80	21.40	22.43	21.52	20.96	22.40	23.28	23.26	22.94	22.88	23.77
1952	24.14	23.26	24.37	23.32	23.86	24.96	25.40	25.03	24.54	24.52	25.66	26.57
1953	26.38	25.90	25.29	24.62	24.54	24.14	24.75	23.32	23.35	24.54	24.76	24.81
1954	26.08	26.15	26.94	28.26	29.19	29.21	30.88	29.83	32.31	31.68	34.24	35.98
1955	36.63	36.76	36.58	37.96	37.91	41.03	43.52	43.18	43.67	42.34	45.51	45.48
1956	43.82	45.34	48.48	48.38	45.20	46.97	49.39	47.51	45.35	45.58	45.08	46.67
1957	44.72	43.26	44.11	45.74	47.43	47.37	47.91	45.22	42.42	41.06	41.72	39.99
1958	41.70	40.84	42.10	43.44	44.09	45.24	47.19	47.75	50.06	51.33	52.48	55.21
1959	55.42	55.41	55.44	57.59	58.68	58.47	60.51	59.60	56.88	57.52	58.28	59.89
1960	55.61	56.12	55.34	54.37	55.83	56.92	55.51	56.96	53.52	53.39	55.54	58.11
1961	61.78	63.44	65.06	65.31	66.56	64.64	66.76	68.07	66.73	68.62	71.32	71.55
1962	68.84	69.96	69.55	65.24	59.63	54.75	58.23	59.12	56.27	56.52	62.26	63.10
1963	66.20	64.29	66.57	69.80	70.80	69.37	69.13	72.50	71.70	74.01	73.23	75.02
1964	77.04	77.80	78.98	79.46	80.37	81.69	83.18	81.83	84.18	84.86	84.42	84.75
1965	87.56	87.43	86.16	89.11	88.42	84.12	85.25	87.17	89.96	92.42	91.61	92.43
1966	92.88	91.22	89.23	91.06	86.13	84.74	83.60	77.10	76.56	80.20	80.45	80.33
1967	86.61	86.78	90.20	94.01	89.08	90.64	94.75	93.64	96.71	93.90	94.00	96.47
1968	92.24	89.36	90.20	97.59	98.68	99.58	97.74	98.86	102.67	103.41	108.37	103.86
1969	103.01	98.13	101.51	103.69	103.46	97.71	91.83	95.51	93.12	97.24	93.81	92.06
1970	85.02	89.50	89.63	81.52	76.55	72.72	78.05	81.52	84.21	83.25	87.20	92.15
1971	95.88	96.75	100.31	103.95	99.63	99.70	95.58	99.03	98.34	94.23	93.99	102.09
1972	103.94	106.57	107.20	107.67	109.53	107.14	107.39	111.09	110.55	111.58	116.67	118.05
1973	116.03	111.68	111.52	106.97	104.95	104.26	108.22	104.25	108.43	108.29	95.96	97.55
1974	96.57	96.22	93.98	90.31	87.28	86.00	79.31	72.15	63.54	73.90	69.97	68.56
1975	76.98	81.59	83.36	87.30	91.15	95.19	88.75	86.88	83.87	89.04	91.24	90.19
1976	100.86	99.71	102.77	101.64	100.18	104.28	103.44	102.91	105.24	102.90	102.10	107.46
1977	102.03	99.82	98.42	98.44	96.12	100.48	98.85	96.77	96.53	92.34	94.83	95.10
1978	89.25	87.04	89.21	96.83	97.24	95.53	100.68	103.29	102.54	93.15	94.70	96.11
1979	99.93	96.28	101.59	101.76	99.08	102.91	103.81	109.32	109.32	101.82	106.16	107.94
1980	114.16	113.66	102.09	106.29	111.24	114.24	121.67	122.38	125.46	127.47	140.52	135.76
1981	129.55	131.27	136.00	132.81	132.59	131.21	130.92	122.79	116.18	121.89	126.35	122.55
1982	120.40	113.11	111.96	116.44	111.88	109.61	107.09	119.51	120.42	133.71	138.54	140.64
1983	145.30	148.06	152.96	164.42	162.39	168.11	162.56	164.40	166.07	163.55	166.40	164.93
1984	163.41	157.06	159.18	160.05	150.55	153.18	150.66	166.68	166.10	166.09	163.58	167.24
1985	179.63	181.18	180.66	179.83	189.55	191.85	190.92	188.63	182.08	189.82	202.17	211.28
1986	211.78	226.92	238.90	235.52	247.35	250.84	236.12	252.93	231.32	243.98	249.22	242.17
1987	274.08	284.20	291.70	288.36	290.10	304.00	318.66	329.80	321.83	251.79	230.30	247.08
1988	257.07	267.82	258.89	261.33	262.16	273.50	272.02	261.52	271.91	278.97	273.70	277.72
1989	297.47	288.86	294.87	309.64	320.52	317.98	346.08	351.45	349.15	340.36	345.99	353.40
1990	329.08	331.89	339.94	330.80	361.23	358.02	356.15	322.56	306.05	304.00	322.22	330.22
1991	343.93	367.07	375.22	375.35	389.83	371.16	387.81	395.43	387.86	392.46	375.22	417.09
1992	408.79	412.70	403.69	414.95	415.35	408.14	424.21	414.03	417.80	418.68	431.35	435.71
1993	438.78	443.38	451.67	440.19	450.19	450.53	448.13	463.56	458.93	467.83	461.79	466.45
1994	481.61	467.14	445.77	450.91	456.50	444.27	458.26	475.49	462.69	472.35	453.69	459.27
1995	470.42	487.39	500.71	514.71	533.40	544.75	562.06	561.88	584.41	581.50	605.37	615.93
1996	636.02	640.43	645.50	654.17	669.12	670.63	639.95	651.99	687.31	705.27	757.02	740.74
1997	786.16	790.82	757.12	801.34	848.28	885.14	954.29	899.47	947.28	914.62	955.40	970.43
1998	980.28	1049.34	1101.75	1111.75	1090.82	1133.84	1120.67	957.28	1017.01	1098.67	1163.63	1229.23
1999	1279.64	1238.33	1286.37	1335.18	1301.84	1372.71	1328.72	1320.41	1282.71	1362.93	1388.91	1469.25
2000	1394.46	1366.42	1498.58	1452.43	1420.60	1454.60	1430.83	1517.68	1436.51	1429.40	1314.95	1320.28
2001	1366.01	1239.94	1160.33	1249.46	1255.82	1224.42	1211.23	1133.58	1040.94	1059.78	1139.45	1148.08
2002	1130.20	1106.73	1147.39	1076.92	1067.14	989.82	911.62	916.07	815.28	885.76	936.31	879.82
2003	855.70	841.15	849.18	916.92	963.59	974.50	990.31	1008.01	995.97	1050.71	1058.20	1111.92
2004	1131.13	1144.94	1126.21	1107.30	1120.68	1140.84	1101.72	1104.24	1114.58	1130.20	1173.82	1211.92
2005	1181.27	1203.60	1180.59	1156.85	1191.50	1191.33	1234.18	1220.33	1228.81	1207.01	1249.48	1248.29
2006	1280.08	1280.66	1294.83	1310.61	1270.09	1270.20	1276.66	1303.82	1335.85	1377.94	1400.63	1418.30
2007	1438.24	1406.82	1420.86	1482.37	1530.62	1503.35	1455.27	1473.99	1526.75	1549.38	1481.14	1468.36
2008	1378.55	1330.63	1322.70	1385.59	1400.38	1280.00	1267.38	1282.83	1166.36	968.75	896.24	903.25
2009	825.88	735.09	797.87	872.81	919.14	919.32	987.48	1020.62	1057.08	1036.19	1095.63	1115.10
2010	1073.87	1104.49	1169.43	1186.69	1089.41	1030.71	1101.60	1049.33	1141.20	1183.26	1180.55	1257.64
2011	1286.12	1327.22	1325.83	1363.61	1345.20	1320.64	1292.28	1218.89	1131.42	1253.30	1246.96	1257.60
2012	1312.41	1365.68	1408.47	1397.91	1310.33	1362.16	1379.32	1406.58	1440.67	1412.16	1416.18	1426.19
2013	1498.11	1514.68	1569.19	1597.57	1630.74	1606.28	1685.73	1632.97	1681.55	1756.54	1805.81	1848.36
2014	1782.59	1859.45	1872.34	1883.95	1923.57	1960.23	1930.67	2003.37	1972.29	2018.05	2067.56	2058.90
2015	1994.99	2104.50	2067.89	2085.51								

NASDAQ COMPOSITE MONTHLY PERCENT CHANGES SINCE 1971

	Jan	Feb	Mar	Apr	May	Jun	Jul	Aug	Sep	Oct	Nov	Dec	Year's Change
1971	10.2	2.6	4.6	6.0	-3.6	-0.4	-2.3	3.0	0.6	-3.6	-1.1	9.8	27.4
1972	4.2	5.5	2.2	2.5	0.9	-1.8	-1.8	1.7	-0.3	0.5	2.1	0.6	17.2
1973	-4.0	-6.2	-2.4	-8.2	-4.8	-1.6	7.6	-3.5	6.0	-0.9	-15.1	-1.4	-31.1
1974	3.0	-0.6	-2.2	-5.9	-7.7	-5.3	-7.9	-10.9	-10.7	17.2	-3.5	-5.0	-35.1
1975	16.6	4.6	3.6	3.8	5.8	4.7	-4.4	-5.0	-5.9	3.6	2.4	-1.5	29.8
1976	12.1	3.7	0.4	-0.6	-2.3	2.6	1.1	-1.7	1.7	-1.0	0.9	7.4	26.1
1977	-2.4	-1.0	-0.5	1.4	0.1	4.3	0.9	-0.5	0.7	-3.3	5.8	1.8	7.3
1978	-4.0	0.6	4.7	8.5	4.4	0.05	5.0	6.9	-1.6	-16.4	3.2	2.9	12.3
1979	6.6	-2.6	7.5	1.6	-1.8	5.1	2.3	6.4	-0.3	-9.6	6.4	4.8	28.1
1980	7.0	-2.3	-17.1	6.9	7.5	4.9	8.9	5.7	3.4	2.7	8.0	-2.8	33.9
1981	-2.2	0.1	6.1	3.1	3.1	-3.5	-1.9	-7.5	-8.0	8.4	3.1	-2.7	-3.2
1982	-3.8	-4.8	-2.1	5.2	-3.3	-4.1	-2.3	6.2	5.6	13.3	9.3	0.04	18.7
1983	6.9	5.0	3.9	8.2	5.3	3.2	-4.6	-3.8	1.4	-7.4	4.1	-2.5	19.9
1984	-3.7	-5.9	-0.7	-1.3	-5.9	2.9	-4.2	10.9	-1.8	-1.2	-1.8	2.0	-11.2
1985	12.7	2.0	-1.7	0.5	3.6	1.9	1.7	-1.2	-5.8	4.4	7.3	3.5	31.4
1986	3.3	7.1	4.2	2.3	4.4	1.3	-8.4	3.1	-8.4	2.9	-0.3	-2.8	7.5
1987	12.2	8.4	1.2	-2.8	-0.3	2.0	2.4	4.6	-2.3	-27.2	-5.6	8.3	-5.4
1988	4.3	6.5	2.1	1.2	-2.3	6.6	-1.9	-2.8	3.0	-1.4	-2.9	2.7	15.4
1989	5.2	-0.4	1.8	5.1	4.4	-2.4	4.3	3.4	0.8	-3.7	0.1	-0.3	19.3
1990	-8.6	2.4	2.3	-3.6	9.3	0.7	-5.2	-13.0	-9.6	-4.3	8.9	4.1	-17.8
1991	10.8	9.4	6.5	0.5	4.4	-6.0	5.5	4.7	0.2	3.1	-3.5	11.9	56.8
1992	5.8	2.1	-4.7	-4.2	1.1	-3.7	3.1	-3.0	3.6	3.8	7.9	3.7	15.5
1993	2.9	-3.7	2.9	-4.2	5.9	0.5	0.1	5.4	2.7	2.2	-3.2	3.0	14.7
1994	3.0	-1.0	-6.2	-1.3	0.2	-4.0	2.3	6.0	-0.2	1.7	-3.5	0.2	-3.2
1995	0.4	5.1	3.0	3.3	2.4	8.0	7.3	1.9	2.3	-0.7	2.2	-0.7	39.9
1996	0.7	3.8	0.1	8.1	4.4	-4.7	-8.8	5.6	7.5	-0.4	5.8	-0.1	22.7
1997	6.9	-5.1	-6.7	3.2	11.1	3.0	10.5	-0.4	6.2	-5.5	0.4	-1.9	21.6
1998	3.1	9.3	3.7	1.8	-4.8	6.5	-1.2	-19.9	13.0	4.6	10.1	12.5	39.6
1999	14.3	-8.7	7.6	3.3	-2.8	8.7	-1.8	3.8	0.2	8.0	12.5	22.0	85.6
2000	-3.2	19.2	-2.6	-15.6	-11.9	16.6	-5.0	11.7	-12.7	-8.3	-22.9	-4.9	-39.3
2001	12.2	-22.4	-14.5	15.0	-0.3	2.4	-6.2	-10.9	-17.0	12.8	14.2	1.0	-21.1
2002	-0.8	-10.5	6.6	-8.5	-4.3	-9.4	-9.2	-1.0	-10.9	13.5	11.2	-9.7	-31.5
2003	-1.1	1.3	0.3	9.2	9.0	1.7	6.9	4.3	-1.3	8.1	1.5	2.2	50.0
2004	3.1	-1.8	-1.8	-3.7	3.5	3.1	-7.8	-2.6	3.2	4.1	6.2	3.7	8.6
2005	-5.2	-0.5	-2.6	-3.9	7.6	-0.5	6.2	-1.5	-0.02	-1.5	5.3	-1.2	1.4
2006	4.6	-1.1	2.6	-0.7	-6.2	-0.3	-3.7	4.4	3.4	4.8	2.7	-0.7	9.5
2007	2.0	-1.9	0.2	4.3	3.1	-0.05	-2.2	2.0	4.0	5.8	-6.9	-0.3	9.8
2008	-9.9	-5.0	0.3	5.9	4.6	-9.1	1.4	1.8	-11.6	-17.7	-10.8	2.7	-40.5
2009	-6.4	-6.7	10.9	12.3	3.3	3.4	7.8	1.5	5.6	-3.6	4.9	5.8	43.9
2010	-5.4	4.2	7.1	2.6	-8.3	-6.5	6.9	-6.2	12.0	5.9	-0.4	6.2	16.9
2011	1.8	3.0	-0.04	3.3	-1.3	-2.2	-0.6	-6.4	-6.4	11.1	-2.4	-0.6	-1.8
2012	8.0	5.4	4.2	-1.5	-7.2	3.8	0.2	4.3	1.6	-4.5	1.1	0.3	15.9
2013	4.1	0.6	3.4	1.9	3.8	-1.5	6.6	-1.0	5.1	3.9	3.6	2.9	38.3
2014	-1.7	5.0	-2.5	-2.0	3.1	3.9	-0.9	4.8	-1.9	3.1	3.5	-1.2	13.4
2015	-2.1	7.1	-1.3	0.8									
TOTALS	123.5	31.8	34.4	63.8	37.2	34.8	6.7	11.3	-22.9	27.3	70.8	85.7	
AVG.	2.7	0.7	0.8	1.4	0.8	0.8	0.2	0.3	-0.5	0.6	1.6	1.9	
# Up	29	25	28	29	26	25	22	24	24	24	29	26	
# Down	16	20	17	16	18	19	22	20	20	20	15	18	

Based on NASDAQ composite; prior to February 5, 1971, based on National Quotation Bureau indices.

157

NASDAQ COMPOSITE MONTHLY CLOSING PRICES SINCE 1971

	Jan	Feb	Mar	Apr	May	Jun	Jul	Aug	Sep	Oct	Nov	Dec
1971	98.77	101.34	105.97	112.30	108.25	107.80	105.27	108.42	109.03	105.10	103.97	114.12
1972	118.87	125.38	128.14	131.33	132.53	130.08	127.75	129.95	129.61	130.24	132.96	133.73
1973	128.40	120.41	117.46	107.85	102.64	100.98	108.64	104.87	111.20	110.17	93.51	92.19
1974	94.93	94.35	92.27	86.86	80.20	75.96	69.99	62.37	55.67	65.23	62.95	59.82
1975	69.78	73.00	75.66	78.54	83.10	87.02	83.19	79.01	74.33	76.99	78.80	77.62
1976	87.05	90.26	90.62	90.08	88.04	90.32	91.29	89.70	91.26	90.35	91.12	97.88
1977	95.54	94.57	94.13	95.48	95.59	99.73	100.65	100.10	100.85	97.52	103.15	105.05
1978	100.84	101.47	106.20	115.18	120.24	120.30	126.32	135.01	132.89	111.12	114.69	117.98
1979	125.82	122.56	131.76	133.82	131.42	138.13	141.33	150.44	149.98	135.53	144.26	151.14
1980	161.75	158.03	131.00	139.99	150.45	157.78	171.81	181.52	187.76	192.78	208.15	202.34
1981	197.81	198.01	210.18	216.74	223.47	215.75	211.63	195.75	180.03	195.24	201.37	195.84
1982	188.39	179.43	175.65	184.70	178.54	171.30	167.35	177.71	187.65	212.63	232.31	232.41
1983	248.35	260.67	270.80	293.06	308.73	318.70	303.96	292.42	296.65	274.55	285.67	278.60
1984	268.43	252.57	250.78	247.44	232.82	239.65	229.70	254.64	249.94	247.03	242.53	247.35
1985	278.70	284.17	279.20	280.56	290.80	296.20	301.29	297.71	280.33	292.54	313.95	324.93
1986	335.77	359.53	374.72	383.24	400.16	405.51	371.37	382.86	350.67	360.77	359.57	349.33
1987	392.06	424.97	430.05	417.81	416.54	424.67	434.93	454.97	444.29	323.30	305.16	330.47
1988	344.66	366.95	374.64	379.23	370.34	394.66	387.33	376.55	387.71	382.46	371.45	381.38
1989	401.30	399.71	406.73	427.55	446.17	435.29	453.84	469.33	472.92	455.63	456.09	454.82
1990	415.81	425.83	435.54	420.07	458.97	462.29	438.24	381.21	344.51	329.84	359.06	373.84
1991	414.20	453.05	482.30	484.72	506.11	475.92	502.04	525.68	526.88	542.98	523.90	586.34
1992	620.21	633.47	603.77	578.68	585.31	563.60	580.83	563.12	583.27	605.17	652.73	676.95
1993	696.34	670.77	690.13	661.42	700.53	703.95	704.70	742.84	762.78	779.26	754.39	776.80
1994	800.47	792.50	743.46	733.84	735.19	705.96	722.16	765.62	764.29	777.49	750.32	751.96
1995	755.20	793.73	817.21	843.98	864.58	933.45	1001.21	1020.11	1043.54	1036.06	1059.20	1052.13
1996	1059.79	1100.05	1101.40	1190.52	1243.43	1185.02	1080.59	1141.50	1226.92	1221.51	1292.61	1291.03
1997	1379.85	1309.00	1221.70	1260.76	1400.32	1442.07	1593.81	1587.32	1685.69	1593.61	1600.55	1570.35
1998	1619.36	1770.51	1835.68	1868.41	1778.87	1894.74	1872.39	1499.25	1693.84	1771.39	1949.54	2192.69
1999	2505.89	2288.03	2461.40	2542.85	2470.52	2686.12	2638.49	2739.35	2746.16	2966.43	3336.16	4069.31
2000	3940.35	4696.69	4572.83	3860.66	3400.91	3966.11	3766.99	4206.35	3672.82	3369.63	2597.93	2470.52
2001	2772.73	2151.83	1840.26	2116.24	2110.49	2160.54	2027.13	1805.43	1498.80	1690.20	1930.58	1950.40
2002	1934.03	1731.49	1845.35	1688.23	1615.73	1463.21	1328.26	1314.85	1172.06	1329.75	1478.78	1335.51
2003	1320.91	1337.52	1341.17	1464.31	1595.91	1622.80	1735.02	1810.45	1786.94	1932.21	1960.26	2003.37
2004	2066.15	2029.82	1994.22	1920.15	1986.74	2047.79	1887.36	1838.10	1896.84	1974.99	2096.81	2175.44
2005	2062.41	2051.72	1999.23	1921.65	2068.22	2056.96	2184.83	2152.09	2151.69	2120.30	2232.82	2205.32
2006	2305.82	2281.39	2339.79	2322.57	2178.88	2172.09	2091.47	2183.75	2258.43	2366.71	2431.77	2415.29
2007	2463.93	2416.15	2421.64	2525.09	2604.52	2603.23	2545.57	2596.36	2701.50	2859.12	2660.96	2652.28
2008	2389.86	2271.48	2279.10	2412.80	2522.66	2292.98	2325.55	2367.52	2091.88	1720.95	1535.57	1577.03
2009	1476.42	1377.84	1528.59	1717.30	1774.33	1835.04	1978.50	2009.06	2122.42	2045.11	2144.60	2269.15
2010	2147.35	2238.26	2397.96	2461.19	2257.04	2109.24	2254.70	2114.03	2368.62	2507.41	2498.23	2652.87
2011	2700.08	2782.27	2781.07	2873.54	2835.30	2773.52	2756.38	2579.46	2415.40	2684.41	2620.34	2605.15
2012	2813.84	2966.89	3091.57	3046.36	2827.34	2935.05	2939.52	3066.96	3116.23	2977.23	3010.24	3019.51
2013	3142.13	3160.19	3267.52	3328.79	3455.91	3403.25	3626.37	3589.87	3771.48	3919.71	4059.89	4176.59
2014	4103.88	4308.12	4198.99	4114.56	4242.62	4408.18	4369.77	4580.27	4493.39	4630.74	4791.63	4736.05
2015	4635.24	4963.53	4900.88	4941.42								

Based on NASDAQ composite; prior to February 5, 1971, based on National Quotation Bureau indices.

	Jan	Feb	Mar	Apr	May	Jun	Jul	Aug	Sep	Oct	Nov	Dec	Year's Change
1979	4.2	-3.5	6.0	0.3	-2.2	4.3	1.1	5.6	0.02	-7.1	5.1	2.1	16.1
1980	5.9	-0.5	-11.5	4.6	5.0	3.2	6.4	1.1	2.6	1.8	10.1	-3.9	25.6
1981	-4.6	1.0	3.8	-1.9	0.2	-1.2	-0.1	-6.2	-6.4	5.4	4.0	-3.3	-9.7
1982	-2.7	-5.9	-1.3	3.9	-3.6	-2.6	-2.3	11.3	1.2	11.3	4.0	1.3	13.7
1983	3.2	2.1	3.2	7.1	-0.2	3.7	-3.2	0.5	1.3	-2.4	2.0	-1.2	17.0
1984	-1.9	-4.4	1.1	0.3	-5.9	2.1	-1.8	10.8	-0.2	-0.1	-1.4	2.2	-0.1
1985	7.8	1.1	-0.4	-0.3	5.4	1.6	-0.8	-1.0	-3.9	4.5	6.5	4.1	26.7
1986	0.9	7.2	5.1	-1.3	5.0	1.4	-5.9	6.8	-8.5	5.1	1.4	-3.0	13.6
1987	12.7	4.0	1.9	-1.8	0.4	4.5	4.2	3.8	-2.4	-21.9	-8.0	7.2	0.02
1988	4.3	4.4	-2.9	0.7	0.2	4.8	-0.9	-3.3	3.9	2.0	-2.0	1.7	13.1
1989	6.8	-2.5	2.0	4.9	3.8	-0.8	8.2	1.7	-0.5	-2.8	1.5	1.8	25.9
1990	-7.4	1.2	2.2	-2.8	8.9	-0.7	-1.1	-9.6	-5.3	-0.8	6.4	2.7	-7.5
1991	4.5	6.9	2.5	-0.1	3.8	-4.7	4.6	2.2	-1.5	1.4	-4.1	11.2	28.8
1992	-1.4	0.9	-2.4	2.3	0.3	-1.9	4.1	-2.5	1.0	0.7	3.5	1.4	5.9
1993	0.7	0.6	2.2	-2.8	2.4	0.4	-0.4	3.5	-0.5	1.2	-1.7	1.6	7.3
1994	2.9	-2.9	-4.5	1.1	1.0	-2.9	3.1	3.9	-2.6	1.7	-3.9	1.2	-2.4
1995	2.4	3.8	2.3	2.5	3.5	2.4	3.7	0.5	3.9	-0.6	4.2	1.4	34.4
1996	3.1	1.1	0.7	1.4	2.1	-0.1	-4.9	2.5	5.5	2.1	7.1	-1.8	19.7
1997	5.8	0.2	-4.6	5.3	6.2	4.0	8.0	-4.9	5.4	-3.4	4.2	1.9	30.5
1998	0.6	7.0	4.9	0.9	-2.3	3.6	-1.3	-15.1	6.5	7.8	6.1	6.2	25.1
1999	3.5	-3.3	3.7	4.2	-2.3	5.1	-3.2	-1.0	-2.8	6.5	2.5	6.0	19.5
2000	-4.2	-0.4	8.9	-3.3	-2.7	2.5	-1.8	7.4	-4.8	-1.2	-9.3	1.1	-8.8
2001	3.2	-9.5	-6.7	8.0	0.5	-2.4	-1.4	-6.2	-8.6	2.0	7.5	0.9	-13.6
2002	-1.4	-2.1	4.0	-5.8	-1.0	-7.5	-7.5	0.3	-10.9	8.1	5.7	-5.8	-22.9
2003	-2.5	-1.7	0.9	7.9	5.5	1.2	1.8	1.9	-1.2	5.7	1.0	4.6	27.5
2004	1.8	1.2	-1.5	-1.9	1.3	1.7	-3.6	0.3	1.1	1.5	4.1	3.5	9.5
2005	-2.6	2.0	-1.7	-2.0	3.4	0.3	3.8	-1.1	0.8	-1.9	3.5	0.01	4.4
2006	2.7	0.01	1.3	1.1	-3.2	0.003	0.1	2.2	2.3	3.3	1.9	1.1	13.3
2007	1.8	-1.9	0.9	4.1	3.4	-2.0	-3.2	1.2	3.7	1.6	-4.5	-0.8	3.9
2008	-6.1	-3.3	-0.8	5.0	1.6	-8.5	-1.3	1.2	-9.7	-17.6	-7.9	1.3	-39.0
2009	-8.3	-10.7	8.5	10.0	5.3	0.1	7.5	3.4	3.9	-2.3	5.6	2.3	25.5
2010	-3.7	3.1	6.0	1.8	-8.1	-5.7	6.8	-4.7	9.0	3.8	0.1	6.5	13.9
2011	2.3	3.3	0.1	2.9	-1.3	-1.9	-2.3	-6.0	-7.6	11.1	-0.5	0.7	-0.5
2012	4.8	4.1	3.0	-0.7	-6.4	3.7	1.1	2.2	2.4	-1.8	0.5	0.8	13.9
2013	5.3	1.1	3.7	1.7	2.0	-1.5	5.2	-3.0	3.3	4.3	2.6	2.5	30.4
2014	-3.3	4.5	0.5	0.4	2.1	2.1	-1.7	3.9	-1.9	2.3	2.4	-0.4	11.1
2015	-2.8	5.5	-1.4	0.6									
TOTALS	38.3	13.7	39.7	58.3	34.1	8.3	21.0	13.6	-21.5	31.3	60.2	59.1	
AVG.	1.0	0.4	1.1	1.6	0.9	0.2	0.6	0.4	-0.6	0.9	1.7	1.6	
# Up	23	23	25	25	24	21	16	23	18	23	26	28	
# Down	14	14	12	12	12	15	20	13	18	13	10	8	

	Jan	Feb	Mar	Apr	May	Jun	Jul	Aug	Sep	Oct	Nov	Dec
1979	53.76	51.88	54.97	55.15	53.92	56.25	56.86	60.04	60.05	55.78	58.65	59.87
1980	63.40	63.07	55.79	58.38	61.31	63.27	67.30	68.05	69.84	71.08	78.26	75.20
1981	71.75	72.49	75.21	73.77	73.90	73.01	72.92	68.42	64.06	67.54	70.23	67.93
1982	66.12	62.21	61.43	63.85	61.53	59.92	58.54	65.14	65.89	73.34	76.28	77.24
1983	79.75	81.45	84.06	90.04	89.89	93.18	90.18	90.65	91.85	89.69	91.50	90.38
1984	88.69	84.76	85.73	86.00	80.94	82.61	81.13	89.87	89.67	89.62	88.36	90.31
1985	97.31	98.38	98.03	97.72	103.02	104.65	103.78	102.76	98.75	103.16	109.91	114.39
1986	115.39	123.71	130.07	128.44	134.82	136.75	128.74	137.43	125.70	132.11	133.97	130.00
1987	146.48	152.29	155.20	152.39	152.94	159.84	166.57	172.95	168.83	131.89	121.28	130.02
1988	135.55	141.54	137.45	138.37	138.66	145.31	143.99	139.26	144.68	147.55	144.59	146.99
1989	156.93	152.98	155.99	163.63	169.85	168.49	182.27	185.33	184.40	179.17	181.85	185.11
1990	171.44	173.43	177.28	172.32	187.66	186.29	184.32	166.69	157.83	156.62	166.69	171.22
1991	179.00	191.34	196.15	195.94	203.32	193.78	202.67	207.18	204.02	206.96	198.46	220.61
1992	217.52	219.50	214.29	219.13	219.71	215.60	224.37	218.86	221.15	222.65	230.44	233.59
1993	235.25	236.67	241.80	235.13	240.80	241.78	240.78	249.20	247.95	250.97	246.70	250.71
1994	258.08	250.52	239.19	241.71	244.13	237.11	244.44	254.04	247.49	251.62	241.82	244.65
1995	250.52	260.08	266.11	272.81	282.48	289.29	299.98	301.40	313.28	311.37	324.36	328.89
1996	338.97	342.56	345.01	349.84	357.35	357.10	339.44	347.79	366.77	374.38	401.05	393.75
1997	416.77	417.46	398.19	419.15	445.06	462.95	499.89	475.33	500.78	483.86	504.25	513.79
1998	517.02	553.14	580.31	585.46	572.16	592.57	584.97	496.66	529.11	570.63	605.31	642.87
1999	665.64	643.67	667.49	695.25	679.10	713.61	690.51	683.27	663.83	707.19	724.66	767.97
2000	736.08	733.04	797.99	771.58	750.98	769.68	755.57	811.17	772.60	763.06	692.40	700.09
2001	722.55	654.25	610.36	658.90	662.39	646.64	637.43	597.67	546.46	557.29	599.32	604.94
2002	596.66	583.88	607.35	572.04	566.18	523.72	484.39	486.08	433.22	468.51	495.00	466.18
2003	454.30	446.37	450.35	486.09	512.92	518.94	528.53	538.40	532.15	562.51	568.32	594.56
2004	605.21	612.58	603.42	591.83	599.40	609.31	587.21	589.09	595.66	604.51	629.26	650.99
2005	633.99	646.93	635.78	623.32	644.28	645.92	670.26	663.13	668.53	656.09	679.35	679.42
2006	697.79	697.83	706.74	714.37	691.78	691.80	692.59	707.55	723.48	747.30	761.43	770.08
2007	784.11	768.92	775.97	807.82	835.14	818.17	792.10	801.22	830.59	844.20	806.44	799.82
2008	750.97	726.42	720.32	756.03	768.28	703.22	694.07	702.17	634.08	522.47	481.43	487.77
2009	447.32	399.61	433.67	476.84	501.95	502.27	539.88	558.21	579.97	566.50	598.41	612.01
2010	589.41	607.45	643.79	655.06	601.79	567.37	606.09	577.68	629.78	653.57	654.24	696.90
2011	712.97	736.24	737.07	758.45	748.75	734.48	717.77	674.79	623.45	692.41	688.77	693.36
2012	726.33	756.42	778.92	773.50	724.12	750.61	758.60	775.07	793.74	779.35	783.37	789.90
2013	831.74	840.97	872.11	886.89	904.44	890.67	937.16	909.28	939.50	979.68	1004.97	1030.36
2014	996.48	1041.36	1046.42	1050.20	1071.96	1094.59	1075.60	1117.71	1096.43	1121.98	1148.90	1144.37
2015	1111.85	1173.46	1156.95	1164.03								

RUSSELL 2000 INDEX MONTHLY PERCENT CHANGES SINCE 1979

	Jan	Feb	Mar	Apr	May	Jun	Jul	Aug	Sep	Oct	Nov	Dec	Year's Change
1979	9.0	-3.2	9.7	2.3	-1.8	5.3	2.9	7.8	-0.7	-11.3	8.1	6.6	38.0
1980	8.2	-2.1	-18.5	6.0	8.0	4.0	11.0	6.5	2.9	3.9	7.0	-3.7	33.8
1981	-0.6	0.3	7.7	2.5	3.0	-2.5	-2.6	-8.0	-8.6	8.2	2.8	-2.0	-1.5
1982	-3.7	-5.3	-1.5	5.1	-3.2	-4.0	-1.7	7.5	3.6	14.1	8.8	1.1	20.7
1983	7.5	6.0	2.5	7.2	7.0	4.4	-3.0	-4.0	1.6	-7.0	5.0	-2.1	26.3
1984	-1.8	-5.9	0.4	-0.7	-5.4	2.6	-5.0	11.5	-1.0	-2.0	-2.9	1.4	-9.6
1985	13.1	2.4	-2.2	-1.4	3.4	1.0	2.7	-1.2	-6.2	3.6	6.8	4.2	28.0
1986	1.5	7.0	4.7	1.4	3.3	-0.2	-9.5	3.0	-6.3	3.9	-0.5	-3.1	4.0
1987	11.5	8.2	2.4	-3.0	-0.5	2.3	2.8	2.9	-2.0	-30.8	-5.5	7.8	-10.8
1988	4.0	8.7	4.4	2.0	-2.5	7.0	-0.9	-2.8	2.3	-1.2	-3.6	3.8	22.4
1989	4.4	0.5	2.2	4.3	4.2	-2.4	4.2	2.1	0.01	-6.0	0.4	0.1	14.2
1990	-8.9	2.9	3.7	-3.4	6.8	0.1	-4.5	-13.6	-9.2	-6.2	7.3	3.7	-21.5
1991	9.1	11.0	6.9	-0.2	4.5	-6.0	3.1	3.7	0.6	2.7	-4.7	7.7	43.7
1992	8.0	2.9	-3.5	-3.7	1.2	-5.0	3.2	-3.1	2.2	3.1	7.5	3.4	16.4
1993	3.2	-2.5	3.1	-2.8	4.3	0.5	1.3	4.1	2.7	2.5	-3.4	3.3	17.0
1994	3.1	-0.4	-5.4	0.6	-1.3	-3.6	1.6	5.4	-0.5	-0.4	-4.2	2.5	-3.2
1995	-1.4	3.9	1.6	2.1	1.5	5.0	5.7	1.9	1.7	-4.6	4.2	2.4	26.2
1996	-0.2	3.0	1.8	5.3	3.9	-4.2	-8.8	5.7	3.7	-1.7	4.0	2.4	14.8
1997	1.9	-2.5	-4.9	0.1	11.0	4.1	4.6	2.2	7.2	-4.5	-0.8	1.7	20.5
1998	-1.6	7.4	4.1	0.5	-5.4	0.2	-8.2	-19.5	7.6	4.0	5.2	6.1	-3.4
1999	1.2	-8.2	1.4	8.8	1.4	4.3	-2.8	-3.8	-0.1	0.3	5.9	11.2	19.6
2000	-1.7	16.4	-6.7	-6.1	-5.9	8.6	-3.2	7.4	-3.1	-4.5	-10.4	8.4	-4.2
2001	5.1	-6.7	-5.0	7.7	2.3	3.3	-5.4	-3.3	-13.6	5.8	7.6	6.0	1.0
2002	-1.1	-2.8	7.9	0.8	-4.5	-5.1	-15.2	-0.4	-7.3	3.1	8.8	-5.7	-21.6
2003	-2.9	-3.1	1.1	9.4	10.6	1.7	6.2	4.5	-2.0	8.3	3.5	1.9	45.4
2004	4.3	0.8	0.8	-5.2	1.5	4.1	-6.8	-0.6	4.6	1.9	8.6	2.8	17.0
2005	-4.2	1.6	-3.0	-5.8	6.4	3.7	6.3	-1.9	0.2	-3.2	4.7	-0.6	3.3
2006	8.9	-0.3	4.7	-0.1	-5.7	0.5	-3.3	2.9	0.7	5.7	2.5	0.2	17.0
2007	1.6	-0.9	0.9	1.7	4.0	-1.6	-6.9	2.2	1.6	2.8	-7.3	-0.2	-2.7
2008	-6.9	-3.8	0.3	4.1	4.5	-7.8	3.6	3.5	-8.1	-20.9	-12.0	5.6	-34.8
2009	-11.2	-12.3	8.7	15.3	2.9	1.3	9.5	2.8	5.6	-6.9	3.0	7.9	25.2
2010	-3.7	4.4	8.0	5.6	-7.7	-7.9	6.8	-7.5	12.3	4.0	3.4	7.8	25.3
2011	-0.3	5.4	2.4	2.6	-2.0	-2.5	-3.7	-8.8	-11.4	15.0	-0.5	0.5	-5.5
2012	7.0	2.3	2.4	-1.6	-6.7	4.8	-1.4	3.2	3.1	-2.2	0.4	3.3	14.6
2013	6.2	1.0	4.4	-0.4	3.9	-0.7	6.9	-3.3	6.2	2.5	3.9	1.8	37.0
2014	-2.8	4.6	-0.8	-3.9	0.7	5.2	-6.1	4.8	-6.2	6.5	-0.02	2.7	3.5
2015	-3.3	5.8	1.6	-2.6									
TOTALS	62.5	46.5	48.3	54.5	47.7	20.5	-16.6	13.8	-15.9	-11.5	63.6	100.9	
AVG.	1.7	1.3	1.3	1.5	1.3	0.6	-0.5	0.4	-0.4	-0.3	1.8	2.8	
# Up	20	22	27	22	23	22	17	21	20	20	23	29	
# Down	17	15	10	15	13	14	19	15	16	16	13	7	

RUSSELL 2000 INDEX MONTHLY CLOSING PRICES SINCE 1979

	Jan	Feb	Mar	Apr	May	Jun	Jul	Aug	Sep	Oct	Nov	Dec
1979	44.18	42.78	46.94	48.00	47.13	49.62	51.08	55.05	54.68	48.51	52.43	55.91
1980	60.50	59.22	48.27	51.18	55.26	57.47	63.81	67.97	69.94	72.64	77.70	74.80
1981	74.33	74.52	80.25	82.25	84.72	82.56	80.41	73.94	67.55	73.06	75.14	73.67
1982	70.96	67.21	66.21	69.59	67.39	64.67	63.59	68.38	70.84	80.86	87.96	88.90
1983	95.53	101.23	103.77	111.20	118.94	124.17	120.43	115.60	117.43	109.17	114.66	112.27
1984	110.21	103.72	104.10	103.34	97.75	100.30	95.25	106.21	105.17	103.07	100.11	101.49
1985	114.77	117.54	114.92	113.35	117.26	118.38	121.56	120.10	112.65	116.73	124.62	129.87
1986	131.78	141.00	147.63	149.66	154.61	154.23	139.65	143.83	134.73	139.95	139.26	135.00
1987	150.48	162.84	166.79	161.82	161.02	164.75	169.42	174.25	170.81	118.26	111.70	120.42
1988	125.24	136.10	142.15	145.01	141.37	151.30	149.89	145.74	149.08	147.25	142.01	147.37
1989	153.84	154.56	157.89	164.68	171.53	167.42	174.50	178.20	178.21	167.47	168.17	168.30
1990	153.27	157.72	163.63	158.09	168.91	169.04	161.51	139.52	126.70	118.83	127.50	132.16
1991	144.17	160.00	171.01	170.61	178.34	167.61	172.76	179.11	180.16	185.00	176.37	189.94
1992	205.16	211.15	203.69	196.25	198.52	188.64	194.74	188.79	192.92	190.90	213.81	221.01
1993	228.10	222.41	229.21	222.68	232.19	233.35	236.46	246.19	252.95	259.18	250.41	258.59
1994	266.52	265.53	251.06	252.55	249.28	240.29	244.06	257.32	256.12	255.02	244.25	250.36
1995	246.85	256.57	260.77	266.17	270.25	283.63	299.72	305.31	310.38	296.25	308.58	315.97
1996	315.38	324.93	330.77	348.28	361.85	346.61	316.00	333.88	346.39	340.57	354.11	362.61
1997	369.45	360.05	342.56	343.00	380.76	396.37	414.48	423.43	453.82	433.26	429.92	437.02
1998	430.05	461.83	480.68	482.89	456.62	457.39	419.75	337.95	363.59	378.16	397.75	421.96
1999	427.22	392.26	397.63	432.81	438.68	457.68	444.77	427.83	427.30	428.64	454.08	504.75
2000	496.23	577.71	539.09	506.25	476.18	517.23	500.64	537.89	521.37	497.68	445.94	483.53
2001	508.34	474.37	450.53	485.32	496.50	512.64	484.78	468.56	404.87	428.17	460.78	488.50
2002	483.10	469.36	506.46	510.67	487.47	462.64	392.42	390.96	362.27	373.50	406.35	383.09
2003	372.17	360.52	364.54	398.68	441.00	448.37	476.02	497.42	487.68	528.22	546.51	556.91
2004	580.76	585.56	590.31	559.80	568.28	591.52	551.29	547.93	572.94	583.79	633.77	651.57
2005	624.02	634.06	615.07	579.38	616.71	639.66	679.75	666.51	667.80	646.61	677.29	673.22
2006	733.20	730.64	765.14	764.54	721.01	724.67	700.56	720.53	725.59	766.84	786.12	787.66
2007	800.34	793.30	800.71	814.57	847.19	833.69	776.13	792.86	805.45	828.02	767.77	766.03
2008	713.30	686.18	687.97	716.18	748.28	689.66	714.52	739.50	679.58	537.52	473.14	499.45
2009	443.53	389.02	422.75	487.56	501.58	508.28	556.71	572.07	604.28	562.77	579.73	625.39
2010	602.04	628.56	678.64	716.60	661.61	609.49	650.89	602.06	676.14	703.35	727.01	783.65
2011	781.25	823.45	843.55	865.29	848.30	827.43	797.03	726.81	644.16	741.06	737.42	740.92
2012	792.82	810.94	830.30	816.88	761.82	798.49	786.94	812.09	837.45	818.73	821.92	849.35
2013	902.09	911.11	951.54	947.46	984.14	977.48	1045.26	1010.90	1073.79	1100.15	1142.89	1163.64
2014	1130.88	1183.03	1173.04	1126.86	1134.50	1192.96	1120.07	1174.35	1101.68	1173.51	1173.23	1204.70
2015	1165.39	1233.37	1252.77	1220.13								

THE ULTIMATE GUIDE TO MARKET-BEATING RETURNS, FROM *STOCK TRADER'S ALMANAC* EDITOR-IN-CHIEF **JEFFREY HIRSCH**

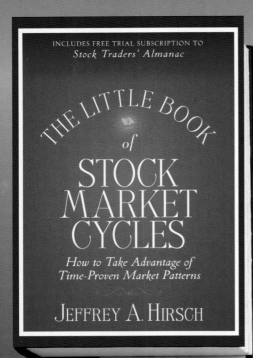

To profit from the stock market, you must be able to predict its patterns. *The Little Book of Stock Market Cycles* brings together everything you need to know about recurring trends in one insightful and accessible volume, backed by the wisdom of the pre-eminent authority on market cycles and seasonal patterns.

The perfect companion to the *Stock Trader's Almanac*, this little book is big on practical advice and proven strategies that you can put to use right away to consistently outperform the market.

 Available wherever books and e-books are sold.

www.littlebook-series.com

10 **BEST** DAYS BY PERCENT AND POINT

	BY PERCENT CHANGE				BY POINT CHANGE		
DAY	CLOSE	PNT CHANGE	% CHANGE	DAY	CLOSE	PNT CHANGE	% CHANGE
DJIA 1901 to 1949							
3/15/33	62.10	8.26	15.3	10/30/29	258.47	28.40	12.3
10/6/31	99.34	12.86	14.9	11/14/29	217.28	18.59	9.4
10/30/29	258.47	28.40	12.3	10/5/29	341.36	16.19	5.0
9/21/32	75.16	7.67	11.4	10/31/29	273.51	15.04	5.8
8/3/32	58.22	5.06	9.5	10/6/31	99.34	12.86	14.9
2/11/32	78.60	6.80	9.5	11/15/29	228.73	11.45	5.3
11/14/29	217.28	18.59	9.4	6/19/30	228.97	10.13	4.6
12/18/31	80.69	6.90	9.4	9/5/39	148.12	10.03	7.3
2/13/32	85.82	7.22	9.2	11/22/28	290.34	9.81	3.5
5/6/32	59.01	4.91	9.1	10/1/30	214.14	9.24	4.5
DJIA 1950 to APRIL 2015							
10/13/08	9387.61	936.42	11.1	10/13/08	9387.61	936.42	11.1
10/28/08	9065.12	889.35	10.9	10/28/08	9065.12	889.35	10.9
10/21/87	2027.85	186.84	10.2	11/13/08	8835.25	552.59	6.7
3/23/09	7775.86	497.48	6.8	3/16/00	10630.60	499.19	4.9
11/13/08	8835.25	552.59	6.7	3/23/09	7775.86	497.48	6.8
11/21/08	8046.42	494.13	6.5	11/21/08	8046.42	494.13	6.5
7/24/02	8191.29	488.95	6.4	11/30/11	12045.68	490.05	4.2
10/20/87	1841.01	102.27	5.9	7/24/02	8191.29	488.95	6.4
3/10/09	6926.49	379.44	5.8	9/30/08	10850.66	485.21	4.7
7/29/02	8711.88	447.49	5.4	7/29/02	8711.88	447.49	5.4
S&P 500 1930 to APRIL 2015							
3/15/33	6.81	0.97	16.6	10/13/08	1003.35	104.13	11.6
10/6/31	9.91	1.09	12.4	10/28/08	940.51	91.59	10.8
9/21/32	8.52	0.90	11.8	3/16/00	1458.47	66.32	4.8
10/13/08	1003.35	104.13	11.6	1/3/01	1347.56	64.29	5.0
10/28/08	940.51	91.59	10.8	9/30/08	1166.36	59.97	5.4
2/16/35	10.00	0.94	10.4	11/13/08	911.29	58.99	6.9
8/17/35	11.70	1.08	10.2	3/23/09	822.92	54.38	7.1
3/16/35	9.05	0.82	10.0	3/18/08	1330.74	54.14	4.2
9/12/38	12.06	1.06	9.6	8/9/11	1172.53	53.07	4.7
9/5/39	12.64	1.11	9.6	8/11/11	1172.64	51.88	4.6
NASDAQ 1971 to APRIL 2015							
1/3/01	2616.69	324.83	14.2	1/3/01	2616.69	324.83	14.2
10/13/08	1844.25	194.74	11.8	12/5/00	2889.80	274.05	10.5
12/5/00	2889.80	274.05	10.5	4/18/00	3793.57	254.41	7.2
10/28/08	1649.47	143.57	9.5	5/30/00	3459.48	254.37	7.9
4/5/01	1785.00	146.20	8.9	10/19/00	3418.60	247.04	7.8
4/18/01	2079.44	156.22	8.1	10/13/00	3316.77	242.09	7.9
5/30/00	3459.48	254.37	7.9	6/2/00	3813.38	230.88	6.4
10/13/00	3316.77	242.09	7.9	4/25/00	3711.23	228.75	6.6
10/19/00	3418.60	247.04	7.8	4/17/00	3539.16	217.87	6.6
5/8/02	1696.29	122.47	7.8	10/13/08	1844.25	194.74	11.8
RUSSELL 1000 1979 to APRIL 2015							
10/13/08	542.98	56.75	11.7	10/13/08	542.98	56.75	11.7
10/28/08	503.74	47.68	10.5	10/28/08	503.74	47.68	10.5
10/21/87	135.85	11.15	8.9	3/16/00	777.86	36.60	4.9
3/23/09	446.90	29.36	7.0	1/3/01	712.63	35.74	5.3
11/13/08	489.83	31.99	7.0	11/13/08	489.83	31.99	7.0
11/24/08	456.14	28.26	6.6	9/30/08	634.08	31.74	5.3
3/10/09	391.01	23.46	6.4	8/9/11	647.85	30.57	5.0
11/21/08	427.88	24.97	6.2	12/5/00	728.44	30.36	4.4
7/24/02	448.05	23.87	5.6	3/23/09	446.90	29.36	7.0
7/29/02	477.61	24.69	5.5	8/11/11	649.44	29.14	4.7
RUSSELL 2000 1979 to APRIL 2015							
10/13/08	570.89	48.41	9.3	10/13/08	570.89	48.41	9.3
11/13/08	491.23	38.43	8.5	9/18/08	723.68	47.30	7.0
3/23/09	433.72	33.61	8.4	8/9/11	696.16	45.20	6.9
10/21/87	130.65	9.26	7.6	11/30/11	737.42	41.32	5.9
10/28/08	482.55	34.15	7.6	10/4/11	648.64	39.15	6.4
11/24/08	436.80	30.26	7.4	11/13/08	491.23	38.43	8.5
3/10/09	367.75	24.49	7.1	10/27/11	765.43	38.28	5.3
9/18/08	723.68	47.30	7.0	5/10/10	689.61	36.61	5.6
8/9/11	696.16	45.20	6.9	8/11/11	695.89	35.68	5.4
10/16/08	536.57	34.46	6.9	12/17/14	1174.83	35.45	3.1

10 <u>WORST</u> DAYS BY PERCENT AND POINT

	BY PERCENT CHANGE				BY POINT CHANGE		
DAY	CLOSE	PNT CHANGE	% CHANGE	DAY	CLOSE	PNT CHANGE	% CHANGE
DJIA 1901 to 1949							
10/28/29	260.64	−38.33	−12.8	10/28/29	260.64	−38.33	−12.8
10/29/29	230.07	−30.57	−11.7	10/29/29	230.07	−30.57	−11.7
11/6/29	232.13	−25.55	−9.9	11/6/29	232.13	−25.55	−9.9
8/12/32	63.11	−5.79	−8.4	10/23/29	305.85	−20.66	−6.3
3/14/07	55.84	−5.05	−8.3	11/11/29	220.39	−16.14	−6.8
7/21/33	88.71	−7.55	−7.8	11/4/29	257.68	−15.83	−5.8
10/18/37	125.73	−10.57	−7.8	12/12/29	243.14	−15.30	−5.9
2/1/17	88.52	−6.91	−7.2	10/3/29	329.95	−14.55	−4.2
10/5/32	66.07	−5.09	−7.2	6/16/30	230.05	−14.20	−5.8
9/24/31	107.79	−8.20	−7.1	8/9/29	337.99	−14.11	−4.0
DJIA 1950 to APRIL 2015							
10/19/87	1738.74	−508.00	−22.6	9/29/08	10365.45	−777.68	−7.0
10/26/87	1793.93	−156.83	−8.0	10/15/08	8577.91	−733.08	−7.9
10/15/08	8577.91	−733.08	−7.9	9/17/01	8920.70	−684.81	−7.1
12/1/08	8149.09	−679.95	−7.7	12/1/08	8149.09	−679.95	−7.7
10/9/08	8579.19	−678.91	−7.3	10/9/08	8579.19	−678.91	−7.3
10/27/97	7161.15	−554.26	−7.2	8/8/11	10809.85	−634.76	−5.6
9/17/01	8920.70	−684.81	−7.1	4/14/00	10305.77	−617.78	−5.7
9/29/08	10365.45	−777.68	−7.0	10/27/97	7161.15	−554.26	−7.2
10/13/89	2569.26	−190.58	−6.9	8/10/11	10719.94	−519.83	−4.6
1/8/88	1911.31	−140.58	−6.9	10/22/08	8519.21	−514.45	−5.7
S&P 500 1930 to APRIL 2015							
10/19/87	224.84	−57.86	−20.5	9/29/08	1106.39	−106.62	−8.8
3/18/35	8.14	−0.91	−10.1	10/15/08	907.84	−90.17	−9.0
4/16/35	8.22	−0.91	−10.0	4/14/00	1356.56	−83.95	−5.8
9/3/46	15.00	−1.65	−9.9	12/1/08	816.21	−80.03	−8.9
10/18/37	10.76	−1.10	−9.3	8/8/11	1119.46	−79.92	−6.7
10/15/08	907.84	−90.17	−9.0	10/9/08	909.92	−75.02	−7.6
12/1/08	816.21	−80.03	−8.9	8/31/98	957.28	−69.86	−6.8
7/20/33	10.57	−1.03	−8.9	10/27/97	876.99	−64.65	−6.9
9/29/08	1106.39	−106.62	−8.8	10/7/08	996.23	−60.66	−5.7
7/21/33	9.65	−0.92	−8.7	8/4/11	1200.07	−60.27	−4.8
NASDAQ 1971 to APRIL 2015							
10/19/87	360.21	−46.12	−11.4	4/14/00	3321.29	−355.49	−9.7
4/14/00	3321.29	−355.49	−9.7	4/3/00	4223.68	−349.15	−7.6
9/29/08	1983.73	−199.61	−9.1	4/12/00	3769.63	−286.27	−7.1
10/26/87	298.90	−29.55	−9.0	4/10/00	4188.20	−258.25	−5.8
10/20/87	327.79	−32.42	−9.0	1/4/00	3901.69	−229.46	−5.6
12/1/08	1398.07	−137.50	−9.0	3/14/00	4706.63	−200.61	−4.1
8/31/98	1499.25	−140.43	−8.6	5/10/00	3384.73	−200.28	−5.6
10/15/08	1628.33	−150.68	−8.5	5/23/00	3164.55	−199.66	−5.9
4/3/00	4223.68	−349.15	−7.6	9/29/08	1983.73	−199.61	−9.1
1/2/01	2291.86	−178.66	−7.2	10/25/00	3229.57	−190.22	−5.6
RUSSELL 1000 1979 to APRIL 2015							
10/19/87	121.04	−28.40	−19.0	9/29/08	602.34	−57.35	−8.7
10/15/08	489.71	−49.11	−9.1	10/15/08	489.71	−49.11	−9.1
12/1/08	437.75	−43.68	−9.1	4/14/00	715.20	−45.74	−6.0
9/29/08	602.34	−57.35	−8.7	8/8/11	617.28	−45.56	−6.9
10/26/87	119.45	−10.74	−8.3	12/1/08	437.75	−43.68	−9.1
10/9/08	492.13	−40.05	−7.5	10/9/08	492.13	−40.05	−7.5
8/8/11	617.28	−45.56	−6.9	8/31/98	496.66	−35.77	−6.7
11/20/08	402.91	−29.62	−6.9	8/4/11	664.65	−34.92	−5.0
8/31/98	496.66	−35.77	−6.7	10/27/97	465.44	−32.96	−6.6
10/27/97	465.44	−32.96	−6.6	10/7/08	538.15	−32.64	−5.7
RUSSELL 2000 1979 to APRIL 2015							
10/19/87	133.60	−19.14	−12.5	8/8/11	650.96	−63.67	−8.9
12/1/08	417.07	−56.07	−11.9	12/1/08	417.07	−56.07	−11.9
10/15/08	502.11	−52.54	−9.5	10/15/08	502.11	−52.54	−9.5
10/26/87	110.33	−11.26	−9.3	10/9/08	499.20	−47.37	−8.7
10/20/87	121.39	−12.21	−9.1	9/29/08	657.72	−47.07	−6.7
8/8/11	650.96	−63.67	−8.9	8/4/11	726.80	−45.98	−6.0
10/9/08	499.20	−47.37	−8.7	8/18/11	662.51	−41.52	−5.9
11/19/08	412.38	−35.13	−7.9	10/7/08	558.95	−36.96	−6.2
4/14/00	453.72	−35.50	−7.3	11/9/11	718.86	−36.41	−4.8
11/14/08	456.52	−34.71	−7.1	2/3/14	1094.58	−36.30	−3.2

10 **BEST** WEEKS BY PERCENT AND POINT

WEEK ENDS	BY PERCENT CHANGE			WEEK ENDS	BY POINT CHANGE		
	CLOSE	PNT CHANGE	% CHANGE		CLOSE	PNT CHANGE	% CHANGE
DJIA 1901 to 1949							
8/6/32	66.56	12.30	22.7	12/7/29	263.46	24.51	10.3
6/25/38	131.94	18.71	16.5	6/25/38	131.94	18.71	16.5
2/13/32	85.82	11.37	15.3	6/27/31	156.93	17.97	12.9
4/22/33	72.24	9.36	14.9	11/22/29	245.74	17.01	7.4
10/10/31	105.61	12.84	13.8	8/17/29	360.70	15.86	4.6
7/30/32	54.26	6.42	13.4	12/22/28	285.94	15.22	5.6
6/27/31	156.93	17.97	12.9	8/24/29	375.44	14.74	4.1
9/24/32	74.83	8.39	12.6	2/21/29	310.06	14.21	4.8
8/27/32	75.61	8.43	12.6	5/10/30	272.01	13.70	5.3
3/18/33	60.56	6.72	12.5	11/15/30	186.68	13.54	7.8
DJIA 1950 to APRIL 2015							
10/11/74	658.17	73.61	12.6	10/31/08	9325.01	946.06	11.3
10/31/08	9325.01	946.06	11.3	12/2/11	12019.42	787.64	7.0
8/20/82	869.29	81.24	10.3	11/28/08	8829.04	782.62	9.7
11/28/08	8829.04	782.62	9.7	3/17/00	10595.23	666.41	6.7
3/13/09	7223.98	597.04	9.0	3/21/03	8521.97	662.26	8.4
10/8/82	986.85	79.11	8.7	2/6/15	17824.29	659.34	3.8
3/21/03	8521.97	662.26	8.4	7/1/11	12582.77	648.19	5.4
8/3/84	1202.08	87.46	7.9	9/28/01	8847.56	611.75	7.4
9/28/01	8847.56	611.75	7.4	7/17/09	8743.94	597.42	7.3
7/17/09	8743.94	597.42	7.3	3/13/09	7223.98	597.04	9.0
S&P 500 1930 to APRIL 2015							
8/6/32	7.22	1.12	18.4	6/2/00	1477.26	99.24	7.2
6/25/38	11.39	1.72	17.8	11/28/08	896.24	96.21	12.0
7/30/32	6.10	0.89	17.1	10/31/08	968.75	91.98	10.5
4/22/33	7.75	1.09	16.4	12/2/11	1244.28	85.61	7.4
10/11/74	71.14	8.80	14.1	4/20/00	1434.54	77.98	5.8
2/13/32	8.80	1.08	14.0	10/24/14	1964.58	77.82	4.1
9/24/32	8.52	1.02	13.6	7/2/99	1391.22	75.91	5.8
10/10/31	10.64	1.27	13.6	3/3/00	1409.17	75.81	5.7
8/27/32	8.57	1.01	13.4	9/28/01	1040.94	75.14	7.8
3/18/33	6.61	0.77	13.2	3/13/09	756.55	73.17	10.7
NASDAQ 1971 to APRIL 2015							
6/2/00	3813.38	608.27	19.0	6/2/00	3813.38	608.27	19.0
4/12/01	1961.43	241.07	14.0	2/4/00	4244.14	357.07	9.2
11/28/08	1535.57	151.22	10.9	3/3/00	4914.79	324.29	7.1
10/31/08	1720.95	168.92	10.9	4/20/00	3643.88	322.59	9.7
3/13/09	1431.50	137.65	10.6	12/8/00	2917.43	272.14	10.3
4/20/01	2163.41	201.98	10.3	4/12/01	1961.43	241.07	14.0
12/8/00	2917.43	272.14	10.3	10/24/14	4483.72	225.28	5.3
4/20/00	3643.88	322.59	9.7	7/14/00	4246.18	222.98	5.5
10/11/74	60.42	5.26	9.5	1/12/01	2626.50	218.85	9.1
2/4/00	4244.14	357.07	9.0	4/28/00	3860.66	216.78	6.0
RUSSELL 1000 1979 to APRIL 2015							
11/28/08	481.43	53.55	12.5	6/2/00	785.02	57.93	8.0
10/31/08	522.47	50.94	10.8	11/28/08	481.43	53.55	12.5
3/13/09	411.10	39.88	10.7	10/31/08	522.47	50.94	10.8
8/20/82	61.51	4.83	8.5	12/2/11	687.44	47.63	7.4
6/2/00	785.02	57.93	8.0	10/24/14	1092.59	43.55	4.2
9/28/01	546.46	38.48	7.6	4/20/00	757.32	42.12	5.9
10/16/98	546.09	38.45	7.6	3/3/00	756.41	41.55	5.8
8/3/84	87.43	6.13	7.5	3/13/09	411.10	39.88	10.7
12/2/11	687.44	47.63	7.4	7/1/11	745.21	39.46	5.6
3/21/03	474.58	32.69	7.4	10/14/11	675.52	38.87	6.1
RUSSELL 2000 1979 to APRIL 2015							
11/28/08	473.14	66.60	16.4	12/2/11	735.02	68.86	10.3
10/31/08	537.52	66.40	14.1	11/28/08	473.14	66.60	16.4
6/2/00	513.03	55.66	12.2	10/31/08	537.52	66.40	14.1
3/13/09	393.09	42.04	12.0	10/14/11	712.46	56.25	8.6
12/2/11	735.02	68.86	10.3	6/2/00	513.03	55.66	12.2
10/14/11	712.46	56.25	8.6	10/31/14	1173.51	54.69	4.9
7/17/09	519.22	38.24	8.0	10/28/11	761.00	48.58	6.8
10/16/98	342.87	24.47	7.7	1/4/13	879.15	47.05	5.7
12/18/87	116.94	8.31	7.7	12/19/14	1195.90	43.45	3.8
3/3/00	597.88	41.14	7.4	7/1/11	840.04	42.25	5.3

10 **WORST** WEEKS BY PERCENT AND POINT

	BY PERCENT CHANGE				BY POINT CHANGE		
WEEK ENDS	CLOSE	PNT CHANGE	% CHANGE	WEEK ENDS	CLOSE	PNT CHANGE	% CHANGE
DJIA 1901 to 1949							
7/22/33	88.42	−17.68	−16.7	11/8/29	236.53	−36.98	−13.5
5/18/40	122.43	−22.42	−15.5	12/8/28	257.33	−33.47	−11.5
10/8/32	61.17	−10.92	−15.2	6/21/30	215.30	−28.95	−11.9
10/3/31	92.77	−14.59	−13.6	10/19/29	323.87	−28.82	−8.2
11/8/29	236.53	−36.98	−13.5	5/3/30	258.31	−27.15	−9.5
9/17/32	66.44	−10.10	−13.2	10/31/29	273.51	−25.46	−8.5
10/21/33	83.64	−11.95	−12.5	10/26/29	298.97	−24.90	−7.7
12/12/31	78.93	−11.21	−12.4	5/18/40	122.43	−22.42	−15.5
5/8/15	62.77	−8.74	−12.2	2/8/29	301.53	−18.23	−5.7
6/21/30	215.30	−28.95	−11.9	10/11/30	193.05	−18.05	−8.6
DJIA 1950 to APRIL 2015							
10/10/08	8451.19	−1874.19	−18.2	10/10/08	8451.19	−1874.19	−18.2
9/21/01	8235.81	−1369.70	−14.3	9/21/01	8235.81	−1369.70	−14.3
10/23/87	1950.76	−295.98	−13.2	3/16/01	9823.41	−821.21	−7.7
10/16/87	2246.74	−235.47	−9.5	10/3/08	10325.38	−817.75	−7.3
10/13/89	2569.26	−216.26	−7.8	4/14/00	10305.77	−805.71	−7.3
3/16/01	9823.41	−821.21	−7.7	9/23/11	10771.48	−737.61	−6.4
7/19/02	8019.26	−665.27	−7.7	8/5/11	11444.61	−698.63	−5.8
12/4/87	1766.74	−143.74	−7.5	7/12/02	8684.53	−694.97	−7.4
9/13/74	627.19	−50.69	−7.5	12/12/14	17280.83	−677.96	−3.8
9/12/86	1758.72	−141.03	−7.4	7/19/02	8019.26	−665.27	−7.7
S&P 500 1930 to APRIL 2015							
7/22/33	9.71	−2.20	−18.5	10/10/08	899.22	−200.01	−18.2
10/10/08	899.22	−200.01	−18.2	4/14/00	1356.56	−159.79	−10.5
5/18/40	9.75	−2.05	−17.4	9/21/01	965.80	−126.74	−11.6
10/8/32	6.77	−1.38	−16.9	10/3/08	1099.23	−113.78	−9.4
9/17/32	7.50	−1.28	−14.6	8/5/11	1199.38	−92.90	−7.2
10/21/33	8.57	−1.31	−13.3	10/15/99	1247.41	−88.61	−6.6
10/3/31	9.37	−1.36	−12.7	3/16/01	1150.53	−82.89	−6.7
10/23/87	248.22	−34.48	−12.2	1/28/00	1360.16	−81.20	−5.6
12/12/31	8.20	−1.13	−12.1	9/23/11	1136.43	−79.58	−6.5
3/26/38	9.20	−1.21	−11.6	1/18/08	1325.19	−75.83	−5.4
NASDAQ 1971 to APRIL 2015							
4/14/00	3321.29	−1125.16	−25.3	4/14/00	3321.29	−1125.16	−25.3
10/23/87	328.45	−77.88	−19.2	7/28/00	3663.00	−431.45	−10.5
9/21/01	1423.19	−272.19	−16.1	11/10/00	3028.99	−422.59	−12.2
10/10/08	1649.51	−297.88	−15.3	3/31/00	4572.83	−390.20	−7.9
11/10/00	3028.99	−422.59	−12.2	1/28/00	3887.07	−348.33	−8.2
10/3/08	1947.39	−235.95	−10.8	10/6/00	3361.01	−311.81	−8.5
7/28/00	3663.00	−431.45	−10.5	10/10/08	1649.51	−297.88	−15.3
10/24/08	1552.03	−159.26	−9.3	5/12/00	3529.06	−287.76	−7.5
12/15/00	2653.27	−264.16	−9.1	9/21/01	1423.19	−272.19	−16.1
12/1/00	2645.29	−259.09	−8.9	12/15/00	2653.27	−264.16	−9.1
RUSSELL 1000 1979 to APRIL 2015							
10/10/08	486.23	−108.31	−18.2	10/10/08	486.23	−108.31	−18.2
10/23/87	130.19	−19.25	−12.9	4/14/00	715.20	−90.39	−11.2
9/21/01	507.98	−67.59	−11.7	9/21/01	507.98	−67.59	−11.7
4/14/00	715.20	−90.39	−11.2	10/3/08	594.54	−65.15	−9.9
10/3/08	594.54	−65.15	−9.9	8/5/11	662.84	−54.93	−7.7
10/16/87	149.44	−14.42	−8.8	9/23/11	627.56	−45.42	−6.8
11/21/08	427.88	−41.15	−8.8	10/15/99	646.79	−43.89	−6.4
9/12/86	124.95	−10.87	−8.0	3/16/01	605.71	−43.88	−6.8
8/5/11	662.84	−54.93	−7.7	5/7/10	611.63	−43.43	−6.6
7/19/02	450.64	−36.13	−7.4	7/27/07	793.72	−41.97	−5.0
RUSSELL 2000 1979 to APRIL 2015							
10/23/87	121.59	−31.15	−20.4	10/10/08	522.48	−96.92	−15.7
4/14/00	453.72	−89.27	−16.4	4/14/00	453.72	−89.27	−16.4
10/10/08	522.48	−96.92	−15.7	10/3/08	619.40	−85.39	−12.1
9/21/01	378.89	−61.84	−14.0	8/5/11	714.63	−82.40	−10.3
10/3/08	619.40	−85.39	−12.1	5/7/10	653.00	−63.60	−8.9
11/21/08	406.54	−49.98	−11.0	9/23/11	652.43	−61.88	−8.7
10/24/08	471.12	−55.31	−10.5	9/21/01	378.89	−61.84	−14.0
8/5/11	714.63	−82.40	−10.3	7/27/07	777.83	−58.61	−7.0
3/6/09	351.05	−37.97	−9.8	10/24/08	471.12	−55.31	−10.5
11/14/08	456.52	−49.27	−9.7	11/25/11	666.16	−53.26	−7.4

164

10 BEST MONTHS BY PERCENT AND POINT

	BY PERCENT CHANGE				BY POINT CHANGE		
MONTH	CLOSE	PNT CHANGE	% CHANGE	MONTH	CLOSE	PNT CHANGE	% CHANGE
DJIA 1901 to 1949							
APR-1933	77.66	22.26	40.2	NOV-1928	293.38	41.22	16.3
AUG-1932	73.16	18.90	34.8	JUN-1929	333.79	36.38	12.2
JUL-1932	54.26	11.42	26.7	AUG-1929	380.33	32.63	9.4
JUN-1938	133.88	26.14	24.3	JUN-1938	133.88	26.14	24.3
APR-1915	71.78	10.95	18.0	AUG-1928	240.41	24.41	11.3
JUN-1931	150.18	21.72	16.9	APR-1933	77.66	22.26	40.2
NOV-1928	293.38	41.22	16.3	FEB-1931	189.66	22.11	13.2
NOV-1904	52.76	6.59	14.3	JUN-1931	150.18	21.72	16.9
MAY-1919	105.50	12.62	13.6	AUG-1932	73.16	18.90	34.8
SEP-1939	152.54	18.13	13.5	JAN-1930	267.14	18.66	7.5
DJIA 1950 to APRIL 2015							
JAN-1976	975.28	122.87	14.4	OCT-2011	11955.01	1041.63	9.5
JAN-1975	703.69	87.45	14.2	APR-1999	10789.04	1002.88	10.2
JAN-1987	2158.04	262.09	13.8	FEB-2015	18132.70	967.75	5.6
AUG-1982	901.31	92.71	11.5	APR-2001	10734.97	856.19	8.7
OCT-1982	991.72	95.47	10.7	OCT-2002	8397.03	805.10	10.6
OCT-2002	8397.03	805.10	10.6	MAR-2000	10921.92	793.61	7.8
APR-1978	837.32	79.96	10.6	NOV-2001	9851.56	776.42	8.6
APR-1999	10789.04	1002.88	10.2	SEP-2010	10788.05	773.33	7.7
NOV-1962	649.30	59.53	10.1	JAN-2013	13860.58	756.44	5.8
NOV-1954	386.77	34.63	9.8	OCT-1998	8592.10	749.48	9.6
S&P 500 1930 to APRIL 2015							
APR-1933	8.32	2.47	42.2	MAR-2000	1498.58	132.16	9.7
JUL-1932	6.10	1.67	37.7	OCT-2011	1253.30	121.88	10.8
AUG-1932	8.39	2.29	37.5	FEB-2015	2104.50	109.51	5.5
JUN-1938	11.56	2.29	24.7	SEP-2010	1141.20	91.87	8.8
SEP-1939	13.02	1.84	16.5	APR-2001	1249.46	89.13	7.7
OCT-1974	73.90	10.36	16.3	AUG-2000	1517.68	86.85	6.1
MAY-1933	9.64	1.32	15.9	OCT-1998	1098.67	81.66	8.0
APR-1938	9.70	1.20	14.1	DEC-1999	1469.25	80.34	5.8
JUN-1931	14.83	1.81	13.9	OCT-1999	1362.93	80.22	6.3
JAN-1987	274.08	31.91	13.2	NOV-2001	1139.45	79.67	7.5
NASDAQ 1971 to APRIL 2015							
DEC-1999	4069.31	733.15	22.0	FEB-2000	4696.69	756.34	19.2
FEB-2000	4696.69	756.34	19.2	DEC-1999	4069.31	733.15	22.0
OCT-1974	65.23	9.56	17.2	JUN-2000	3966.11	565.20	16.6
JAN-1975	69.78	9.96	16.6	AUG-2000	4206.35	439.36	11.7
JUN-2000	3966.11	565.20	16.6	NOV-1999	3336.16	369.73	12.5
APR-2001	2116.24	275.98	15.0	FEB-2015	4963.53	328.29	7.1
JAN-1999	2505.89	313.20	14.3	JAN-1999	2505.89	313.20	14.3
NOV-2001	1930.58	240.38	14.2	JAN-2001	2772.73	302.21	12.2
OCT-2002	1329.75	157.69	13.5	APR-2001	2116.24	275.98	15.0
OCT-1982	212.63	24.98	13.3	OCT-2011	2684.41	269.01	11.1
RUSSELL 1000 1979 to APRIL 2015							
JAN-1987	146.48	16.48	12.7	OCT-2011	692.41	68.96	11.1
OCT-1982	73.34	7.45	11.3	MAR-2000	797.99	64.95	8.9
AUG-1982	65.14	6.60	11.3	FEB-2015	1173.46	61.61	5.5
DEC-1991	220.61	22.15	11.2	AUG-2000	811.17	55.60	7.4
OCT-2011	692.41	68.96	11.1	SEP-2010	629.78	52.10	9.0
AUG-1984	89.87	8.74	10.8	APR-2001	658.90	48.54	8.0
NOV-1980	78.26	7.18	10.1	JUL-2013	937.16	46.49	5.2
APR-2009	476.84	43.17	10.0	FEB-2014	1041.36	44.88	4.5
SEP-2010	629.78	52.10	9.0	OCT-1999	707.19	43.36	6.5
MAY-1990	187.66	15.34	8.0	DEC-1999	767.97	43.31	6.0
RUSSELL 2000 1979 to APRIL 2015							
FEB-2000	577.71	81.48	16.4	OCT-2011	741.06	96.90	15.0
APR-2009	487.56	64.81	15.3	FEB-2000	577.71	81.48	16.4
OCT-2011	741.06	96.90	15.0	SEP-2010	676.14	74.08	12.3
OCT-1982	80.86	10.02	14.1	OCT-2014	1173.51	71.83	6.5
JAN-1985	114.77	13.28	13.1	FEB-2015	1233.37	67.98	5.8
SEP-2010	676.14	74.08	12.3	JUL-2013	1045.26	67.78	6.9
AUG-1984	106.21	10.96	11.5	APR-2009	487.56	64.81	15.3
JAN-1987	150.48	15.48	11.5	SEP-2013	1073.79	62.89	6.2
DEC-1999	504.75	50.67	11.2	JAN-2006	733.20	59.98	8.9
JUL-1980	63.81	6.34	11.0	JUN-2014	1192.96	58.46	5.2

10 <u>WORST</u> MONTHS BY PERCENT AND POINT

	BY PERCENT CHANGE				BY POINT CHANGE		
MONTH	CLOSE	PNT CHANGE	% CHANGE	MONTH	CLOSE	PNT CHANGE	% CHANGE
DJIA 1901 to 1949							
SEP-1931	96.61	–42.80	–30.7	OCT-1929	273.51	–69.94	–20.4
MAR-1938	98.95	–30.69	–23.7	JUN-1930	226.34	–48.73	–17.7
APR-1932	56.11	–17.17	–23.4	SEP-1931	96.61	–42.80	–30.7
MAY-1940	116.22	–32.21	–21.7	SEP-1929	343.45	–36.88	–9.7
OCT-1929	273.51	–69.94	–20.4	SEP-1930	204.90	–35.52	–14.8
MAY-1932	44.74	–11.37	–20.3	NOV-1929	238.95	–34.56	–12.6
JUN-1930	226.34	–48.73	–17.7	MAY-1940	116.22	–32.21	–21.7
DEC-1931	77.90	–15.97	–17.0	MAR-1938	98.95	–30.69	–23.7
FEB-1933	51.39	–9.51	–15.6	SEP-1937	154.57	–22.84	–12.9
MAY-1931	128.46	–22.73	–15.0	MAY-1931	128.46	–22.73	–15.0
DJIA 1950 to APRIL 2015							
OCT-1987	1993.53	–602.75	–23.2	OCT-2008	9325.01	–1525.65	–14.1
AUG-1998	7539.07	–1344.22	–15.1	AUG-1998	7539.07	–1344.22	–15.1
OCT-2008	9325.01	–1525.65	–14.1	JUN-2008	11350.01	–1288.31	–10.2
NOV-1973	822.25	–134.33	–14.0	SEP-2001	8847.56	–1102.19	–11.1
SEP-2002	7591.93	–1071.57	–12.4	SEP-2002	7591.93	–1071.57	–12.4
FEB-2009	7062.93	–937.93	–11.7	FEB-2009	7062.93	–937.93	–11.7
SEP-2001	8847.56	–1102.19	–11.1	JAN-2014	15698.85	–877.81	–5.3
SEP-1974	607.87	–70.71	–10.4	MAY-2010	10136.63	–871.98	–7.9
AUG-1974	678.58	–78.85	–10.4	MAY-2012	12393.45	–820.18	–6.2
JUN-2008	11350.01	–1288.31	–10.2	FEB-2000	10128.31	–812.22	–7.4
S&P 500 1930 to APRIL 2015							
SEP-1931	9.71	–4.15	–29.9	OCT-2008	968.75	–197.61	–16.9
MAR-1938	8.50	–2.84	–25.0	AUG-1998	957.28	–163.39	–14.6
MAY-1940	9.27	–2.92	–24.0	FEB-2001	1239.94	–126.07	–9.2
MAY-1932	4.47	–1.36	–23.3	JUN-2008	1280.00	–120.38	–8.6
OCT-1987	251.79	–70.04	–21.8	SEP-2008	1166.36	–116.47	–9.1
APR-1932	5.83	–1.48	–20.2	NOV-2000	1314.95	–114.45	–8.0
FEB-1933	5.66	–1.28	–18.4	SEP-2002	815.28	–100.79	–11.0
OCT-2008	968.75	–197.61	–16.9	MAY-2010	1089.41	–97.28	–8.2
JUN-1930	20.46	–4.03	–16.5	SEP-2001	1040.94	–92.64	–8.2
AUG-1998	957.28	–163.39	–14.6	FEB-2009	735.09	–90.79	–11.0
NASDAQ 1971 to APRIL 2015							
OCT-1987	323.30	–120.99	–27.2	NOV-2000	2597.93	–771.70	–22.9
NOV-2000	2597.93	–771.70	–22.9	APR-2000	3860.66	–712.17	–15.6
FEB-2001	2151.83	–620.90	–22.4	FEB-2001	2151.83	–620.90	–22.4
AUG-1998	1499.25	–373.14	–19.9	SEP-2000	3672.82	–533.53	–12.7
OCT-2008	1720.95	–370.93	–17.7	MAY-2000	3400.91	–459.75	–11.9
MAR-1980	131.00	–27.03	–17.1	AUG-1998	1499.25	–373.14	–19.9
SEP-2001	1498.80	–306.63	–17.0	OCT-2008	1720.95	–370.93	–17.7
OCT-1978	111.12	–21.77	–16.4	MAR-2001	1840.26	–311.57	–14.5
APR-2000	3860.66	–712.17	–15.6	SEP-2001	1498.80	–306.63	–17.0
NOV-1973	93.51	–16.66	–15.1	OCT-2000	3369.63	–303.19	–8.3
RUSSELL 1000 1979 to APRIL 2015							
OCT-1987	131.89	–36.94	–21.9	OCT-2008	522.47	–111.61	–17.6
OCT-2008	522.47	–111.61	–17.6	AUG-1998	496.66	–88.31	–15.1
AUG-1998	496.66	–88.31	–15.1	NOV-2000	692.40	–70.66	–9.3
MAR-1980	55.79	–7.28	–11.5	FEB-2001	654.25	–68.30	–9.5
SEP-2002	433.22	–52.86	–10.9	SEP-2008	634.08	–68.09	–9.7
FEB-2009	399.61	–47.71	–10.7	JUN-2008	703.22	–65.06	–8.5
SEP-2008	634.08	–68.09	–9.7	MAY-2010	601.79	–53.27	–8.1
AUG-1990	166.69	–17.63	–9.6	SEP-2002	433.22	–52.86	–10.9
FEB-2001	654.25	–68.30	–9.5	SEP-2011	623.45	–51.34	–7.6
NOV-2000	692.40	–70.66	–9.3	SEP-2001	546.46	–51.21	–8.6
RUSSELL 2000 1979 to APRIL 2015							
OCT-1987	118.26	–52.55	–30.8	OCT-2008	537.52	–142.06	–20.9
OCT-2008	537.52	–142.06	–20.9	SEP-2011	644.16	–82.65	–11.4
AUG-1998	337.95	–81.80	–19.5	AUG-1998	337.95	–81.80	–19.5
MAR-1980	48.27	–10.95	–18.5	JUL-2014	1120.07	–72.89	–6.1
JUL-2002	392.42	–70.22	–15.2	SEP-2014	1101.68	–72.67	–6.2
AUG-1990	139.52	–21.99	–13.6	JUL-2002	392.42	–70.22	–15.2
SEP-2001	404.87	–63.69	–13.6	AUG-2011	726.81	–70.22	–8.8
FEB-2009	389.02	–54.51	–12.3	NOV-2008	473.14	–64.38	–12.0
NOV-2008	473.14	–64.38	–12.0	SEP-2001	404.87	–63.69	–13.6
SEP-2011	644.16	–82.65	–11.4	NOV-2007	767.77	–60.25	–7.3

10 __BEST__ QUARTERS BY PERCENT AND POINT

	BY PERCENT CHANGE				BY POINT CHANGE		
QUARTER	CLOSE	PNT CHANGE	% CHANGE	QUARTER	CLOSE	PNT CHANGE	% CHANGE
DJIA 1901 to 1949							
JUN-1933	98.14	42.74	77.1	DEC-1928	300.00	60.57	25.3
SEP-1932	71.56	28.72	67.0	JUN-1933	98.14	42.74	77.1
JUN-1938	133.88	34.93	35.3	MAR-1930	286.10	37.62	15.1
SEP-1915	90.58	20.52	29.3	JUN-1938	133.88	34.93	35.3
DEC-1928	300.00	60.57	25.3	SEP-1927	197.59	31.36	18.9
DEC-1904	50.99	8.80	20.9	SEP-1928	239.43	28.88	13.7
JUN-1919	106.98	18.13	20.4	SEP-1932	71.56	28.72	67.0
SEP-1927	197.59	31.36	18.9	JUN-1929	333.79	24.94	8.1
DEC-1905	70.47	10.47	17.4	SEP-1939	152.54	21.91	16.8
JUN-1935	118.21	17.40	17.3	SEP-1915	90.58	20.52	29.3
DJIA 1950 to APRIL 2015							
MAR-1975	768.15	151.91	24.7	MAR-2013	14578.54	1474.40	11.3
MAR-1987	2304.69	408.74	21.6	DEC-2013	16576.66	1446.99	9.6
MAR-1986	1818.61	271.94	17.6	DEC-1998	9181.43	1338.81	17.1
MAR-1976	999.45	147.04	17.2	DEC-2011	12217.56	1304.18	12.0
DEC-1998	9181.43	1338.81	17.1	SEP-2009	9712.28	1265.28	15.0
DEC-1982	1046.54	150.29	16.8	JUN-1999	10970.80	1184.64	12.1
JUN-1997	7672.79	1089.31	16.5	DEC-2003	10453.92	1178.86	12.7
DEC-1985	1546.67	218.04	16.4	DEC-2001	10021.50	1173.94	13.3
SEP-2009	9712.28	1265.28	15.0	DEC-1999	11497.12	1160.17	11.2
JUN-1975	878.99	110.84	14.4	JUN-1997	7672.79	1089.31	16.5
S&P 500 1930 to APRIL 2015							
JUN-1933	10.91	5.06	86.5	DEC-1998	1229.23	212.22	20.9
SEP-1932	8.08	3.65	82.4	DEC-1999	1469.25	186.54	14.5
JUN-1938	11.56	3.06	36.0	DEC-2013	1848.36	166.81	9.9
MAR-1975	83.36	14.80	21.6	MAR-2012	1408.47	150.87	12.0
DEC-1998	1229.23	212.22	20.9	MAR-2013	1569.19	143.00	10.0
JUN-1935	10.23	1.76	20.8	SEP-2009	1057.08	137.76	15.0
MAR-1987	291.70	49.53	20.5	MAR-1998	1101.75	131.32	13.5
SEP-1939	13.02	2.16	19.9	JUN-1997	885.14	128.02	16.9
MAR-1943	11.58	1.81	18.5	DEC-2011	1257.60	126.18	11.2
MAR-1930	25.14	3.69	17.2	JUN-2003	974.50	125.32	14.8
NASDAQ 1971 to APRIL 2015							
DEC-1999	4069.31	1323.15	48.2	DEC-1999	4069.31	1323.15	48.2
DEC-2001	1950.40	451.60	30.1	MAR-2000	4572.83	503.52	12.4
DEC-1998	2192.69	498.85	29.5	DEC-1998	2192.69	498.85	29.5
MAR-1991	482.30	108.46	29.0	MAR-2012	3091.57	486.42	18.7
MAR-1975	75.66	15.84	26.5	DEC-2001	1950.40	451.60	30.1
DEC-1982	232.41	44.76	23.9	DEC-2013	4176.59	405.11	10.7
MAR-1987	430.05	80.72	23.1	SEP-2013	3771.48	368.23	10.8
JUN-2003	1622.80	281.63	21.0	JUN-2001	2160.54	320.28	17.4
JUN-1980	157.78	26.78	20.4	JUN-2009	1835.04	306.45	20.0
JUN-2009	1835.04	306.45	20.0	SEP-2009	2122.42	287.38	15.7
RUSSELL 1000 1979 to APRIL 2015							
DEC-1998	642.87	113.76	21.5	DEC-1998	642.87	113.76	21.5
MAR-1987	155.20	25.20	19.4	DEC-1999	767.97	104.14	15.7
DEC-1982	77.24	11.35	17.2	DEC-2013	1030.36	90.86	9.7
JUN-1997	462.95	64.76	16.3	MAR-2012	778.92	85.56	12.3
DEC-1985	114.39	15.64	15.8	MAR-2013	872.11	82.21	10.4
JUN-2009	502.27	68.60	15.8	SEP-2009	579.97	77.70	15.5
DEC-1999	767.97	104.14	15.7	DEC-2011	693.36	69.91	11.2
SEP-2009	579.97	77.70	15.5	JUN-2009	502.27	68.60	15.8
JUN-2003	518.94	68.59	15.2	JUN-2003	518.94	68.59	15.2
MAR-1991	196.15	24.93	14.6	DEC-2010	696.90	67.12	10.7
RUSSELL 2000 1979 to APRIL 2015							
MAR-1991	171.01	38.85	29.4	DEC-2010	783.65	107.51	15.9
DEC-1982	88.90	18.06	25.5	DEC-2014	1204.70	103.02	9.4
MAR-1987	166.79	31.79	23.5	MAR-2013	951.54	102.19	12.0
JUN-2003	448.37	83.83	23.0	DEC-2011	740.92	96.76	15.0
SEP-1980	69.94	12.47	21.7	SEP-2013	1073.79	96.31	9.9
DEC-2001	488.50	83.63	20.7	SEP-2009	604.28	96.00	18.9
JUN-1983	124.17	20.40	19.7	MAR-2006	765.14	91.92	13.7
JUN-1980	57.47	9.20	19.1	DEC-2013	1163.64	89.85	8.4
DEC-1999	504.75	77.45	18.1	MAR-2012	830.30	89.38	12.1
SEP-2009	604.28	96.00	18.9	JUN-2009	508.28	85.53	20.2

10 <u>WORST</u> QUARTERS BY PERCENT AND POINT

	BY PERCENT CHANGE			BY POINT CHANGE			
QUARTER	CLOSE	PNT CHANGE	% CHANGE	QUARTER	CLOSE	PNT CHANGE	% CHANGE
DJIA 1901 to 1949							
JUN-1932	42.84	–30.44	–41.5	DEC-1929	248.48	–94.97	–27.7
SEP-1931	96.61	–53.57	–35.7	JUN-1930	226.34	–59.76	–20.9
DEC-1929	248.48	–94.97	–27.7	SEP-1931	96.61	–53.57	–35.7
SEP-1903	33.55	–9.73	–22.5	DEC-1930	164.58	–40.32	–19.7
DEC-1937	120.85	–33.72	–21.8	DEC-1937	120.85	–33.72	–21.8
JUN-1930	226.34	–59.76	–20.9	SEP-1946	172.42	–33.20	–16.1
DEC-1930	164.58	–40.32	–19.7	JUN-1932	42.84	–30.44	–41.5
DEC-1931	77.90	–18.71	–19.4	JUN-1940	121.87	–26.08	–17.6
MAR-1938	98.95	–21.90	–18.1	MAR-1939	131.84	–22.92	–14.8
JUN-1940	121.87	–26.08	–17.6	JUN-1931	150.18	–22.18	–12.9
DJIA 1950 to APRIL 2015							
DEC-1987	1938.83	–657.45	–25.3	DEC-2008	8776.39	–2074.27	–19.1
SEP-1974	607.87	–194.54	–24.2	SEP-2001	8847.56	–1654.84	–15.8
JUN-1962	561.28	–145.67	–20.6	SEP-2002	7591.93	–1651.33	–17.9
DEC-2008	8776.39	–2074.27	–19.1	SEP-2011	10913.38	–1500.96	–12.1
SEP-2002	7591.93	–1651.33	–17.9	MAR-2009	7608.92	–1167.47	–13.3
SEP-2001	8847.56	–1654.84	–15.8	JUN-2002	9243.26	–1160.68	–11.2
SEP-1990	2452.48	–428.21	–14.9	SEP-1998	7842.62	–1109.40	–12.4
MAR-2009	7608.92	–1167.47	–13.3	JUN-2010	9774.02	–1082.61	–10.0
SEP-1981	849.98	–126.90	–13.0	MAR-2008	12262.89	–1001.93	–7.6
JUN-1970	683.53	–102.04	–13.0	JUN-2008	11350.01	–912.88	–7.4
S&P 500 1930 to APRIL 2015							
JUN-1932	4.43	–2.88	–39.4	DEC-2008	903.25	–263.11	–22.6
SEP-1931	9.71	–5.12	–34.5	SEP-2011	1131.42	–189.22	–14.3
SEP-1974	63.54	–22.46	–26.1	SEP-2001	1040.94	–183.48	–15.0
DEC-1937	10.55	–3.21	–23.3	SEP-2002	815.28	–174.54	–17.6
DEC-1987	247.08	–74.75	–23.2	MAR-2001	1160.33	–159.95	–12.1
DEC-2008	903.25	–263.11	–22.6	JUN-2002	989.82	–157.57	–13.7
JUN-1962	54.75	–14.80	–21.3	MAR-2008	1322.70	–145.66	–9.9
MAR-1938	8.50	–2.05	–19.4	JUN-2010	1030.71	–138.72	–11.9
JUN-1970	72.72	–16.91	–18.9	SEP-1998	1017.01	–116.83	–10.3
SEP-1946	14.96	–3.47	–18.8	DEC-2000	1320.28	–116.23	–8.1
NASDAQ 1971 to APRIL 2015							
DEC-2000	2470.52	–1202.30	–32.7	DEC-2000	2470.52	–1202.30	–32.7
SEP-2001	1498.80	–661.74	–30.6	SEP-2001	1498.80	–661.74	–30.6
SEP-1974	55.67	–20.29	–26.7	MAR-2001	1840.26	–630.26	–25.5
DEC-1987	330.47	–113.82	–25.6	JUN-2000	3966.11	–606.72	–13.3
MAR-2001	1840.26	–630.26	–25.5	DEC-2008	1577.03	–514.85	–24.6
SEP-1990	344.51	–117.78	–25.5	JUN-2002	1463.21	–382.14	–20.7
DEC-2008	1577.03	–514.85	–24.6	MAR-2008	2279.10	–373.18	–14.1
JUN-2002	1463.21	–382.14	–20.7	SEP-2011	2415.40	–358.12	–12.9
SEP-2002	1172.06	–291.15	–19.9	SEP-2000	3672.82	–293.29	–7.4
JUN-1974	75.96	–16.31	–17.7	SEP-2002	1172.06	–291.15	–19.9
RUSSELL 1000 1979 to APRIL 2015							
DEC-2008	487.77	–146.31	–23.1	DEC-2008	487.77	–146.31	–23.1
DEC-1987	130.02	–38.81	–23.0	SEP-2011	623.45	–111.03	–15.1
SEP-2002	433.22	–90.50	–17.3	SEP-2001	546.46	–100.18	–15.5
SEP-2001	546.46	–100.18	–15.5	SEP-2002	433.22	–90.50	–17.3
SEP-1990	157.83	–28.46	–15.3	MAR-2001	610.36	–89.73	–12.8
SEP-2011	623.45	–111.03	–15.1	JUN-2002	523.72	–83.63	–13.8
JUN-2002	523.72	–83.63	–13.8	MAR-2008	720.32	–79.50	–9.9
MAR-2001	610.36	–89.73	–12.8	JUN-2010	567.37	–76.42	–11.9
SEP-1981	64.06	–8.95	–12.3	DEC-2000	700.09	–72.51	–9.4
JUN-2010	567.37	–76.42	–11.9	SEP-2008	634.08	–69.14	–9.8
RUSSELL 2000 1979 to APRIL 2015							
DEC-1987	120.42	–50.39	–29.5	SEP-2011	644.16	–183.27	–22.1
DEC-2008	499.45	–180.13	–26.5	DEC-2008	499.45	–180.13	–26.5
SEP-1990	126.70	–42.34	–25.0	SEP-2001	404.87	–107.77	–21.0
SEP-2011	644.16	–183.27	–22.1	SEP-2002	362.27	–100.37	–21.7
SEP-2002	362.27	–100.37	–21.7	SEP-1998	363.59	–93.80	–20.5
SEP-2001	404.87	–107.77	–21.0	SEP-2014	1101.68	–91.28	–7.7
SEP-1998	363.59	–93.80	–20.5	MAR-2008	687.97	–78.06	–10.2
SEP-1981	67.55	–15.01	–18.2	MAR-2009	422.75	–76.70	–15.4
MAR-2009	422.75	–76.70	–15.4	JUN-2010	609.49	–69.15	–10.2
MAR-1980	48.27	–7.64	–13.7	DEC-1987	120.42	–50.39	–29.5

10 **BEST** YEARS BY PERCENT AND POINT

	BY PERCENT CHANGE				BY POINT CHANGE		
YEAR	CLOSE	PNT CHANGE	% CHANGE	YEAR	CLOSE	PNT CHANGE	% CHANGE
DJIA 1901 to 1949							
1915	99.15	44.57	81.7	1928	300.00	97.60	48.2
1933	99.90	39.97	66.7	1927	202.40	45.20	28.8
1928	300.00	97.60	48.2	1915	99.15	44.57	81.7
1908	63.11	20.07	46.6	1945	192.91	40.59	26.6
1904	50.99	15.01	41.7	1935	144.13	40.09	38.5
1935	144.13	40.09	38.5	1933	99.90	39.97	66.7
1905	70.47	19.48	38.2	1925	156.66	36.15	30.0
1919	107.23	25.03	30.5	1936	179.90	35.77	24.8
1925	156.66	36.15	30.0	1938	154.76	33.91	28.1
1927	202.40	45.20	28.8	1919	107.23	25.03	30.5
DJIA 1950 to APRIL 2015							
1954	404.39	123.49	44.0	2013	16576.66	3472.52	26.5
1975	852.41	236.17	38.3	1999	11497.12	2315.69	25.2
1958	583.65	147.96	34.0	2003	10453.92	2112.29	25.3
1995	5117.12	1282.68	33.5	2006	12463.15	1745.65	16.3
1985	1546.67	335.10	27.7	2009	10428.05	1651.66	18.8
1989	2753.20	584.63	27.0	1997	7908.25	1459.98	22.6
2013	16576.66	3472.52	26.5	1996	6448.27	1331.15	26.0
1996	6448.27	1331.15	26.0	1995	5117.12	1282.68	33.5
2003	10453.92	2112.29	25.3	1998	9181.43	1273.18	16.1
1999	11497.12	2315.69	25.2	2014	17823.07	1246.41	7.5
S&P 500 1930 to APRIL 2015							
1933	10.10	3.21	46.6	2013	1848.36	422.17	29.6
1954	35.98	11.17	45.0	1998	1229.23	258.80	26.7
1935	13.43	3.93	41.4	1999	1469.25	240.02	19.5
1958	55.21	15.22	38.1	2003	1111.92	232.10	26.4
1995	615.93	156.66	34.1	1997	970.43	229.69	31.0
1975	90.19	21.63	31.5	2009	1115.10	211.85	23.5
1997	970.43	229.69	31.0	2014	2058.90	210.54	11.4
1945	17.36	4.08	30.7	2006	1418.30	170.01	13.6
2013	1848.36	422.17	29.6	2012	1426.19	168.59	13.4
1936	17.18	3.75	27.9	1995	615.93	156.66	34.1
NASDAQ 1971 to APRIL 2015							
1999	4069.31	1876.62	85.6	1999	4069.31	1876.62	85.6
1991	586.34	212.50	56.8	2013	4176.59	1157.08	38.3
2003	2003.37	667.86	50.0	2009	2269.15	692.12	43.9
2009	2269.15	692.12	43.9	2003	2003.37	667.86	50.0
1995	1052.13	300.17	39.9	1998	2192.69	622.34	39.6
1998	2192.69	622.34	39.6	2014	4736.05	559.46	13.4
2013	4176.59	1157.08	38.3	2012	3019.51	414.36	15.9
1980	202.34	51.20	33.9	2010	2652.87	383.72	16.9
1985	324.93	77.58	31.4	1995	1052.13	300.17	39.9
1975	77.62	17.80	29.8	1997	1570.35	279.32	21.6
RUSSELL 1000 1979 to APRIL 2015							
1995	328.89	84.24	34.4	2013	1030.36	240.46	30.4
1997	513.79	120.04	30.5	1998	642.87	129.08	25.1
2013	1030.36	240.46	30.4	2003	594.56	128.38	27.5
1991	220.61	49.39	28.8	1999	767.97	125.10	19.5
2003	594.56	128.38	27.5	2009	612.01	124.24	25.5
1985	114.39	24.08	26.7	1997	513.79	120.04	30.5
1989	185.11	38.12	25.9	2014	1144.37	114.01	11.1
1980	75.20	15.33	25.6	2012	789.90	96.54	13.9
2009	612.01	124.24	25.5	2006	770.08	90.66	13.3
1998	642.87	129.08	25.1	2010	696.90	84.89	13.9
RUSSELL 2000 1979 to APRIL 2015							
2003	556.91	173.82	45.4	2013	1163.64	314.29	37.0
1991	189.94	57.78	43.7	2003	556.91	173.82	45.4
1979	55.91	15.39	38.0	2010	783.65	158.26	25.3
2013	1163.64	314.29	37.0	2009	625.39	125.94	25.2
1980	74.80	18.89	33.8	2006	787.66	114.44	17.0
1985	129.87	28.38	28.0	2012	849.35	108.43	14.6
1983	112.27	23.37	26.3	2004	651.57	94.66	17.0
1995	315.97	65.61	26.2	1999	504.75	82.79	19.6
2010	783.65	158.26	25.3	1997	437.02	74.41	20.5
2009	625.39	125.94	25.2	1995	315.97	65.61	26.2

10 <u>WORST</u> YEARS BY PERCENT AND POINT

	BY PERCENT CHANGE				BY POINT CHANGE		
YEAR	CLOSE	PNT CHANGE	% CHANGE	YEAR	CLOSE	PNT CHANGE	% CHANGE
DJIA 1901 to 1949							
1931	77.90	–86.68	–52.7	1931	77.90	–86.68	–52.7
1907	43.04	–26.08	–37.7	1930	164.58	–83.90	–33.8
1930	164.58	–83.90	–33.8	1937	120.85	–59.05	–32.8
1920	71.95	–35.28	–32.9	1929	248.48	–51.52	–17.2
1937	120.85	–59.05	–32.8	1920	71.95	–35.28	–32.9
1903	35.98	–11.12	–23.6	1907	43.04	–26.08	–37.7
1932	59.93	–17.97	–23.1	1917	74.38	–20.62	–21.7
1917	74.38	–20.62	–21.7	1941	110.96	–20.17	–15.4
1910	59.60	–12.96	–17.9	1940	131.13	–19.11	–12.7
1929	248.48	–51.52	–17.2	1932	59.93	–17.97	–23.1
DJIA 1950 to APRIL 2015							
2008	8776.39	–4488.43	–33.8	2008	8776.39	–4488.43	–33.8
1974	616.24	–234.62	–27.6	2002	8341.63	–1679.87	–16.8
1966	785.69	–183.57	–18.9	2001	10021.50	–765.35	–7.1
1977	831.17	–173.48	–17.3	2000	10786.85	–710.27	–6.2
2002	8341.63	–1679.87	–16.8	1974	616.24	–234.62	–27.6
1973	850.86	–169.16	–16.6	1966	785.69	–183.57	–18.9
1969	800.36	–143.39	–15.2	1977	831.17	–173.48	–17.3
1957	435.69	–63.78	–12.8	1973	850.86	–169.16	–16.6
1962	652.10	–79.04	–10.8	1969	800.36	–143.39	–15.2
1960	615.89	–63.47	–9.3	1990	2633.66	–119.54	–4.3
S&P 500 1930 to APRIL 2015							
1931	8.12	–7.22	–47.1	2008	903.25	–565.11	–38.5
1937	10.55	–6.63	–38.6	2002	879.82	–268.26	–23.4
2008	903.25	–565.11	–38.5	2001	1148.08	–172.20	–13.0
1974	68.56	–28.99	–29.7	2000	1320.28	–148.97	–10.1
1930	15.34	–6.11	–28.5	1974	68.56	–28.99	–29.7
2002	879.82	–268.26	–23.4	1990	330.22	–23.18	–6.6
1941	8.69	–1.89	–17.9	1973	97.55	–20.50	–17.4
1973	97.55	–20.50	–17.4	1981	122.55	–13.21	–9.7
1940	10.58	–1.91	–15.3	1977	95.10	–12.36	–11.5
1932	6.89	–1.23	–15.1	1966	80.33	–12.10	–13.1
NASDAQ 1971 to APRIL 2015							
2008	1577.03	–1075.25	–40.5	2000	2470.52	–1598.79	–39.3
2000	2470.52	–1598.79	–39.3	2008	1577.03	–1075.25	–40.5
1974	59.82	–32.37	–35.1	2002	1335.51	–614.89	–31.5
2002	1335.51	–614.89	–31.5	2001	1950.40	–520.12	–21.1
1973	92.19	–41.54	–31.1	1990	373.84	–80.98	–17.8
2001	1950.40	–520.12	–21.1	2011	2605.15	–47.72	–1.8
1990	373.84	–80.98	–17.8	1973	92.19	–41.54	–31.1
1984	247.35	–31.25	–11.2	1974	59.82	–32.37	–35.1
1987	330.47	–18.86	–5.4	1984	247.35	–31.25	–11.2
1981	195.84	–6.50	–3.2	1994	751.96	–24.84	–3.2
RUSSELL 1000 1979 to APRIL 2015							
2008	487.77	–312.05	–39.0	2008	487.77	–312.05	–39.0
2002	466.18	–138.76	–22.9	2002	466.18	–138.76	–22.9
2001	604.94	–95.15	–13.6	2001	604.94	–95.15	–13.6
1981	67.93	–7.27	–9.7	2000	700.09	–67.88	–8.8
2000	700.09	–67.88	–8.8	1990	171.22	–13.89	–7.5
1990	171.22	–13.89	–7.5	1981	67.93	–7.27	–9.7
1994	244.65	–6.06	–2.4	1994	244.65	–6.06	–2.4
2011	693.36	–3.54	–0.5	2011	693.36	–3.54	–0.5
1984	90.31	–0.07	–0.1	1984	90.31	–0.07	–0.1
1987	130.02	0.02	0.02	1987	130.02	0.02	0.02
RUSSELL 2000 1979 to APRIL 2015							
2008	499.45	–266.58	–34.8	2008	499.45	–266.58	–34.8
2002	383.09	–105.41	–21.6	2002	383.09	–105.41	–21.6
1990	132.16	–36.14	–21.5	2011	740.92	–42.73	–5.5
1987	120.42	–14.58	–10.8	1990	132.16	–36.14	–21.5
1984	101.49	–10.78	–9.6	2007	766.03	–21.63	–2.7
2011	740.92	–42.73	–5.5	2000	483.53	–21.22	–4.2
2000	483.53	–21.22	–4.2	1998	421.96	–15.06	–3.4
1998	421.96	–15.06	–3.4	1987	120.42	–14.58	–10.8
1994	250.36	–8.23	–3.2	1984	101.49	–10.78	–9.6
2007	766.03	–21.63	–2.7	1994	250.36	–8.23	–3.2

DOW JONES INDUSTRIALS ONE-YEAR SEASONAL PATTERN CHARTS SINCE 1901

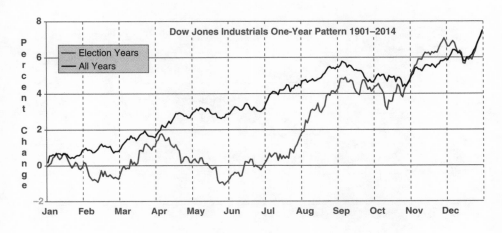

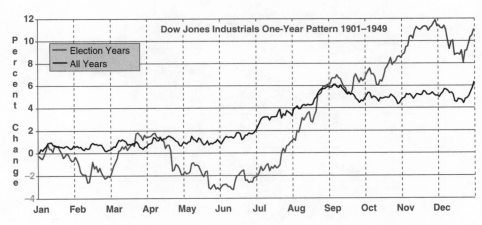

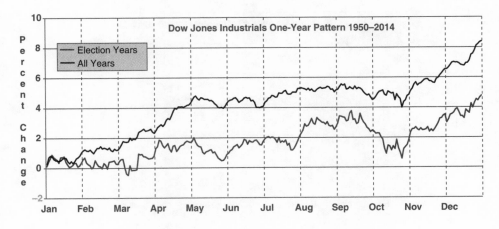

S&P 500 ONE-YEAR SEASONAL PATTERN CHARTS SINCE 1930

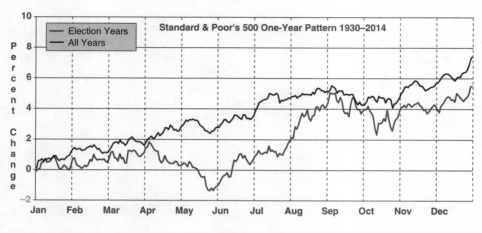

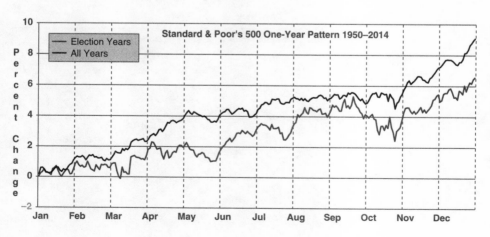

NASDAQ, RUSSELL 1000 & 2000 ONE-YEAR SEASONAL PATTERN CHARTS SINCE 1971

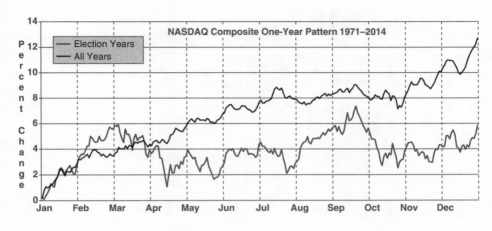

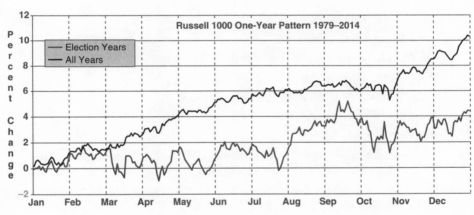

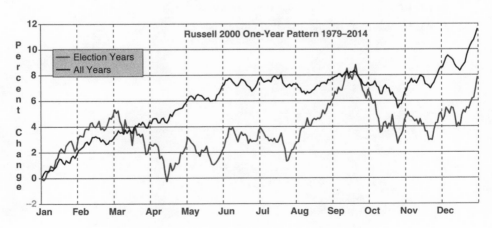

STRATEGY PLANNING AND RECORD SECTION

CONTENTS

These forms are available at our website www.stocktradersalmanac.com.

PORTFOLIO AT START OF 2016

DATE ACQUIRED	NO. OF SHARES	SECURITY	PRICE	TOTAL COST	PAPER PROFITS	PAPER LOSSES

ADDITIONAL PURCHASES

DATE ACQUIRED	NO. OF SHARES	SECURITY	PRICE	TOTAL COST	REASON FOR PURCHASE PRIME OBJECTIVE, ETC.

ADDITIONAL PURCHASES

DATE ACQUIRED	NO. OF SHARES	SECURITY	PRICE	TOTAL COST	REASON FOR PURCHASE PRIME OBJECTIVE, ETC.

SHORT-TERM TRANSACTIONS

Pages 178–181 can accompany next year's income tax return (Schedule D). Enter transactions as completed to avoid last-minute pressures.

NO. OF SHARES	SECURITY	DATE ACQUIRED	DATE SOLD	SALE PRICE	COST	LOSS	GAIN

TOTALS:
Carry over to next page

178

SHORT-TERM TRANSACTIONS (continued)

NO. OF SHARES	SECURITY	DATE ACQUIRED	DATE SOLD	SALE PRICE	COST	LOSS	GAIN

TOTALS:

179

LONG-TERM TRANSACTIONS

Pages 178–181 can accompany next year's income tax return (Schedule D). Enter transactions as completed to avoid last-minute pressures.

NO. OF SHARES	SECURITY	DATE ACQUIRED	DATE SOLD	SALE PRICE	COST	LOSS	GAIN

TOTALS:
Carry over to next page

LONG-TERM TRANSACTIONS *(continued)*

NO. OF SHARES	SECURITY	DATE ACQUIRED	DATE SOLD	SALE PRICE	COST	LOSS	GAIN

TOTALS:

INTEREST/DIVIDENDS RECEIVED DURING 2016

SHARES	STOCK/BOND	FIRST QUARTER		SECOND QUARTER		THIRD QUARTER		FOURTH QUARTER	
		$		$		$		$	

BROKERAGE ACCOUNT DATA 2016

	MARGIN INTEREST	TRANSFER TAXES	CAPITAL ADDED	CAPITAL WITHDRAWN
JAN				
FEB				
MAR				
APR				
MAY				
JUN				
JUL				
AUG				
SEP				
OCT				
NOV				
DEC				

WEEKLY PORTFOLIO PRICE RECORD 2016 (FIRST HALF)

Place purchase price above stock name and weekly closes below.

STOCKS	1	2	3	4	5	6	7	8	9	10
Week Ending	1	2	3	4	5	6	7	8	9	10

JANUARY

Week	1	2	3	4	5	6	7	8	9	10
8										
15										
22										
29										

FEBRUARY

Week	1	2	3	4	5	6	7	8	9	10
5										
12										
19										
26										

MARCH

Week	1	2	3	4	5	6	7	8	9	10
4										
11										
18										
25										

APRIL

Week	1	2	3	4	5	6	7	8	9	10
1										
8										
15										
22										
29										

MAY

Week	1	2	3	4	5	6	7	8	9	10
6										
13										
20										
27										

JUNE

Week	1	2	3	4	5	6	7	8	9	10
3										
10										
17										
24										

WEEKLY PORTFOLIO PRICE RECORD 2016 (SECOND HALF)

Place purchase price above stock name and weekly closes below.

STOCKS / Week Ending	1	2	3	4	5	6	7	8	9	10
JULY 1										
8										
15										
22										
29										
AUGUST 5										
12										
19										
26										
SEPTEMBER 2										
9										
16										
23										
30										
OCTOBER 7										
14										
21										
28										
NOVEMBER 4										
11										
18										
25										
DECEMBER 2										
9										
16										
23										
30										

WEEKLY INDICATOR DATA 2016 (FIRST HALF)

	Week Ending	Dow Jones Industrial Average	Net Change for Week	Net Change on Friday	Net Change Next Monday	S&P or NASDAQ	NYSE Advances	NYSE Declines	New Highs	New Lows	CBOE Put/Call Ratio	90-Day Treas. Rate	Moody's AAA Rate
JANUARY	8												
	15												
	22												
	29												
FEBRUARY	5												
	12												
	19												
	26												
MARCH	4												
	11												
	18												
	25												
APRIL	1												
	8												
	15												
	22												
	29												
MAY	6												
	13												
	20												
	27												
JUNE	3												
	10												
	17												
	24												

WEEKLY INDICATOR DATA 2016 (SECOND HALF)

Week Ending		Dow Jones Industrial Average	Net Change for Week	Net Change on Friday	Net Change Next Monday	S&P or NASDAQ	NYSE Advances	NYSE Declines	New Highs	New Lows	CBOE Put/Call Ratio	90-Day Treas. Rate	Moody's AAA Rate
JULY	1												
	8												
	15												
	22												
	29												
AUGUST	5												
	12												
	19												
	26												
SEPTEMBER	2												
	9												
	16												
	23												
	30												
OCTOBER	7												
	14												
	21												
	28												
NOVEMBER	4												
	11												
	18												
	25												
DECEMBER	2												
	9												
	16												
	23												
	30												

MONTHLY INDICATOR DATA 2016

	DJIA% Last 3 + 1st 2 Days	DJIA% 9th to 11th Trading Days	DJIA% Change Rest of Month	DJIA% Change Whole Month	% Change Your Stocks	Gross Domestic Product	Prime Rate	Trade Deficit $ Billion	CPI % Change	% Unemployment Rate
JAN										
FEB										
MAR										
APR										
MAY										
JUN										
JUL										
AUG										
SEP										
OCT										
NOV										
DEC										

INSTRUCTIONS:

Weekly Indicator Data (pages 185–186). Keeping data on several indicators may give you a better feel of the market. In addition to the closing DJIA and its net change for the week, post the net change for Friday's Dow and also the following Monday's. A series of "down Fridays" followed by "down Mondays" often precedes a downswing (see page 80). Tracking either the S&P or NASDAQ composite, and advances and declines, will help prevent the Dow from misleading you. New highs and lows and put/call ratios (www. cboe.com) are also useful indicators. All these weekly figures appear in weekend papers or *Barron's*. Data for 90-day Treasury Rate and Moody's AAA Bond Rate are quite important for tracking short- and long-term interest rates. These figures are available from:

> Weekly U.S. Financial Data
> Federal Reserve Bank of St. Louis
> P.O. Box 442
> St. Louis MO 63166
> **http://research.stlouisfed.org**

Monthly Indicator Data. The purpose of the first three columns is to enable you to track the market's bullish bias near the end, beginning, and middle of the month, which has been shifting lately (see pages 92, 145, and 146). Market direction, performance of your stocks, gross domestic product, prime rate, trade deficit, Consumer Price Index, and unemployment rate are worthwhile indicators to follow. Or, readers may wish to gauge other data.

PORTFOLIO AT END OF 2016

DATE ACQUIRED	NO. OF SHARES	SECURITY	PRICE	TOTAL COST	PAPER PROFITS	PAPER LOSSES

IF YOU DON'T PROFIT FROM YOUR INVESTMENT MISTAKES, SOMEONE ELSE WILL

No matter how much we may deny it, almost every successful person in Wall Street pays a great deal of attention to trading suggestions—especially when they come from "the right sources."

One of the hardest things to learn is to distinguish between good tips and bad ones. Usually, the best tips have a logical reason in back of them, which accompanies the tip. Poor tips usually have no reason to support them.

The important thing to remember is that the market discounts. It does not review, it does not reflect. The Street's real interest in "tips," inside information, buying and selling suggestions, and everything else of this kind emanates from a desire to find out just what the market has on hand to discount. The process of finding out involves separating the wheat from the chaff—and there is plenty of chaff.

HOW TO MAKE USE OF STOCK "TIPS"

- The source should be **reliable**. (By listing all "tips" and suggestions on a Performance Record of Recommendations, such as the form below, and then periodically evaluating the outcomes, you will soon know the "batting average" of your sources.)

- The story should make sense. Would the merger violate antitrust laws? Are there too many computers on the market already? How many years will it take to become profitable?

- The stock should not have had a recent sharp run-up. Otherwise, the story may already be discounted, and confirmation or denial in the press would most likely be accompanied by a sell-off in the stock.

PERFORMANCE RECORD OF RECOMMENDATIONS

STOCK RECOMMENDED	BY WHOM	DATE	PRICE	REASON FOR RECOMMENDATION	SUBSEQUENT ACTION OF STOCK

INDIVIDUAL RETIREMENT ACCOUNT (IRA): MOST AWESOME MASS INVESTMENT INCENTIVE EVER DEVISED

MAX IRA INVESTMENTS OF $5,500* A YEAR COMPOUNDED AT VARIOUS INTEREST RATES OF RETURN FOR DIFFERENT PERIODS

Annual Rate	5 Yrs	10 Yrs	15 Yrs	20 Yrs	25 Yrs	30 Yrs	35 Yrs	40 Yrs	45 Yrs	50 Yrs
1%	$28,336	$58,118	$89,418	$122,316	$156,891	$193,230	$231,423	$271,564	$313,752	$358,093
2%	29,195	61,428	97,016	136,308	179,690	227,587	280,469	338,855	403,318	474,490
3%	30,076	64,943	105,363	152,221	206,542	269,515	342,518	427,148	525,258	638,994
4%	30,981	68,675	114,535	170,331	238,215	320,806	421,291	543,546	692,288	873,256
5%	31,911	72,637	124,616	190,956	275,624	383,684	521,600	697,619	922,268	1,208,985
6%	32,864	76,844	135,699	214,460	319,860	460,909	649,665	902,262	1,240,295	1,692,658
7%	33,843	81,310	147,884	241,258	372,221	555,902	813,524	1,174,853	1,681,635	2,392,423
8%	34,848	86,050	161,284	271,826	434,249	672,902	1,023,562	1,538,796	2,295,843	3,408,195
9%	35,878	91,082	176,019	306,705	507,782	817,164	1,293,186	2,025,605	3,152,523	4,886,426
10%	36,936	96,421	192,224	346,514	595,000	995,189	1,639,697	2,677,685	4,349,374	7,041,647
11%	38,021	102,088	210,045	391,958	698,493	1,215,022	2,085,404	3,552,048	6,023,428	10,187,848
12%	39,134	108,100	229,643	443,843	821,337	1,486,609	2,659,047	4,725,283	8,366,697	14,784,112
13%	40,275	114,479	251,195	503,085	967,176	1,822,233	3,397,621	6,300,172	11,647,933	21,500,837
14%	41,445	121,245	274,892	570,726	1,140,330	2,237,054	4,348,701	8,414,497	16,242,841	31,315,649
15%	42,646	128,421	300,946	647,956	1,345,916	2,749,763	5,573,401	11,252,746	22,675,938	45,652,055
16%	43,876	136,031	329,588	736,123	1,589,985	3,383,389	7,150,149	15,061,631	31,678,448	66,579,439
17%	45,138	144,100	361,069	836,762	1,879,695	4,166,271	9,179,470	20,170,648	44,268,235	97,100,943
18%	46,431	152,653	395,665	951,616	2,223,497	5,133,252	11,790,069	27,019,253	61,859,935	141,566,978
19%	47,756	161,720	433,676	1,082,661	2,631,368	6,327,131	15,146,529	36,192,731	86,416,412	206,267,876
20%	49,115	171,327	475,432	1,232,141	3,115,075	7,800,418	19,459,052	48,469,462	120,656,646	300,281,459

* At Press Time - 2016 Contribution Limit will be indexed to inflation

190

G. M. LOEB'S "BATTLE PLAN" FOR INVESTMENT SURVIVAL

LIFE IS CHANGE: Nothing can ever be the same a minute from now as it was a minute ago. Everything you own is changing in price and value. You can find that last price of an active security on the stock ticker, but you cannot find the next price anywhere. The value of your money is changing. Even the value of your home is changing, though no one walks in front of it with a sandwich board consistently posting the changes.

RECOGNIZE CHANGE: Your basic objective should be to profit from change. The art of investing is being able to recognize change and to adjust investment goals accordingly.

WRITE THINGS DOWN: You will score more investment success and avoid more investment failures if you write things down. Very few investors have the drive and inclination to do this.

KEEP A CHECKLIST: If you aim to improve your investment results, get into the habit of keeping a checklist on every issue you consider buying. Before making a commitment, it will pay you to write down the answers to at least some of the basic questions—How much am I investing in this company? How much do I think I can make? How much do I have to risk? How long do I expect to take to reach my goal?

HAVE A SINGLE RULING REASON: Above all, writing things down is the best way to find "the ruling reason." When all is said and done, there is invariably a single reason that stands out above all others, why a particular security transaction can be expected to show a profit. All too often, many relatively unimportant statistics are allowed to obscure this single important point.

Any one of a dozen factors may be the point of a particular purchase or sale. It could be a technical reason—an increase in earnings or dividend not yet discounted in the market price—a change of management—a promising new product—an expected improvement in the market's valuation of earnings—or many others. But, in any given case, one of these factors will almost certainly be more important than all the rest put together.

CLOSING OUT A COMMITMENT: If you have a loss, the solution is automatic, provided you decide what to do at the time you buy. Otherwise, the question divides itself into two parts. Are we in a bull or bear market? Few of us really know until it is too late. For the sake of the record, if you think it is a bear market, just put that consideration first and sell as much as your conviction suggests and your nature allows.

If you think it is a bull market, or at least a market where some stocks move up, some mark time, and only a few decline, do not sell unless:

✓ You see a bear market ahead.
✓ You see trouble for a particular company in which you own shares.
✓ Time and circumstances have turned up a new and seemingly far better buy than the issue you like least in your list.
✓ Your shares stop going up and start going down.

A subsidiary question is, which stock to sell first? Two further observations may help:

✓ Do not sell solely because you think a stock is "overvalued."
✓ If you want to sell some of your stocks and not all, in most cases it is better to go against your emotional inclinations and sell first the issues with losses, small profits, or none at all, the weakest, the most disappointing, etc.

Mr. Loeb is the author of *The Battle for Investment Survival*, John Wiley & Sons.

G. M. LOEB'S INVESTMENT SURVIVAL CHECKLIST

OBJECTIVES AND RISKS

Security		Price	Shares	Date

"Ruling reason" for commitment	Amount of commitment
	$_____
	% of my investment capital
	_____%

Price objective	Est. time to achieve it	I will risk _____ points	Which would be $_____

TECHNICAL POSITION

Price action of stock:

❑ Hitting new highs   ❑ In a trading range

❑ Pausing in an uptrend   ❑ Moving up from low ground

❑ Acting stronger than market   ❑ _____

Dow Jones Industrial Average

Trend of market

SELECTED YARDSTICKS

	Price Range		Earnings Per Share Actual or Projected	Price/Earnings Ratio Actual or Projected
	High	Low		
Current year Previous year				

Merger possibilities	Years for earnings to double in past
Comment on future	Years for market price to double in past

PERIODIC RE-CHECKS

Date	Stock Price	DJIA	Comment	Action taken, if any

COMPLETED TRANSACTIONS

Date closed	Period of time held	Profit or loss

Reason for profit or loss